German and Central European Emigration
Monograph Number 1

RECONSTRUCTED PASSENGER LISTS FOR 1850: HAMBURG TO AUSTRALIA, BRAZIL, CANADA, CHILE, AND THE UNITED STATES

Part 1: Passenger Lists 1 through 25
Part 2: Passenger Lists 26 through 42
Part 3: Passenger Lists 43 through 60
Part 4: Supplemental Notes on Emigrants'
        Places of Origin

by
Clifford Neal Smith

CLEARFIELD

German and Central European Emigration
Monograph Number 1, Part 1

RECONSTRUCTED PASSENGER LISTS FOR 1850:

HAMBURG TO AUSTRALIA, BRAZIL, CANADA, CHILE,

AND THE UNITED STATES

Part 1: Passenger Lists 1 through 25

Clifford Neal Smith

Reprinted, 1983
Reprinted, 1984
Reprinted, 1990
Reprinted, 1993   u

CONTENTS

INTRODUCTION

The passenger lists preserved in the files of the Hamburg police authorities are the single most important genealogical research link between the Old and New Worlds, for they record the birthplaces and the destinations of millions of central European emigrants. Neither the naturalization files nor the port of entry records in lands of settlement consistently contain this information in such detail.[1] It must be noted with regret that similar files maintained by Bremen police authorities were destroyed in the *Feuersturm* of 1945, when the city itself went up in flames. The Bremen files probably were considerably larger than those of Hamburg and contained the names of most of the emigrants from western Germany and Switzerland.[2] Consequently, the reconstruction of nineteenth-century western German emigration records can only be approached by analysis of the files of each *Gemeinde* (community) in the country, a formidable task which proceeds at a slow and opportunistic pace.[3]

The Hamburg police lists are divided into two series, Direct and Indirect. The Direct series, in 399 volumes, begins in 1850 and includes all ships leaving Hamburg (and associated minor ports) without stopping at other European ports to take on emigrant passengers. The Indirect series, in 118 volumes, beginning in 1855, includes ships which made intermediate European and British ports of call. For purposes of genealogical research, the distinction does not seem to be significant, excepting that some emigrants may have been taken aboard at other ports and, therefore, are unlisted in these passenger lists. Consequently, the lists for each year of both series will be presented together in these monographs.

During the first years in which names of emigrants were recorded, the actual passenger lists apparently were not preserved. Instead, the police clerks entered the data from these original lists in large bound registers in a quasi-alphabetical fashion. This makes it difficult for researchers to determine who among the emigrants may have accompanied the subject of research. Extended family or support groups and coreligionists frequently emigrated together, a matter of significance to the researcher. To remedy this defect, the 1850

passenger lists have been reconstructed from the quasi-alphabetical entries to be found in the registers.

All the reconstructed lists for 1850 have been abstracted from microfilm roll number 1 (Library of Congress, Manuscript Division, shelf number 10,897) made of the following archival materials:

Hamburg. Staatsarchiv. Bestand Auswandereramt. Auswanderer Listen, Direkt, 1850.

The Library of Congress has microfilms of both the Direct and Indirect volumes for the period 1850-1873. The Genealogical Society of Utah, Salt Lake City, has the entire 517 volumes on microfilm, from 1850 to 1913, when the series was discontinued.

There are a total of 4,074 entries in the Direct series for 1850. Some entries record only one emigrant, other entries list entire families. It seems likely that the total number of individuals emigrating via Hamburg in 1850 may have been about 7,000 (of which almost 2,500 are listed in this monograph). Later passenger lists contain more information than do those of 1850, notably the names and ages of all family members. For the 1850 entries, the information hereinafter is as follows:

Column

1   Surname
2   Given names
3   Occupation. Some of the terms used are those of Hamburg dialect, rather than modern *Hochdeutsch*, and may not be correctly translated. For example a commonly reported occupation is that of *Oeconom*. This means farmer or manager. In these monographs the term has been uniformly translated as manager.
4   Birthplace. See the section at the end of Part 3 for notes thereon.
5   Reference number/Page number in register. The reference number has been assigned by this compiler and is not to be found in the registers. The number will probably have little use to researchers, other than indicating place on the register page relative to nearby names.

Having found a surname of interest, researchers should consider all other emigrants on the ship for possible accompanying extended-family members and coreligionists. These relationships may occasionally be inferred by considering also the birthplaces common to a number of passengers. The Index to Birthplaces can also be used to identify persons from the same birthplaces who have traveled on different ships. Occasionally, names listed herein may supplement data missing in other emigrant lists. For example, in the monograph entitled *Nineteenth-Century Emigration of "Old Lutherans"* . . .[4] it is reported that the names of 98 emigrants to Australia had not been found in German administrative files. Some of these persons may be included among the passengers of the three ships which sailed from Hamburg to Australia in 1850.

---

1. A detailed description of the Hamburg emigration files will be found in Clifford Neal Smith and Anna Piszczan-Czaja Smith, *Encyclopedia of German-American Genealogical Research* (New York: R. R. Bowker, 1976), pp. 199-200. Additional information on supplementary research materials in the Hamburg Staatsarchiv can be found in Smith & Smith, *American Genealogical Resources in German Archives* (Munich: Verlag Dokumentation, 1977), p. 227, et seq.

2. Of the nearly 79,000 persons emigrating from Germany to the United States in 1850, only about 7,000 passed through the port of Hamburg. Thus the great majority of Germans must have emigrated via the ports of Bremen and LeHavre. U.S. Bureau of the Census, *Historical Statistics of the United States: Colonial Times to 1957* (Washington, D.C.: Government Printing Office, 1960), p. 57.

3. See the back cover of this monograph for a listing of monographs in the German-American Genealogical Research series having to do with communal records on emigration.

---

4. Clifford Neal Smith, *Nineteenth-Century Emigration of "Old Lutherans" from Eastern Germany (Mainly Pomerania and Lower Silesia) to Australia, Canada, and the United States.* German-American Genealogical Research Monograph 7 (McNeal, AZ: Westland Publications, 1980), p. 46.

ABBREVIATIONS USED

b	born	Po	Poland
Ba	Bavaria, a state now in West Germany; formerly included lands in Rheinlad-Pfalz	Pm	Pomerania, a former Prussian province, now in Poland
Bi	Birkenfeld, a former principality, which in 1850 belonged to Oldenburg; territory now in Rheinland-Pfalz, West Germany	Pr	Prussia; in 1850 a kingdom with lands now in East and West Germany and Poland
Bo	Bohemia, former kingdom, now part of Czechoslovakia	Ru	Rudolstadt; Schwarzburg-Rudolstadt a former principality in Thuringia, now in East Germany
c	child, children	s	son
Ca	Cassel (now Kassel); Hessen-Cassel was a principality, also known as Electoral Hesse, now in state of Hessen, West Germany	Sa	Saxony, a former kingdom, now mainly in East Germany
d	daughter	Sb	Swabia, a region, now in Baden-Wuerttemberg, West Germany
De	Detmold; Lippe-Detmold, a former principality, now in Nordrhein-Westfalen, West Germany	Sc	Schwarzburg. *See* Rudolstadt and Sondershausen
Go	Gotha, a principality also called Sachsen-Coburg-Gotha, now in East Germany	Si	Silesia, a Prussian province in 1850, now part of Poland
Ha	Hannover, a sovereign territory, now in Niedersachsen, West Germany	Sl	Schleswig, a former province, now in Schleswig-Holstein, West Germany
He	Hessen, a former principality, now in Hessen, West Germany	Sn	Sondershausen; Schwarzburg-Sondershausen, a former principality in Thuringia, now in East Germany
Ho	Holstein, now in Schleswig-Holstein, West Germany	Sw	Sweden
Hu	Hungary; in 1850 a part of the Austro-Hungarian Empire	Sz	Switzerland
		Th	Thuringia, a region, now in East Germany
Li	Lippe; Lippe-Detmold, a former principality, now in Nordrhein-Westfalen, West Germany	Ty	Tyrol, a region in Austria
		We	Weimar; Sachsen-Weimar-Eisenach, a principality, now in East Germany
Mk	Mecklenburg, a former principality, now in East Germany	Wu	Wuerttemberg, a former kingdom, now in Baden-Wuerttemberg, West Germany
Ol	Oldenburg, a former principality, now in Niedersachsen, West Germany	y	year, years

List 1

Ship *Aeolus*, Captain J. D. Steffen,
Departing Hamburg 16 May 1850 for Quebec (Direct)

APPEL	C. F.	--?	Tiefurt	0043/003
BAUMBACH	Catherine	12 y (with J. F. Ermisch)	Grumbach, Pr	0258/012
BECKER	W.	laborer	Seehausen, Pr	0260/012
BESE	Carl	mason	Krackow, Mk	0255/012
BORNSCHIN	Mikel	--	Kleinau, Th	0259/012
BUCHMANN	J. A. Christiane	manager wife	Walschleben?	0254/012
BUECHNER	Dorothea	15 y (with J. F. Ermisch)	Grumbach, Pr	0256/012
BUECHNER	Friederike	13 y (with J. F. Ermisch)	Grumbach, Pr	0257/012
ERMISCH	J. F. -- -- --	laborer wife 4 children 3 children (*see* Baumbach, Buechner)	Grumbach, Pr	0720/034
GALANDER	Carl -- --	laborer wife child	Kleinau, Th	1037/048
GEBANER	Joseph	mason	Grossmandern, Pr	1036/048
HAAS	Gottfried	baker	Erfurt	1289/058
HAUCKE	F. M.	mechanic	Leipzig	1288/058
HELBING	H. Auguste	shoemaker wife	Braunschweig	1287/058
KECHOR	J.	mason	Grossmandern, Pr	1732/078
KOENIG	Christian	miller	Saalburg, Sa-We	1731/078
LIEBETRAU? [LIEBETRAN?]	Friedrich -- --	laborer wife 3 children	Honingsleben	2044/092
MACK	H.	carpenter	Hasslow, Ho	2296/103
MEISSNER	C. W. Johanna	mason --	Kleinau, Th	2297/103
MEISSNER	Fritz Franz Johanna	child child child	Kleinau, Th	2298/103

List 1 (continued)

MEISSNER	Friedrich	child	Kleinau, Th	2299/103
	Carolina	¼ y		
NOTT	Ernst	cigar maker	Celle	2544/114
OLDENBURG	A. G.	--?	Schwabstedt	2628/118
SCHMID	--	glazier	S[achsen] Weimar	3263/146
SCHUHMANN	J. Friedrich	manager	Walschleben, Sa	3262/146
	--	wife		
	--	4 children		
SCHUMANN	Theodor?	laborer	Tiefurt	3264/146
TOEPFER	Joachim	--	Ahrendsee, Th	3654/163

List 2

Ship *Alfred*, Captain N. Storkenbecker
Departing Hamburg 11 Sep 1850 for Valdivia & San Francisco

ANCHELL	Levin	tailor	Bromberg	0091/005
ANDERSSEN	Andreas	shoemaker	Hellbeck	0093/005
ASTFULCK	Lothar	pharmacist	Berlin	0092/005
EXSS	Hugo	official	Ullersdorf	0778/036
EXSS	Heinrich	official	Ullersdorf	0779/036
	--	wife		
	--	2 d, 19 & 24 y		
FALKENHAGEN	Joachim	--?	Berlin	0927/043
	Carl	s, 15 y		
HINSCH	Richard	businessman	Hamburg	1432/064
HOFFMANN	Carl	manager	Frankfurt/Oder	1433/064
	Amalia			
HOLTERMANN	Eller?	businessman	Drautheim? [Drant-heim?]	1434/064
HOSTEDT	Wilhelm	ship's carpenter	Buxtehude	1431/064
JEPSEN	Thomas	saddler	Tondern	1580/071
KRAUSE	Hermann	landscape gardener	Leipzig	1921/086
KROKE	Wilhelm	businessman	Berlin	1920/086
LARSSON	Jens	--?	Christianstat, Sw	2163/097
LAWACK	Adolph	manager	Camenz	2162/097

List 2 (continued)

LORENZ	Carl	--?	Crossen am Oder	2161/097
	--	wife		
	--	d, 1½ y		
MELLSTEDT	Wilhelm	--?	Berlin	2465/110
MEYER	Ludwig	--?	Muenchen	2466/110
PAUSENBERGER	Theodor	storekeeper	Breslau	2781/125
QUAPPE	Julius	farm hand	Francfurt/Oder	2819/127
RATZ	Carl	machinist	Cassel	3020/136
RETTIG	Moritz	shoemaker	Breslau	3021/136
	--	wife		
	--	4 c, 7 to 10 y		
SANDER	Julius	businessman	Kitzingen	3523/157
SCHRIEVER	Dorothea	widow?	Neuhaus an der Osts[ee?]	
	--	d, 3/4 y* [born here?]		
SCHUSTER	August	businessman	Luebben	3520/157
SEEBOECK	Johann	businessman	Wien	3521/157
STEGMOELLER	Carl	machinist	Cassel	3522/157
SWENSON	Ewen?	farmer? [builder?]	Christiansthal, Sw	3524/157
TAVERNIER	Gustav	businessman	Hamburg	3697/165
UDBYE	Esten	blacksmith	Dronsheim	3730/166
WAECHTER	Carl	businessman	Berg	3990/179
WIEBERIG	Julius	businessman	Hamburg	3989/179

List 3

Ship *Amalia*, Captain J. W. Radmann
Departing Hamburg 10 May 1850 for Quebec (Direct)

ANSCHUETZ	H. A.	peasant	Guntersleben	0039/003
	--	wife		
	--	3 children		
BEHRENS	Johann	laborer	Bramberg	0236/011

List 3 (continued)

BERG	Johann Simon	manager	Brueheim	0235/011
	--	wife		
	--	son		
	--	daughter		
	(*See also* stepchildren, Anna, Johann, & August Kuehn)			
BERTHELMANN	Hermann	businessman	Hamburg	0238/011
BIERMANN	Johann	plowman	Goldberg	0237/011
	--	wife		
	--	2 children		
BILZ	Joseph	beer brewer	Waldthur	0234/011
	--	wife		
	--	7 c, 4-20 y		
BORCHARDT	Auguste	--	Goldberg	0242/012
BRANDT	Friedrich	laborer	Neisse	0240/011
BUHRKAMP	C. F.	shoemaker	Rahden	0239/011
BUSCHENHAGEN	Friedrich	tailor	Berlin	0241/012
	Amalia	wife		
CASPAR	Franz	cabinetmaker	Reine	0528/024
DAUBMERKEL	Barbara	manager [!]	Waldthurn	0603/028
DOBMEYER	Anna	Frau	Waldthurn, Ba	0605/028
FELDER	Carolina	--?	Tennis, Mk	0842/039
FRUECHTMICHT	Matte	--	Sethersmuehlen, Ho	0843/039
GOERDLER	Friedrich	laborer	Louisenhoff, Mk	1028/047
GRAF	Johann	manager	Waldthurn	1027/047
	--	wife		
	--	2 children		
GREIMER	Theodor	tailor	Johenrieth, Ba	1026/047
	--	wife		
	--	4 children		
HALBSKAT	Friedrich	blacksmith	Krakow	1276/058
HOLMSTROEM	Christoph	cabinetmaker	Franzburg	1275/058
	Maria	wife		
JACOBS	Johann Michel	peasant	Guntersleben, Sa-Go	1527/069
	--	wife		
	--	4 children		

List 3 (continued)

KANNEWURF	J. H. -- --	miller wife 3 children	Langensalza	1707/077
KEUER	Wilhelm	laborer	Banrow, Mk	1709/077
KOELN	Johann	baker	Goldberg	1712/077
KOLBE	N. H. -- --	mason wife 2 children	Niedersimmer?	1710/077
KUEHN	Anna Johann Aug- ust	31 y* 20 y*	Brueheim	1708/077
	(*Stepchildren of Johann Simon Berg)			
KUEHN	Martha Catharina	--	Niederzimmer	1711/077
LANGLATZ		*See* Weber		3862/173
LEHMANN	Magdalena	maid	Niendorf	2033/091
LIEBETRAN		*See* Weber		3863/173
MANDEWETT	Simon -- --	mason wife 3 children	Bruheim, Sa-Go	2282/103
MORITZ	Paul	(*See* Paul Moritz Roch)	--	2283/103
OTTO	Heinrich --	tailor? wife	Grossmelzen	2624/117
OTTO	Franz Theodor	book printer	Dresden	2625/118
PAPPE	Wilhelm	baker	Minden	2691/121
PEPKE	Carl Friedrich	businessman	Jener? [Tener?]	2694/121
POIR	Barbara	--	Lemesrith? [Hemes- rith?]	2693/121
PRESLER	Christian	peasant	Sonneborn? [Sanne- born?]	2692/121
REICHMANN	H. -- --	book printer wife 2 children	Schleswig	2879/130
ROCH	Paul Moritz	bookbinder	Dresden	2880/130
ROOSE	Franz	cabinetmaker	Retsch	2882/130
RUGE	C. F.	manufacturer	Grossretbach	2881/130

8

RUSS	Carl	laborer	Tessin	2878/130
SAEUBERT	Clara	--	Dunepfl	3226/144
SCHIPPER	Moritz	glazier	Neukloster	3225/144
	Louise	--		
SCHLEGEL	Johann Val-[entin]	peasant	Sanneborn? [Sonne-born?]	3227/145
	--	wife		
	--	6 children		
SCHMIDT	Johann Hein-rich	carpenter	Niederzimmer	3219/144
SCHOENEMANN	Johann Adolph	manager	Molschleben, Sa-Go	3222/144
	--	wife		
	--	8 children		
SCHREYER	Anna	Frau	Waldthur	3216/144
	--	daughter		
	--	son		
SCHUCHERT	Ad[olphu]s?	peasant	Brueheim, Sa-Go	3217/144
	--	wife		
	--	8 c, 2-16 y		
SCHULTZ	Johann	laborer	Heydefried	3218/144
SCHULTZ	Johann	laborer (same person as above?)	Hadefinen? [Hadef-men?]	3230/145
SCHULZE	Benjamin	manager	Sitzerode, Sa	3228/145
	--	wife		
	--	9 children		
SEIBERT	J. C. Eber-hard	shoemaker	Hannover	3229/145
	--	wife		
	--	2 children		
STAUBE	Gotth[ilf?]	peasant	Waldthur, Ba	3221/144
STIER	C. J. Hein-rich	laborer	Hofgrabau	3220/144
STREIGEL	Catharina	--	Baérenrieth, Ba	3223/144
	Joseph			
STROBEL	Joseph	--	Ottenrieth	3224/144
TAEGTOW	Friedrich	laborer	Krakow	3649/163
TIEDE	Johann	laborer	Zehna	3646/163
	Maria	wife		
	--	2 children		

List 3 (continued)

TIMMERMANN	Wilhelm Henriette* Friederike*	-- (*Not clear whether one or two persons)	Rothkirchen	3647/163
WALTHER	C. F. -- --	manager wife 3 c, 4-17½ y	Tangsdorf, Sa-Go	3857/173
WALTHER	Andreas -- --	peasant wife 3 c, 3-7 y	Guntersleben, Sa-Go?	3858/173
WARKENTIN	Wilhelm -- --	laborer wife 3 children	Grabow	3856/173
WEBER	Georg --	peasant wife	Sonneborn	3860/173
WEBER	Christiane Elisabeth? Heinrich Ernst	--	Sonneborn	3861/173
WEBER	August Lang- lotz? Christian Friedrich	--	Sonneborn	3862/173
WEBER	Philipp Libe- tran Catharina Libe- tran Mart[in] Carl Libetran	--	Sonneborn	3863/173
WESTPHAL	F. J. J.	laborer	Grebbin	3859/173
WILLMANN	Christoph	shoemaker	Waldau	3855/173

List 4

Ship *Brasilien*, Captain J. Hinrichsen
Departing Hamburg 2 Sep 1850 for Galveston, Texas (Direct)

BAER	Friedrich	--?	Spandau	0456/020
BARGFELDT	Friedrich	--?	Stolpe	0455/020
BLOHM	Christoph --	--? mother	Wandsbeck	0457/021

List 4 (continued)

BURMESTER	Friedrich	farmer	Wandsbeck	0458/021
DUEHREN	Hans --	farmer? wife	Wandsbeck	0665/031
GLASS	Theodor Anna	farmer wife	Braunsberg	1140/052
GLASS	Hugo Maria --	farmer wife son, 1¼ y	Braunsberg	1141/052
GRAB	Auguste Ottilia Charlotte	Frau d, 18 y d, 21 y	Perleberg	1142/052
HAYER	Richard	pharmacist	Posen	1429/064
HEINICKE	Nicolas -- --	tailor wife 4 children, 5-8 y	Wentdorf	1426/064
HEINS	Charles -- --	shoemaker wife 3 children, 11-14 y	Hamburg	1425/064
HERMS	Wilhelm -- --	miller wife 3 children, 17-26 y	Pantin	1427/064
HERMS	Adam Friederike	miller wife	Patin	1428/064
HUTH	Peter Julia	farmer --	Marienwaerder	1430/064
JAHN	H. A. F. -- --	jeweler? wife 4 children 4-8 y	Hamburg	1579/071
KIECKE	August	cabinetmaker	Schilde	1916/086
KOPP	Christoph Anna	cabinetmaker wife	Kressbach, Wu	1919/086
KORTE	Friedrich	laborer	Boetzow	1918/086
KOSCHEL	Samuel	cabinetmaker	Breslau	1917/086
LEIB	--	--	Perleberg	2160/097
MACH	Carl	farmer (in English)	Garz	2460/110
MEINCKE	Ernst -- --	carpenter wife son, 3 y	Gueltzow	2463/110

List 4 (continued)

MEITZEN	Laura	--	Koenigsberg	1462/110
MEYER	Julius	bookbinder	Caslin? [Coslin?]	2461/110
	--	wife		
MEYER	Friedrich	farmer (in English)	Butterstieg	2464/110
MILATZ	Johann	farmer (in English)	Perleburg	2459/110
NUERMANN	Carl	--	Perleberg	2591/116
	Adolph	son, 8 y		
NUERNBERG	F. L. H.	mechanic?	Hamburg	2590/116
	--	wife		
	--	5 children, 3/4-8 y		
PAGEL	Gottfried	carpenter	Kortenhagen	2778/125
	--	wife		
	--	8 c, ¼-16 y		
PEPLAU	Martin	farmer (in English)	Marienwaerder	2779/125
	Ottilia	wife		
PRANGE	Friedrich	distiller	Berlin	2780/125
	Louise	wife		
RICKSEN	Wilhelmine	--	Wandsbeck	3019/136
RIEP	Carl	die caster?	Alt Batkop	3018/136
SCHEPPER	Louis	butcher	Gueltzow	3518/157
SCHWERTFEGER	Heinrich	blacksmith	Coeslin	3517/157
TESCH	Johann Lud-wig	gardener	Nebelin	3696/165
	--	wife		
	--	4 c, 1?-8 y		
VAHL	Alexander	farmer (in English)	Wolgast	3778/168
	Elisabeth	wife		
WALTER	Heinrich	farmer (in English)	Wolgast	3984/179
	--	wife		
WENDEL	Gottfried	shoemaker	Schweksznen?	3988/179
WENDLING	Heinrich	cabinetmaker	Wittstock	3987/179
	--	wife		
	--	5 children, ½-8 y		
WERBACH	August	--	Pausin	3986/179
	--	wife		
	--	daughter, 3 y		
WILMS	Joachim	farmer (in English)	Perleberg	3985/179

List 4 (continued)

ZERBST	Carl Wilhelm	--	Boetzow	4070/183
	--	wife		
	--	2 children, 9 & 16 y		
ZOBEL	Christine	--	Butterstieg, Ho	4071/183

List 5

S. S. *British Queen* (English ship) Captain J. R. Ball
Departing Hamburg 1 Apr 1850 for New York (Direct)

ACKERMANN	Auguste	--	Breslau	0019/002
	--	son		
	--	daughter		
BIRGHEIM	Adolph	businessman	Breslau	0150/008
BLUM	Carl L. Aug-ust	manager	Binde	0155/008
BLUMENBERG	Louis	businessman	Braunschweig	0154/008
BOLTE	Wilhelm	businessman	Hofgeismar	0152/008
BUFFLE	Jean Pierre Henry	--	Gent [Geneva] Sz	0151/008
BUNSENTHAL	Helene?	Fraeulein	Cassel	0156/008
BURMESTER	Heinrich	carpenter	Breitenfeld	0153/008
CROSTA	Peter	businessman	Erfurt	0515/024
DRESSELT	Nicholas? Ad[olphu]s?	carpenter	Langenvilsen? Sn	0578/027
DUSSLER	Wilhelm	miller	Thielbeen, Pr	0577/027
EHRLICH	Jacob	businessman	Breslau	0696/033
FRIEDRICH	Margaretha	--	Bayersdorf	0814/038
FRITZSCHE	Eduard Her-mann	manager	Oppurg	0813/038
GOEDIKE	Elise	--	Herrenhausen	0972/045
	--	2 small daughters		
GOEDIKE	Friedrich Friederike	-- wife s & d, both small	Herrenhausen	0973/045
GOETTLICH	Carl	manager	Gosewitz	0975/045
GOLDSCHMIDT	Peter	businessman	Kiel	0974/045
GOTTINGER	Isador	student	Filene	0971/045

List 5 (continued)

GUENTHER	Rosenthal	gold worker	Nordhausen	0970/045
JAEGER	Adelheid	Frau	Hamburg	1508/068
	--	2 sons		
	--	1 baby		
JENTZSCH	F. M.	miller	Meissen	1509/068
KIRCHHUEBEL	Hermann	machinist	Dresden	1637/074
	Auguste, b	wife		
	KOCH			
KOCH	Eduard	gold worker	Hagdeburg	1634/074
	--	wife		
	--	3 children		
von KOENIGS-	Heinrich	--?	Hamburg	1639/074
LOEF				
KREIN	Vinzenz M.	business agent	Cilli, Styria	1635/074
KUEKELHAHN	Carl	--?	Denstorf	1638/074
KURTH	Heinrich	--?	Pyrmont	1636/074
LEUTHIEN	C. Ehrich	miller	Gruenau	1984/089
LINDENBERG	Charlotte	Frau	Genthien	1987/089
	Bisky?	brother		
	--	4 sons		
	--	3 daughters		
LOEKNING?	Johanna	--	Stollberg	1986/089
[LOEHNING?]	--	2 daughters, small		
LORENZEN	Paul	candidate [for aca-	Wilster	1983/089
		demic degree]		
LUCAS	Wilhelm	manager	Kietz, Pr	1985/089
MAEKE	Carolina	--	Meissen	2241/101
MARTIN	Carl	businessman	Hofgeismar	2238/101
MENKE	Mikas	businessman	Giffhorn	2235/101
MERTENS	Dorothea	--	Kietz, Pr	2237/101
MEYER	Claus	shoemaker	Uelzen	2234/101
MOELLER	H. F.	soldier	Hamburg	2233/101
MOLLER	Heinrich	manager	Pennewitz	2239/101
	Jonas			
	--	wife		
	--	3 daughters		
	--	1 son		

14

MONTAG	Johann Heinrich	businessman	Cassel	2240/101
MUEHLENBRUCH	Eduard	manager	Lueneburg	2242/101
MUELLER	Josephine?	--	Stollberg	2236/101
OELMANN	Wilhelm	cabinetmaker	Braunschweig	2610/117
	Henriette?	wife		
	--	baby		
von OTTO	Heinrich Friedrich	manager	Crimitzschau	2612/117
OXENNIUS	Carl	businessman	Aroldsen	2611/117
PAPE	E. W.	businessman	Dudenhausen, Li-De	2655/120
PEETZ	Richard?	butcher	Lehesten, Sa	2656/120
REIMANN	Ernst Ludwig	cabinetmaker	Frankfurt/Oder	2838/128
REIMANN	Theodor	--	Frankfurt/Oder	2839/128
REINFELD	Catharina	--	Bayersdorf	2841/128
REINHARD	Eduard	businessman	Cassel	2840/128
RIECKMANN	E. H.	shoemaker	Klenzow	2837/128
RINGEL	Heinrich	cabinetmaker	Schoeningen	2836/128
ROSENTHAL	Guenther	gold worker	Nordhausen	2835/128
ROSENTHAL	Jacob	businessman	Temeswar, Hu	2842/128
SCHAMMEL	August	manager	Bayersdorf	3111/140
SCHELLER	Sophia Dorothea	--	Pennewitz	3107/140
SCHLEGEL	August Wilhelm	wood turner	Brandis	3105/139
	--	wife		
	--	2 daughters		
	--.	1 son		
SCHLEGEL	Louis	bookbinder	Sondershausen	3109/140
	Ida	wife		
SCHLUETER	Carolina	--	Derenthal	3100/139
SCHLUETER	Julia	--	Derenthal	3102/139
SCHMIDT	E. W. E.	doctor & --?	Dresden	3097/139
SCHMIDT	Carl Friedrich	manager	Rukhahn	3110/140

List 5 (continued)

SCHOLZ	Richard	confectioner	Frankenstein	3098/139
SCHUPP	P. A.	cabinetmaker	Hamburg	3104/139
	Maria	wife		
	--	child		
SEIDLER	Henriette	--	Braunschweig	3101/139
SIEBELIST	Catharina	--	Pennewitz	3108/140
SIEVERS	Adolph	soldier	Hamburg	3103/139
STEINTHAL	Eduard	businessman	Berlin	3112/140
STUERMER	Carl	blacksmith	Schoenemark	3099/139
	Sabina	wife		
STUERMER	August	blacksmith	Schoenemark	3099a/139
	Carl	blacksmith		
	Carolina	--		
	Carolina	child		
SUPPANTSCHITSCH	Josep	businessman	Laibach	3106/139
TRUNNITZ	Ferdinand	painter	Wilster	3626/162
von VASSOLD	August	manager	Gotha	3737/167
WEYER	Martin	peasant	Schoenemark	3806/171
WILLWEBER	Johanna?	--	Canhaven? [Can-husen?]	3807/171
	Maria?			
WITTMARK? [WITTMACK?]	Heinrich	blacksmith	Kiel	3808/171
WOELCK? [WOELOK?]	Rudolph	confectioner	Marienwerder	3810/171
WOHLFAHRT	Friedrich	manager	Klein Goerlitz	3809/171
ZIMMERMANN	Friedrich	carpenter	Passow	4030/181
ZINAU	Christian August	miller	Gardelen	4031/181

List 6

Ship *Bryant*, Captain J. Bryant
Departing Hamburg 3 Jul 1850 for New York (Direct)

BAUER	--?	--	Gillersdorf	0364/017
	--	wife		
	--	child, ¼? y		

List 6

BAUER	Elisabeth	--	Gillersdorf	0365/017
	Wilhelm	child		
BOCK	Joachim	shoemaker	Roebel	0367/017
BOEDECKER	Martin	clothmaker	Eschwegen	0366/017
BRUNN	Michael	tailor	Posen	0363/017
DAWSON	Wilhelm	soldier	Landau	0640/030
EADENBECKER?	Caspar	manager	Heina, Th	0750/035
[EADENBECHER?]				
	--			
	--	son, 7 y		
FOCKS? [FACKS?]	Salomon	tailor	Czrikhof	0890/041
FREITAG	J. J.	--?	Wismar	0892/041
FRISCHMUTH	Wilhelm	soldier	Gotha	0891/041
GILLES	Johann	clothmaker	Eupern	1091/050
GOLDMANN	Moritz	baker	Jarwin	1092/050
GRAHM	C. F.	industrialist	St. Petersburg	1094/050
	Johanna	wife		
GUTSCHE	August	brewer	Obsendorf	1093/050
HACCIUS	Georg	mechanic	Rostock	1356/061
HALLER	C. W. F.	waiter	Rostock	1358/061
HERBST	Christian	hunter	Bochow? [Rochow?]	1357/061
JANS	Heinrich	saddler	Neustad Leberswalde?	1560/070
KESSELRING	Andreas	manager	Rosenlubwitz?	1822/082
KOCH	K. A.	miller	Guestrow	1824/082
KRESEWETHER	Bernhard	butcher	Breitenbach	1823/082
KUEHN	Carl	cabinetmaker	Greisenberg	1821/082
LANGGUTH	August	tailor	Willernbach	2097/094
LIEM	Fritz	mason	Loburg	2098/094
	--	wife		
	--	4 children, 1¼-7½ y		
MATHEAS	Carl	miller	Schwersenz	2392/107
MEISSNER	Carl	businessman	Berlin	2395/107
MICHALSKY	Hermann	plumber	Javorin, Pr	2393/107
MUELLER	Carl Eduard	toolmaker?	Heinrotha?	2394/107

List 6 (continued)

MUELLER	Christian -- --	manager wife 3 children, ¼-20 y	Wotz	2396/107
MUND	G. E.	tailor	Leipzig	2391/107
NEITHASE	Hermann	clothmaker	Paesneck	2567/115
PAUL	Otto	cigarmaker	Friedland	2744/123
RIEBEN	Carl	tailor	Domitz	2962/133
ROSENTHAL	Adolph	--?	Warschau	2963/133
SALOMON	Siegurd?	--? manufacturer	Helmstedt	3394/152
SAUERBEER	Henriette?	--	Schlottheim	3395/152
SCHALKHAUSER	Lob.?	businessman	Schwabach	3392/152
SCHARFENBERG	Carl	miller	Hermannstorf? [Hermannsdorf?]	3396/152
SCHULT	John (in Eng- lish)	master tailor	Breslau	3390/151
SCHULTZ	C. A.	cablemaker	Rostock	3393/152
SCHUTZ	F. Adolph Jz.?	cigarmaker	Schwerin	3391/151
SUELZER	Emanuel	soldier	Breslau	3389/151
THOMAS	Johann Gott- fried	shoemaker	Lohburg, Pr	3676/164
THOMS	Fritz Philipp	wheelwright laborer	Wahlow	3675/164
TOLLST	Balthasar	wagoner	Uthstadt	3674/164
TREPPNER	C. F. T.	tailor	Markfiebach	3673/164

List 7

Ship *Choctaw*, Captain J. C. Flitner
Departing Hamburg 15 Aug 1850 for New York (Direct)

ALM	Carl Chris- tian?	sailor	Rostock	0081/005
AMON	Johann	baker	Adelsdorf	0080/005
BACHMANN	Julia	--	Frankfurt/Oder	0413/019

List 7 (continued)

BASTIAN	Johann J.	manager	Tessin	0414/019
	--	wife		
	--	5 children, 3½-15 y		
BAUMANN	Isidor	tailor	Schneidemuehle	0421/019
BAYER	Margaretha	--	Mantel	0415/019
BECKMANN	Christian	carpenter	Zarrentien	0418/019
BESCH	Friedrich	manager	Malchow	0416/019
	--	wife		
BESCH	Maria	--	Laasch	0417/019
BEUTLER	Heymann	tailor	Schwersenz	0420/019
BRAASCH	J. J. Ch.	farmhand	Bentwisch	0422/019
BUSCH	August	--	Altona	0419/019
ENGEL	Mina	--	Malchow	0766/036
	Carl	shepherd		
ERDMANN	C. L. F.	farmhand	Gustrow	0767/036
FISCHER	Israel	businessman	Wreschen	0914/042
FLATOW	Ascher	furrier	Strassburg	0915/042
GAEDKE	Friedrich	dyer	Hagenow	1124/051
GUELDNER	Ernst	sweeper	Rossnow	1125/051
GUENTHER	Pauline	--	Gnesen	1123/051
	--	4 children, 1-9 y		
HEILBRONN	Julius	businessman	Gnesen	1400/063
HEYMANN	Wolff	businessman	Schneidemuehle	1401/063
HOEPPNER	J. C. M.	shoe repairman	Monckhagen	1402/063
JUERSS	J. J. F. T.	coachman	Wolfsberg	1575/071
	--	wife		
KATTE	Christian	tailor	Berlin	1884/084
KOHSOW	H. J. C.	saddler	Tessin	1881/084
	--	wife		
	--	3 children		
KRAUSE	Wilhelm	tailor	Berlin	1883/084
KROENCKE	J. W.	manager	Pomeiske	1882/084
LAHN	Friedrich	manager	Laasch	2131/095
LUETH	Christoph	laborer	Schossin, Mk	2132/095
	Dorothea	--		
	Dorothea	--		

List 7 (continued)

LUETH	Anna Christian --	-- -- 4 children, 3/4-11 y	Schossin, Mk	2133/095
MARCKWARDT	Johannes	manager	Malchow	2427/109
MARCKWARDT	Friedrich? Johannes?	--	Malchow	2428/109
MARKUS	Aron	businessman	Schneidemuehle	2430/109
MEHRING	Heinrich -- --	cabinetmaker wife 2 children	Ahle	2432/109
MERGERLEIN	J. G. -- --	peasant wife 3 children, ½-9 y	Plau, Mk	2429/109
MEYER	Anton	shoemaker	Neustadt, Ho	2431/109
MEYER	W.	tailor	Ehrenfriedersdorf	2426/109
OSTERMANN	Franz	machine builder	Iserlohn	2642/118
OTTO	Hermann	gardener	Halle	2643/118
OTTO	C. E. F.	carpenter	Fredenhagen	2644/118
PERSAIL	Mina	--	Malchow	2760/124
POEHLMANN	Joseph	carpenter	Mantel	2759/124
POHL	Adelbert	tailor	Pilsen	2761/124
SAN	Adam	tailor	Nethra	3461/154
SCHARFF	F.	shoemaker	Halle	3463/154
SCHERE	Christian	carpenter	Berlin	3460/154
SCHIFF	Gerson	tailor	Schwersenz	3459/154
SCHLEICHER	Ignatz	brewer? [Kohlen- brauer]	Weihersdorf, Ba	3456/154
SCHLEICHER	Elisabeth Joseph --	-- -- 2 children, ¼-2½ y	Weihersdorf, Ba	3457/154
SCHRICKER	August	architect	Wunsiedel	3455/154
SCHULTZ	Johann Fried- rich	farmhand	Appelhagen	3462/154
STEINFELD	C. F. M.	manager	Tessin	3458/154
UHLICH	C. A.	businessman	Brusow	3725/166

List 7 (continued)

WENDELMUTH	Ernst	businessman	Tannenrode	3969/178
	--	wife		
	--	2 children, ½-3½ y		
WERTH	C. J. Christian	weaver	Petrow	3970/178
WILKE	Martin Friedrich	peasant	Poratz	3966/178
	--	wife		
	--	5 children, 8-19 y		
WILKE	Johann	6 y	Poratz	3967/178
	Carl Heinrich	4 y		
WILKE	Michael	80 y	Poratz	3968/178
ZULKOWSKI	Samuel	tailor	Znin, Pr	4065/182
ZWINGER	J. J. H.	farmhand	Strahlendorf	4066/182

List 8

Ship *Clara Anna*, Captain William Reed
Departing Hamburg 13 Nov 1850 for New York (Direct)

ANDRE	Carl	shoemaker	Hamburg	0114/006
ANDRESEN	Georg	--?	Copenhagen	0115/006
BADI	H. J. G.	--?	Rosenthal	0507/023
BAEDECKER	Carl	cabinetmaker	Celle, Ha	0506/023
BEHRENS	Wilhelm	mechanic?	Rechenberg, Pr	0508/023
BENJAMINSON	Salomon	cigarmaker	Suwalky, Po	0503/022
BRANDES	Elisabeth	--	Hamburg	0504/022
BRAUN	C. E.	book binder	Erlangen, Ba	0505/022
ELLERBROCK	J. A.	laborer	Barmbeck bei Hamburg	0801/037
FREIS	Johanna	--	Bies, Ho	0957/044
GITTELSON	Isaac	businessman	Kalway, Po	1163/053
GROHE? [GROBE?]	C. F.	manager	Hersgehoefel	1164/053
JACOB	Heinrich	soapmaker	Gross Glogau, Si	1600/072

List 8 (continued)

KOELLING	J. F. L	mechanic	Hamburg	1959/087
LIND	Charles --	manager? wife	New York	2204/098
MARCUS	Moritz	--	Berlin	2504/112
MEYER	Friedrich	houseboy	Drackenburg, Ha	2503/112
MUELLER	Friedrich	butcher	Annaberg	2505/112
PRAHL	Johann	farmhand	Vretz, Mk	2814/126
RITZ	Blasius	sculptor	Braunschweig	3058/137
SCHEUER	Heinrich	farmhand	Vietz, Mk	3610/161
VIERTH	Julius Fried- rich	baker	Meissen	3781/169
WARNECKE	Gustav	wheelwright	Danzig	4019/180

List 9

Ship *Colon*, Captain C. Hassell
Departing Hamburg 9 Dec 1850 for Brazil and San Francisco (Direct)

AULFES	Willrand? -- --	-- wife son	Bramsche, Ol	0113/006
BARLAGE	Friedrich	--	Epel, Ol	0499/022
BAUER	Baptist	--	Sarmensdorf? Sz	0497/022
BOCKELMANN	J. H. -- --	-- wife 2 children	Epe, Ol	0500/022
BOEHMANN	Anna Maria Maria Wilhelmina	-- -- --	Hesepe, Ol	0502/022
BOELICKE	J. C. E. --	-- wife	Frankfurt/Oder, Pr	0498/022
BRACHMANN	Wilhelm	--	Bramsche, Ol	0501/022
ENGEL	H. H. -- --	-- wife 2 daughters	Cappeln, Ol	0800/037

List 9 (continued)

FELDER	Gustav	businessman	Petschkau	0812/038
	Anna	--		
FREUDENBERG	Rudolph	--	Buehren, O1	0956/044
	--	wife		
	--	5 children		
GILGEN	Christian	--	Rueggisberg, Sz	1162/053
	--	wife		
	--	6 children		
HEISLAGE	Friedrich	--	Hemke, O1	1493/067
HUMMERT	Gerhard	--	Ankum, O1	1492/067
LANGENEGGER	Heinrich	--	Gais, Sz	2203/098
LODER	Wilhelm	--	Aetigen? Sz	2202/098
	--	wife		
	--	5 children		
MAEOHLER?	Joseph	--	Innerweggithal?	2498/112
	--	wife	[Innaweggithal?] Sz	
	--	2 children		
MOERKING	Johann	--	Bramsche, O1	2502/112
	Heinrich			
MORELL	Christel	--	Bramsche, O1	2501/112
MORIKOFER	Carl	--	Frauenfeld, Sz	2497/112
	--	wife		
	--	4 children		
MUELLER	Johann	--	Siblingen, Sz	2499/112
	--	wife		
	--	7 children		
MUELLER	Georg	--	Siblingen, Sz	2500/112
ROSKAMP	Johann	--	Bramsche, O1	3057/137
	Heinrich			
	--	wife		
	--	7 children		
SCHACK	Johann	--	Amt Geringen, Sc-Ru	3609/161
	Wolfgang			
SCHELLING	Alexander	--	Siblingen, Sz	3605/160
	--	wife		
	--	4 children		
SCHELLING	Jacob	nephew (of Alexander? or accompanied by his own nephew?)	Siblingen, Sz	3606/160

List 9 (continued)

SCHMIDLI	Bartholomaeus	--	Siblingen, Sz	3604/160
	--	wife		
	--	5 children		
SCHMIDLI	Johann	--	Siblingen, Sz	3607/160
STORRER	Gottlieb	--	Siblingen, Sz	3608/161
TANNER	Conrad	--	Siblingen, Sz	3709/165
	--	wife		
	--	8 children		
TANNER	Franz	--	Siblingen, Sz	3709a/165
ULM	--?	--	Bramsche, Ol	3732/166
	--	2 sons		
VOELCKER	H. H.	--	Fuerstenau, Ol	3780/169
WEBER	Jacob	--	Siblingen, Sz	4015/180
WEBER	Sebastian	--	Siblingen, Sz	4016/180
	--	wife		
	--	5 children		
WEBER	Conrad	--	Siblingen, Sz	4017/180
	--	wife		
	--	5 children		
WEBER	Jacob	--	Siblingen, Sz	4018/180

List 10

Ship *Colonist* (Hamburg flag) Captain H. P. Juergensen
Departing Hamburg 28 Mar 1850 for Galveston, Texas (Direct)

ALTMANN	Carl	chimney sweep	Frankenstein	0017/002
	Dorothea	--		
	Ida	--		
	Bertha	--		
APPEL	August	sailmaker	Hamburg	0015/002
	Christian?	--		
	Bernhard	--		
	August	--		
APPEL	Elisabeth	--	Hamburg	0016/002
	Elisabeth	--		
	Carolina	--		
ARNOLD	Julius	tailor	Breslau	0018/002
	Carolina	--		

List 10 (continued)

BARMISCH? [BAEMISCH?]	August	carpenter	Breslau	0148/008
BISCHOFF	Fritz	carpenter	Breslau	0149/008
BROSIG	Theodor Joseph	--? businessman	Neisse	0146/008
BUNGE	Christian Wilhelmine Wilhelm Wilhelmine	machinist -- -- --	Perleberg	0147/008
CORETH	Ernst Agnes --	-- -- (total of 9 persons in party)	Tyrol	0514/024
DAMUS	Adolph	businessman	Pr[eussich] Holland	0576/027
von GILGENHEIMB	Ferdinand	--	Breslau	0966/045
GROSSE	Louis	--?..	Auma, Sa-We	0967/045
GROSSE	Julius Ernst Franz	--	Auma, Sa-We	0968/045
GUTTNER	Carl	butcher (did not go)	Dittersbach	0969/045
HASSELNORSCH? [HASSELHORSCH?]	Juliana	--	Reichenbach	1199/055
HAUDE	Julius Bertha Louise --	peasant little girl?	Reichenbach	1198/055
von HEDEMANN	August	hunter	Poppelau	1195/054
HEGG	Friedrich	--	Gebersdorf	1196/055
von HIPPEL	Moritz	--?	Breslau	1197/055
JACOB	Wilhelm	baker?	Breslau	1507/068
JASCHKE	Rudolph	tanner	Frankenstein	1506/068
KATTNER	August	--?	Breslau	1631/074
KATTNER	Henriette Blanka	-- --	Breslau	1632/074
KAUFFMANN	Adolph	carpenter	Breslau	1629/074
KISELING	Carl	cabinetmaker	Frankenstein	1626/074

List 10 (continued)

KOCH	Louis	official	Osnabrueck	1630/074
KRUG	Heinrich	Ph.D.	Breslau	1627/074
KRUG	Sophie	--	Breslau	1633/074
LUEDTKE	Friedrich	laborer	Perleberg	1982/089
MALITZKY	Louis	--	Langenbuelau	2231/101
MARCI	Bertha	--	Perleberg	2230/101
MICHAELIS	Henriette	--	Perleberg	2229/100
MUELLER	Ottakar	--	Schoenberg	2232/101
NECKER	Carl	shoemaker	Perleberg	2519/113
REITSCH	Albert	--?	Breslau	2834/128
SCHIEVER	Johann Friedrich	distiller	Perleberg	3090⅟139
SCHIMKE	Gottfried	businessman	Neusalz	3087/139
SCHIMKE	Friedrich	peasant	Fischbach	3088/139
SCHMIDT	Carl Friederike	shoemaker	Perleberg	3086/139
SCHMIDT	--	wheelwright	Breslau	3093/139
SCHOTT	Wilhelm Auguste Emil	mason	Breslau	3094/139
SCHULZ	--	--?	Reichenbach	3095/139
SCHWARZ	Liborius	mason	Breslau	3084/139
SCHWARZBACH	Gottl[ieb?]	weaver	Ober Lichtenau	3091/139
SEJA	Gustav	brewer	Juliusburg	3089/139
SIEGERT	Berthold	businessman	Neisse	3092/139
STENZEL	Carl Bertha Hermann Emilie	carpenter -- -- --	Reichenbach	3096/138
STUWINSKY	Friederike --? Robert Adolph	-- -- --	Breslau	3085/139
VOGES	Diedrich	laborer	Bissendorf	3736/167
WEILSHAEUSER	Emil	--	Oppeln	3805/170

List 10 (continued)

WOLTERSDORF	Carl	butcher	Perleberg	3803/170
WUESTHOFF	Robert	--	Perleberg	3804/170

List 11

Ship *Dockenhuden*, Captain Jacob Meyer
Departing Hamburg 20 Oct 1850 for Port Adelaide and Sydney

AUGSTEIN	Eduard	baker	Danzig	0103/006
BOECKMANN	Heinrich	peasant	Sievern, Ha	0477/021
	--	wife		
	--	4 children, 15-29 y		
DUEBELL	G. H.	physician	Schleswig	0678/031
	--	wife		
	--	2 children, 2 & 7 y		
FICHTER	Christian	--	Sievern, Ha	0948/044
	--	wife		
	--	son, ½? y		
FITTER	Hinrich	--	Sievern, Ha	0947/044
GEPHARD	G. H.	businessman	Magdeburg	1156/053
	C. L.	son, businessman		
GOLDSMITH	Alfred	businessman	Paris	1157/053
	Eduard	businessman		
HELLMENS	Heinrich	peasant	Filsen, Ha	1464/066
	--	wife		
	--	son, 11 y		
JACOBS	Heinrich	businessman	Damgarten	1590/071
	Albertine	--		
KRUEGER	Matthias	peasant	Cottbus	1947/087
	--	wife		
	--	7 children, 4-23 y		
NEUHAUS	Otto	businessman	Berlin	2595/116
RIETZCHLER	Carl A.	miner	Bautzen, Sa	3040/137
ROEDIGER	Julius	mason	Berlin	3039/137
RUNGE	Heinrich	cabinetmaker	Wedendorff	3041/137
	--	4 children, 19-28 y		
SCHULTZ	Johann	peasant	Cottbus	3575/159

List 11 (continued)

| SEIFFERT | Alexander | physician | Sonneberg, Pr | 3576/159 |
| WIESE | Wilhelm | cabinetmaker | Wedendorff, Mk | 4007/180 |

List 12

Ship *Elbe* (Hamburg flag) Captain F? A. Heydtmann
Departing Hamburg 16 Mar 1850 for New York (Direct)

ADAM	Paul	businessman	Saalfeld	0012/002
ANNENMUELLER	Friedrich	weaver	Kaulsdorf	0010/002
APPELFELDER	Christian	laborer	Unterhain	0008/002
ARNOLD	Georg A.	mason	Kaulsdorf	0009/002
AXT	Wilhelmine	--	Blankenberg	0011/002
BAUMANN	Christiane?	--	Zello, Th	0135/007
BAUMANN	Elisabeth --	-- baby	Zello, Th	0136/007
BAUMGARTEN	C. C.	weaver	Koenigssee	0131/007
BRAEUNER	Johanna --	-- baby	Volkstedt	0132/007
BRAEUNLICH	E. E.	carpenter	Oppurg	0134/007
BREHME	E. J. H. C. J. C.	wagoner manager	Kaulsdorf	0133/007
DIETZEL	August	barrelmaker?	Kaulsdorf	0572/027
DUEMMLER	J. G. H. D.	manager	Reschwitz	0573/027
EHLE	C. E.	laborer	Blankenburg	0694/033
EHLE	Nicolas Gotth[ilf?] Const[antin?]	laborer -- --	Meuselbach	0692/033
ERDMANN	C. A. --	manager family	Dornfeld	0693/033
FORSTER	J. C.	weaver	Gebstedt	0808/038
FUCHS	--?	blacksmith	Hamburg	0896/041
GERBERT	Louis Amalia?	businessman --?	Oberweissbach	0963/045
GOETZE	Gustav Wilhelm	painter? tailor	Oberweissbach	0964/045

List 12 (continued)

GRUNENSFELDT	J. H. F.	shoemaker	Pflanzvirbach	0962/045
HARTUNG	Gustav	surgeon	Blankenburg	1187/054
HAUKE	J. C. L.	manager	Unterhain	1188/054
HAUSCHILD	M. L. Amalia	butcher sister	Blankenburg	1189/054
HAUSCHILD	Hermann	-- (son of Amalia Hau- schild)	Blankenburg	1191/054
HOPFE	C. G. W.	laborer	Wickendorf	1185/054
HOPFE	Anton Christian Friederike	laborer -- --	Wickendorf	1186/054
HUSCH	Heinrich	--	Oberwellnborn	1190/054
JAHN	August	furrier?	Oberweissbach	1500/068
JAHN	J? N.	carpenter	Meusselbach	1502/068
JAUCH	Caroline?	--	Kaulsdorf	1501/068
KAEMMER	Carl --	butcher family	Saalfeld	1616/073
KAESTNER	Christian B.	--	Weischwitz	1618/073
KESSEL	J. F.	shoemaker	Breternitz	1619/073
KIRCHNER	Johann M. --	manager family	Doeschnitz	1613/073
KIRCHNER	Leonhard	baker	Ranis	1620/073
KIRCHNER	C. F.	cabinetmaker	Gross Goelitz	1621/073
KLETT	Bernhard	mason	Obernitz	1615/073
KOENIG	Oscar Justin	shoemaker tanner	Blankenburg	1614/073
KORN	Wilhelmine	Frau	Kaulsdorf	1617/073
LOHSE	Friedrich	wagoner	Wittenberg	1980/089
MACHELEIDT	Ferdinand	businessman	Rohrbach	2219/100
MITHFESSEL?	Carolina	--	Hirzbach? [Herzbach]	2217/100
MITSCHE	Michael	cabinetmaker	Zello, Th	2221/100
MOELLER	Ferdinand	brewer	Oberweissbach	2216/100
MOELLER	Johann W.	weaver	Blankenburg	2218/100

MUELLER	Cordes?	dyer	Zello, Th	2220/100
NEUBERT	J? Friedrich	laborer	Unterhain	2516/113
NOETHLICH	Albert	cablemaker	Saalfeld	2517/113
ORTLOFF	Gustav	laborer	Saalfeld	1609/117
OSCHMANN	J. C. F. W.	--	Oberweissbach	2608/117
OSCHWITZ	J? G. C?	laborer	Hirzbach	2607/117
PROPPE	Valentin --	laborer family?	Hochheim	2653/120
ROESSEL	C. F.	saddler	Oppurg	2826/128
ROSE	Heinrich --	master butcher? family	Rockendorf	2827/128
SCHAAF	August	mason	Kranichfeld	3079/138
SPINDLER	Johann Heinrich --	manager family	Dietrichshuette	3078/138
TREMPERT	J. G. --	blacksmith family	Saalfeld	3623/162
TROPEL	Christiane	--	Beilwitz	3622/162
ULRICH	J. E. F. --	master weaver wife	Oberweissbach	3714/166
ULRICH	E. M. R.	weaver	Oberweissbach	3715/166
VOIGT	J. H. A.	surgeon	Blankenburg	3735/167
VOLCK	Christine	--	Oberweissbach	3734/167
WALTHER	Henriette	--	Oberweissbach	3799/170
WEIDERMANN	August	mason	Gossitz	3798/170
WOLFRAM	Friederike	--	Burglemnitz	3800/170
ZIENER	C. H. F.	manager	Markelitz	4024/181

List 13

Ship *Elbe*, (Hamburg flag) Captain F? A. Heydtmann
Departing Hamburg 27 Jul 1850 for New York (Direct)

ADAM	Louis	baker	Erfurt	0071/004
ALBRECHT	Johann	tailor	Stralsund	0073/005
ALLSTROM?	Olha?	--?	Copenhagen	0072/004
ARNOLD	Johannes	shoemaker	Vechta	0070/004
BADT	--?	--	Graetz	0385/018
BECKER	J. C. H.	wheelwright	Schwerin	0386/018
	--	wife		
	--	son, 1½ y		
BERLIN	Georg	blacksmith	Neustadt	0377/017
	--	wife		
	--	daughter, 22 y		
BERWIN	Heymann	--	Schwersitz	0387/018
BETTIG	C. A.	peasant	Zwerga	0383/017
	--	wife		
	--	baby		
BLUMENTHAL	Friedrich	--	Muchow	0378/017
BOCKNER	A. A.	manager	Etzebach	0382/017
	--	wife		
	--	4 children, 5-24 y		
BOLLER	Sophia	14 y (with Gottfried Sperling)	Abbenrode	0380/017
BORNSCHEIN	Emma	--	Erfurth	0384/017
von BORSTEL	J.	peasant	Ritsch	0388/018
BROCK	Veila	Frau	Ruppin	0381/017
	Meyer	businessman		
BULLMANN	Friederike	--	Veckenstedt	0389/018
BULS	Maria	--	Parchim	0379/017
DABOGITZKY	Rosalia	--	Krotoschin	0647/030
ECKBOHM	J. F.	cook	Wien	0754/035
ECKEL	Johann	peasant	Duhrnleiss	0756/035
EHLERS	Carolina	--	Hamburg	0753/035
EHRICHS	Peter	peasant	Vollersaade	0757/035
ERNST	Louis	soapmaker	Schlieben	0755/035

List 13 (continued)

FERSENHEIM	Gustav	clothmaker	Frankfurt	0901/042
FISCHER	G. W.	--?	Parchim	0895/041
FRANCK	Magnus Hermann	businessman, 18 y businessman, 22 y	Kuestrin	0897/041
FRANCK	Gustav	13 y	Kuestrin	0898/041
FREUND	Wilhelm Sophia	--	Lengsfeld	0899/042
FRIEDLANDER	Wilhelm Louis	distiller --?	Chodziesen	0900/042
GANSCHOW	C. F. -- --	cabinetmaker wife 3 children, 6 to 7-3/4 y	Reiffenhagen	1107/051
GIESE	Albert	glazier	Liebenau	1106/051
GOECKEN	G. F.	manager	New York	1104/051
GROTTCKE	F. W.	sieve maker	Hamburg	1103/051
GUELDNER	C. G. -- --	--? wife 4 children, 2½-14 y	Erfurt	1105/051
HAAGE	J. G. -- --	manufacturer? wife 7 children, to 21 y	Erfurt	1377/062
HAMCKE? [KAMCKE?]	Friedrich	businessman	Altenlohm	1849/083
HAMMANN	Clara	--	Wallendorf	1373/062
HANSEN	Hermann Carolina	businessman --	Hamburg	1380/062
HARDING	Bay?	businessman	Hamburg	1379/062
HELSEBECK	Heinrich	hoodlum?	New York	1371/062
HENCKE	Fritz Ludwig	stable boy stable boy	Riepl? [Riepe?]	1375/062
HENKE	Dorothea	7 y	Riepl? [Riepe?]	1376/062
HENKE	Christiane	--	Riepe	1381/962
HENKEN	J. J.	hoodlum?	New York	1372/062
HERTWIG	Wilhelm --	businessman son, 14 y	Leipzig	1378/062

List 13 (continued)

HIRSCH	--?	--	Sakolker	1369/062
	Simon	5 y		
HOLST	Johann Heinrich	hoodlum?	New York	1370/062
HOWELING	Wilhelm	mechanic	Koenigsberg	1374/062
	--	wife		
	--	2 children, to 1½ y		
ISAACK	Samuel	--?	Grajewo	1566/070
JACHELT? [JACHELL?]	Jutta	--	Ruppin	1567/070
	--	daughter		
	--	baby		
JARESKI	Gustav	goldsmith	Posen	1568/070
KADEN	Wilhelm	hammer? smith	Laussnitz	1852/083
	--	5 children, 6-19 y		
KAMCKE? [HAMCKE?]	Friedrich	businessman	Altenlohm	1849/083
KAPFER	J. H.	cabinetmaker	Albany am S? [L?]	1843/083
	--	wife	Hamburg	
	--	daughter, 3 y		
KATZSCH	Caroline	--	Leipzig	1844/083
	--	2 children, to 4 y		
KATZSCH	Heinrich	cabinetmaker	Wurzen	1845/083
KAVEL	H. A.	shoemaker	Parchim	1841/083
	--	wife		
KICK?	George	tailor	Waldthurm	1846/083
KILLING	Louis	cigarmaker	Hamburg	1850/083
KNABE	Friedrich	laborer	Kallenda	1847/083
KOST	H. F.	student	Tansberg	1851/083
KROEPLIN	Fritz	saddler	Parchim	1842/083
	--	wife		
KUECKS	Matta	--	Vollersaade	1853/083
KUTSCHER	Leopold	furrier	Koenigsberg	1848/083
LANDAUER	Ernestine	Frau	Rawitsch	2114/095
	--	son, 5 y		
LANG	--	--	--	2105/094
LEONHARDT	W. L.	shoemaker	Nordheim	2106/094

List 13 (continued)

LIEBAS	Robert	saddler	Zdony	2115/095
LIEBIG	Eduard	cigarmaker	Leipzig	2111/095
LOCK	Maria	--	Parchim	2103/094
LOCK	Fritz	saddler	Parchim	2104/094
	David	--		
LOEBEN	Eva?	Frau	Schmiegel	2110/094
	--	baby		
LOEWENSTEIN	Julius	gold worker	Chodziesen	2112/095
LOFSTROM	Peter	machine builder	Copenhagen	2113/095
LOHEIM	Traugott	shoemaker	Sorau	2108/094
LUDRU	Bertha	maid	Koenigsberg	2109/094
LUTZ	W.	tailor	West Rhoda	2107/094
MARTENS	Carl	tailor	Goldberg	2403/108
	--	wife		
MEHRCKENS	N. D.	teacher	Cuxhaven	2404/108
	--	wife		
MEYER	Johann	tailor?	Neustadt	2401/108
	--	4 children, 3-10 y		
MEYER	Christine?	--	Neustadt	2402/108
	--	2 babies		
MEYER	Joseph	tailor	Heithausen	2405/108
MEYER	Broet?	furrier	Ruppin	2406/108
MEYER	Ludwig?	--?	Fordau	2408/108
	Joseph			
MOSES	Bernhard	tailor	Graetz	2407/108
	--	wife		
	--	daughter, 4½ y		
NIETSCHMANN	Friedrich	baker	Weimar	2574/115
NORDHAUSEN	Elias	--?	Veckenstedt	2573/115
	--	wife		
PINGEL	Johann	peasant	Domsuehl	2752/124
RAMCKE	J. M.	wagoner	Kolbe	2972/134
	--	wife		
	--	6 children, to 25 y		
REUMANN	J.	manager	New York	2969/134
ROSENTHAL	C. H.	saddler	Leipzig	2971/134

List 13 (continued)

ROST	Eduard	shoemaker	Reisdorf	2970/134
	--	wife		
RUDOLPH	Carl	businessman	Stettin	2973/134
RUDOLPH	Fritz	businessman	Berlin	2974/134
SAMUEL	Julius	tailor	Kurnick	3419/153
SCHEUFFLER	Ernst	book printer	Meissen	3416/153
SCHOENBRUNN	Julius	pharmacist	Brieg	3415/152
SCHROETER	H. H.	baker	Thorn	3418/153
SCHUETT	Johann	tailor	Stralsund	3417/153
SCHUMACHER	Wilhelmine	Frau	Hamburg	3413/152
	--	2 daughters, 11 & 23 y		
SEIDEL	August	storekeeper	Hamburg	3411/152
SPERLING	Gottfried	miller	Abbenrode	3412/152
	--	wife		
	--	2 children, 11 & 13 y		
		(also Sophia Boller)		
SPRINGER	Isaac	tailor	Scherkow	3410/152
STAHN	Julius	butcher	Koenigsberg	3414/152
TAUSEND	Michael	baker	Wien	3678/164
	--	wife		
	--	child		
von THUN	J. H.	peasant	Vollersaade	3679/164
TUNELL	Friedrich	peasant	Garleben	3695/165
VERSELLE	Samuel	organ builder	Yverdon	3768/168
WEISS	Heinrich	weaponsmaker	Copenhagen	3949/177
WIESE	Carl	baker	Schwersitz	3951/178
WOLFF	Johann	plumber	Hamburg	3950/178
ZACHOW	Jacob	peasant	Domsuhl	4057/182

List 14

Ship *Elbe* (Hamburg flag) Captain F? A. Heydtmann
Departing Hamburg 30 Nov 1850 for New York (Direct)

BANNEBERGER?	Auguste	--	Saalfeld	0494/022
[BONNEBERGER?]	Fridrike baby			
[RONNEBERGER?]				

List 14 (continued)

BERTELSEN	N. L.	businessman	Ballum	0496/022
BRUHNS	Friedrich	businessman	Luebeck	0495/022
CARLSEN	--	--	Deutschkrona	0561/025
CLAUSEN	--hilde?	--	Tondern	0562/025
DOLSCH	E. H.	soldier	Rostock	0684/031
ECKARDT	C. G.	cabinetmaker	Linda bei Friedberg	0799/037
FISCHER	Hermann	--?	Meissen	0955/044
GRAUL	--	shoemaker	Rudolstadt	1161/053
HAENSEL	C. F.	-- wine maker?	Hamburg	1487/067
HAMMER	E?	tailor	Binnlau	1490/067
HANSEN	Nicolas	laborer	Deestrup	1491/067
HERBST	J. H. -- --	gardener wife 3 children, 3-7 y	Schoeningen	1488/067
HERBST	F. W.	weaver	Immenrode	1489/067
HEUBEL	Fritz -- --	house painter wife 8 children, to 18 y	Rudolstadt	1484/066
HIRSCH	Itzig	book printer	Berlin	1485/067
HOFFMANN	Th. C.	manufacturer's sales- man	Rendsburg	1486/067
JACOBSEN	H. O. --	--? wife	Ballam	1599/072
KRAUSE	Adolph	manager	Freiberg	1958/087
LIEVRE	L? A? L?	--?	Hamburg	2201/098
MARTENS	Charlotte	--	Schmegel	2496/112
MAUCKSCH	Johann	miller	Finkwaerder	2495/112
PELZ	Joseph	tailor	Grossnossen	2811/126
PICKER	J. F.	wheelwright	Ploen	2813/126
PROZELLE	Carl	teacher	Friedland	2812/126
REIF	Georg	--	Gommatshausen	3056/137
RONNEBERGER	Auguste --	-- baby	Saalfeld	3054/137
RUTENICK	Nathanael	landscape gardener	Neulevin	3055/137

36

SASS? [SALZ?]	Heinrich	peasant	Fehmarn	3602/160
SCHOLZ	A. A.	gardener	Eisleben	3601/160
SEIDLER	W. F.	wheelwright	Finsterwalde	3603/160
TESKE	Johann	tailor	Deutschkrona	3708/165
UMSCHLAG	J. J.	tailor	Reindorf	3731/166
WEBER	Maria S.	--	Altona	4014/180
WIESTNER	J. H. F.	blacksmith	Rostock	4013/180

List 15

Ship *Ellen,* Captain W. Knaggs
Departing Hamburg 1 Jun 1850 for New York (Direct)

ALEXANDER	Selig	shoemaker	Thorn	0052/004
	Bertha	--		
BEIN	Sebastian	saddler	Ilsenburg, Pr	0303/014
	--	wife		
	--	5 children, ¼-10 y		
BERWALD	Ernst	blacksmith	Neisse	0300/014
	Anna	--		
BETHGE	G. Ad[olph?]	printer?	Gnadenfrey, Pr	0302/014
	Pauline	--		
BIEBASS	C. W.	carpenter	Ruppersdorf, Sa	0301/014
BOLTE	Chr[istian?]	plumber	Schwerin	0305/014
	--	wife		
BUEDWECH	J. A.	--?	Elbing	0304/014
DAENIN	Catherine	--	Koenigshofen	0622/029
DAVIDSOHN	J?	dyer	Geroschin	0621/029
ECKSTEIN	Isaack	furrier	Rawitz	0731/034
ERIKSEN	Martin	baker	Astadkarget?	0732/034
FRIESE	Carl	metal worker [*Gelb-gieser*]	Parchim	0869/040
FRIESKE	J.	peasant	Tischkauer, Pr	0868/040
GASSARIEL	E.	cap maker	Posen	1061/049
GEISSEL	Caspar	coachman	Koenigshofen	1060/049

List 15 (continued)

GOLDBAUM	Leopold	soldier	Strenze	1062/049
HASSE	Eduard	cabinetmaker	Bitan? [Bitow?]	1320/060
HOLM	Carl	coppersmith	Parchim	1321/060
	Adolphine?	--		
KANBA	Friedrich	glazier	Bennsdorf	1779/080
KOTHWITZ? [KATHWITZ?]	Isedor	--?	Posen	1778/080
KERCHER	L.	butcher	Altsheim	1775/080
KLIETZ	Leopold	peasant	Dadersheim	1780/080
	Friederike	--		
	Christoph	--		
KLIETZ	Christian?	peasant	Dadersheim	1781/080
	Friederike	wife		
KOLSTADT	Hans	baker	Nas? [Mas?]	1777/080
KUSCH	Samuel	soldier	Rosengarth	1776/080
LENOWSKY	M.	businessman?	Suwanck	2074/093
LENSCHEL	W.	peasant	Benndorf	2075/093
LESTEN	Carl	manager	Wismar	2072/093
LEWIN	Hermann	soldier	Kobal	2071/093
LINDENBERG	Louise	girl	Badenhausen	2073/093
LINDENBERG	L.	businessman	Badenhausen	2076/093
LINDENBERG	C.	sculptor	Badenhausen	2077/093
MEYNECKE	Johann	peasant	Tampow	2344/105
	--	wife		
	--	child, ½ y		
MEYNECKE	Wilhelm	cabinetmaker	Tampow	2345/105
OPITZ	Johann	brewer	Neisse	2636/118
PIMM?	H. J.	stone mason	Thomasburg, Pr	2723/122
RAUBOLD	C. F.	blacksmith	Benndorf?	2919/132
	--	wife		
ROSENBAUM	M.	soldier	Bromberg	2916/132
ROSENTHAL	H?	master --?	Nevershausen	2917/132
ROTH	J.	dyer	Berlin	2918/132

List 15 (continued)

THIEDE	Katinka	--	Parchim	3660/163
WOLF	J. C.	carpenter	Schleswig	3916/176
	Louise	wife		

List 16

Ship *Elise* (Hamburg flag) Captain H. D. N. Trautmann
Departing Hamburg 27 Apr 1850 for New York (Direct)

ALTMANN	Stephan	--	Karbach, Ba	0037/003
AUGE	Dorothea	--	Rheinfeld, Ho	0036/003
BAUER	J. G.	--	Karbach, Ba	0207/010
	--	3 persons		
BECKER	Wilhelm	--?	Thuringia	0206/010
	Christiane	wife		
	August	baby		
BECKURTS	H. F.	--	Braunschweig	0212/010
BERTRAND	Therese	--	Apolda	0208/010
	--	child		
BIBELGE	Carl Georg	brewer	Grabow	0211/010
BORGER	Friedrich	basketmaker	Berthelsdorf	0209/010
BROCKMANN	Heinrich	cabinetmaker	Luebs	0210/010
DENICKE	H. W.	--	Hamburg	0595/028
DIETRICH	C. G.	cabinetmaker	Willsdorf	0593/028
	--	wife		
	--	adopted son (W. Zumpfe)		
DOMNECH	H.	--	Meiningen	0594/028
EHRLICH	Ernst	miller	Nemditz?	0708/033
FIEDLER	A.	peasant	Wellwarn? Bo	0835/039
	Maria	wife		
	Wenzel	son		
	--	baby		
FISCHER	Carl Gott-fried	--?	Herzogswalde	0836/039
	--	wife		
	--	2 children		

List 16 (continued)

FLECK	Heinrich	mason	Munschwitz, Th	0833/039
	Irma	wife		
	Erdmann	son		
FLECK	Christian	weaver	Kleingeschwinda, Th	0834/039
	Rosa	wife		
	--	3 children		
GELPCKE	Friedrich	--	Lenzen	1019/047
	Otto	--		
GOEDICKE	J. S? [L?]	wagon master	Nekewitz	1015/047
GOETZE	Wilhelm	butcher	Rechmannsdorf	1018/047
GREDE	Arnold	tailor	Uttershausen	1014/047
GROSCH	Dorothea	--	Grosslandorf	1017/047
	Pauline	--		
	--	daughter, 4 y		
GUTHEIL	H. F.	--	Garnsdorf	1016/047
HARNISCH	Johann Gott-1[ieb?]	miller	Kossmannsdorf	1248/057
HEIL	Heinrich	servant [*Dienstknecht*]	Modlich	1253/057
HEINERT	Wilhelm	--	Lippelsdorf, Th	1252/057
HELD	Louise	Frau	Hamburg	1250/057
	Eleanor?	daughter		
	Josephine	daughter		
	Julia	daughter		
HOFFMANN	J. A.	--	Erlenbach	1251/057
HOHENECK	J. E.	--?	Tharand	1247/057
HOPFE	Carl	journeyman carpenter	Loehma	1249/057
JAEGER	Jacob	businessman	Uttershausen, He-Ca	1519/068
JUNGHANS	Carl	cabinetmaker	Schwarzburg	1520/068
KAERGER	Eugen	--	Zuellichau	1687/076
KAISER	C. G. F.	ropemaker?	Saalfeld	1679/076
KATZENBERGER	H.	tailor	Hamburg	1681/076
KATZENSTEIN	Lina	--	Hamburg, Ha [!]	1683/076
	Emanuel	--		
KIRCHHOF	Elise	--	Luebs	1685/076
KLAHR	Heinrich	laborer	Lenzen	1678/076
	Sophia	wife		

List 16 (continued)

KOENIG	Louise	--	Koeditz	1682/076
KOESELOW	Friedrich	saddler	Roempen	1680/076
KOTTA	Julius	tanner	Breslau	1684/076
KRAMER	C. F.	baker	Oschatz	1686/076
LEISER	Ascher	tailor	Loebau	2016/091
LEHNER	Erhardt	technician	Wien	2014/090
LEITHARDT	J. G. D.	manager	Koeditz	2017/091
LERCHE	Theodor	butcher	Saalfeld	2015/091
MARTIN	Christian	basketmaker	Thunis	2265/102
MUELLER	D.	--	Dresden	2266/102
OHNESORGE	Johann?	--	Lenzen	2618/117
	Catharina	--		
OHNESORGE	Johann	shipper [Schiffer]	Lenzen	2619/117
OHNESORGE	Wilhelm	soap manufacturer	Lenzen	2620/117
OHNESORGE	Christian	miller	Lenzen	2622/117
OWES	Johann	peasant	Wellwarn	2621/117
	--	wife		
	--	2 children		
PAPENDIECK	--	Mad[am?]	Magdeburg	2683/121
	--	sister [nurse?]		
	--	5 children		
PICK	C. H.	--	Dresden	2682/121
	Henriette*	--		
	Wilhelmine*	--		
	Maria	--		
	Theodor	--		
	*[May be one person]			
PIETSCH	Friedrich Ludwig	tanner	Wilsdorf	2681/121
REISS	Samuel	potter?	Bremen	2869/130
ROESCH	J. G.	laborer	Obersteinach	2868/130
ROSSTAEUSCHER	A.	businessman	Oels	2870/130
SCHILLING	Christian?	--	Koeditz	3185/143
	Johanna Cn.	wife		
	--	2 small children		
SCHILLING	Johanna Caro-lina	--	Koeditz	3186/143

List 16 (continued)

SCHMIDT	H. F.	peasant	Futtercamp, Ho	3190/143
SCHOENE	Julius	tanner	Heinsberg	3183/143
SCHOENHEIT	Johanna?	--	Schmiedefeld	3184/143
SCHRUT	F. E.	tailor	Dresden	3189/143
SCHUMANN	H.	model builder?	Kossmannsdorf	3182/143
SIEGLITZ	J. W.	mechanic	Jena	3188/143
SPIRO	J. N.	shoemaker	Hamburg	3187/143
TAMRATH	Wilhelmine	Frau	Weimar	3640/162
	Carl	child		
	Louise	child		
VOERTMANN	J. Heinrich	peasant	Retheim	3751/167
VOGEL	G.	laborer	Wien	3748/167
	--	wife		
	Theodor	laborer		
VOGEL	Franz	miller	Frankenstein	3748a/167
	Auguste	--		
	Therese	--		
VORSATZ	Johanna	--	Gleima	3749/167
	--	2 small children		
VORSATZ	Maria	--	Gleima	3750/167
WAACK	Georg	manager	Carlsburg?	3840/172
WALDENBURG	L.	upholsterer	Gross Glogau	3836/172
WALTHER	Margaretha	--	Koeditz	3837/172
WEBER	Georg	manager	Landseedorf	3839/172
WIETZ	August	carpenter	Warnow	3838/172
WINTER	C. F. M.	--	Saalfeld	3833/172
	C. F. W.	--		
WOLFF	Ernst	miller	Schieritz	3832/172
WOZACK	Wenzel	blacksmith	Leschau	3834/172
	--?	wife		
WOZACK	Rosalie	child of W. Wozack	Leschau	3835/172
	Barbara	child of W. Wozack		
	Johann	child of W. Wozack		
ZUMPFE	Wilhelm	14 y (*see* C. G. Dietrich)	Willstruff	4036/181

42

List 17

Ship *Elise* (Hamburg flag) Captain H. D. N. Trautmann
Departing Hamburg 31 Aug 1850 for New York (Direct)

ALBRECHT	Carl	shoemaker	Zella	0088/005
ALBRECHT	Johann	--	Ruest	0090/005
APEL	Gustav	businessman	Schweinfurt	0089/005
BARTH	J. H. Carl	cabinetmaker tailor	Wilmersdorf	0450/020
BASCH	Jutta	--	Loewenberg	0452/020
BEREL	Mathilde	--	Breslau	0454/020
BERNSDORF	H.	carpenter	Bissendorf	0445/020
BIEDERMANN	C. C.	baker	Berlin	0451/020
BOEHM	Joseph	butcher	Leipe	0453/020
BREIDERT	J. A. L.	tailor	Berlin	0448/020
BREIDING	Carl	painter	Braunschweig	0446/020
BRETHSCHNEIDER	Juliane? --	-- baby boy	Coblentz	0449/020
BRUHN	Carl Friederike	wagoner daughter, 7 y	Bordesholm	0447/020
CLASEN	Johann Carolina	butcher --	Parber	0549/025
DRAEUSDORF	C.	--	Plau	0664/031
DREISSE? [DREISPE?]	F. W.	baker	Schmiedeberg	0663/031
ECKOLDSTEIN	Alexander	businessman	Leipzig	0775/036
EHLERT	Wilhelm	manager	Kuckuck	0777/036
ELIASZEWICZ	Carl	painter	Posen	0776/036
ENGEL	Wilhelm	laborer	Helmstedt	0774/036
ENGELS	Heinrich	--	Moelln	0773/036
FALCK	Ricka?	--	Wandsbeck	0921/042
FELDTMANN	Rosa Salomma -- --	-- -- 2 children, 3 & 5 y 1 baby	Posen	0926/043
FLEISCHER	J. W. C.	shoemaker	Berlin	0922/042
FREUNDTEN	Maria	--	Kladrum?	0925/043

List 17 (continued)

FRIEDMANN	Jacob	baker	Baronow	0923/043
	Greta	wife		
FUCHS	Joseph	shoemaker	Wien	0924/043
GLAETZNER	Adolph	tailor	Hamburg	1139/052
GROSSE	August	mechanic	Kirchheim	1138/052
HAENSGEN	Friedrich	cabinetmaker	Naumburg	1421/064
HAGEN	Friedrich	laborer	Grabow	1418/064
HAMBURG	Lorenz	saddler	Cassel	1415/064
HARNITZKY	A. F.	furrier	Berlin	1419/064
HARTWIG	J. E. H.	button maker	Hamburg	1414/064
HEILBRUNNER	Abraham	tailor	Oettingen	1424/064
HELLMER	Barbara	--	Feldsberg	1422/064
HELLWEGE	Therese	6 y [a note says "see F. L." of unknown meaning]	Wien	1417/064
HENNING	G. C.	laborer	Dingelstedt	1420/064
	--	wife		
HEYLAND	A. H.	gardener	Stadtilm	1416/064
HORN	J. C. F.	mechanic	Schwerin	1423/064
	--	wife		
JACOB	Gabriel	tailor	Hamburg	1578/071
	--	wife		
KALB	Jacob	teacher	Breitenbach	1904/085
KEGEL	Heinrich	shoemaker	Erfurt	1915/086
KELLER	Gbr. [= Gebrueder? or brothers?]	--	Leipzig	1913/086
KLEIN	Susmann	tanner	Uitwa	1907/085
KLEINKOPF	Julius	baker	Hirschheim	1905/085
KLUGE	Eduard	tanner	Pritzwalk	1914/086
KOERNER	Theodor	businessman	Leipzig	1911/085
KOHN	Julius	--	Markisch	1909/085
KOHRS	L.	tailor	Hamburg	1912/085
KORMANN	Friedrich	--?	Koenigsee	1908/085
KRAUSE	Johann	cabinetmaker	Wandsbeck	1903/085

List 17 (continued)

KROENCKE	Caroline	--	Hamburg	1906/085
KUCKEMATZWY	Michael	private	Pesth	1910/085
LAMPE	Joachim	--	Altona	2155/096
LARENTZEN? [LORENTZEN?]	Pauline	--	Bredstedt	2152/096
LEITEL	Catharine	--	Uelsen	2156/096
LEMBURG?	Joachim	shoemaker	Burdesholm	2159/097
LEWISOHN	Adolph	soldier	Rosenberg	2157/096
LEWOHL	Joseph	chemist	Szerd	2158/096
LORENZEN	H. C.	Miller	Weddingstedt	2151/096
	J. C.	--		
LOTZE	Elisabeth	--	Koenigsee	2153/096
	Catharina	--		
LOTZE	August	miller	Eichfeld	2154/096
MAENELL	Hermann	bookbinder	Plau	2456/110
MATHIAS	Rosalie	--	Wien	2453/110
	Franziska	--		
MESTER	J. F.	laborer	Volsrade	2457/110
MEYER	C.	tailor	Hamburg	2452/110
MEYER	Friedrich	saddler	Wittenburg	2458/110
MICHALOWSKA	--	Frau	Kempen	2455/110
	Rosa	11 y		
MILCKE	Michael	tailor	Ahrensfelde	2454/110
MUELLER	Gustav	machine builder	Koenigsberg	2451/100
NATHAN	Betty?	--	Hamburg	2589/116
PFEFFERKORN	Valentin	shoemaker	Kreutzberg	2777/125
RAABE	Joachim	tin worker	Zuelckow	3010/135
RADZXATKOWSKY	Joseph	--?	Pesth	3017/136
	--	wife		
RATH	Emil	tailor	Hamburg	3011/135
REHLENDER	Ferdinand	tailor	Neu Strelitz	3008/135
RETHLIN	Wilhelm	tailor	Karbo	3016/136
REUMANN? [RENMANN?]	Paulus	weaver	Schaffhausen	3007/135

List 17 (continued)

RICKOFF	H.	baker	Tribbow	3014/136
RICKOFF	J. H.	laborer	Tribbow	3015/136
RODECK	Julius	court servant? [*Folgediener*]	Berlin	3012/136
ROENNECKE	F. W. -- --	laborer wife 2 children, to 6 y	Dingelstedt	3013/136
RUST	Johann Heinrich	shoemaker	Hamburg	3009/135
SASSE	Amalia --	-- 2 babies	Friedrichsberg	3505/156
SASSE	Friedrich	laborer	Friedrichsberg	3506/156
SCHMIDT	J. F. F. A.	carpenter tailor	Niederzimmern	3515/157
SCHRECK	Dorothea	--	Erfurt	3511/156
SCHROEDER	Wilhelmine	--	Hamburg	3508/156
SCHROEDER	Friedrich	lithographer?	Breslau	3516/157
SCHULTZE	Anton	businessman	Berlin	3510/156
SCHWARTZ	Mathilde Heinrich	Frau son, 7 y	Berlin	3509/156
SELL	Carl --	manager wife	Hohenschoenau	3507/156
SILBERMANN	Moses -- --	furrier daughter, 18 y son, 13 y	Schneidemuehl	3514/157
STAHL	Jochen -- --	blacksmith wife 5 children, 11-19 y	Severin	3512/157
STEINBEISSER	Franz -- -- --	manager wife 2 babies stepdaughter, 6 y [note says "see H.?]	Wien	3513/157
ULRICH	Julius	businessman	Torgau	3729/166
UNGER	Anton	--	Graben	3728/166
WEISS	Christian	--	Heidesbach	3983/179
WETTIG	Friedrich	tailor	Hamburg	3982/179
ZUEHL	Carl	mason	Wangeriehm	4069/183

List 18

Ship *Emma and Louise*, Captain Viereck
Departing Hamburg 8 Jun 1850 for Brazilian Ports (Direct)

ADAM	Christian	-- (to Rio Grande)	Weickenrodt, Bi	0060/004
BOETTCHER	J. A.	--? (to Desterro)	Gross Oerner?	0330/015
BOSSLE	Maria Anna Elisabeth	-- -- (to Rio Grande)	Kollweiler, Ba	0331/015
CROME	J. F.	-- (to Rio Grande)	--	0538/025
DEIENSIG?	Minna	-- (to Rio Grande)	Bartenhausen	0629/029
DRESSEL	Friedrich	-- (to Desterro)	Osterfeld	0628/029
ENGEL	Charlotte	-- (to Desterro)	Wallbeck? [Wall- beik?]	0739/035
FRIEDENREICH	C. W. --	-- family (4 persons, including baby) (to Desterro)	Hettstadt	0879/041
GAERTNER	R. J. C.	-- (to Desterro)	Blankenburg	1073/049
GEIER	--	-- (to Desterro)	Mansfeld	1077/049
GROSSE	Ferdinand Gotth[ilf?] --	-- wife (to Desterro)	Mansfeld	1074/049
GROSSE	J. S? F.	-- (to Desterro)	Mansfeld	1075/049
GROSSE	Lina? Louise -- --	-- daughter baby (to Desterro)	Mansfeld	1076/049
HARMS	Christiane Anna	-- 3 y (to Rio de Janeiro)	Magdeburg	1346/061
HENNECKE	Henriette	-- (to Rio de Janeiro)	Hamburg	1337/060

List 18 (continued)

HEYDTMANN	Anna Sophia	--	Hamburg	1336/060
	Max	--		
	Hugo	--		
		(to Rio Grande)		
HOFFMANN	Ehrig?	--	Osterfeld	1345/061
		(to Desterro)		
KELLNER	Johann Paul	--	Barbecke	1797/081
KOHLMANN	J. F. C.	--	Gross Oerner?	1798/081
	--	wife		
		(to Desterro)		
MOELLER	Adele	--	Hamburg	2365/106
		(to Rio de Janeiro)		
PERSUHN	Hermann	--	Braunschweig	2734/123
		(to Desterro)		
PFAFFENDORFF	J. C. D.	--	Klein Endersdorf	2735/123
		(to Desterro)		
RIMER	Friedrich	--	Osterfeld	2941/133
	August	(to Desterro)		
RITSCHER	J. H. F.	--	Lauterberg	2940/133
		(to Desterro)		
RUFF	L. F.	--	Schelklingen	2942/133
		(to Rio Grande)		
SALLENTIEN	Franz	--	Braunschweig	3350/150
		(to Desterro)		
SCHNEIDER	Philip	--	Wickenrodt	3352/150
		(to Rio Grande)		
SEYDEL	Hermann	--	Magdeburg	3351/150
		(to Rio de Janeiro)		
ULLRICH	Gottfried	--	Wullbeck	3722/166
		(to Desterro)		

List 19

Ship *Emmy*, Captain J. Homeyer
Departing Hamburg 23 Nov 1850 for Valparaiso (Direct)

ANDERSSEN	J.	shoemaker	Luna, Sb	0108/006
ANDERSSEN	L.	laborer	Luna, Sb	0109/006

48

ANDERSSON	A. F.	soldier	Westervick, Sw	0112/006
ANDERSSON	F.	businessman	Skaraborgslaen, Sw	0111/006
ANDERSSON	W.	soldier	Elfbargslaen, Sw	0110/006
BEAUMONT	Eduard	gardener	Kornthal, Wu	0489/022
BENEDIXON	Magnus Andreas	--? --	Joenkoepingslaen, Sw	0492/022
BERGGREN	J. A.	soldier	Joenkoepingslaen, Sw	0493/022
BIELHUBER	Otto	--	Vahingen, Wu	0491/022
BOHNHOLZER	M.	potter	Lauffen am Neckar, Wu	0488/022
BRUNN? [BRUUN?]	T. A.	businessman	Copenhagen	0487/022
BUEHLER	Fritz	beer brewer	Vahingen am Neckar, Wu	0490/022
DANZ	F.	miner	Bieber, He-Ca	0683/031
DUHN	Margaretha Elisabeth	-- --	Hamburg	0682/031
ECKSTROEM	A. A.	petty officer	Joenkoepingslaen, Sw	0795/037
von EKENSTEEN	B. A. L.	soldier --	Hallund, Sw	0796/037
ELG	G.	businessman	Stockholm	0798/037
ENGGVIST	C.	soldier	Westervick, Sw	0797/037
GUNDLACH	Jacob	businessman	Lohr, Ba	1160/053
HAGELQVIST	Samuel? [Lemuel?]	peasant	Wexsa	1482/066
HAMMARSTRAND	M. W.	miner	Stockholm	1483/066
JENSEN	J.	businessman	Flensburg, Sl	1597/072
JETTER?	Jacob	carpenter	Balingen	1595/072
JOHANSON	C. J.	laborer	Tonkoepingslaen? [Joenkoepingslaen?] Sw	1596/072
JOHANSON	J.	laborer	Stockholm	1598/072
LANDSTROEM	R? [B?]	soldier	Stockholm	2200/098
MAGNUSON	J.	soldier	Bohuslaen, Sw	2494/112

List 19 (continued)

MESSER	Kilian	businessman	Lohr, Ba	2492/111
MICHAELSEN	J. D.	businessman	Copenhagen	2493/111
OSBECK	C. A.	soldier	Bohuslaen, Sw	2651/119
SCHEIBLE	Friederike	--	Lauffen am Neckar, Wu	3596/160
SCHIEK	Heinrich	--?	Heilbronn, Wu	3597/160
SCHMIDT	E. H.	businessman	Hamburg	3593/160
SCHUETZ	Ernst	farmer	Butigheim, Wu?	3598/160
SCHULER	Daniel	manufacturer	Waldorf	3599/160
SODERLING	G. E.	peasant	Westervick, Sw	3600/160
SOEDLING	C. E.	doctor	Westervick, Sw	3594/160
STROEM	Jacob C.	businessman	Aalesund	3595/160
TAUBE	Eduard	cabinetmaker	Gera	3707/165
WARMARK	C. A.	soldier	Bohnslaen, Sw	4012/180
WILHELMI	Wolrad	baker	Yersberg, He-Ca	4011/180

List 20

Ship *Esther*, Captain R? Hartnoll
Departing Hamburg 2 Nov 1850 for Rio Grande do Sul, Brazil (Direct)

ADAM	Johann	shoemaker	Parchau	0107/006
	--	wife		
	--	son, 2 y		
ANDERS	Gottl[ieb?]	miller	Gohlau	0106/006
BAATZ	Carl	businessman	Belitz, Pr	0486/022
	Friederike	wife		
	Rosalia	daughter, 3/4 y		
BECKER	Gottlob	laborer	Kosel	0485/022
BECKER	Heinrich Friedrich	laborer	Kosel, Pr	0484/022
	--	son, 12 y		
ECKARDT	Anton	pupil	Kutlau, Pr	0794/037
HANSEL	Franz	--	Luckau? [Suckau?]	1480/066
	Joseph	--		

List 20 (continued)

HANSEL	Johann Carl	farmer	Luckau? [Suckau?]	1479/066
	Therese	--		
HENNIG	Johann	butcher	Quaritz	1481/066
	--	wife		
	--	2 children, 2 & 16 y		
HILBIG	Franz	glazier	Klopschen, Pr	1478/066
	--	wife		
	--	6 children, ½-10 y		
JACOB	Ignatz	plowman	Klopschen, Pr	1594/072
JOHN	Hedwig	maid	Klopschen, Pr	1593/072
KARL	Alexander	saddler	Klopschen, Pr	1956/087
	--	wife		
	--	2 sons, 9 & 17 y		
KLIMANN	Franz	gardener	Klopschen, Pr	1957/087
	--	wife		
	--	6 children, ½-14 y		
LANGE	Julius	--?	Beuthen, Pr	2198/098
LUDWIG	Christian	laborer	Leipe, Pr	2199/098
	--	wife		
	--	2 children, 4 & 9 y		
MUELLER	Gottl[ieb?]	wheelwright	Quaritz	2491/111
	Heinrich	mill builder		
OHLAND	Joseph	cabinetmaker	Klopschen, Pr	2650/119
	Johanna	wife		
PAETZOLD	Franz	carpenter	Gohlau, Pr	2810/126
PRAETZEL	Joseph	cabinetmaker	Kotzemenschel	2809/126
	August	butcher		
PREUSS	August	brewer? [builder?]	Klopschen	2807/126
PRITSCH	Bernhard	farmhand	Froebel, Pr	2808/126
PUTZKE	Christian?	gardener	Klopschen, Pr	2805/126
	--	wife		
	--	3 children, 4-6 y		
PUTZKE	Franz	mover?	Klapschen [Klop- 2806/126	
	Ambrosius	--	schen]	
RABUSKE	Carolina	maid	Ransdorf, Pr	3051/137
RABUSKE	Anton	gardener	Ransdorf, Pr	3052/137
	--	wife		
	--	6 children, 4-19 y		

List 20 (continued)

RASCHKE	Wilhelm	miller	Kleinlogisch, Pr	3053/137
SCHULZ	Ernst	tailor	Klopschen, Pr	3592/160
SCHUNDER	Ernestine?	maid	Klopschen, Pr	3589/160
SEIPOLD	Joseph	merchant	Leipe, Pr	3591/160
	--	wife		
	--	2 children, 3 & 9 y		
STANDKE	Joseph	farmhand	Kosiadel, Pr	3590/160
TULCKE	Florian	weaver	Suckau? [Luckau?] Pr	3706/165
WINKELMANN	Anton	merchant	Klopschen, Pr	4010/180
	--	wife		
	--	2 children, 16 & 20 y		

List 21

Ship *Fortunatus* (Prussian flag) Captain N. G. Claasen
Departing Hamburg 16 Apr 1850 for Quebec (Direct)

ADERHOLD	Gottfried	glazier	Kelbra, Pr	0031/003
	--	wife		
ADERHOLD	Christian	--	Kelbra, Pr	0032/003
	Friederike	--		
	Auguste	--		
	Hermann	--		
APEL	J. C. F.	--	Lebra	0033/003
	--	wife		
	Carl Christian	--		
	August	--		
	Jutta?	--		
	Franz	--		
BEHRENS	Daniel	cabinetmaker	Goldberg	0189/009
	--	wife		
BEHRENS	Fritz	--	Goldberg	0190/009
	Heinrich	--		
	Georg	--		
	Maria	--		
BECKER	G. H.	mason	Weimar	0181/009
	--	wife		

List 21 (continued)

BECKER	Julie	--	Weimar	0182/009
BEHR	Pauline	--	Weimar	0183/009
BLASIG	Joseph	cloth cutter	Oppeln, Ho	0180/009
BLUETHMANN	J. C.	shepherd	Osterburg	0184/009
BLUETHMANN	Elisabeth	--	Osterburg	0185/009
	Christine	--		
BLUNCK	Conrad	laborer	Goldberg	0188/009
BOCKE	H. J.	machinist	Lichtenhain	0186/009
BOHN	Carl F.	mechanic	Langensalza	0187/009
BRESSEL	Carl August	--	Gobitz	0191/009
	Johanne			
	Sophie	--		
DIECKMANN	--	--?	Niehof	0588/027
EICKELBERG	Louise	--	Goldberg	0703/033
FEIGE	Heinrich	shoemaker	Leipzig	0826/038
	--	wife		
FEIGE	Friederike	--	Leipzig	0827/039
	Amalia	--		
	Heinrich	--		
	Richard	--		
	Theodor	--		
FROEHLICH	C. F.	comb maker	Jena	0825/038
GERTZ	Hans	shoemaker	Rena	1001/046
GODECKE	Wilhelm	blacksmith	Osterburg	1002/046
GRAMBOW	Friedrich	peasant	Niehof	1004/046
GUENTHER	Heinrich	mason	Weimar	1003/046
	Wilhelm			
HAHN	Wilhelm	painter	Magdeburg	1229/056
HEMMING	Friedrich	brickmaker	Malsdorf	1232/056
HEMMY	Ernest [so	--	Molsdorf	1231/056
	spelled]			
	August	--		
	Christoph	--		
HINSKE	E. R.	rope maker?	Fraustadt, Pr	1228/056
HINSKE	August	furrier	Fraustadt, Pr	1230/056
	--	wife		
	Carl	--		
	Amalia	--		

List 21 (continued)

JUNG	Carl	tailor	Kirchkogel, Ho	1515/068
KAEMPF	Carl	shoemaker	Luechow, Pr	1658/075
KOBERMANN	Eberhard	businessman	Marienwerder	1657/075
KOENIG	Elisabetha	--	Kleinau, Pr	1654/075
KRAGEL	Wilhelm	cabinetmaker	Salzwedel	1659/075
KRUMPE	C. A.	--	Liederstadt	1660/075
	--	wife		
	Christian	--		
	Wilhelm	--		
KRUMPE	Julia	--	Liederstadt	1661/075
	Charlotte	--		
	Emma	--		
	Carl	--		
KUHL	J. W?	manager	Gispersleben	1655/075
	--	wife		
	Elisabeth	--		
	Catharina	--		
KUHL	Benjamin	child	Gispersleben?	1656/075
	Carl			
	Louise	child		
LAMMERTS	P. C. D.	blacksmith	Tetenbuell, Ho	2007/090
LEHMANN	Anton	businessman	Burkhaslach, Pr	2010/090
	--	son		
LEHNIS	Maria Rebecca	--	Elexleben	2009/090
LUTKENMEYER	C. L.	businessman	Herford	2008/090
MEISTER	Eduard	tailor	Kelbra	2259/102
MESSER	Wilhelm	laborer	Gispersleben	2260/102
	--	wife		
MESSER	Carolina	child	Gispersleben	2261/102
	Maria	child		
NEIMANN	Sophia	--	Goldberg	2530/113
NEUSS	C? B?	butcher?	Weimar	2531/113
NEUSS	Carl	--	Weimar	2532/113
	Albert	--		
	Anna	--		
NUERNBERGER	J. F.	laborer	Rodo	2529/113
OBERDIECK	C. H.	glazier	Wustrow	2617/117
OETERER	Carl	miller	Treffurt, Ho	2616/117

List 21 (continued)

PETERSEN	Jacob	tailor	Kleinbenebeck	2668/120
REIMER	Friedrich	tailor	Doppertin	2856/129
RICHHOFF	A. L.	tailor	Schwerin	2857/129
RICHTER	A.	shoemaker	Braunschweig	2858/129
RUPPRECHT	Barbara	--	Salzungen	2859/129
SCHIMCKE	Christian	wheelwright	Janischwalde	3158/142
SCHINKE	Michael	laborer	Zachow	3159/142
SCHIRMER	Friedrich	blacksmith	Pritschen	3161/142
SCHLAFMANN	Dorothea	--	Kleinau? [Kleman?] Pr	3160/142
SCHMIDT	W. G.	shoemaker	Hamburg	3156/142
SCHMIDT	J. H.	shoemaker	Mellingen	3157/142
SCHNEIDER	Jacob	soldier	Marienwerder	3163/142
SCHULTZ	Carl	shoemaker	Oberbilau	3155/142
SCHWENDT	Carl	shoemaker	Hannover	3154/141
SIERING	G. C. W.	cabinetmaker	Gamstadt	3162/142
SUCKAU	Johann	soldier	Marienwerder	3164/142
TACKMANN	Johann	tailor	Goldberg	3636/162
TACKMANN	Lisette Josephine	-- child	Goldberg	3637/162
TAPPERT	Heinrich	laborer	Hochheim	3638/162
TONNDORF	J. A. C. --	shoemaker wife	Weimar	3634/162
TONNDORF	Pauline Maria	-- --	Weimar	3635/162
VORBECK	Christian	laborer	Andorf? [Audorf?] Ho	3746/167
WARNECKE	Carl --	carpenter wife	Kleinau, Pr	3822/171
WIMMER	Ernestine	--	Mellingen	3821/171

List 22

Ship *Franklin* (Hamburg flag) Captain C. F. Rohlueffs?
Departing Hamburg 16 Apr 1850 for New York (Direct)

ALBRAND	W. F? T.	peasant	Luebow	0026/003
AMBERG	Christian	peasant	Mendhausen	0028/003
ANDREASEN	Caroline?	girl	Foehr	0029/003
ARFSTEN	J. Christian	peasant	Foehr	0030/003
ARNOLD	B. A.	tailor	Meuselbach	0027/003
	--	wife		
	Franz August	--		
	Maria	--		
	Ernst	--		
BAEHRING	Heinrich	mechanic	Koenigsee	0179/009
BASOLD	Franz	miller	Rembden	0176/009
BEHREND	D.	cabinetmaker	Bevensdorf	0178/009
BLUMENSTANGEL	Carl	manager	Helmstedt	0177/009
CZARENTZKY	Alexander	--?	Breslau	0519/024
	--	wife		
	Emma	child		
DENKER	J. P.	laborer	Hoseldorf? [Haseldorf?]	0587/027
EBENER	Horenz?	carpenter	Saal	0701/033
ENGELMANN	Robert	furrier	Lissa	0702/033
FISCHER	Moritz	metal worker [*Gelbgiesser*]	Berlin	0822/038
FRANZEL	Joseph	peasant	Gutwitz	0821/038
FUCHS	Hermann	merchant	Wien	0824/038
FUGLI	C.	businessman	Zuerich	0823/038
GOTTEL	J.	barrel maker?	Leipzig	1000/046
	Clemens	barrel maker?		
GRABOW	Otto	businessman	Roebel, Mk	0999/046
GROSSMEYER	J.	plumber	Gadebusche	0998/046
HAGEN	Adolph	--	Schwerin	1227/056
	--	baby		
HAMMELMANN	Barbara	--	Dietersdorf	1224/056
	Heinrich	--		
HERZ	Heymann	soldier	Strassburg	1221/056

List 22 (continued)

HEYMANN	J.	soldier	Neumark	1220/056
HIRT	Hermann	sailmaker	Remden	1218/055
HOFFMANN	Dorothea	--	Hannsheim	1226/056
	Heinrich	--		
HOFMANN	H.	dyer	Hannsheim	1225/056
	--	wife		
HOLTZ	Moritz	tailor	Posen	1222/056
HOPSTOCK	Adolph	soldier	Grimen	1219/055
HUCKE	G. G.	writer?	Langershausen	1223/056
JACOBY	Salomon	baker	Posen	1513/068
JOHN	Johann	machinist?	Muehlenberg	1514/068
JOSEPH	Moses	shoemaker	Strassburg	1512/068
KAISER	F.	furrier	Lissa	1653/075
KLEBER	W. L.	cabinetmaker	Kolberg	1652/075
KOENIG	Friedrich	--	Coeln	1651/075
LINKE	H.	brewer	Erfurt	2005/090
LOBEDANZ	Ludwig	soldier	Nassau	2003/090
LOEFBLAD	A. F.	soldier	Hamburg	2006/090
LUBLIN	David	furrier	Lissa	2004/090
MAYENBERG	K.	businessman	Adelebsen	2258/102
MEISSNER	Otto	cook	Coethen	2254/102
METZL	Siegmund?	--	Brake	2257/102
MOVES	Clemens	carpenter?	Cottbus	2255/102
	--	wife		
MUELLER	Elise	--	Schwerin	2256/102
NACK	J?	saddler	Langerhausen [San-genhausen?]	2528/113
NEUMANN	N.	furrier	Lissa	2527/113
NOAK	Albert	butcher	Berlin	2526/113
NOWACK	Johann	master baker	Petersdorf	2525/113
	Ernestine	(illegible notation)		
ORLAWSKY	Friedrich	brush maker	Marienwerder	2615/117
PUTZIGER	Salomon	soldier	Alt Huette	2667/120
ROBERT	Adolph	blacksmith	Schwerin	2855/129

List 22 (continued)

ROCKSER	Otto	brewer	Marienwerder	2854/129
ROSSMER	Georg	mason	Sesslach	2853/129
SACHER	Gottl[ieb?]	wood turner	Brelsau	3141/14
SALOMON	C. A. F. Maria	doctor? wife	Schwerin	3151/141
SALOSCHIN	Gabriel	tailor	Lissa	3149/141
SCHAEDEL	Dorothea	--	Sassbach	3148/141
SCHAEFER	Carl	plumber	Schwerin	3153/141
SCHARETZKY	Roesche?	--	Posen	3147/141
SCHULTZE	Johann	laborer	Schwerin	3150/141
SCHWINDEMANN	Andreas	mechanic	Speyer	3142/141
SOLTMANN	Christian	shoemaker	Coethen	3143/141
STAEDLER	Adolph	--	Eisenach	3145/141
STEIN	Eleanora	--	Schoenbrunn	3139/141
STEIN	Anton Franz	shoemaker shoemaker	Schoenbrunn	3140/141
STEUBER	Friederike?	Mad[am?]	Eisenach	3144/141
STOLLEG? [STOLLEY?]	L?	teacher	Segeberg	3146/141
SUSSMANN	Julius	soldier	Glueckstadt	3152/141
TEECK? [TEECKE?]	Adolph	peasant	Gossdorf	3632/162
TRALLES	Friedrich	cabinetmaker	Kistrinchen	3631/162
TRINKAUS	W.	cabinetmaker	Sangerhausen? [Langerhausen?]	3633/162
UHRBACH	C. F. --	tailor wife	Lueneburg	3716/166
VIEDEBRANDT	E. A. H. J. A. G.	high school student high school student	Berlin	3745/167
VIEDT	Friedrich	houseboy	Grassleben	3741/167
VOLCKER	Louis	soldier	Grimmen	3740/167
VOSS	Johann --	peasant wife	Junien	3742/167
VOSS	Anna Marga- retha Dorothea Claus Catharina	-- -- -- --	Junien	3743/167

58

List 22 (continued)

VOSS	Johann	--	Junien	3744/167
	--	wife		
	Anna Catharina	[perhaps wife's name]		
	--	baby		
WEIDNER	J. G.	cabinetmaker	Seifersdorf	3819/171
WILKEN	Franz	blacksmith	Malchow	3820/171
ZIMMERMANN	Wilhelm	cabinetmaker	Feinsberg, Si	4034/181
	--	wife		

List 23

Ship *Franklin* (Hamburg flag) Captain C. F. Rohlueffs?
Deparging Hamburg 15 Aug 1850 for New York (Direct)

ASCHER	Carl	manager	Ribnitz	0082/005
BAGGERT	C. E. L.	--	Wismar	0428/019
BARTELS	Elise	--	Otterndorf	0425/019
BASCH	Heymann	tailor	Posen	0423/019
	Maria? [Minna?]	wife		
BOHN	Ludwig	tanner?	Parchim	0426/019
BOHN	Carl	dyer	Parchim	0427/019
BUCHIN	Friedrich	shoemaker	Krackow	0424/019
COHEN	August	soldier	Hamburg	0547/025
DAHNCKE	Christian	--?	Luebz	0657/030
	--	wife		
	--	3 children, 5-10 y		
EBERT	H.	manager	Lesen	0769/036
	--	wife		
	--	3 children, 10-19 y		
EBERT	Carl	manager	Wittenburg	0770/036
ELCKIN	Eduard	businessman	Philadelphi	0768/036
	Jacob	8 y		
GECK	Heinrich	--	Marwitz	1129/052
GEICK	Dorothea	--	Sichelkow	1128/052
GROSSMANN	Carl	cabinetmaker	Schwerin	1127/052
	--	wife		
	--	daughter, ½ y		

List 23 (continued)

GRUBERT	G. F.	manager	Tauchwitz	1126/052
	--	wife		
	--	3 children, 8½-18 y		
HECHT	Joseph	shoemaker	Wiesaw? [Wiesau?]	1403/063
HEMMINGS	Johann	laborer	Tessin	1405/063
HERR	Fritz	footman	Parchim	1404/063
JANTZEN	--	teacher	Glashagen	1576/071
KAMPF	Johann	laborer	Roth	1891/085
KEMPIEN	Wilhelm	shoemaker	Duemerhuette	1887/084
KOENIG	Fritz	--	Wittenburge	1889/085
KROEDL	Franz	--?	Altenburg	1890/085
KRONENBERG	Bertha	--	Hamburg	1885/084
KRUEGER	Friedrich Gotthilf	furrier	Senftenberg	1888/084
KRULL	Carl	tailor	Howisch	1886/084
	--	wife		
	--	2 children, ¼ & 2 y		
LEUCHTER	Isaac	cigarmaker	Krackow	2134/095
LIEBERMANN	Eleanora	--	Graefenthal	2136/096
LORENZ	Louis	businessman	Hamburg	2135/096
MARTICKE	Heinrich Eduard	miller	Grockow	2434/109
MUELLER	Johanna	--	Grossnenndorf	2433/109
MUELLER	Christian	tailor	Grossnenndorf	2435/109
NEGENDANCK	Friederike	--	Krackow	2586/116
NOEBEL	Hugo A.	architect	Harthan, Sa	2587/116
PAGELS	J.	bricklayer	Marnitz	2766/124
	Maria	--		
PETERS	Wilhelm	--	Wustrow	2762/124
POREP	Carl	shoemaker	Grabow	2767/124
PRAHL	Sophia	--	Schwerin	2765/124
PREHN	C. N.	wheelwright	Stannsdorf	2763/124
	F. J. J.	--		
PRESTIN	Ludwig	cabinetmaker	Buchholz	2764/124
REMAK	Julius	furrier	Posen	2986/134

List 23 (continued)

RITZ	Nicolaus	wagoner	Walldorf	2991/135
RODEIM	Anna	--	Friedenfels	2987/134
ROTHLANDER	Otto	manager	Lesen	2988/135
	Sophia	wife		
SANDER	Rosina	--	Posen	3464/155
SATTLER	Friedrich	cabinetmaker	Neustadt	3475/155
SCHIKOROWSKY	Wilhelm	saddler	Marienwerder	3468/155
SCHROEDER	J. F.	shoemaker	Carow	3472/155
SCHUBERT	H.	weaver	Hildburghausen	3476/155
SCHUETT	C. J.	clothmaker	Malchow	3470/155
	Maria	wife		
SCHULZ	Christian	peasant	Romanshof	3465/155
	--	wife		
	--	daughter, 2 y		
SCHULZ	Andreas	peasant	Romanshof	3466/155
	--	wife		
	--	3 children, 2, 6, & 25 y		
SCHULZ	Gottl[ieb?]	peasant	Romanshof	3467/155
	--	wife		
	--	5 children, 1½-13 y		
SEIDEMANN	B.	soldier	Warschau	3469/155
SEIDENSCHNUR	J. W. C.	--	Wismar	3477/155
SONTAG	G. Conrad	manager	Steinbach	3471/155
	--	wife		
	--	3 children, 5½-11 y		
STOLLE	Ernst	cabinetmaker	Cramow	3474/155
SYDOW	Adolph	weaponsmaker	Otterndorf	3473/155
VETTERLEIN	Ch. F.	--	Oelmitz	3771/168
	Friederike	--		
	Wilhelmine	--		
VOSS	Christian	tailor	Kassbade	3770/168
WEHRMANN	Wilhelm	businessman	Zwickau	3973/178
WESTPHAL	Emil	--	Hamburg	3971/178
WIGGES	Dick	laborer	St. Margarethen, Ho	3972/178
WITTINGEN	Carolina	--	Grafenthal	3975/179
WORTMANN	C. F.	glazier	Grabow	3974/179
ZAHN	G.	cabinetmaker	Berlin	4067/182

List 24

Ship *Gellert*, Captain H. Ihlder
Departing Hamburg 18 May 1850 for San Francisco, California (Direct)

von APPEN	Christian	--?	Hamburg	0045/003
BARKHAUS	H.	houseboy	Hamburg	0277/013
BARKHAUS	Dorothea	--?	Hamburg	0278/013
BARTUSCH	Johann	businessman	Stachal? Sa	0281/013
BEHRENDT	Vincent	manager	Braunsberg	0275/013
BEHRENDT	Juliann	--?	Braunsberg	0276/013
BIEL	P. C.	agent	Hamburg	0282/013
BLASSMANN	C. E?	ship's doctor	Barmen	0273/013
BOEHRT	Julius	architect?	Hamburg	0274/013
BOHEMANN	Alb	cabinetmaker	Hamburg	0280/013
BOLLMAYER	Conrad	businessman	Altona	0272/013
BROCKER	Dorothea	--?	Hamburg	0279/013
DIETZE	August	miller	Torgau	0617/029
DUVE	Rudolph	businessman	Hamburg	0616/029
EBERWALD	F. W.	miller	Waimar [so spelled]	0724/034
ELBORG	Julius	businessman	Hamburg	0723/034
ENDEL	Carl	miller	Torgau	0722/034
ENGERT	A. F. C.	businessman	Hamburg	0725/034
FREWERT	H.	cabinetmaker	Flotow, Pr	0854/040
FRUECHTENICH	Jacob	--?	Gross Nordende	0852/040
GALSTER	C. F.	cabinetmaker	Berlin	1048/048
GOETZ	George	waiter	Nuernberg	1044/048
GOETZE	A.	businessman	Berlin	1046/048
GRASS	W. L?	seaman	Gothenburg	1045/048
GRASSHOFF	F.	cabinetmaker	Burg, Pr	1047/048
GRUND	C. F. R.	architect	Hamburg	1043/048
HAAKER	A. F. W.	plumber	Altona	1301/059
HANSSEN	H. P.	businessman	Flensburg	1297/059
HARBORDT	Ferdinand	businessman	Hamburg	1298/059
HENSING	Otto	businessman	Lichtenberg, Grand-duchy of ?	1300/059

List 24 (continued)

HEYER	August	baker	Hamburg	1302/059
HOLLANDER	Daniel --	ship's carpenter wife	Hamburg	1303/059
HOLZENBACHER	Carl Otto	miller	Torgau?	1299/059
HOMEYER	Max --	--? wife	Muenchen	1304/059
JAHNKE	Carl August -- --	master mason wife 3 children, 5-9 y	Hamburg	1540/069
JUSTH	E.	lithographer	Verboca, Hu	1539/069
KLAUS	Friedrich	machinist	Eger, Bo	1753/079
KLUTHE	George	cabinetmaker	Stade	1748/079
KOESER	Dietrich	seaman	Hamburg	1747/079
KRAKUHN	August	see Michael Wobbe	Braunsberg	1749/079
KRAUSE	F. W.	cabinetmaker	Darkehmen, Pr	1751/079
KRIPPENSTAPEL	Gottfried? Gotth[ilf?]	machinist? --	Lauenburg	1750/079
KUEHNELL	F. C. R.	ship's carpenter	Hamburg	1752/079
LANGE	C. F. A.	peasant	Copenhagen	2055/092
LETH	W. P.	architect	Kopenhagen	2053/092
LIMPRECHT	August	coachman	Schwerborn, Pr	2054/092
LUEDERS	Johanna	maid	Hamburg	2058/092
LUND	H. Peter	mason	Copenhagen	2056/092
LUND	Niels Alex- ander	mason	Copenhagen	2057/092
MARTENS	Christian	--?	Kiel	2314/104
MEYER	Albertus -- --	businessman wife 3 daughters, 12-20 y	Bremen	2315/104
MEYER	L. Ferdinand -- --	businessman wife mother	Hamburg	2309/104
MEYER	Johann Fried- rich	architect	Kopenhagen	2310/104
MONTAIGUE	C.	businessman	Heiligenstadt, --?	2313/104
MOSHEIMER	I? [J?]	master builder	Heiligenstadt, --?	2312/104

List 24 (continued)

MUELLER	Johann	businessman	Hamburg	2311/104
MUELLER	N.	cabinetmaker	Oberhoechstedt, Ba	2316/104
NACHMANN	Adolph	--?	Riga	2546/114
NEYDHARDT	J. P. W.	cabinetmaker	Hamburg	2548/114
NEIMANN	Robert	businessman	Rheda, Pr	2545/114
NOERENBERG? [NORENBERG?]	Wilhelm August	cabinetmaker	Neukirchen, Pm	2547/114
OETTL	Franz Nanny?	singer? wife	Landeck, Ty Prepwitz, Bo	2631/118
OHMS	M.	Doctor Philologicae	Ploen	2629/118
OLDEHUS	Peter	seaman	Uetersen	2630/118
PETERSEN	L? F.	real estate agent	Kopenhagen	2712/122
PEYNE	Julius	businessman	Kopenhagen	2713/122
PLOETZ	J. C.	butcher	Hamburg	2714/122
REILS	J. H.	businessman	Hamburg	2896/131
REINECKE	H. C.	ship's carpenter	Hamburg	2898/131
RODE	G.	seaman	Gothenburg	2897/131
SCHERPEL	Rudolph	cabinetmaker	Hamburg	3282/147
SCHIFF	Bertha	--	Altona	3291/147
SCHMIDT	Carl	miller	Targau	3283/147
SCHMIDT	H. W.	businessman	Lueneburg	3287/147
SCHNABEL	C. H.	wheelwright	Hamburg	3289/147
SCHOLZ	George	cabinetmaker	Hamburg	3288/147
SCHREVE	Carl Gustav	businessman	Hamburg	3292/147
SCHROEDER	Christian	businessman	Copenhagen	3281/147
SCHUVOIGT	G. H.	pharmacist	Ratzeburg	3286/147
SCHYTHE? [SCHIJTHE?]	Juergen Christian	--?	Copenhagen	3280/147
STADLER	H.	cabinetmaker	Hamburg	3290/147
STAHL	Claus	seaman	Uetersen	3284/147
STAPPENBECK	H.	carpenter	Luechow	3293/147
STOCK	C. H. *or* Frewert --	carpenter wife	Hamburg	3285/147

List 24 (continued)

THODE	Hinrich	horseshoer	Altona	3655/163
USLAR	Franz	businessman	Harburg	3718/166
WAGENER	Joseph	painter	Hamburg	3894/175
	--	wife		
	--	small child		
WEGENER	F. O.	architect	Hamburg	3890/175
WEIDEL	Louis	illustrator?	Wien	3899/175
WENDELSTADT	C. F. A.	physician	Stade	3889/175
WESSELS	Hinrich	--?	Hamburg	3896/175
WILHELMI	Johann[es?]	--?	Hamburg	3897/175
	Elisabeth	--		
WINKLER	Eduard	businessman	Stockholm	3900/175
WITMANN	Carl	cabinetmaker	Hamburg	3895/175
WITT	C. H.	goldsmith	Hamburg	3898/175
WOBBE	Michael	carpenter	Braunsberg	3893/175
	--	wife		
	--	child		
	--	foster child, August Krakuhn, 15 y		
WOLFF	Carl Heinrich	cloth--?	Torgau, Pr	3892/175
WOLLMER	Minna	--	Hamburg	3891/175
ZIMMERN	Georg	gold worker	Hamburg	4043/181

List 25

Ship *Gustav*, Captain G. J. v. Santen
Departing Hamburg 10 Jun 1850 for San Francisco (Direct)

AVERBERG	Carl Theodor	businessman	Hamburg	0059/004
	--	wife, b Krauss		
BAUER	Moritz	artist	Hamburg	0328/015
BRODERSEN	B.	businessman	Flensburg	0327/015
BUDEY	Joseph	industrialist	Presburg	0329/015
BULLING	Maria	--?	Falkenburg	0326/015
CRAMER	Carl	--?	Dresden	0537/025
EISFELD	--	cook.	Hamburg	0738/035
	--	wife		

List 25 (continued)

GEBHARDT	Carl Joseph	--?	Odenheim	1071/049
GROENEWALD	Theodor	--?	Neunkirchen	1072/049
HAACKER	W.	plumber	Hamburg	1343/061
HADLIG	Louis	waiter	Guestrow	1342/061
HELLMER	Ferdinand	businessman	Berlin	1340/061
HENSCHEL	H. L.	businessman	Hamburg	1338/060
HERMANN	H. F.	--?	Hamburg	1339/060
	--	wife		
HOLST	Carl	businessman	Guestrow	1341/061
HUBENER	Adolph	businessman	Bremen	1344/061
KERDEL	Rudolph	manager?	Hamburg	1796/081
KRAUSS	Carl	--?	Bueckeburg	1795/081
KUEHL	Elise	--	Hamburg	1794/081
LUESCHOW?	C. D. A.	businessman	Hamburg	2082/093
MARTIN	--	--?	Hamburg	2363/106
MAURICE	Eduard	soldier	Hamburg	2362/106
MEYER	H.	businessman	Teterow	2364/106
PESTNER	Ernst	--?	Harburg	2733/123
POHLMANN	E. H. W.	gold worker	Hamburg	2732/123
RESTNER	Ernst	printer?	Harburg	2938/132
ROTHHAR	H. H.	businessman	Bremen	2939/132
SCHONDORFF	R.	businessman	Teherow [Teterow?]	3347/150
SCHWABE	--	physician	Hamburg	3346/150
SIBBERS	M. S.	businessman	Chr. Alb Koog, Sl	3349/150
SLATAPER	A.	clothmaker	Triest	3345/150
SOMMER	Johann	ship's --?	Assel am Stade, Kedingen? [Gdingen?]	
THULIN	--	Mad[am?]	Hamburg	3666/163
UMLAUFF	J. G.	cabinetmaker	Hamburg	3721/166
WEISS	Carl Ludwig	maitre d'hotel	Cassel	3925/176
WESTERICH	Albrecht	businessman	Harburg	3923/176
WOLFF	A. J.	jeweler	Hamburg	3924/176
WOLLHEIM	J. H.	businessman	Hamburg	3922/176

SURNAME INDEX
By Ship-List Number

HINSKE, 21
von HIPPEL, 10
HIRSCH, 13
HIRSCH, 14
HIRT, 22
HOEPPNER, 7
HOFFMANN, 2, 14, 16, 18, 22
HOFMANN, 22
HOHENECK, 16
HOLLANDER, 24
HOLM, 15
HOLMSTROEM, 3
HOLST, 13, 25
HOLTERMANN, 2
HOLTZ, 22
HOLZENBACHER, 24
HOMEYER, 24
HOPFE, 12, 16
HOPSTOCK, 22
HORN, 17
HOSTEDT, 2
HOWELING, 13
HUBENER, 25
HUCKE, 22
HUMMERT, 9
HUSCH, 12
HUTH, 4

ISAACK, 13

JACHELL, 13
JACHELT, 13
JACOB, 8, 10, 17, 20
JACOBS, 3, 11
JACOBSEN, 14
JACOBY, 22
JAEGER, 5, 16
JAHN, 4, 12
JAHN. *See also* JOHN
JAHNKE, 24
JANS, 6
JANTZEN, 23
JARESKI, 13
JASCHKE, 10
JAUCH, 12
JENSEN, 19
JENSEN. *See also* JANTZEN
JENTZSCH, 5

JEPSEN, 2
JETTER, 19
JOHANSON, 19
JOHN, 20, 22
JOHN. *See also* JAHN
JOSEPH, 22
JUERSS, 7
JUNG, 21
JUNGHANS, 16
JUSTH, 24

KADEN, 13
KAEMMER, 12
KAEMPF, 21
KAERGER, 16
KAESTNER, 12
KAISER, 16, 22
KALB, 17
KAMCKE, 13
KAMPF, 23
KAMPF. *See also* KAEMPF
KANBA, 15
KANNEWURF, 3
KAPFER, 13
KARL, 20
KARLSEN. *See* CARLSEN
KASPAR. *See* CASPAR
KATHWITZ, 15
KATTE, 7
KATTNER, 10
KATZENBERGER, 16
KATZENSTEIN, 16
KATZSCH, 13
KAUFFMANN, 10
KAVEL, 13
KECHOR, 1
KEGEL, 17
KELLER, 17
KELLNER, 18
KEMPIEN, 23
KERCHER, 15
KERDEL, 25
KESSEL, 12
KESSELRING, 6
KEUER, 3
KICK, 13
KIECKE, 4
KILLING, 13

KIRCHHOF, 16
KIRCHHUEBEL, 5
KIRCHNER, 12
KISELING, 10
KLAHR, 16
KLAUS, 24
KLAUSEN. *See* CLASEN, CLAUSEN
KLEBER, 22
KLEIN, 17
KLEINKOPF, 17
KLETT, 12
KLIETZ, 15
KLIMANN, 20
KLUGE, 17
KLUTHE, 24
KNABE, 13
KOBERMANN, 21
KOCH, 5, 6, 10
KOELLING, 8
KOELN, 3
KOENIG, 1, 12, 16, 21, 22, 23
von KOENIGSLOEF, 5
KOERNER, 17
KOESELOW, 16
KOESER, 24
KOHLMANN, 18
KOHN, 17
KOHRS, 17
KOHSOW, 7
KOLBE, 3
KOLSTADT, 15
KOPP, 4
KORETH. *See* CORETH
KORMANN, 17
KORN, 12
KORTE, 4
KOSCHEL, 4
KOST, 13
KOTHWITZ, 15
KOTTA, 16
KRAGEL, 21
KRAKUHN, 24
KRAMER, 16
KRAMER. *See also* CRAMER
KRAUSE, 2, 7, 14, 17, 24
KRAUSS, 25
KREIN, 5
KRESEWETHER, 6

INDEX TO BIRTHPLACES
By Ship-List Number

This is a temporary index. At the end of Part 3 geographical notes have been appended which should be consulted by the researcher.

CARLSBURG, 16

CAROW, 23

CASLIN, COSLIN, 4

CASSEL, 2, 5, 17, 25

CELLE, Hannover, 1, 8

CHODZIESEN, 13

CHR. ALB KOOG, Schleswig, 25

CHRISTIANSTAT, Sweden, 2

CHRISTIANSTHAL, Sweden, 2

CILLI, Styria, 5

COBLENTZ, 17

COELN, 22

COESLIN, 4

COETHEN, 22

COPENHAGEN, 8, 13, 19, 24

COTTBUS, 11, 22

CRAMOW, 23

CRIMITZSCHAU, 5

CROSSEN AM ODER, 2

CUXHAVEN, 13

CZRIKHOF, 6

DADERSHEIM, 15

DAMGARTEN, 11

DANZIG, 8, 11

DARKEHMEN, Prussia, 24

DENSTORF, 5

DERENTHAL, 5

DEUTSCHKRONA, 14

DIETERSDORF, 22

DIETRICHSHUETTE, 12

DINGELSTEDT, 17

DITTERSBACH, 10

DOESCHNITZ, 12

DOESTRUP, 14

DOMITZ, 6

DOMSUEHL, DOMSUHL, 13

DOPPERTIN, 21

DORNFELD, 12

DRACKENBURG, Hannover, 8

DRANTHEIM, DRAUTHEIM, 2

DRESDEN, 3, 5, 16, 25

DRONSHEIM, 2

DUDENHAUSEN, Lippe-Detmold, 5

DUEMERHUETTE, 23

DUENPFL, 3

DUHRNLEISS, 13

EGER, Bohemia, 24

EHRENFRIEDERSDORF, 7

EICHFELD, 17

EISENACH, 22

EISLEBEN, 14

ELBING, 15

ELEXLEBEN, 21

ELFBARGSLAEN, Sweden, 19

EPE, Oldenburg, 9

ERFURT, 1, 5 13, 17, 22

ERLANGEN, Bavaria, 8

ERLENBACH, 16

ESCHWEGEN, 6

ETZEBACH, 13

EUPERN, 6

FALKENBURG, 25

FEHMARN, 14

FEINSBERG, Silesia, 22

FELDSBERG, 17

FILENE, 5

FILSEN, Hannover, 11

FINKWAERDER, 14

FINSTERWALDE, 14

FISCHBACH, 10

FLENSBURG, Schleswig, 19, 24, 25

FLOTOW, Prussia, 24

FOEHR, 22

FORDAU, 13

FRANKENSTEIN, 5, 10, 16

FRANKFURT AM ODER, 2, 5 7, 9

FRANKFURT [AM ODER or MAIN] 13

FRANZBURG, 3

FRAUENFELD, Switzerland, 9

FRAUSTADT, Prussia, 21

FREDENHAGEN, 7

FREIBERG, 14

FRIEDENFELS, 23

FRIEDLAND, 6, 14

FRIEDRICHSBERG, 17

FROEBEL, Prussia, 20

FUERSTENAU, Oldenburg, 9

FUTTERCAMP, Holstein, 16

GADEBUSCHE, 22

GAIS, Switzerland, 9

GAMSTADT, 21

GARDELEN, 5

GARLEBEN, 13

GARNSDORF, 16

GARZ, 4

GEBERSDORF, 10

GEBSTEDT, 12

GENT [GENEVA] Switzerland, 5

GENTHIEN, 5

GERA, 19

GEROSCHIN, 15

GIFFHORN, 5

GILLERSDORF, 6

GISPERSLEBEN, 21

GLASHAGEN, 23

GLEIMA, 16

GLUECKSTADT, 22

GNADENFREY, Prussia, 15

GNESEN, 7

GOBITZ, 21

GOHLAU, Prussia, 20

GOLDBERG, 3, 13, 21

GOMMATSHAUSEN, 14

GOSEWIT, 5

GOSSDORF, 22

GOSSITZ, 12

GOTHA, 5, 6

GOTHENBURG, 24

GRABEN, 17

GRABOW, 3, 16, 17, 23

GRAEFENTHAL, 23

GRAETZ, 13

GRAJEWO, 13

GRASSLEBEN, 22

GREBBIN, 3

GREISENBERG, 6

GRIMEN, GRIMMEN, 22

GROCKOW, 23

GROSS GLOGAU, Silesia, 8, 16

GROSS GOELITZ, 12

GROSSLANDORF, 16

GROSSMANDERN, Prussia, 1

GROSSMELZEN, 3

GROSSNENNDORF, 23

GROSS NORDENDE, 24

GROSSNOSSEN, 14

GROSS OERNER, 18

GROSSRETBACH, 3

German and Central European Emigration
Monograph Number 1, Part 2

RECONSTRUCTED PASSENGER LISTS FOR 1850:

HAMBURG TO AUSTRALIA, BRAZIL, CANADA, CHILE,

AND THE UNITED STATES

Part 2: Passenger Lists 26 through 42

Clifford Neal Smith

Reprint, 1983
Reprint, 1984
Reprint, 1989
 Reprint, August 1991   u
Reprint, January 1996   u

CONTENTS

INTRODUCTION

The passenger lists preserved in the files of the Hamburg police authorities are the single most important genealogical research link between the Old and New Worlds, for they record the birthplaces and the destinations of millions of central European emigrants. Neither the naturalization files nor the port of entry records in lands of settlement consistently contain this information in such detail.[1] It must be noted with regret that similar files maintained by Bremen police authorities were destroyed in the *Feuersturm* of 1945, when the city itself went up in flames. The Bremen files probably were considerably larger than those of Hamburg and contained the names of most of the emigrants from western Germany and Switzerland.[2] Consequently, the reconstruction of nineteenth-century western German emigration records can only be approached by analysis of the files of each *Gemeinde* (community) in the country, a formidable task which proceeds at a slow and opportunistic pace.[3]

The Hamburg police lists are divided into two series, Direct and Indirect. The Direct series, in 399 volumes, begins in 1850 and includes all ships leaving Hamburg (and associated minor ports) without stopping at other European ports to take on emigrant passengers. The Indirect series, in 118 volumes, beginning in 1855, includes ships which made intermediate European and British ports of call. For purposes of genealogical research, the distinction does not seem to be significant, excepting that some emigrants may have been taken aboard at other ports and, therefore, are unlisted in these passenger lists. Consequently, the lists for each year of both series will be presented together in these monographs.

During the first years in which names of emigrants were recorded, the actual passenger lists apparently were not preserved. Instead, the police clerks entered the data from these original lists into large bound registers in a quasi-alphabetical fashion. This makes it difficult for researchers to determine who among the emigrants may have accompanied the subject of research. Extended family or support groups and coreligionists frequently emigrated together, a matter of significance to the researcher. To remedy this defect, the 1850 passenger lists have been reconstructed from the quasi-alphabetical entries to be found in the registers.

All the reconstructed lists for 1850 have been abstracted from microfilm roll number 1 (Library of Congress, Manuscript Division, shelf number 10,897) made of the following archival materials:

Hamburg. Staatsarchiv. Bestand Auswandereramt. Auswanderer Listen, Direkt, 1850.

The Library of Congress has microfilms of both the Direct and Indirect volumes for the period 1850-1873. The Genealogical Society of Utah, Salt Lake City, has the entire 517 volumes on microfilm, from 1850 to 1913, when the series was discontinued.

There are a total of 4,074 entries in the Direct series for 1850. Some entries record only one emigrant, other entries list entire families. It seems likely that the total number of individuals emigrating via Hamburg in 1850 may have been about 7,000 (of which almost 2,500 are listed in this monograph). Later passenger lists contain more information than do those of 1850, notably the names and ages of all family members. For the 1850 entries, the information hereinafter is as follows:

Col-
umn

1   Surname
2   Given names
3   Occupation. Some of the terms used are those of Hamburg dialect, rather than modern *Hochdeutsch*, and may not be correctly translated. For example a commonly reported occupation is that of *Oeconom*. This means farmer or manager. In these monographs the term has been uniformly translated as manager.
4   Birthplace. See the section at the end of Part 3 for notes thereon.
5   Reference number/Page number in register. The reference number has been assigned by this compiler and is not to be found in the registers. The number will probably have little use to researchers, other than indicating place on the register page relative to nearby names.

Having found a surname of interest, researchers should consider all other emigrants on the ship for possible accompanying extended-family members and coreligionists. These relationships may occasionally be inferred by considering also the birthplaces common to a number of passengers. The Index to Birthplaces can also be used to identify persons from the same birthplaces who have traveled on different ships. Occasionally, names listed herein may supplement data missing in other emigrant lists. For example, in the monograph entitled *Nineteenth-Century Emigration of "Old Lutherans"* . . .[4] it is reported that the names of 98 emigrants to Australia had not been found in German administrative files. Some of these persons may be included among the passengers of the three ships which sailed from Hamburg to Australia in 1850.

---

1. A detailed description of the Hamburg emigration files will be found in Clifford Neal Smith and Anna Piszczan-Czaja Smith, *Encyclopedia of German-American Genealogical Research* (New York: R. R. Bowker, 1976), pp. 199-200. Additional information on supplementary research materials in the Hamburg Staatsarchiv can be found in Smith & Smith, *American Genealogical Resources in German Archives* (Munich: Verlag Dokumentation, 1977), p. 227, et seq.

2. Of the nearly 79,000 persons emigrating from Germany to the United States in 1850, only about 7,000 passed through the port of Hamburg. Thus the great majority of Germans must have emigrated via the ports of Bremen and LeHavre. U.S. Bureau of the Census, *Historical Statistics of the United States: Colonial Times to 1957* (Washington, D.C.: Government Printing Office, 1960), p. 57.

3. See the back cover of this monograph for a listing of monographs in the German-American Genealogical Research series having to do with communal records on emigration.

4. Clifford Neal Smith, *Nineteenth-Century Emigration of "Old Lutherans" from Eastern Germany (Mainly Pomerania and Lower Silesia) to Australia, Canada, and the United States.* German-American Genealogical Research Monograph 7 (McNeal, AZ: Westland Publications, 1980), p. 46.

ABBREVIATIONS USED

Am   America; usually meaning the United States

Au   Austria

b   born (maiden name)

Ba   Bavaria, a state now in West Germany; formerly included lands in Rheinland-Pfalz

Bd   Baden; now part of the state of Baden-Wuerttemberg in West Germany

Bi   Birkenfeld, a former principality, which in 1850 belonged to Oldenburg; territory now in Rheinland-Pfalz, West Germany

Bo   Bohemia, former kingdom, now part of Czechoslovakia

c   child, children

Ca   Cassel (now Kassel); Hessen-Cassel was a principality, also known as Electoral Hesse, now in the state of Hessen, West Germany

d   daughter

De   Detmold; Lippe-Detmold, a former principality, now in Nordrhein-Westfalen, West Germany

Di   Ditmarschen, a region in the state of Schleswig-Holstein, West Germany

Ds   Dassau, formerly a political unit in Saxony, now in East Germany

Fr   France

Go   Gotha, a principality also called Sachsen-Coburg-Gotha, now in East Germany

Gr   Goerlitz, an administrative district now in East Germany and Poland

Ha   Hannover, a sovereign territory, now in Niedersachsen, West Germany

He   Hessen, a former principality, now in the state of Hessen, West Germany

Ho   Holstein, now in Schleswig-Holstein, West Germany

Hu   Hungary; in 1850 a part of the Austro-Hungarian Empire

La   Lauenburg, a former principality, now part of the state of Schleswig-Holstein, West Germany

Li   Lippe; Lippe-Detmold, a former principality, now in Nordrhein-Westfalen, West Germany

Mk   Mecklenburg, a former principality, now in East Germany

Mn   Meiningen; Sachsen-Meiningen, a former principality, now in East Germany

No   Norway

Ol   Oldenburg, a former principality, now in Niedersachsen, West Germany

Pm   Pomerania, a former Prussian province, now in Poland

Po   Poland

Pr   Prussia; in 1850 a kingdom with lands now in East and West Germany and Poland

Ps   Posen; in 1850 a Prussian province, now in Poland

Ru   Rudolstadt; Schwarzburg-Rudolstadt a former principality in Thuringia, now in East Germany

s   son, sons

Sa   Saxony, a former kingdom, now mainly in East Germany

Sb	Swabia, a region, now in Baden-Wuerttemberg, West Germany
Sc	Schwartzburg. *See* Rudolstadt and Sondershausen
Si	Silesia, a Prussian province in 1850, now part of Poland
Sl	Schleswig, a former province, now in Schleswig-Holstein, West Germany
Sn	Sondershausen; Schwarzburg-Sondershausen, a former principality in Thuringia, now in East Germany
St	Strelitz; Mecklenburg-Strelitz, a former principality, now in East Germany
Sw	Sweden
Sz	Switzerland
Th	Thuringia, a region, now in East Germany
Ty	Tyrol, a region in Austria
We	Weimar; Sachsen-Weimar-Eisenach, a former principality, now in East Germany
Wu	Wuerttemberg, a former kingdom, now in Baden-Wuerttemberg, West Germany
y	year, years

List 26

Ship *Guthenberg* (or *Gutenberg*) Captain O. H. Flor
Departing Hamburg 15 May 1850 for New York (Direct)

ALEXANDER	Samuel	tailor	Nagel, Pr	0041/003
ARLAND	Ernst	brewer	Schkeuditz	0042/003
ASCH	Leo	businessman	Posen	0040/003
BADE	Johannes	--	Buxtehude	0249/012
BAUER	Robert	businessman	Leipheim	0245/012
BAUMBACH	Wilhelm	peasant	Weberstedt	0243/012
BAUMGARTEN	Wilhelm	--	Lalchow	0252/012
BENNY	Bernhard	soldier	Hamburt	0244/012
BERGMANN	C. F.	--?	Barningen	0250/012
	--	wife		
	--	child		
BIELFELDT	Chr[istian?]	artist?	Krem	0251/012
BILLING	Fr.	baker	Bottendorf	0248/012
BROCKMANN	F.	soldier	Bergen	0247/012
BROCKMANN	H. F.	gold worker	Bentzin	0253/012
	--	wife		
	--	3 children, 16-29 y		
BUTTIG?	F.	shoemaker	Glogau	0246/012
CADOW	Chr[istian?]	blacksmith	Friedland	0529/024
DEICKE	Eduard	lithographer	Franitz	0608/028
DISSEN	Wilhelm	plumber	Berlin	0607/028
DREGE	J. Friedrich	commissioner?	Hamburg	0609/028
DRESDNER	Michaelis	furrier	Lissa	0606/028
	--	wife		
	--	2 children, small		
EFFNER	Magdalene	--	Gruenberg	0717/034
	Albertine	--		
EGGERS	Friedrich	soldier	Klesebach	0716/034
ELITT	Christian	laborer	Barckow	0718/034
	--	wife		
	--	2 children		
ENGEL	Christian	wheelwright	Luebz	0719/034
FALLER	Johann	cabinetmaker	Hamburg	0847/039

FISCHEL	Hersch	tailor	Altfracknick, Pr	0845/039
FLOEDER	Th. Eugen	peasant	Guchen, Pr	0848/039
	--	wife		
	--	4 children, 3-12 y		
FRAENKEL	Isaac	--?	Lissa	0844/039
FRICKE	A. F. L.	--?	Braunschweig	0846/039
GEBHARDT	Mathilde	--	Grafenthal, Pr	1035/048
	--	3 children, 5-15 y		
GEHRMANN	Maria	--	Klesebeck	1029/047
GIESE	Wilhelm	peasant	Tangendorf	1031/048
GRENA	Solomon	soldier	Boionocow, Mk	1030/048
GROLLPFEIFER	G. F.	cabinetmaker	Imenhausen	1032/048
	Johanna	--		
GROLLPFEIFER	Emma	--	Imenhausen	1033/048
	Heinrich	--		
GUENTHER	Ernst	--	Goldlauter	1034/048
HABERSTROH	Carl	waiter?	Doerflas	1281/058
HAHN	Johann	mason	Heinrichau	1279/058
HALL	Johann	helmsman	Grabow	1286/058
HARLESS	Adam	manager	Schoenbrunn	1282/058
HESS	J. M.	blacksmith	Kirchzell	1284/058
HINSPETER	H.	stable hand	Rebentin	1285/058
HIRSCH	Elias	--?	Filehne	1277/058
	Ernestine	--		
	Amalia	--		
HIRSCH	Hirsch	tailor	Filehne	1278/058
	Ephraim Jacob	--		
HIRSCHFELDT	Jonas	soldier	D[eutsch] Crone, Pr	1283/058
HOCHHEIM	C. L.	manager	Eisenach	1280/058
JACKMANN	Liebmann?	businessman	Filehne	1528/069
JACOB	Levin?	baker	Szarnakow	1529/069
JAHN	J. H.	--	Baringau? Th	1530/069
	Juliana	--		
JAHN	Ferdinand	tailor	Baringau? Th	1531/069
JAHN	J. N.	--?	Baringau? Th	1532/069

List 26 (continued)

JORCK	L.	cap maker	Wreschen	1533/069
KAHLERT	J.	businessman	Eisenach	1718/077
KAROWSKY	Johann	peasant	Birnbaum	1719/077
KAROWSKY	Johann	peasant [second person of same name?]	Birnbaum	1724/078
KELLER	Heinrich -- --	-- wife child	Goldlander	1725/078
KEMPE	Raphael Rike	tailor --	Kamin	1714/077
KIEHRT	N. F.	carpenter	Schoenflies	1716/077
KLEINFELD	T.	mechanic	Rebentin	1729/078
KLUBE	Gustav -- --	saddler wife 2 children	Oldischleben	1721/078
KLUBE	Hermann	--	Oldischleben	1722/078
KOCH	Julius	tanner	Eisleben	1730/078
KOJETZKY	Hermann Nepema Kov- na?	lithographer [this may be the surname of a woman; if so, it is Nepemakovna]	Posen	1728/078
KOLB	Siegfried	laborer	Goldlander	1726/078
KOTTEK	Leiser	furrier	Kamin	1715/077
KRAUSE	Barthold	manager	Wallenburg	1720/077
KRICK	Maria Heinrich	girl child	Muenchen	1713/077
KROEGER	J. F.	coachman	Menkhagen	1723/078
KRUEGER	Johann	laborer	Cunern	1717/077
KRUSCHKE	Anton	bookbinder	Braunsberg	1727/078
LECHERT	Ludwig	glovemaker	Berlin	2034/091
LEMKE	L.	butcher	Luebz	2042/092
LEMPKE	H.	plumber	Berlin	2040/092
LERCHE	Otmin?	shoemaker	Oldisleben	2041/092
LESCHINSKA	Dorothea	--	Szidowa, Pr	2038/091
LEVY	Maria	--	Goldschin	2039/092

LICHTENSTERN	Hermann	furrier	Lebow	2035/091
LINIENTHAL	Joseph	--	Golin, Pr	2036/091
LIPINSKI	Hermes	shoemaker	Loebau	2037/091
LOHGERBER	Louis	--	Dermisdorf, Th	2043/092
MANASSE	Moses	businessman	Filehne	2287/103
MATTWICH	___	girl?	Hamburg	2290/103
MEYER	Benjamin	soldier	Berlin	2288/103
MEYER	C. A. F.	peasant	Cismar	2291/103
MEYER	Jetta	--	Hamburg	2292/103
MOCK	Anton	musician	Wolffmannshausen	2295/103
MOSES	Abraham Grischel	businessman --	Kempen	2285a/103
MOSES	Mina	--	Corneck? [Car-neck?] Pr	2294/103
MOTHS	Heinrich -- --	-- wife 5 children, ½-9 y	Zimmer	2284/103
MUCKE	Eduard	tanner	Zilchau	2289/103
MUELLER	F. A.	butcher	Niederndorf	2286/103
MUELLER	Dorothea	--	Kesschendorf? [Ketschendorf?]	2293/103
MUSIKER	Abraham Loebel	businessman	Kempen	2285/103
NIEDLANDT	Christian -- --	bricklayer wife 3 children, 8-20 y	Karbow	2543/114
OBST	August	--	Neuhof	2626/118
OTTO	Heinrich	blacksmith	Heinrichau	2627/118
PARISER	Roeschia? Hanna	-- --	Szidona, Pr	2699/121
PFAFFEN-SCHLAGER	Franz Eduard	--?	Gruenberg	2697/121
PITSCH	J. C.	peasant	Langensalza	2700/122
POHLMANN	Barbara	--	Fasseldorf, Ba	2701/122
PRACHT	Johann Christian -- --	peasant wife 8 c, 3/4-15 y	Zimmer	2695/121

List 26 (continued)

PROSCH	Ludwig Christian	shoemaker	Crewitz, Mk	2702/122
PROSCH	Ludwig	tailor	Crewitz, Mk	2703/122
PROSCH	Sophia	--	Crewitz, Mk	2704/122
PULS	A.	--?	Rendsburg, Ho	2698/121
	Julia	--		
PURUCKER	Matthias	blacksmith	Ober Rosslau?	2696/121
RASCHKE	Heinrich	furrier	Lissa	2884/130
RAUCHFUSS	August	mason	Genetzsk	2890/130
RICHTER	Robert	furrier	Munsterberg	2885/130
	Minna	--		
RIES	H.	cabinetmaker	Rodwitz	2888/130
ROBISCH	G.	baker	Ober Rosslau	2887/130
ROCKSTROP	J. F.	baker	Rodwitz	2889/130
RODE	Carl Ludwig	--	Leipzig	2883/130
	Louise	--		
	Hermann	child		
RUPPEL	Christian	shoemaker	Ober Rosslau	2886/130
SALINGER	Saul	soldier	D[eutsch] Crone, Pr	3242/145
SAUER	Carolina	Mad[am?]	Stettin	3231/145
SAUER	J. G. F.	cabinetmaker	Weimar	3237/145
SCHABBEL	Maria	--	Luebz	3254/146
SCHMIDT	Johann	--?	Rothenburg, Pr	3244/145
SCHMIDT	W. F.	manager	Bosdorf, Pr	3245/145
SCHMULL	Itzig	hatter	Corneck	3257/146
SCHNORR	Matth[ias]	--?	Diemersdorf	3238/145
SCHOBERT	Johanna	--	Ober Rosslau	3239/145
SCHOLTZ	Carl	soldier	Posen	3248/145
SCHONBILD	F.	butcher	Luebz	3253/146
SCHRADER	Hermann	manager	Weimar	3234/145
SCHRICKER	Heinrich	--	Ober Rosslau	3240/145
SCHROEDER	J.	peasant	Luebz	3241/145
SCHUBERT	Louise	--	Muensterberg	3236/145

SCHUEBEL	Benjamin	laborer	Goldlauter	3249/145
SCHULTZ	Johann	shoemaker	Berg	3246/145
SCHULTZ	Christian	cabinetmaker	Berg, Mk	3251/146
SCHWARZ	J. H.	tailor	Tacken	3255/146
SEIDEL	Reinhard	innkeeper	Kottsberg	3243/145
SEITZ	Anna	--	Imenhausen	3247/145
SELLMANN	Christian	peasant	Brock	3252/146
SOLMS	Salomon	--	Filehne	3235/145
	Hanna	6 y		
	Carolina	10 y		
SORGENFREI	Johann	mason	Tangendorf	3256/146
STEHM	Georg? E.	peasant	Fahrenrode, Sa	3258/146
STEHM	Maria	--	Fahrenrode, Sa	3259/146
STEHM	Andreas	peasant	Fahrenrode, Sa	3260/146
STEHM	Lisabetha	--	Fahrenrode, Sa	3261/146
STIEG	Ernst	laborer	Kleefeld	3250/145
	Doris	--		
STRENG	Adam	butcher	Memelsdorf	3233/145
SUCKERT	F. W.	businessman	Warschau	3232/145
	--	wife		
	--	3 grown children		
TECHNER	Johanna	--	Grueneberg, Pr	3653/163
THOMY	August	peasant	Grueneberg, Pr	3652/163
	--	wife		
TIETGENS	Claus	farmhand	Kampe	3651/163
TOMHAGEN	J. A.	farmhand	Kampe	3650/163
VERCH	Carl August	brewer	Teetz	3755/167
VOIGT	Rosina?	--	Oldischleben, Sl	3754/167
	Maria	--		
	Johann	--		
WAGNER	Franz	architect	Leipzig	3866/173
	Agnes	--		
WEBER	F. H.	businessman	Kemnitz	3864/173
WEISE	F. C.	saddler	Dermsdor, Th	3875/173
	--	wife		
	--	3 children, 10-16 y		

List 26 (continued)

WEISS	Catharina	--	Goldlauter, Th	3868/173
	Gustav	--		
WEISS	Marianne	--	Goldlauter, Th	3869/173
	Laurete?			
WEISS	Gottfried	laborer	Goldlauter, Th	3870/173
WEISS	A. W.	laborer	Goldlauter, Th	3871/173
	F.	laborer		
WELTZIEN	Johann	plumber	Rebentin	3873/173
WERNER	Joseph	musician	Wolfmannshausen	3876/173
WIENER	Adolph	--	Altona	3872/173
WILDSCHINSKY	Tobias	tailor	Inowraslow, Pr	3864a/173
WILDSCHINSKY	Marcus	soldier	Inowraslav, Pr	3865/173
WITTKAUER	Wolf	--?	Posen	3874/173
WOLF	Carl L.	wheelwright	Gloetz, Mk	3867/173
	Sophia	--		
ZEIDLER	Margarethe	--	Ober Rosslau	4039/181
ZERRENNER	Jacob	mason	Baringen	4041/181
	--	wife		
	--	3 children, 3/4-16? y		
ZICKELKOW	Johann	nailsmith	Bruell	4040/181

List 27

Ship *Guthenberg* (or *Gutenberg*) Captain J. Peters
Departing Hamburg 1 Oct 1850 for New York (Direct)

APPEL	Ignatz	--?	Pesth	0100/006
BADER	Rudolph	businessman	Berlin	0474/021
BARTH	Friedrich	manager	Wakendorf	0472/021
BAU	Johann Christian	manager	Wolfshagen	0470/021
BECKER	J. F. Th.	manager	Penzlin	0471/021
BERG	Julius	businessman	Hamburg	0475/021
BUSS	C. J. G?	mason	Priegnitz	0473/021

List 27 (continued)

CARL	J. H.	mason	Sternkrug, Mk	0556/025
	--	wife		
	--	3 children, 4-16 y		
COHN	Simon	cigarmaker	Liegnitz, Pr	0555/025
	Bertha	--		
von COTTI	Eduard	mechanic	Hamburg	0557/025
	Elise	wife		
DANCKERT	Friedrich	mason	Bprlin	0672/031
DITTMAR	A.	architect	Pritzwalk	0671/031
ECKERT	Gottfried	clothmaker	Chodziesen, Pr	0785/037
	August	--		
EVERS	Knuth	cabinetmaker	Christiani, No	0784/036
FAHRENHOLZ	W.	cloth manufacturer	Pritzwalk	0937/043
FAHRENHOLZ	Maria	--	Pritzwalk	0938/043
	Minna	--		
	Ferdinand	--		
FAHRENHOLZ	August	--	Pritzwalk	0939/043
	Ludwig	--		
FINGER	Friedrich	manager	Albertsdorf, Mk	0941/043
	--	wife		
FRESSDORF	August	tailor	Abendorf	0940/043
FREUND	Carl	baker	Friedland, Pr	0936/043
	--	wife		
	--	3 children, 13-17 y		
GABELIN	Anna	--	Frickenhausen, Ba	1151/053
GIESE	Friedrich	manager	Seldin	1149/052
	--	wife		
	--	6 children, 4-20 y		
GRAEFNER	R. Th.	carpenter	Keuschberg, --?	1148/052
GUTKIND	Simon	tailor	Scharpenort	1150/053
	--	wife		
	--	son, 14 y		
HACKER	Carl	manager, 61 y	Parchim, Mk	1454/065
	--	5 children, 9-38 y		
HAGEN	C. T. W.	manager	Lehsten, Mk	1447/065
	--	wife		
	--	2 children, ½-11 y		

12

HAGEN	F. A.	manager	Lehsten, Mk	1446/065
HAMANN	Joachim	manager	Warnow	1453/065
HANSEN	Forgel	mason	Draemen, No	1445/065
HANSEN	Hermann	cabinetmaker	Mass, No	1444/065
HANSEN	P.	captain	New York	1457/065
HEMPRICH	Ludwig	barber	Hagenow	1448/065
HERZ	H.	soldier	Hamburg	1456/065
HEYDTMANN	Christian -- --	laborer wife 2 c, 2 & 11½ y	Grabow	1451/065
HEYDTMANN	J.	laborer	Grabow	1450/065
HIEBERT	Johann -- --	manager wife 3 children	Frickenhausen	1455/065
HOFFMANN	Cornel[ius]	cake baker	Chodziesen	1452/065
HOLZ	Christine	--	Rostock	1449/065
JAGEMANN	G. Ph.	tailor	Hamburg	1585/071
JAHNCKE	Johann	goat herder?	Wissendorf, Mk	1586/071
JANSEN	F. M.	tailor	Lutjenburg, Ho	1588/071
JANSEN	Wilhelmine Dorothea	-- --	Lutjenburg, Ho	1589/071
JUNGE	Cler? -- --	carpenter wife daughter, 3 y	Luebz	1587/071
KANZLER	Wilhelmine --	Frau 6 children, ¼-14 y	Selchow, Pr	1935/086
KOEHLER	Christian	blacksmith	Grabow, Mk	1937/087
KOEHLER	Ernst	waiter	Grabow, Mk	1938/087
KOEPCKE	Johann	manager	Waeten, Mk	1934/086
KNUTH	Evers	cabinetmaker	Christiani, No	1933/086
KOPITZ	Georg	musician	Reinfeld, Ho	1939/087
KRUEGER	Adolph	tailor	Malchow	1936/086
LADENDORF	Christian	wheelwright	Dobbertin, Mk	2179/097
LADENDORF	Maria	--	Penzlin	2181/097
LASCH	Johann -- --	wheelwright wife 8 children, ½?-30 y	Langenhagen	2180/097

List 27 (continued)

LAU	Johann Friedrich	peasant	Fralkenhagen, Mk	2178/097
	--	wife		
	--	son [age illegible]		
LEHNERT	Ludwig	Doctor	Friedland, Mk	2184/098
LEINE	Rudolph	bookdealer	Leipzig	2176/097
LENTZING	Friedrich	--	Bochzoff?	2177/097
LICHEWSKY	Heinrich	carpenter	Graudenz, Pr	2183/098
LORENTZ	Gottl[ieb?]	tailor?	Schoenwalde	2174/097
LORENZ	Ludwig	furrier	Schoenwalde	2175/097
LOY	Hermann	tailor	Scharffenow, Pr	2182/098
MALLEIS	Wilhelm	businessman	Mardenwaerder, Pr? [Marienwerder?]	2481/111
	Hulda	--		
	Peter	cabinetmaker		
MAMEROW	Johannes	manager	Hofhagen	2478/111
	--	wife		
	--	5 children, 2-12 y		
MARTIES	J. C. F.	manager	Ventschow	2480/111
MATTHIAS	Benjamin	--?	Hamburg	2476/111
MENDEL	Theresa	--	Schernejava	2477/111
MEYER	Ernst	manager	Salzwedel	2475/111
MEYER	Johann	baker	BOITZENBURG, Mk	2479/111
NAUMANN	Richard	--	Lembach, Ba	2594/116
PFEIFER	Christian	manager	Fritzenhausen?	2795/126
POLTER	J.	seaman	New York	2794/126
PRIESTER	Paulina	--	Malkwitz, Ho	2792/125
PULS	Friedrich	manager	Goldenitz	2793/125
RATZEL	C. T.	barber?	Oranienburg, Pr	3028/136
	--	wife		
	--	3 children, 13-17 y		
RAWOHL	J. W.	hatter	Hamburg	3026/136
REMER	Emilia	--	Berlin	3027/136
RICHTER	Friedrich	cabinetmaker	Kletzke, Pr	3031/136
ROHDE	Johann Jacob	laborer	Langenhagen	3030/136
		--		

14

ROHM	Samuel	manager	Frickenhausen, Ba	3032/136
ROSE	Carl B.	cigarmaker	Hamburg	3029/136
SAKAN	Andreas	manager	Marienwerder	3565/159
SASS	Wilhelm	paperhanger	Kiel	3563/159
	--	wife		
	--	2 children, ½ & 4 y		
SCHNELL	Friedrich	mill builder	Kogel	3558/158
SCHORBAHN	Johann	manager	Mestlin? [Mettlin?] Mk	3559/158
SCHROEDER	H. P.	cabinetmaker	Rostock	3560/159
SELS	Eduard	candidate [for academic de-gree]	Lauchstadt, Pr	3562/159
	Walesia?	wife		
SIEVERT	Heinrich	machine builder	Marienwerder	3564/159
SKAMPER	Ernestine	--	Posen	3554/158
	Mina	--		
SPEER	E. F.	brewer	Greiburg	3557/158
SPOERER	Bruno	book binder	Nordhausen, Pr? [Ps?]	3555/158
STAEBELOW	F. J. C.	manager	Gielow	3561/159
STEINHAEUSER	Carl	soldier	Pritzwalck, Pr	3553/158
STRASSENBURG	Dorothea	--	Pritzwalck, Pr	3552/158
STUEWE	Friedrich	tailor	Neu Zachnin? [Zachuen?]	3556/158
	--	3 children 2½-7½ y		
TREWES	F. R.	captain?	Hamburg	3702/165
WEBER	Seb[astian]	cabinetmaker	Lyon	3996/179
WEDEL	C. F. J.	laborer	Klein Beesen	3998/180
WULKOW	Wilhelm	cabinetmaker	Brun	3997/179

List 28

S.S. Helene Sloman, Captain P. N. Paulsen
Departing Hamburg 28 May 1850 for New York (Direct)

ADAMI	Hermann Bertha	rope maker? wife	Grueneberg	0050/004
AISCHBERG	H.	--	Illfeld	0046/003
ALTSCHUL	Antonia	--	Leibach	0049/004
ANGERMANN	B.	watchmaker	Altenkundstadt	0047/003
ARNSTEIN	Louise? [Lewin?]	--	Leibach, Ba?	0048/003
BECKED	Chr[istian] Julia? [Julius?]	--?	Koenigsbach	0285/013
BERGROTH	L.	landowner	Stockholm	0284/013
BETTMANN	B.	soldier	Weidnitz	0289/014
BEUCHEL	Charlotte Wilhelm	-- boy	Erfurt	0291/014
BLECH	J. C. Louise	plumber --	Thorn	0286/013
BLECH	Theodor Henriette	carpenter? --	Thorn	0287/013
BLUME	Ferdinand -- --	--? wife son, ½ y	Magdeburg	0293/014
BRANDENSTEIN	J.	soldier	Himmel, Pr	0290/014
BRAUM	J. C. F.	businessman	Frankenhausen	0288/013
BRAUN	G.	book binder	Erlangen	0292/014
BURGER	Joseph	--?	Kanth	0283/013
COHN	Fan[n]y?	--	Meineck	0533/024
BOHN	Babette?	--	Horb	0534/024
COHN	Justus -- --	-- wife 3 children, 1½-5 y	Landen	0535/024
CONRAD	Emilie?	--	Berlin	0532/024
CRESSIEN	H. R?	carpenter	Dithmar	0536/025
DALBERG	Abraham	businessman	Beverungen	0618/029

List 28 (continued)

DROESEN	H. C.	carpenter	Dithmar	0619/029
ECKERT	Henriette	--	Erlangen	0727/034
ELLERT	Moritz	manager	St. Micheln, Pr	0730/034
ERBE	Georg	weaver	Meiningen	0726/034
EVERS	E. F.	sweeper?	Rendsburg	0729/034
EWERT	J.	tailor	Stettin	0728/034
	Mathilde	wife		
	--	child, 3/4 y		
FISCHER	H.	basketmaker	Burkersdorff	0856/040
FOERSTER	L.	dyer	Zeulenrode	0858/040
FRANCKEL	Amalia	--	Micheln, Pr	0859/040
	--	3 children, 3/4, 2½, & 5 y		
FRANK	J.	basketmaker	Weidnitz	0855/040
FRIEDRICH	Christian	manager	Micheln, Pr	0860/040
FRIEDSAM	Babette	--	Memelsdorf	0857/040
GARBING	H.	surveyor	Weimar	1054/049
GEIERSHOFER	A.	soldier	Weimar	1049/048
GOMPERTZ	Th[eodor]	lithographer	Hamburg	1051/048
GOTTHOLD	Moritz	--	Posen	1050/048
GRAETZED	F. A.	glazier	Roemhild	1052/048
GROSSMANN	Albert	cake baker	Carlshafen, Pr	1053/048
GRUNDMANN	F. E.	--?	Mittweida	1055/049
HANKE	Joseph	businessman	Aussig	1307/059
HASSENFELD	H.	--	Copenhagen	1313/059
HAUDEGEN	Carolina	--	Zechau	1315/059
HECKEL	Eduard	--	Muehlhausen	1312/059
HELLER	David	baker	Oberleutersdorf	1306/059
HERMANN	Rica	--	Fassoldshof	1308/059
HESSELBEIN	Louise	--	Thorn	1309/059
HILBINGER	Margarethe?	--	Erlangen	1311/059
	--	child, 3 y		
HOEPPNER	Franz	manager	Erfurt	1310/059

List 28 (continued)

HOLZHAUSEN	F. August	blacksmith	Kemberg, Pr	1314/059
HONEGGER	Rudolph Babette	businessman wife	Constanz	1316/060
HOPPE	F. August	shoemaker	Oberstrosse	1305/059
JACOBI	F.	mason	Kemberg	1543/069
JACOBY? [JACOLY?]	Otto	distiller	Berlin	1542/069
JAENSCH	Julius	businessman	Gnadenfeld	1544/069
JANSSEN	O.	businessman	Stockholm	1541/069
JETTE	Amalia	--	Micheln, Pr	1545/070
KAESTNER	Wilhelm	tailor	Camenz	1757/079
KAPPER	Christian	laborer	Micheln, Pr	1765/079
KASTEN	Carl	cake baker	Erfurt	1759/079
KAVE	--	painter	Braunschweig	1767/079
KLAGES	Carl	mechanic	Celle	1763/079
KLEIN	Ludwig	businessman	Wald	1756/079
KLINGSAHR	Victor	businessman	Muenden	1760/079
KOCH	Carl August Sophia --	cake baker -- her? mother	Micheln, Pr	1764/079
KOCH	Felix	manager	Weimar	1754/079
KOCH	F. A.	hunter	Segeberg	1762/079
KORALL	J. W.	peasant	Gunzerode	1761/079
KRAKOWIZER	--	physician	Steyer, Au	1766/079
KUH	Rette?	--	Redwitz	1755/079
KUMMERT	M? [N?]	peasant	Erlangen	1758/079
LEHMANN	C.	businessman	Schamwecht?	2059/092
LEHNERT	Carl Johann?	laborer laborer	Erlangen	2062/092
LESSER	Bertha	--	Schwersenz	2060/092
LEVIN	Rosalia	--	Altona	2065/093
LEVY	Emma	--	Altona	2066/093

18

LIEBSCHNER	Carl	businessman	Forchheim	2063/093
	--	wife		
	--	7 children, 3/4-12 y		
LIEBSCHER	C. F.	teacher	Doebel	2064/093
	--	wife		
LINDNER	C. F. W.	cabinetmaker	Reichenbach, Sa	2068/093
LITHAUER	Augusta	--	Posen	2061/092
LUDWIG	Maria Alvinna?	girl [unmarried] daughter	Landeshut, Si	2067/093
MAERZ	Friedrich	manager	Beverangen	2326/105
MAITAG	Friedrich	tailor	Grabow	2330/105
	--	wife		
	--	son, 19 y		
MAMMEN?	Carl	soldier	Graden	2324/104
MANDELBAUM	Carolina	--	Illfeld	2321/104
MARTENS	Hermann	peasant	Brossbuettel	2329/105
MATSCHINSKI	J? [I?]	--	Neisse	2333/105
	--	wife		
	--	child		
MAYER	J? [I?]	furrier	Inowraclaw, Ps	2317/104
MEISSNER	Adolph?	clothmaker	Bitterfeld	2323/104
MELZNER	Maria	--	Frauenanna, Ba	2327/105
MELZNER	F? [J?] A.	tanner	Pesneck, --?	2338/105
MENDEL	Rachel	--	Ludwigslust	2334/105
MEUSEL	B.	manager	Weissenfels	2331/105
MEYER	Th[eodor?]	manager	Annaberg	2320/104
MEYERFELD	Moritz	plumber	Beverangen	2328/105
MEYNCKE	C.	confectioner	Neubrandenburg, Mk	2339/105
MICHAELIS	Pauline	--	Schwersenz	2325/105
MISSELHARN	F. L.	machinist	Celle	2337/105
	Charlotte?	wife		
MUECK	Johannes	confectioner	Oberleutersdorf	2319/104
	--	wife		
MUELLER	Benjamin	mason	Kanth	2318/104

List 28 (continued)

MUELLER	Sophia	--	Altenknudstadt	2322/104
MUELLER	Gotthelf	shoemaker	Annaberg	2332/105
MUELLER	Franz	dyer	Weimar	2335/105
MUELLER	H.	peasant	Degritz	2336/105
NUERNBERGER	F? A.	laborer	Zorbau	2549/114
OEHME	Emilia	--	Doebel	2634/118
OPPENHEIMER	J? [T?]	--	Kahnstadt	2632/118
OPPENHEIMER	M.	--	Burgkunstadt	2633/118
PEIN	Carl	--?	Neisse	2719/122
PESCHKE	Carl	--?	Annaberg, Sa	2715/122
PESCHKE	Samuel	tailor	Mielbock	2718/122
PETER	Simon	brewer	Hartenberg	2716/122
PFAFF	Johann	basket dealer	Micheln	2717/122
RAEBEL	Hermann -- --	-- wife child	Bitterfeld, Goerlitz	2901/131
RAEBEL	Hermann	--	Goerlitz	2903/131
RECHENBACH	C. G. Rebecca	shoemaker --	Muehlhausen	2905/131
REICHERT	Carolina	--	Mettkan? [Nettkan?]	2899/131
REICHERT	G. C. Ernst	master --? wife son, 23 y	Doebel, Sa	2907/131
REINHARD	Christian	peasant	Gunzerode	2906/131
RICHTER	August Christina	teacher wife	Kemberg	2911/131
RIEDEL	J. E.	businessman	Leipzig	2908/131
RIEGELMANN	Mayer	soldier	Arndorf	2900/131
RIEHME	Adelfriede	--	Camenz	2904/131
RIPS	Theodor	--	Magdeburg	2913/131
RITTER	H.	pharmacist	Lueneburg	2910/131
RITZ	Philippina --	Mad[am?] 2 children, 6 & 4 y [2 words illegible]	Berlin	2914/131

20

ROSENFELD	Lippmann	--	Illfeld	2902/131
ROST	F.	tanner	Doebeln	2909/131
RUPPRECHT	Wilhelmine	--	Kemberg	2912/131
SALOMON	R.	dentist	Hamburg	3304/148
SCHLEGEL	Gustav	--?	Landstreit, Au	3307/148
SCHLEGEL	Julius	manager	Landstreit, Au	3308/148
SCHLESINGER	H.	businessman	Inowravslaw [!] Ps	3294/147
SCHMIDT	J. F.	innkeeper	Frankenhausen	3295/147
SCHOMANN	S.	businessman	Stockholm	3312/148
	Christine	wife		
SCHROEDER	Ernst	peasant	Meckern	3305/148
SCHUETZE	Johann	pharmacist	Uetersen	3311/148
SCHULTZ	Emilia	--	Camenz	3299/148
SIMON	Peter	brewer	Hartenberg	3306/148
SIMON	George	cabinetmaker	Zechau	3309/148
SOLLMANN	W.	laborer?	Cassel	3296/147
STEIN	Isa[a]c	businessman	Beverungen	3300/148
STEINECKE	August	peasant	Guenzerode	3303/148
STEINHOF	A.	cabinetmaker	Engellade	3298/147
STEINWEG	H.	instrument maker	Seesen, Ha	3297/147
	--	wife		
	--	7 children, 7-23 y		
STOCK	Wilhelm	gold worker	Weimar	3310/148
	--	wife		
	--	2 children, ½ & 3 y		
STUERMER	Maria	--	Ansbach	3301/148
SUDHEIM	Moritz	tanner	Beverungen	3302/148
TAMB	Wilhelm	pharmacist	Herrenberg	3659/163
THEURICH	Carl	saddler	Goerlitz	3656/163
THEURICH	Amalie	--	Annaberg	3658/163
TIEGERSFELDER	Rica	--	Horb	3657/163
VELDER	--	physician	Weissenkuechen	3760/168
VOIGT	Henriette	--	Leipzig	3758/168
	--	4 children, 2-7 y		

VORKELLER	C.	musician	Frankenhausen	3759/168
WAERNECKE	J. J. G. H.	peasant	Moedlich, Pr	3907/176
	--	wife		
	--	4 children, 1¼–7 y		
WALLROTH	Maria	--	Guenzerode	3903/176
WECHSLER	Wilhelm	dyer	Camenz	3902/176
WEIDENMUELLER	Bernhard	--	Langenfeldt	3909/176
WEIL	Moses	butcher	North [!] Loeder	3908/176
WILKEN	F. T. G.	needle maker?	Tessin	3910/176
WILSDORF	Louis	tanner	Doebel, Sa	3905/176
WILSDORF	August	butcher	Doebel, Sa	3906/176
WITTIG	Wilhelmine	--	Goelmgen	3904/176
WOLDENBERG	M. L.	soldier	Gnesen	3901/175
ZAHN	Friedrich	saddler	Redwitz	4046/182
ZAHN	Carl	dyer	Redwitz	4047/182
ZINN	Siegmund	--?	Redwitz	4044/181
ZIPPRECHT	S.	saddler	Cassel	4045/182
ZSCHOCKE	Ernst	manager	Erfurt	4048/182
ZSCHOCKELT	J. C. G.	wheelwright	Erlbach, Sa	4050/182
	--	wife		
	--	2 children, 7 & 15 y		
ZSCHOCKELT	C. G.	master wagoner	Mittweida?	4051/182
	--	wife		
	--	3 children, 10, 6, 5 y		
ZUBER	Franz	brewer	Elbogen, Bo	4049/182

List 29

S.S. Helene Sloman, Captain P. N. Paulsen
Departing Hamburg 10 Aug 1850 for New York (Direct)

ARON	Joachim	businessman	Belgard	0078/005
BAEBENROTH	Friedrich	book binder	Erxleben	0396/018
BARTHELS	H. E.	sculptor	Ebersdorf	0397/018
BIBO	Charles	cigarmaker	Graet	0402/018
BIEHL	R.	book binder	Rotenburg	0394/018
BOETTCHER	Wilhelm	manager	Dankerode	0407/018
	--	wife		
	--	2 sons, 16 & 26 y		
BORMANN*	Christine	--	Dankerode	0409/018
		*So spelled		
BORRMANN*	Christian?	shoemaker	Dankerode	0408/018
	--	wife		
	--	daughter, 5 y		
	--	son, 3/4 y		
		*So spelled		
von der BOSCH	James	farmer	South America	0401/018
BRAND	Franz	pharmacist	Bisperode	0399/018
BRANDT	C?	tailor	Below	0395/018
BRUHN	Johann	peasant	Warnitz	0406/018
BUERSTEN-	Minna	--	Wittenberge	0400/018
BINDER	Minna	--		
BUHSE	Johann	--	Warnitz	0403/018
	--	wife		
	--	daughter, 5½ y		
BUHSE	Dorothea	--	Warnitz	0404/018
BULL	Johannes	peasant	Warnitz	0405/018
BUNEMEYER	C.	--?	New York	0398/018
COHN	Gustav	businessman	Berlin	0546/025
COHN	Simon	soldier	Euthhausen	0545/025
DARMSTAEDT	--	Frau	Leipzig	0653/030
	--	5 children, 1-3/4 -15 y		
DETHJENS	Joachim	peasant	Lestermuehl	0651/030

DIETRICHS	Lisette	--	Grabow	0652/030
DOELTZ	Wilhelm	--	Osnabrueck	0654/030
DOERR	J. F.	peasant	Rendsburg	0649/030
DOHR	Joachim --	-- wife	Hernsteinfeld	0650/030
EBERLEIN	Christian --	miller wife	Crailsheim	0765/036
EHRLICH	Rudolph	businessman	Neustadt	0764/036
ESBACH	Heinrich	--?	Klingenthal	0763/036
FASS	Sophia	--	Crivitz	0903/042
FELLNER	Friedrich	businessman	Kiel	0907/042
FIEDLER	Carl	manager	Dobbertin, Mk	0909/042
FRANCK	Moses	soldier	Parrweisach	0905/042
FRANK	--	girl	Cuestrin, Pr	0911/042
FRANKE	Friedrich	businessman	Mempshier? [Mernp- shier?]	0906/042
FREUND	Samuel	soldier	Andenhausen, Ba	0904/042
FRIEDRICH	Laphus? -- --	pharmacist? wife twins, 15 y	Dankerode	0910/042
FUTH	Christian	manager	Boltenhagen	0908/042
GEBHARDT	Caroline	--	Dankerode	1115/051
GEORG	Elise	--	Rotenburg	1112/051
GLAS	F. W.	wheelwright	Aldorf, Sa	1111/051
GOGE	Marianne	--	Liegnitz	1117/051
GOSSOW	Eduard --	businessman son, 10 y	Berlin	1113/051
GROTHHUSEN	Louise --	-- son, 11 y	Neustrelitz	1116/051
GRUMSEN	H.	--	Goettingen	1118/051
GUSTLOFF	J.	manager	Boltenhagen	1114/051
HAMM	H.	musician	Hof	1391/063
HANKE	W. A. -- --	mechanic wife son, 3/4 y	Herrnhuth	1392/063

24

HARLESS	Adolph	pharmacist	Bunde	1389/063
HASSNER	Ph[ilipp?] H.	miller	Grafenthal	1394/063
HEIM	Hermann	businessman	Neustadt, Pr	1393/063
HESSE	C. W.	businessman	Jostadt? [Jastadt?]	1388/062
HEUCHELBACHER	N.	soldier	Parweisach?	1387/062
HOFFMANN	Ernst	--?	Treppeln	1390/063
	--	wife		
	--	family		
HUESEMANN	L.	businessman	New York	1395/063
	--	wife		
	--	2 children, ½ & 2½ y		
JACOBSEN	Henriette	--	Potsdam	1573/071
	--	daughter, 7 y		
JANSSEN	C, Ktin?	--	New York	1571/071
JENSEN	Emma	--	Copenhagen	1572/071
KAEFERSKIN	Wilhelm	manager	Sinzleben	1863/083
KALITTA	Julius	miller	Goschuetz	1866/084
	Ernestine	wife		
KLESER	Carl	manager	Baltenhagen	1868/084
	Lina?	wife		
KLOEVEKORN	Bernhardine	--	Vechter	1872/084
KLOTH	Ludwig	milled	Tessdorf	1869/084
KOCH	Caroline	--	Grueneberg	1871/084
	--	son, 9 y		
	--	daughter, 3/4 y		
KOECKRIT	Friedrich	soldier	Klein Rosenthal	1865/084
KOEHLER	Carl	musician	Grabow	1867/084
KOHN	Max	businessman	Aidhausen	1870/084
KOTH	J. F. H.	cabinetmaker	Copenhagen	1864/083
	--	wife		
KRUSE	Sophie	--	--	1862/083
KURTZ	Carl	businessman	Reutlingen	1873/084
	--	daughter, 7 y		
LANDSCHUTZ	C. A.	butcher	Sol	2120/095

List 29 (continued)

LANE	Hermann	watchmaker	Neustrelitz	2125/095
LANGBEIN	H. W.	wheelwright	Coburg	2121/095
LEDERGERW?	M.	businessman	St. Gallen	2122/095
LEVISON	William	sailor	New York	2119/095
LINKE	F.	wheelwright	Reichenbach	2124/095
LIPPMANN	E.	manager	Gebersdorf	2126/095
LOW	Josephine	--	Erbach	2127/095
LUECK	Johann -- Johann	manager wife son, 22 y	Grabow	2123/095
MARTIN	Eduard	high school student	Coburg	2413/108
MAZZUCKI	Cisare? Giovanni?	art dealer --	Phazzona? [Stazzona?] Hu	2418/108
MELCHES	G. W.	--?	Varel	2411/108
MENDHEIM	H.	soldier	Cuestrin	2421/108
MENTZEL	Friederike	--	Herrnhuth	2420/108
MEYER	August --	shoemaker wife	Micheltondern	2412/108
MICHEL	J. B.	tailor	Niesky, Pr	2414/108
MUEHLENDORF	Adolph?	soldier	Filehne	2416/108
MUELLER	Robert	brewer	Tirschenreuth, Ba	2415/108
MUELLER	C. F.	businessman	Gruneberg	2417/108
MUELLER	J. H. F.	tailor	Rinteln	2419/108
MUELLER	Alexander	businessman	Saalfeld	2422/109
NEUMANN	E? Th?	[woman?]	Berlin	2579/115
NEUMEISTER	Franz	tanner	Neustadt	2582/115
NIEMANN	Dietrich	--	Grabow	2580/115
NIENBURG	Caspar	sailor	Uetersen	2583/115
NOELKE	Gustav	art dealer	Berlin	2581/115
OBERFELD	Johann	manager	Boltenhagen	2640/118
OBERNFELD	Anna --	-- 2 daughters, 3/4 & 3 y	Wendorf	2641/118

List 29 (continued)

PEECK	Adolph Paul	tailor miller	Tessdorf	2755/124
PEECK	Louise	--	Tessdorf	2756/124
PFEIFFER	Alexander	businessman	Berlin	2757/124
PHILIPP	Bertha	--	Berlin	2754/124
PINKUS	Michael	tailor	Posen	2753/124
POSPSCHILL	Joseph	--?	Wien	2758/124
QUAST	F. W.	businessman	Louisville, Am	2817/127
REINCKE	A? G.	manager	Memel	2981/134
RICHTER	Emil	physician	Leipzig	2983/134
RICKHOF	Christian?	manager	Boltenhagen	2982/134
RIESMANN	Carl	manager	Topper	2984/134
ROSENBERG	J. F. E.	baker	Lobau	2980/134
SCHAEFER	C.	soldier	Rotenburg	3441/154
SCHANDER	C. G.	--	Sangershausen	3448/154
SCHERZER	J. A.	weaver	Arnsgrun, Sa	3440/154
SCHMIDT	Johann --	steerman wife	New York	3439/153
SCHMIDT	Friedrich	--	Sangershausen	3449/154
SCHMUTTE	Heinrich	businessman	Hunteburg	3443/154
SCHUMACHER	H.	manager	Boltenhagen	3445/154
SOLTMANN	Heinrich Gustav	mechanic --	Hattorf, Ha	3442/154
STAGGE	Friedrich	--?	Hunteburg	3444/154
STAGGENBERG	J.	manager	Dinklan? [Dinklau?]	3450/154
STEINFELD	Ernestine	tanner	Neustadt	3446/154
STEINHARD	Rosalia	--	Berlin	3447/154
THOMAS	Joseph	peasant	Namay? [Nomay?]	3684/164
TRESSENHUSEN	Hermann? C.	manager	Boltenhagen	3682/164
TRIPPENBACH	W.	manager	Knese	3683/164
VOLGER	C. W. O. A. -- --	businessman wife 4 children, 3/4-4 y	Hamburg	3769/168

List 29 (continued)

WAGNER	August? [Auguste?]	wheelwright	Zschopan	3956/178
WALTHER	J. A.	gardener	Doebeln	3959/178
WARSCHAU	J. J.	tailor	Kempen	3957/178
WOLFFER	Maria -- --	-- daughter, 5½ y son, 4 y	Luebeck	3958/178
ZELARIUS	Heinrich	high school student	Obernhagn? [Obernhayn?]	4061/182
ZOELLNER	Hannchen?	--	Berlin	4062/182

List 30

S.S. Helene Sloman, Captain P. N. Paulsen
Departing Hamburg 25 Oct 1850 for New York (Direct)

ASMUS	C. J. A.	businessman	Hamburg	0104/006
BELLING	Heinrich	--?	Weiderstab? Pr	0481/021
BERG	Marcus	businessman	Hamburg	0480/021
BIENTZEL	Mathilde	--	Hamburg	0479/021
BOSCHKE	H. S. -- --	farmer wife 2 children, 20 & 22 y	Washington, Am	0478/021
CASPARI	A.	pharmacist	Reading, Am	0559/025
CLARNER	E. Chr.	dyer	Kirchenlamitz	0560/026
DANNENBERG	J.	businessman	Trendelberg, Ha	0679/031
DEIMEL	Adolph	miner	Wien	0680/031
EBNER	Friedrich	student	Weder, Pr	0791/037
EHLERS	--	Doctor	Hamburg	0792/037
ELDER	August Bertha	businessman wife	Eldagsen, Ha	0793/037
FISCHER	Johann Wilhelm	cantor	Brieg, Pr	0949/044
FISCHER	Wilhelm E.	--	Brieg, Pr	0950/044

List 30 (continued)

FISCHER	Eduard	businessman	Berlin	0951/044
FOERSTER	F.	shoemaker	Ludwigslust	0952/044
FRANKE	Theodor	--?	Saalfeld, Th	0953/044
GUDEMANN	Julius	businessman	Bosseborn, Ol	1158/053
GUINSCHE?	Christian	shepherd	Saalfeld	1159/053
HAGEN	L. -- --	gold worker wife 3 children, 3/4- 6 y	Hagenow	1469/066
HAGEN	Dietrich --	surgeon wife	Hagenow	1470/066
HANSEN	Ludwig	businessman	Itzehoe, Ho	1473/066
HEGEWISCH	Louise	--	Hamburg	1467/066
HIRSCH	Bertha	--	Malchin, Mk	1468/066
HOFFMANN	Anna Margaretha	-- --	Graefenberg, Pr	1465/066
HOLGERSON	Anna --	-- daughter, 2 y	Copenhagen	1472/066
HOLMLAE	A. B.	businessman	Ollesund, No	1466/066
HOPPERT	Wilhelm	butcher	Breslau? Sa [!]	1474/066
HUCK	F.	master machinist	Altenlatow, Pr	1471/066
JENA	H. Michaelis	businessman	Detmold	1591/071
KARSTEN	Joachim	--?	Kronskamp	1952/087
KLOSTERMANN	Heinrich	miller	Gramzow	1948/087
KNOBLOCH	C. E. C. W.	tanner --	Mittweyda	1951/087
KNOCH	Catharina	--	New York	1953/087
KOELBL	Theresia --	-- 2 daughters, 17 & 20 y	Wien	1954/087
KRUEGER	F. G. Ludwig	shoemaker --	Guben, Pr	1949/087
KRUG	Georg August	brewer son	Mildenberg, Ba	1950/087
LICHTENHEIM	Ansel	--	Koenigsberg, Pr	2196/098

List 30 (continued)

LINDENAU	Christoph -- --	cabinetmaker wife 2 children, 10 & 12 y	Loebau, Pr	2193/098
LOLL	Ludwig	mechanic	Breslau, Sa [!]	2195/098
LUTZ	Eduard	physician	Heilbronn	2194/098
MAAS	Heinrich	businessman	Oldenburg, Duchy	2488/111
MAIER	Johannes -- --	blacksmith wife 3 children, 4-12 y	Kirchheim, Wu	2489/111
MEYER	N. D.	peasant	Lahre, Ditmarschen?	2487/111
NELSEN	P. -- --	soapmaker wife 5 children, 2-17 y	Hagenow	2596/116
NOWACK	Emil	soldier	Valkenberg	2597/116
OTTENBURG	H. C.	butcher	Luechow, Mk	2649/119
PEMUELLER	Carl	--	Hagenow	2802/126
POMPEJUS	Adolph	book dealer	Glatz, Hu	2803/126
PUDER	Franz	miller	Neumuehle, Pr	2801/126
RATHJENS	Jacob	painter	Elmshorn	3047/137
REICHARDT	Augusta	--	Ditmannsrieth, Ba	3042/137
RICHTER	Max	businessman	Breslau	3050/137
ROSE	Carl Louise	bird? dealer wife	Gruenenplau? [Gruenenplan?]	3044/137
ROSE	Ferdinand	investor	St. Louis, Am	3045/137
ROSENBUSCH	August	manager	Schlagerthal, Thu	3048/137
ROTH	Carl	confectioner	Coblenz, Pr	3049/137
RUEBKE	Johann	manager	Rastow, Mk	3046/137
RULLMANN	Eduard	businessman	Oldenburg	3043/137
SANDER	August	businessman	Peine, Ha	3579/159
SCHAEFFEL	Maria	--	New York	3583/159
SCHLIETER	Martha?	--	Kellinghusen, Ho	3578/159
SCHMIDT	August	--	Harburg	3582/159
SCHONAT	Wilhelm	pastor	Cincinnaty, Am	3580/159

List 30 (continued)

SCHWARZ	Theodor? Wilhelm	plumber	Coblenz	3584/160
SOMMER	Adolph	--	Hamburg	3581/159
STIER	Gustav	--?	Sonneberg, Pr	3577/159
TEEGN	Marsow?	storekeeper?	Hasenmoor, Ho	3704/165
WENTZEL	Heinrich -- --	pharmacist wife son, ½ y	Bartenstein, Pr	4009/180
WINKLER	F. A. F. A.	weaver --	Rachlitz, Sa	4008/180

List 31

Ship *Herrmann* (Russian flag) Captain H. Hanker
Departing Hamburg 18 May 1850 for New York (Direct)

ABRAHAM	Fischel	tailor	Hamburg	0044/003
ASSMY	Adolph	manager	Potsdam	0038/003
BADE	Heinrich	wheelwright	Gartow? [Gartau?]	0270/013
BAHRT	Heinrich -- --	mason wife 5 children, 3-18 y	Reschwitz, Th	0261/012
BAUER	G. F.	laborer	Eisenberg, Th	0264/012
BAUMGARTEN	F. C.	mason	Eisenberg, Th	0265/013
BAYER	--?	--?	Dresden	0266/013
BEESEMANN	Ernst --	tailor wife	Cammin, Pr	0268/013
BENICKE	August	glazier	Gartow? [Gartau?]	0271/013
BINDER	C. W.	cabinetmaker	Marburg	0269/013
BOCK	Henriette	--	Lehesten	0262/012
BUCHMANN	F. A. -- --	tailor wife child	Eisenberg, Th	0263/012
BURO	Christian	tailor	Thore bei Zerbst, Th	0267/013

List 31 (continued)

CALISCH	Ernestine	Frau	Kratoschin, Po	0530/024
CALISCH	Lotte	--	Kratoschin, Po	0531/024
DAUTERSTEDT	Carl W.	baker	Eisenberg	0610/028
DETLOF	C. F.	blacksmith	Falkenwalde, Pr	0614/029
	--	wife		
	--	6 children, 7-24 y		
DETLOF	Friedrich	blacksmith	Justow	0615/029
	--	wife		
DIETRICH	Christian	tailor	Seehausen	0613/029
DROEGE	G. W?	cabinetmaker	Garstow, Pr	0611/028
DUPONT	August W.	shoemaker	Camin	0612/028
ERDMANN	C. Friedrich	peasant	Plathe, Pr	0721/034
	--	wife		
	--	3 children, 3-9 y		
FICKE	Carl August	--?	Commin? [Cammin?] Pr	0849/039
FISCHEL	Abraham	tailor	Hamburg	0851/040
FREWERT	C. H.	carpenter	Hamburg	0853/040
	--	wife		
FRICK	A. F. W.	--	Hamburg	0850/039
	--	wife		
	--	small child		
GABLER	Julius Ernst	shoemaker	Klein Poterwitz, Th	1038/048
GARMSEN	A.	book binder	Flensburg	1042/048
GROSSE	Johanna	--	Grosswitz	1039/048
GRUNERT	Heinrich	shepherd	Danndorf	1040/048
GUTMANN	Ernestine	Frau	Grossenhayn	1041/048
	--	2 small children		
HAVELMANN	Carl	peasant	Zimmerhausen	1295/059
	Wilhelmine	wife		
HAVELMANN	Gotth[ilf?]	--	Zimmerhausen	1296/059
	--	wife		
	--	3 children		
HERTZ	--?	--	Hamburg	1290/058
HILLER	Mine	--	Posen	1292/059
HOPFGARTEN	Louise	--	Blankenhain	1294/059

32

List 31 (continued)

HORWITZ	Sophia	--	Saraczewa	1293/059
	Rieke	daughter		
	Maria	daughter		
HUFELAND	Leonhard	book dealer	Dresden	1291/058
	--	mother		
JACOB	Leopold	tailor	Schoeps, Pr	1534/069
JACOBY	Michael	soldier	Rosenberg	1538/069
JANGER? [JAUGER?]	Carl Fried-rich	manager	Soldikow	1535/069
JENISCH	G. F.	sculptor	Berlin	1537/069
JUNGMANN	Auguste	--	Blankenhain	1536/069
KATELHOHN	Jochen	adopted son of E. F. Paul	Dallberg, Mk	1737/078
KATZENSTEIN	Rieke	--	Hamburg	1733/078
KIRSCHBAUM	Moses	tailor	Poljewo	1742/078
KISTER	Wilhelm	weaver	Boehlen	1738/078
KNAPE	Friedrich	clothmaker	Millrowe	1743/078
	--	wife		
	--	2 children, 8 & 18 y		
KRETSCHMANN	Paul	armorer?	Eisenberg	1735/078
	Bertha	sister		
KREUTZFELD	Auguste C. L.	--	Altona	1739/078
KRUEGER	F. D.	cabinetmaker	Zewitz	1736/078
KRUEGER	Ludwig	peasant	Schnittrige?	1840/078
	--	wife		
	--	small child		
KRUMBUS	Michael	servant	Grambow	1745/079
KUECKHOEFEL	C. G.	laborer	Grabow	1744/078
	--	wife		
	--	2 small children		
KUNZHALS	Christian	Postillion	Allstedt	1734/078
KURTH	Johann	peasant	Triegelhof	1741/078
	--	wife		
	--	7 children, 6-20 y		
KURZHALS	Friedrich	laborer	Allstedt	1746/079
LANGHALS	Friedrich	shoemaker	Neubrandenburg, Mk-St	2045/092

List 31 (continued)

LEMCKE	Wilhelm	peasant	Schnittrige	2049/092
LEMM	Philipp	peasant	Schnittrige	2050/092
	Elisabeth	--		
	--	5 children, 6-13 y		
LENAU	Augusta	--	Gartow, Pr	2046/092
LINDOW	Wilhelm	cabinetmaker	Polsen, Pr	2051/092
	--	wife		
	--	2 children, 3 & 7 y		
LINDOW	Christian	cabinetmaker	Polsen, Pr	2052/092
	--	wife		
	--	3 children, 2½-11 y		
LUEBKE	Johann	peasant	Schwessow	2047/092
	Charlotte	wife		
	Sophia	--		
LUEBKE	Carl	--	Schwessow	2048/092
	Charlotte	--		
	August	--		
	Wilhelmine	--		
	Augusta	--		
	Maria	--		
MAAS	Johann	peasant	Schnithrige?	2305/104
MANN	Ernst	--? 18 y	Dresden	2300/103
MARKIEWITZ	David	businessman	Hamburg	2308/104
MARTHON	Joseph	tailor	Hamburg	2307/104
MATERNE	Hermann?	manager	Stroppen	2302/104
MENGE	Bernhard	master mason	Weimar, Th	2303/104
MEYER	August	manager	Klenze, Pr	2301/104
MEYER	Johanna?	--	Hamburg	2306/104
	--	7 y		
	--	16 y		
MUELLER	Friedrich	--	Schnithrige?	2304/104
	Ernst?			
PAULS	C. F.	--	Dallberg, Mk	2708/122
	Carolina	wife		
	--	adopted son, *see* KATELHOHN		
PEWESDORF	Wilhelm	miller	Gartow	2707/122
PIEPERS	C. W.	carpenter	Rupperdorf	2711/122
	--	wife		

List 31 (continued)

PITSCH? [PETSCH?]	F. G. W.	--	Cassel	2706/122
PLESS	Anna Maria	--	Hamburg	2705/122
PRITZLAFF	Elisabeth Maria	--	Schnittrige	2709/122
PRIWE	C. O. F.	saddler	Treptow	2710/122
REISE	Carolina	--	Wildenspring, Th	2892/131
ROEMER	Andreas	--?	Wien	2894/131
ROEPER	Henriette	--	Hamburg	2895/131
ROSENTHAL	Hermann	tailor	Poljewo	2893/131
RUDOLPH	Anton --	Doctor, pastor 3 children, 15-21 y	Visselbach	2891/130
SACHSE	Hermann	soldier	Bischofswerder	3277/147
SALCHE	Moritz	tailor	Hamburg	3266/146
SCHANTZ	Christian	servant	Roehrenfahrt	3269/146
SCHEIBE	Friedrich Julius	mason	Eisenberg	3267/146
SCHRADER	H. J.	houseboy	Hamburg	3276/147
SCHROEDER	Carl	laborer	Plathe	3273/146
SCHUMACHER	Joachim	--	Gartow	3271/146
SCHUMACHER	J. C.	laborer	Anker? [Auker?] La	3279/147
SEELMANN	Johann Pauline --	-- -- daughter, 7 y	Ober Oppurgdor? Th	3272/146
STEDEFELD	Max	manager	Blankenhain	3274/146
STEINMETZ	Johann	manager	Donndorf? [Danndorf?]	3275/147
STEINMETZ	Mattheus Maria	manager wife	Gutendorf	3278/147
STENDAL	Maria	--	Gartow, Pr	3268/146
STENDAL	Johann	--	Gartow	3270/146
SUEDEKUM	H. --	mason wife	Dransfeld, Ha	3265/146
VETTER	Christoph	daguerrotypist [photographer]	Rehan, Ba	3756/168

List 31 (continued)

VOIGT	Franz	--	Schwessow	3757/168
WALDENBURG	L.	upholsterer	Grossglogau	3887/175
WEBER	August	--?	Berlin	3888/175
	--	wife		
	--	small child		
WEISSBACH	Charlotte	--	Muencherholzen	3885/175
WIMMLER	Juliana	--	Ober Oppurg	3880/175
WITHMANN	Friedrich	blacksmith	Gartow, Pr	3877/173
WOELFEL	Sophia	--	Grossbammsdorf	3881/175
WOHLFAHRT	Albert	shoemaker	Blankenstein	3882/175
WOLFF	Jetta?	--	Rogasen	3883/175
WOLFF	Adolph	tailor	Rogasen	3884/175
WOLFF	G. A.	mason	Mellingen, Th	3886/175
WUERTZBERGER	J. C. F.	farm laborer	Birckicht	3878/175
WUERTZBERGER	G. E.	laborer	Birckicht	3879/175
ZIMMERMANN	Christian	tailor	Goldberg	4042/181
	--	wife		
	--	2 children		

List 32

Ship *Herrmann* (Russian flag) Captain H. Hanker
Departing Hamburg 21 Sep 1850 for New York (Direct)

ABARBANELL	Julius	weaver	Berlin	0098/006
ANGERMANN	Caroline	Frau	Erlau	0099/006
	--	5 children, 1½-11 y		
ANTHOR	Auguste	--	Dresden	0097/006
	--	5 children, 4-18 y		
BLIEMEISTER	H.	--	--	0468/021
BURY?	Maria Friede- rike	--	Hamburg	0469/021
DRUT	Louise	--	Lyon	0670/031
	--	son, 6 y		
FINN	Gottliebe B.	--	Moehrenbach	0933/043
FISCHER	Carl	businessman	Rudolstadt	0934/043

36

FRIEDEMANN	Moritz	businessman	Hamburg	0935/043
GRAMANN	Heinrich	miller	Gehren	1147/052
	--	wife		
	--	daughter, 21 y		
HASSLINGER	Therese	--	Wien	1443/065
HEINRICHS	Theodor	businessman	--	1442/065
JAENICKE	Friedrich	soapmaker?	Stettin	1583/071
JOURTAN	Friedrich	butcher	Berlin	1584/071
KOLB	Johann	grocer	Funfhaus bei Wien	1932/086
	--	wife		
	--	4 children, to 4½ y		
KRAUSE	C. P.	manager	Ziegemueck	1929/086
	Eleanore	wife		
KRAUSE	Wilhelm	manager	Ziegemueck	1930/086
	Eva	wife		
KRAUSE	Gottlob	manager	Ziegemueck	1931/086
	Christine	wife		
	--	4 children, 3-12 y		
	--	1 baby		
LINDENBAUM	Is[aac?] M.	--?	Hannover	2172/097
LINDENBAUM	--?	--	Hannover	2173/097
LUDWIG	Hermann	cabinetmaker	--?	2171/097
MAHN	A? J.	tailor	Drabischau? [Drobischau?]	2473/111
MUNTEN	Wilhelmine	--	Nordhausen	2474/111
	--	2 sons, 7 & 8 y		
PETRAM	Franz	cabinetmaker	Hohenmasch?	2790/125
PUTZ	Leopold	flower maker	Wien	2791/125
RAABE	Detlev	--?	Uetersen	3024/136
RAMPENDAHL	Johannes?	weaver	Ebeleben	3025/136
RUDOLPH	J. P. D.	cabinetmaker	Berlin	3023/136
	Wilhelmine	wife		
SCHKLIEBA	Adalbert	saddler	Reichenau	3550/158
SCHOENHEIT	H. Friedrich	cabinetmaker	Egelsdorf	3546/158
SCHULTZE	A. F.	tobacconist? [Tabagist]	Landsberg	3548/158

List 32 (continued)

SCHUETZ	Paulina	--	Schwerin	3549/158
SCHUETZ	G. H.	tobacco manufac-turer	Schwerin	3544/158
	--	wife		
SESSMANN	Sophia	--	Meiningen	3543/158
	--	3 children, to 8 y		
SONNENSCHMIDT	Doris	maid	Dannenberg	3542/158
STEIN	H. August	construction worker	Dresden	3551/158
STREESEMANN	Gottl[ieb?]	tailor	Hammerspring	3545/158
	--	wife		
	--	child		
STRENG	Sophia	--	Weickersheim	3547/158
THIESS	A. H.	tailor	Luechow	3700/165
	--	wife		
TIMM	Carl	houseboy	Hamburg	3701/165
VOGEL	Carl H.	shoemaker	Mupten? [Muchten?]	3779/168
WARDT	P. A.	wheelwright	Helmsdorf	3994/179
WEBER	Catharina	--	Riegelsdorf	3993/179
WEBER	Heinrich	mason	Klinge	3995/179

List 33

Ship *Howard*, Captain J. H. Jacobs
Departing Hamburg 1 Jul 1850 for New York (Direct)

BAUER	Christian	wheelwright	Arnstadt	0353/016
BEHRENDT	J.	peasant	Duez	0357/016
von BEINHOF	E.	--	Wien	0356/016
BERNHARD	Paul	businessman	Leipzig	0355/016
	Theodor	businessman		
BIERMANN	J.	wheelwright	Dobbertin, Mk	0358/016
BLANSKY	Heinrich	shoemaker	Kl[ein] Welke	0354/016
BOHSE	J. B.	tailor	Berlin	0359/016
	Dorothea	wife		

List 33 (continued)

BORCHARD	Friedrica	--	Hamburg	0361/017
BRASSLER	Carl	soldier	Ludwigslust	0360/016
BURR	Friedrich	laborer	Kreyln	0362/017
CLEMENS	--	baker	Schwerin	0541/025
CRULL	Maria	--	Apenrade	0542/025
DANIELS	Peter	manager	Rosenkranz	0634/029
	--	wife		
	--	5 children, 3-19 y		
DANIELS	Johann	manager	Rosenkranz	0635/029
DAUCK	Johann Joachim	peasant	Garwitz	0639/030
	--	wife		
	--	child, 3/4 y		
DOHRN	C. L. Ch.	laborer	Ehlerstorf	0636/029
DONNER	G.	physician	Drogdersen	0637/030
DREIER	Johann Joachim	peasant	Garwitz	0638/030
	--	wife		
	--	2 children, 2 & 5 y		
EBERLE	Gustav	soapmaker	Niesky	0744/035
EHLERS	Johann	--	Apenrade	0749/035
ERPENSTEIN	Johann	tailor	Schonlamke, Pr	0745/035
EURICH	Carolina	--	Waldenburg	0747/035
	--	3 children, 1-3/4 to 5 y		
EURICH	August	painter	Waldenburg	9747/035
	--	wife		
	--	daughter, 3 y		
EVERS	J. D. L.	soldier	Hamburg	0746/035
FARBACH	Alfred	--?	Wien	0888/041
FELTEN	Johann Maria	laborer --	Krabow	0889/041
FIEDLUND	J. G. Louise? [Linne?]	cigarmaker	Stockholm	0887/041
FUERGANG	Ch. F.	pharmacist	Wien	0886/041
	--	wife		
	--	4 children, 4-13 y		

List 33 (continued)

FUERSTE	Wilhelm	button maker	Tangermunde	0885/041
GRAGERT	Carl -- --	councilman? wife 4 children, 2-12 y	Stuer, Mk	1089/050
GRISCHOW	F.	manager	Stavenhagen	1088/050
GROH	Willfried	furrier	Hohenebe	1085/050
GROOTH	Christian -- --	-- wife 2 children, 9 & 12 y	Kreyen	1090/050
GUENTHER	Friedrich	--	Lehesdorf	1086/050
GULICHSRUD	H. H. -- --	peasant wife 6 children, 7-23 y	Kangersagen? [Kaugersagen?] No	1087/050
HAMISCH	Ernst Friedrich	butcher	Bartelsdor	1354/061
HOFFMANN	Heinrich	--	Gnanzien	1355/061
JAEGER	Carl	--?	Neubuckow?	1556/070
de JAGER	Henry	soldier	Hamburg	1557/070
JENS	Johann -- --	laborer wife 2 children, 3/4 & 4 y	Stuer	1559/070
JENSEN	Trol? Conrad	butcher?	Husum	1555/070
JOACHIMI	L. Caroline --	manager wife 3 children, 5-7 y	Lienitz	1558/070
KAPPMEYER	Johannes	brush maker	Lueneburg	1812/081
KATOLEINS	Adolph -- --	blacksmith wife 2 children, 4 & 9 y	Luebz	1818/082
KIENCKE	Heinrich	miller	Kluetz	1820/082
KLEINHEMPEL	F. A.	rein maker?	Neusalza	1814/081
KREFFT	Ch. R. J.	--	Goldberg	1816/081
KRUSEMARCK	W.	soldier	Wittenberg	1819/082
KUEHN	Andreas	peasant	Zemitz, Sa?-Ds	1815/081

List 33 (continued)

KUFMANN	C. L.	wheelwright	Stradun	1813/081
KUHL	Christian Sophia	tailor wife	Klein Rogahn	1817/082
LAU	Hermann	machinery builder	Treptow	2089/094
LAUBNER? [LANBNER?]	Alexina? --	-- 2 children, 4 & 6 y	Altenburg	2096/094
LAUENROTH	Dorothea	--	Herrnhuth	2090/094
LEHMANN	Ferdinand	rifle maker	Waren	2091/094
LEMBCKE	Louis Louise	cabinetmaker wife	Luebz	2093/094
LEMKE	Christian Sophia	shepherd wife	Grabow	2094/094
LERCHE	Daniel -- --	teacher wife 4 children, 17-21 y	Copenhagen	2092/094
LITTMANN	Louis	businessman	Salzwedel	2095/094
LUBAN	Wilhelm	tailor	Grafenhagen, Pr	2205/098
MAHN	Eduard	manager	Rechlin	2382/107
MAHN	Amandus	tailor	Rechlin	2390/107
MARTIN	Theodor Louise	tanner wife	Herrnhuth	2378/107
MAYER	Fanny	--	Rendsburg	2381/107
MOELLER	Daniel -- --	peasant wife 5 children, 6-20 y	Luebz	2383/107
MOELLER	Friedrich	laborer	Grussow	2385/107
MOELLER	Catharina	--	Garwitz	2386/107
MOELLER	Johann	peasant	Garwitz	2387/107
MOELLER	Wilhelm Joachim?	peasant peasant	Garwitz	2388/107
MOELLER	Johann Jacob Johann Fried- rich	peasant peasant	Garwitz	2389/107
MUELLER	Johann -- --	laborer wife 2 children, 2½ & 4 y	Stuer	2384/107

List 33 (continued)

MUHLMEISTER	H.	cabinetmaker	Bueckeburg	2380/107
MUHSFELD	A.	barber?	Hamburg	2379/107
NEITHARDT	Johann	butcher	Wien	2566/115
OSTBYE	Zacharias?	peasant	Kongsberg	2639/118
PINK	Louis	businessman	Hamburg	2741/123
POEHL	J. D.	baker	Parchim	2740/123
	--	wife		
POHLMANN	J.	blacksmith	Luebz	2742/123
	--	wife		
	--	2 children, 3/4 & 4 y		
POLCHOW	Wilhelm Christian?	peasant	Marslow? [Maerslow?]	2743/123
	--	wife		
	--	6 children, 4-18 y		
RATH	H.	--?	Stuer	2961/133
	--	wife		
	--	2 children, 4 & 6½ y		
ROHLOFF	Christian	brewer	Dablerstein	2959/133
	Hanna?	wife		
ROSENBERG	H.	baker	Niesky	2957/133
RUBOW	Johann	wheelwright	Suckwitz	2960/133
RUPPINS	Amalia	--	Waldenburg	2958/133
	==	2 children, 3/4 & 3 y		
SAUERHERING	F. A.	pharmacist	Stargard	3387/151
SCHEELKE	Johann	soldier	Glueckstadt	3384/151
SCHLAG	Friedrich	butcher	Goldberg	3381/151
SCHMIDT	Gottl[ieb?]	gold worker	Stuttgart	3374/151
SCHMIDT	F.	painter	Dobbertin	3376/151
SCHNELL	Johann	laborer	Satow	3385/151
SCHNELL	Christiane	--	Stuer	3386/151
SCHOENFELD	Ferdinand	machine builder	Coburg	3388/151
	--	wife		
	--	2 children, 4 & 8 y		

42

SCHRODT	Paul Robert	tanner	Zillichau	3373/151
SCHROEDER	Christian	laborer	Stuer	3377/151
	Elisabeth	wife		
	--	3 children, 7-12 y		
SCHUETT	F. C. C.	tailor	Schwerin	3375/151
SCHULT	H.	--	Luebz	3379/151
SCHULTZ	Sophia	--	Krogen	3382/151
SEIFERT	Johann	peasant	Gleichenwiessen, Th	3372/151
SOERENSON	Adolph	manager	Copenhagen	3383/151
	Hanna	--		
SOHR	Ludwig	blacksmith	Goldberg	3380/151
	Julia	wife		
STARK	Fritz	tailor	Robel	3378/151
TECHANT	J. H. W.	glazier	Hagenow	3672/164
TIMM	Adolph	wheelwright	Rambow? [Raumbuw?]	3671/164
VOGT	Christian	--	Marslow	3767/168
	Carolina	--		
VOSS	H.	businessman	Altona	3766/168
WAGNER	Adolph	shoemaker	Prenzlin	3939/177
WALLERSTEIN	Lisette	--	Berlin	3942/177
WETTERHALL	Carl	dyer	Sevanger, No	3944/177
WICHMANN	J.	miller	Rossin	3943/177
	--	wife		
	--	child, 3/4 y		
WIENER	Salomon	tailor	Posen	3936/177
WIENER	Goetz	tailor	Posen	3937/177
WIENER	Maria	--	Posen	3938/177
	--	2 children, 7 & 9 y		
WIENER	Emilia	--	Berlin	3940/177
	Renate	--		
	Rosalia	--		
WIENER	Max	--	Berlin	3941/177
	Ludwig	12 y		
	Theodor	7 y		

List 33 (continued)

WILHELMS	Amalia	--	New York	3933/177
WISKORIL	Victor	butcher	Lehesdorf	3934/177
	--	wife		
	--	2 children, 3/4 & 3½ y		
WISKORIL	Francisca	--	Lehesdorf	3935/177
WITTMACK	Carl	gold worker	Altona	3945/177

List 34

Ship *Howard*, Captain J. H. Jacobs
Departing Hamburg 27 Nov 1850 for New York (Direct)

AHRENS	J. H.	--	N. Lueblow, Mk	0116/006
	--	wife		
	--	daughter, 10 y		
AHRENS	Carl	laborer	Lehsen, Pr	0117/006
EICHACKER	C. F.	--	Coblenz	0802/037
GERHARDT	J.	butcher	Wittenburg, Mk	1169/053
	--	wife		
	--	daughter, 5 y		
GIESECKE	W.	butcher	Bursinghausen, Ha	1167/053
GIESECKE	Friedrich	mechanic	Bursinghausen, Ha	1168/053
GLANDER	Gottfried	tailor	Berlin	1165/053
GROFELMANN	H.	brewer	Gramstaedt	1166/053
HIGELSTROEM	J. R.	paperhanger	Stockholm	1494/067
KROEGER	Johann	--?	Lueneburg	1960/087
KROGICK	Francisca	--	Bohrschuetz	1961/088
MALLEIS	Cornelius	carpenter	Marienwerder, Pr	2506/112
NEUMANN	Marcus	butcher	Dobrawitz, Bo	2598/116
NIBBE	Johann	manager	Opland, Ha	2599/116
PFEFFER	Conrad	cabinetmaker	Walshausen, Sa	2815/126
SCHAECKEL	F. W.	blacksmith	Petershagen, Pr	3611/161
TROBE	G. B.	baker	Lueda, Ha	3710/165
WENDHEIM	F	farmhand	Runnstadt	4020/180

List 35

Ship *Hermann*, Captain J. Simonsen
Departing Hamburg 29 Jun 1850 for Valdivia (Direct)

ALSDORF	Heinrich	book printer	Berlin	0061/004
ALSDORF	Johanna	teacher	Berlin	0062/004
ANWANDTER	Carl Hermann	pharmacist pharmacist	Colau	0064/004
ANWANDTER	Wilhelm	cabinetmaker	Colau	0065/004
ANWANDTER	Otto -- --	cabinetmaker child, 12 y child, 7 y	Colau	0066/004
AUNAS	Wilhelm	shoe repairman	Berlin	0063/004
BADTKE	H.	manager	Landsberg am W.	0332/015
BECHER	Albert	--?	Berlin	0334/015
BLUFERT	Louise? E. Carl	-- 8 y	Berlin	0333/015
BUENCHLER	Ernestine	--	Frankfurt am Oder	0336/015
BURSCH	Christian	artist?	Ullersdorf	0335/015
EICHLER	Juliane, b HARNISCH	teacher	Berlin	0740/035
GRIMM	F. A.	peasant	Nordhausen	1078/050
HAEBERLE	Georg	manager	Faurnidau, Wu	1349/061
HERMANN	August	clothmaker	Guben	1347/061
HETTICH	G. S?	vinedresser	Unterturkheim	1348/061
KASKEL	F. J. M.	physician	Berlin	1802/081
KELLER	J. J. Catherine	mason --	Untertuerkheim	1805/081
KINDERMANN	W. M.	peasant	Fekfh To?	1800/081
KLEIN	G. J.	small gardener	Wangen	1804/081
KOERNER	Theodor	actuary?	Colau	1799/081
KSCHINKA	Christian	farm hand	Ullensdorf	1803/081
KUNSTMANN	H. H.	businessman	Dresden	1801/081
LANGE	H. F.	baker	Landsberg am W.	2083/093
LINCK	Xaver	pharmacist?	Leutkirch	2084/093
MENZEL	Hermann?	businessman	Frankfurt/Oder	2369/106

List 35 (continued)

METZDORF	H. L.	teacher	Frankfurt/Oder	2366/106
METZDORF	Pauline August Paul Maria --	-- peasant, 21 y 6 y 3 y baby	Frankfurt/Oder	2367/106
MOSER	Ludwig	businessman	Berlin	2368/106
MOSER	R.	gardener	Stuttgart	2370/106
NICOLAI	Carl	manager	Luebben	2562/115
NOACK	Christian -- --	-- wife 3 children, 10-22 y	Schadewitz	2561/114
PAUER	Friedrich	businessman	Colau	2736/123
REUTER	Jacob	--?	Baelingen?	2948/133
REWALD	G.	carpenter	Nieder Eldungen	2947/133
RIBBECK	Wilhelm	manager	Neuzelle	2944/133
RIBBECK	Friedrich Heinrich	storekeeper businessman (in Stettin)	Neuzelle	2945/133
RICHTER	Carl G.	butcher	Dresden	2943/133
RICHTER	Friedrich	butcher	Calau, Hinter? [Nieder?] Lausitz	2946/133
ROSENTHAL	C. W.	cabinetmaker	Hamburg	2949/133
SCHLEGEL	W. A. Maria	book binder wife	Vetschau	3354/150
SCHMIDT	Carl	businessman	Osterwitz	3353/150
SCHROEDER	W. F.	peasant	Wismar	3359/150
SCHULTZ	Wilhelmine	servant girl	Ullersdorf	3355/150
SEISSMANN	Wilhelmine	--	Hamburg	3358/150
STROBEL	E. P. A. -- --	miller wife 4 children, 6-19 y	Langenau	3356/150
STROBEL	Catharina	--	Langenau	3357/150
TIEDEMANN	Carl	peasant	Neuhaus	3667/164
ULEMANN? [UHEMANN?]	Rudolph	businessman	Berlin	3723/166

List 35 (continued)

WINKLER	Eduard	manager	Gay	3926/177
WISWEDE	H.	businessman	Neu Haldensleben	3927/177
	Mathilde	--		

List 36

Ship *Herschel* (Hamburg flag) Captain J. C. Edenholtz
Departing Hamburg 30 Apr 1850 for New York (Direct)

BACHMANN	August	--?	Hemerrichs, --?	0222/011
BAEHR	Salomon	cap maker	Schwersenz	0218/011
BARTH	Josef	peasant	Wulkemin, Mk	0219/011
BAUM	Marcus	cap maker	Schwersenz	0217/011
BEISE	H. G.	peasant	Fernosfeld, Pr	0223/011
	Friederike	wife		
BEISE	Alvina	child	Fernosfeld, Pr	0224/011
	August	child		
	Minna	child		
	Wilhelm	child		
	Carl*	child		
	Albert	child		
	Carl*	child		
	Emilia	child		
		*So stated		
BERENT	Friederike	--	Fernosfeld, Pr	0225/011
	Carolina	--		
BEUTLER	M.	carpenter	Gruetzendorf	0221/011
BIENENFREUND	Clara	--	Waltershausen, Ba	0226/011
	Rebecca	--		
BISCHHEISTER	August	manager	Dohren	0228/011
BLANKE	Wilhelm	carpenter	Berlin	0213/010
BLUMANN	Clara	--	Inowraclaw?	0220/011
BORNHOEFT	--	girl	Malchow	0227/011
	Maria	child		
	Friederike	child		
BUSCH	Nina?	--	Posen	0215/010
	Jacob	boy		
BUSCH	Rosalchen?	child	Posen	0216/010
	Cizilchen?	child		
	Raphael	child		

List 36 (continued)

BUSSENIUS	August	pharmacist	Bevesen, Pr	0214/010
CARDINAHL	Th.	--	Stade	0527/024
CHRISTENSEN	Peter	tailor	Kopenhagen	0526/024
COHN	Gotthelf	soldier	Inowraclav	0525/024
	Bernhard	soldier		
COWITZ	David Juda	teacher	Garkowo	0524/024
DARMSOW	Albertine	--	Fernosfeld	0599/028
	Johann Lud- wig	child		
	August	child		
	Albert	child		
	Rinke?	child		
DENNER	J. C.	peasant	Gantersleben	0604/028
	--	wife		
DETTLOFF	Christian	peasant	Fernosfeld, Pr	0597/028
	Anna	wife		
DETTLOFF	Friederike	--	Fernosfeld	0598/028
	Carl	--		
	Caroline*	--		
	Wilhelm	--		
	Caroline*	--		
	Emma	--		
		*So shown		
DIRCKS	Helene A.	--	St. Georg	0600/028
DRAPPIEL	Carl Ferdinand	tailor	Plauszig	0601/028
DREYER	Carl Wilhelm	brick maker	Salzwedel	0596/028
	Friederike	wife		
	--	2 children		
DREYER	Sophia	--	Malchow	0602/028
EHEMANN	Theodor	tailor	Gross Breitenbach	0710/033
EHRENDRICH	Johann	manager	Yorksrow, Pr	0712/034
	Louise	--		
ELKUS	Rosalia	--	Schwersenz	0709/033
ENGELHARDT	R?	book binder	Gross Breitenbach	0711/033
ERNST	F.	shoemaker	Neuhaus, Pr	0714/034
EWALD	Christian	shoemaker	Yorksrow, Pr	0713/034
	Johanna	--		
	Wilhelm	child		
	Johanne	child		

List 36 (continued)

FEDERLEIN	M.	peasant	Eichenhausen	0841/039
FEYBUSCH	Simon	shoemaker	Lebow	0837/039
FLOEDER	Heinrich	wheelwright	Marienwerder	0838/039
FRIEDLAENDER	J. M.	dyer	Hamburg	0839/039
FRIEDRICH	D. Carolina --	shoemaker wife 6 children	Neu Ruppin	0840/039
GANS	--?	--	Schwersenz	1020/047
GEISSEL	Georg	soldier	Pr[eussisch] Eylau	1022/047
GOLDSCHMIDT	Babette	--	Wilmars	1021/047
GRIMM	Pauline	--	Kiel	1023/047
HASEBALG	F.	sculptor	Steinfurth	1268/058
HECHT	Esther	--	Northeim, Ba	1265/057
HEINDEL	Joseph	paper manufac- turer	Regensburg	1264/057
HEISS	Theodor	seminarist	Dewitz	1259/057
HEITMANN	N.	soldier	Potsdam	1254/057
HEITMANN	C. N.	cake baker	Potsdam	1255/057
HEYMANN	Ostrow	tailor	Janova? Po	1258/057
HIFFNER	Theodor Carl Ottilia	-- -- --	Stameln	1266/057
HIFFNER	Pauline Eduard	-- --	Stameln	1267/057
HIRSCH	Ernestine	--	Nagol, Pr	1256/057
HIRSCH	Joseph	tailor	Exin, Pr	1260/057
HOFMANN	Carl	waiter	Kemel, Pr	1257/057
HOFMANN	Theodor	--	Gross Breitenbach	1261/057
HOFSCHILD	Wilhelmine	--	Fernosfeld, Pr	1263/057
HOLAND	August	butcher	Gross Breitenbach	1262/057
IBSOHN	Fritz	--?	Hamburg	1526/069
JACOBI	Moritz	soldier	Kopenhagen	1524/069
JACOBSOHN	Adolph	peasant	Milwauki [Milwaukee] Am	1522/069

List 36 (continued)

JAEGER	Justus	shoemaker	Utershausen	1521/069
JAFFE	Mina Ruha?	--	Inowraclav	1523/069
JANTZ	Augustin	--	Marienwerder	1525/069
KAHLMANN	Kallon A.	tanner	Nagol, Pr	1689/076
KEILING	Wilhelm	stocking maker	Hotzenplutz	1688/076
KNUEBBEL	J. L. Albertine	-- --	Fernosfeld, Pr	1693/076
KOCK	F. W.	tailor	Grunow	1690/076
KOEHLER	Regina	--	Fernosfeld, Pr	1694/076
KOLLER	B.	carpenter	Frauenburg	1692/076
KOPH	H.	manager	Winsen, Pr	1695/076
KOTTLOW	Jette Ernestine Helene?	--	Gnosen	1697/077
KROG	Albert	baker	Hohenzieritz	1698/076
KRUEGER	Dorothea	--	Salzwedel	1691/076
KUEBER	Eduard	painter	Glauchau	1696/076
LANGE	--	--	Neu Strelitz	2019/091
LEHMANN	J.	--	Hameln	2031/091
LEISE	Moses	tanner	Lebow, Pr	2023/091
LEOPOLD	Franz	butcher	Sekkenditz	2029/091
LEUSCHOW	J.	fisherman	Malchow	2028/091
LEVIN	Anna	--	Inowraclau	2024/091
LEVY	David	dyer	Hamburg	2030/091
LEVY	M. David	tailor	Eckzin, Pr	2020/091
LEVY	Caroline --	Frau 3 children	Eckzin, Pr	2021/091
LEVY	Eva --	-- 3 children	Eckzin, Pr	2022/091
LOEPER	F.	manager	Stargaard	2025/091
LUBENSKY	Adolph	cigarmaker	Berlin	2018/091
LUX	Joseph	butcher	Frankenstein	2026/091
LUX	Francisca	--	Frankenstein	2027/091

List 36 (continued)

MACHEL	Johann	--	Fernosfeld, Pr	2276/102
	Hanna?	wife		
	--	child		
MAGAWITZ	Ferdinand	--	Fernosfeld, Pr	2275/102
	Wilhelmine	--		
	Carl	--		
MANHEIMER	--	soldier	Schwersenz	2271/102
MARCKUSY	Nathan Meyer	--	Lebow	2267/102
MARCUS	Johann? [Jette?]	--	Nagol, Pr	2268/102
	Roeschen	--		
MARWEDEL	H. A.	carpenter	Stade	2277/102
MOELLER	Anna	--	Hamburg	2270/102
	Maria	--		
MOORES	Ernst	manager	Martenwerder	2269/102
MORGENSTERN	Adolph	businessman	Inowraclow	2273/102
MORGENSTERN	Elkan	butcher	Inowraclaw	2274/102
MOSESCHEYER?	--	sailmaker	Golkowko	2272/102
NADLER	Joseph	weapons maker	Pilsen	2536/113
NADLER	Veronica	--	Pilsen	2537/113
NATHANN	Lohse	trader	Heinerichs, Pr	2538/114
NEUDECK	Carl Eduard	glazier	Peltzig, Sa	2540/114
NEUDORF	Louis	gold worker	Marienwerder	2535/113
NIEMANN	C. H.	butcher	Hagenow	2539/114
NOLL	Elise	--	Geinsen	2542/114
NOWACK	Johann	baker	Petersdorf	2541/114
	Ernestine	--		
OLDACH	Rudolph	cabinetmaker	Neubrandenburg	2623/117
PESCHKY	Robert	gold worker	Frankenstein	2687/121
	Bertha?	wife		
PESTER	Eduard	journeyman shoe-maker	Hameln? [Stameln?]	2689/121
	Wilhelmine	--		
PETSCH	Anton	shoemaker	Schloetersdorf	2686/121
	Carolina	--		
PITTINS? [PITTIUS?]	Ludwig	carpenter	Schoenfeld	2684/121

List 36 (continued)

POHLMANN	B.	--	Fasseldorf	2690/121
PRESINSKY	Elkan	tailor	Inowraclaw	2685/121
	Malchan?	wife		
	Ernestine	--		
PUFF	Carl	basketmaker	Krausheim	2688/121
RATZE	Diedrich	carpenter	Hannover	2875/130
REINHARD	Trina	--	Bitzfleth	2872/130
REINHARDT	Friedrich	gold worker	Sondershausen	2877/130
RESER	J. D.	agent?	Hamburg	2876/130
RIMON	Babette	--	Oettingen	2873/130
ROSENKRANZ	Ludwig	--	Neustadt, Ho	2871/130
	Ferdinand	--		
RUEDIGER	Leopold	farmer	Neuhaus	2874/130
SAGER	Carl	painter	Brunstadt	3207/144
SCHLOSS	Isac	weaver	Oberlauringen, Ba	3206/144
SCHOR	Samuel	soldier	Inowraclaw	3194/143
SCHRADER	Carolina	--	Permund	3209/144
SCHROEDER	Friedrich	blacksmith	Klein Luechow	3201/143
SCHROEDER	C.	manager	Neu Strelitz	3210/144
SCHUBERT	Minna	Mad[am?]	Berlin	3192/143
	Maria	child		
	Albert	child		
	Heinrich	child		
	Minna	child		
SCHULTZ	Christoph	miller	Salzwedel	3197/143
	Sophia	wife		
	Maria	child		
	Dorothea	child		
SCHULTZ	H.	--	Salzwedel	3198/143
SCHULZ	Juergen H.	peasant	Volzendorf	3199/143
	Dorothea	wife		
SCHULZ	Christoph	--	Volzendorf	3200/143
	Maria	--		
SCHWARZ	Carolina	--	Schleswig?	3205/144
	Doris	--		

52

SELLE	August	laborer	Schoenemark	3202/143
SENGER	Philipp	weaver	Seeberg, Ha	3208/144
SPINTZ	Ephraim	soldier	Inowraclaw	3193/143
SPOTT	J. F.	--	Merseburg	3211/144
SPRING	-- Clara	Mad[am?]	Waltershausen	3203/144
SPRING	Rebecca	--	Waltersahusen	3204/144
STIPPE	Carl Eduard	finishing dyer [*Schoenfaerber*]	Gruenberg	3191/143
SUESSENGUTH	F.	clothmaker	Lobenstein	3196/143
SZAMOTUTSKY	Gustav	tailor	Schwersenz	3195/143
TELZ	Franz Thusla? --	baker wife 5 children	Riegersdorf	3642/162
TELZ	Barbara	--	Riegersdorf	3643/162
TEPPERT	Carl H. A.	shoemaker	Breslau	3641/162
TIRKS	Carl Friederike August Friedrich Caroline Wilhelm	peasant -- -- -- -- --	Fernosfeld, Pr	3644/163
UCIESZYNSKI	Franz	shoemaker	Posen	3717/166
VOGEL	C. F. -- Maria Paul	--? librarian wife child child	Leipzig	3752/167
VOLBEHR	Ph[ilipp?] H.	--	Kiel	3753/167
WARSCHAUER	Eva	--	Inowraclow	3843/172
WEEGANT	Caspar	peasant	Sonnenburg	3849/172
WEINSTOCK	Elias	tanner	Roetelmeier, Ba	3842/172
WERNER	Nicolas	shoemaker	Gross Breitenbach	3844/172
WERNER	Christian Adolph	glazier	Carlsruhe	3847/172
WILLMER	August -- --	cabinetmaker wife 3 children	Berlin	3841/172

List 36 (continued)

WINKLER	Johanna? [Johannes?]	--	Straubitz	3845/172
WINKLER	Wilhelm	cabinetmaker	Knautheim	3848/172
WOLF	Racha Lisette	-- --	Posen	3851/172
WOLFSOHN	A.	teacher	Glueckstadt	3850/172
WURO	Caroline	--	Fernosfeld, Pr	3846/172
ZIMMERMANN	Friedrich	bricklayer	Schonemark	4037/181

List 37

Ship *Herschel* (Hamburg flag) Captain J. C. Edenholtz
Departing Hamburg 16 Sep 1850 for New York (Direct)

ABICHT	Carl	wheelwright	Koeleda, Duchy of	Ru0096/005
ARONS	Leopold	businessman	Teserow	0095/005
ASCHHEIM	Henriette	--	Posen	0094/005
BEHRENS	H.	tailor	Ruest	0461/021
BLOCK	Carl	mason	Greifswald	0462/021
BOETTCHER	Hans	businessman	Rehna	0463/021
BOGE	Peter N.	seaman?	Foehr	0467/021
BOYSEN	A.	pharmacist	Grabow	0459/021
BRANDT	Hermann	businessman	Ziekel, Pr	0466/021
BRANDT	J. M.	weaver	Weibzbach [Waebz- bach]	0465/021
BREDT	J. C. F.	tailor	Beckadel	0464/021
BUDIN	Julius	--	Greifswald	0460/021
CALISKY	Jacob	--?	Posen	0551/025
CELLMANN	J.	farmhand	Brock, Mk	0553/025
COEHN	Heinrich	distiller	Wuesteyersdorff, Sa	0554/025
COHN	Johanne	--	Berlin	0550/025
COHN	Blume? --	-- 2 children, 5½ & 7½ y	Botschow, Pr	0552/025

List 37 (continued)

DASE	Johann	--	Karchow	0667/031
DENNING	Anna	--	Hamburg	0666/031
DEUERLING	Sophia	--	Burgkandstedt	0668/031
DISSEN	Wilhelmine	Frau	Berlin	0669/031
EBENSPERGER	C.	businessman	Alshoff?	0782/036
EICHHORST	Heinrich	--	Helm	0781/036
EISICH	H.	shoemaker	New York	0783/036
ELBLEIN	Andreas	cabinetmaker	Arnstadt	0780/036
FABER	Friedrich	soapmaker	Kreuzburg, Sa-We	0929/043
FISCHER	Carl	laborer	Brackensdorf	0931/043
FRANKE	Jacob Carl	--?	Astronow, Pr	0928/043
FREITAG	Christian -- --	weaver wife daughter, 13 y	Neuhaltensleben, Pr	0932/043
FUCHS	Simon	tailor	Vitkover	0930/043
GEHLE	Fritz	weaver	Cohlenfeld	1143/052
GLISSMANN	Wilhelm	laborer	Schwerin, Mk	1146/052
GOERS	Christianna	--	Plate	1144/052
GURKER	Isaac	tailor	Wreschen, Pr	1145/052
HAASE	Friedrich	tailor	Rampe	1438/065
HAASE	Christian -- --	manager wife 3 children, 3/4- 6 y	Crewitz, Mk	1441/065
HASS	J.	saddler	Althoff, Ba	1440/065
HEFTER	Heym[ann]	businessman	Pleschen	1435/064
HEISE	F. W. Fried- rich	tailor	Neumassow	1437/065
HEITER	Ferdinand	barber	Astronow, Pr	1439/065
HORN	Anna Wilhelm	-- son, 6 y	St. Petersburg	1436/064
JACOBS	Carl -- --	shepherd wife 4 children, 5-14 y	Dobbin	1581/071

List 37 (continued)

JUCH	Wilhelm	mason	Sachsa, Pr	1582/071
KELLNER	Carl	teacher	Nordheim	1928/086
KIENKE	Heinrich	manager	N[eu] Zachum, Mk	1923/086
KLOCKOW	Johann	farmhand	Klinken, Mk	1925/086
KNORDTS	Johann	shoemaker	Wuebzbach, Ba	1924/086
KOCH	Theodor	laborer	Neubrandenburg	1927/086
KOCKERT	Jacob	tailor	Bareck	1922/086
KORCK	Louis	tailor	Thorn	1926/086
LEHRNITZ?	H.	manager	Marsow	2165/097
LEMBCKE	J.	tailor	Brack	2167/097
LESCHNISKY	Jacob	tailor	Danzig	2168/097
LINDNER	Ferdinand	tailor	Aschersleben	2166/097
LITTNER	J. G.	weaver	Thimetz?	2164/097
LOHFING?	Fritz -- --	laborer wife 4 children, 3-11 y	Krackow, Mk	2169/097
LOHFING?	Dorothea --	Frau 3? children, 1-3/4-8½ y	Krackow, Mk	2170/097
MAHNERT	Albert	manager	Grosswich	2469/110
von MALIGNON? [MALIGNAN?]	Franz	businessman	Bagnols, France	2471/111
MEDANS	Friedrich -- --	laborer wife son, 4 y	Mettin	2467/110
MEYER	Heymann Abraham	businessman businessman	Filehne	2468/110
MOELLER	C. --	-- 2 children, 3/4 & 3 y	Hamburg	2470/111
MUELLER	Maria	--	Friedland, Mk	2472/111
NICKELSEN	Boye Peter	seaman	Foehr	2593/116
NOLT	Friedrich Johanna	tailor mother	Malchow	2592/116
OELZE	Heinrich -- --	shoemaker wife 3 children, 1-9 y	Neuhaltensleben, Pr	2648/118

OERTEL	F.	copper engraver	Waebzbach, Ba	2647/118
OPPENHEIM	Julius	businessman	Berlin	2646/118
PAULANGER	Paulina	--	Werdau	2783/125
PAUSEWEIN	F.	tailor	Lueneburg	2784/125
PETTER? [PITTER?]	Franz	brewer	Welmarn	2782/125
PFOTENHAUER	J. H. C.	laborer	Zeigerheim	2788/125
POHERT?	J. H.	--	Leutenberg	2789/125
PRAHL	Johann	manager	Gruenhoff, Mk	2785/125
	--	wife		
	--	2 children, ¼-7 y		
PRALOW	Friedrich	mason	Malchow	2786/125
	--	wife		
	--	2 children, ½-3 y		
PRALOW	Christian	farmhand	Stuer	2787/125
RUSDORF	Philip	laborer	Plahsen? [Plassew?] Mk	3022/136
SALOMON	Martin	businessman	Teterow	3527/157
SCHIRMER	G. A.	--?	Hamburg	3526/157
	--	wife		
	--	daughter, 7 y		
SCHREYER	Martin	--	Zellin	3525/157
	--	wife		
	--	3 children, 7-13 y		
SCHROEDER	Maximilian	wheelwright	Butzow, Mk	3538/158
SCHULDT	Johann	laborer	Henrichsberg	3540/158
SCHULTZ	J. C. G.	tailor	Moedlich	3528/157
SCHULTZ	H.	blacksmith	Kitz	3529/157
SCHULTZ	Carl	clothmaker	Braunschweig	3530/157
	--	wife		
	--	son, 5 y		
SEEMANN	Johann	manager	Pamperin, Mk	3534/157
	--	wife		
	--	3 children, 2-7¼ y		
SEEMANN	Sophia	--	Pamperin, Mk	3535/157
SIEVERT	Hans H.	manager, 50 y	Schwaberow, Mk	3531/157

List 37 (continued)

SIEVERT	Dorothea*	30 y	Schwaberow, Mk	3532/157
	Dorothea*	22 y		
	Sophia	20 y		
	*So shown			
SIEVERT	Maria	17 y	Schwaberow, Mk	3533/157
	Ludwig	14 y		
	Elise	7 y		
	Mina	3/4 y		
SIMON	Maria	--	Hamburg	3536/158
SPRINKSTUB	W. L.	shoemaker	Braunschweig	3541/158
STILLER	John W.	seaman	Danzig	3539/158
STOBBE	Emilia	--	Leipzig	3537/158
THIEL	Louise	--	Lipna, Po	3699/165
TIMM	J. H.	businessman	Helgoland	3698/165
WIETING	P.	laborer	Rothen	3992/179
WISPELHORN	Carolina	--	Braunschweig	3991/179
	Johanna	--		

List 38

Ship *Johann Friedrich*, Captain J. F. C. Behrens
Departing Hamburg 12 Oct 1850 for Galveston & Indianola, Texas

ARNIM	Edmund	laborer	Kyritz, Pr	0101/006
BOLDT	Christian	--	Moellenbeck, Mk	0476/021
CUSTODIS	Leopold	peasant	Duesseldorf	0558/025
	Johanna	--		
DELFF	Friedrich	peasant	Wittstock	0673/031
DUEBEL	Johann	mason	Proettlin, Pr	0674/031
	--	wife		
	--	2 children, 2 & 4 y		
EBERHARD	Friedrich	saddler	Greiffenau	0788/037
ELLERBUSCH	J. A.	laborer	Hamburg	0787/037
	--	wife		
	--	2 children		
EULE	Adolph	cabinetmaker	Bautzen, Sa	0786/037

List 38 (continued)

FALKENHAGEN	Georg -- --	peasant wife 2 children, 5-14 y	Wittstock, Pr	0942/043
FALKENHAGEN	Ludwig Wilhelmine	wheelwright --	Wittstock, Pr	0943/043
FROST	Carl	--	Bautzen, Sa	0944/043
FUCHS	Friedrich -- --	peasant wife 4 children, 9-21 y	Penzlin	0945/043
GRUENBEIN	Friedrich -- --	peasant wife 2 children, 7 & 9 y	Wittstock, Pr	1152/053
HAASE	Dorothea Ferdinand	-- son, 13 y	Wittstock, Pr	1459/065
HAMANN	Maria	--	Moellenbeck, Pr	1460/065
HILLERT	-- -- --	*Feldmeister* wife son, 10 months	Neu Ruppin	1458/065
KOCH	Carl	plumber	Hamburg	1942/087
KOCH	Christian	cake baker	Hamburg	1943/087
KOHN	Bernhard	hunter	Polzin	1941/087
KOLBOW	Carl -- --	peasant wife 3 children, ½-10 y	Moellenbeck, Pr	1944/087
KUNDE	Johann -- --	peasant wife 6 children, 1-12 y	Polzin	1940/087
LAFIN	Ernst	wheelwright	Polzin	2186/098
LANGE	Carl -- --	carpenter wife 2 children [ages illegible]	Ham bei Hamburg	2187/098
LENTH	Johann Fried- rich	peasant	Moellenbeck	2188/098
LENTH	Juergen Magdalena --	-- wife child, ½? y	Moellenbeck	2189/098
LISTICH	Engelhard -- --	peasant wife 4 children, 10-15 y	Polzin, Pr	2185/098

List 38 (continued)

MASUR	Gottfried	carpenter	Polzin, Pr	2482/111
MINKE	Christine	--	Holzminden	2484/111
MOERER	Fritz	peasant	Moellenbeck, Pr	2483/111
POLL	Fritz	--	Moellenbeck	2796/126
PRILL	Fritz	peasant	Zierzow	2797/126
REMMIN?	Christian	peasant	Mollenbeck, Pr	3033/136
SCHUETZE	Wilhelm	instrument maker	Hannover	3570/159
	--	wife		
SCHULTZ	--	tailor	Werle	3567/159
	--	wife		
	--	4 children, 6 weeks to 24 y		
SOMMER	Pauline	--	Jauer	3566/159
STRUWE	Johann Friedrich	peasant	Moellenbeck	3568/159
	--	wife		
	--	daughter, 8 y		
STRUWE	Maria	36 y	Moellenbeck	3569/159
TOEPPERWEIN	Ferdinand	teacher	Neu Ruppin	3703/165
	--	wife		
	--	6 children, 4-15 y		
WASSERMANN	Georg	--	Kaltenlengsfeld, Sa-Mn	4000/180
	Catharina	15 y		
WESENBERG	Carl	peasant	New Ruppin	3999/180
ZERBST	Carl Wilhelm	cabinetmaker	Boetzow	4073/183
ZWESCH	Franz	cabinetmaker	New Ruppin	4972/183

List 39

Ship *Kossuth*, Captain John Fisher
Departing Hamburg 15 Jul 1850 for New York (Direct)

ASBROCK	Sophia	--	Wittenburg	0069/004
	--	4 children, 3/4-12 y		
BLENCK	Johann	miller	Doemitz	0372/017

List 39 (continued)

BLENCK	Anna	--	Wosten	0373/017
	Wilhelm	miller		
BOBSIN	Johann	shoemaker	Goldberg	0369/017
BOLDT	H. H. D.	businessman	Luebeck	0375/017
BROCK	R--?	--	Kazmin	0370/017
BROCKMANN	Wilhelmine	--	Goldberg	0376/017
	Maria	--		
BUBLITZ	C. J. F.	brewer	Fredenwalde	0371/017
BUETHNER	Robert	gold worker	Breslau	0368/017
BURMEISTER	Friedrich	butcher	Goldberg	0374/017
	--	wife		
	--	5 children, 3/4- 12 y		
COHN	Meyer Wolff	tailor	Neumark	0543/025
COHN	Hirsch	--	Frandke	0544/025
	Ernestine	wife		
DAUER	F. R.	blacksmith	Stoessen?	0642/030
	--	wife		
	--	7 children, ½-15 y		
DEMPE	Franz	manager	Strelsen	0645/030
	Maria	wife		
DESSAUER	Bertha	--	Brinkum, Ol	0646/030
DREHBAUM	August	--	Ziegelrade	0641/030
DREYER	Heinrich	shepherd	Geppersdorf	0644/030
	--	wife		
	--	son, 10 y		
DUESENBERG	Ludwig	shoemaker	Dasse	0643/030
EGGERT	Andreas	--?	Klein Treppow, Mk	0752/035
EWERS	Carolina	--	Slatel, Mk	0751/035
FESKY	Ernst	peasant	Friedrichsthal, Mk	0894/041
FRIESE	Carl	painter	Magdeburg	0893/041
	--	wife		
	--	2 children, 3/4- 1-3/4 y		
GABEL	J.	soldier	Hamburg	1098/050
GERSON	Joseph	tailor	Krotoschin	1099/050

List 39 (continued)

GILLWALD	H.	--	Magdeburg	1102/051
GOELDNER	Julius	--	Strelslen [so	1101/050
	Carl	--	spelled]	
	Carl?	--		
	Joseph	7 y		
GRAEFE	Carl	--	Glueckstadt	1100/050
GRIEPENKIEL	--	physician	--	1097/050
GRUNAR	--	businessman	Berlin	1095/050
	--	wife		
	--	4 children		
GUENTHER	A. D.	helmsman	Luebeck	1096/050
HALBIG	Christian	--	Raebel	1359/061
	Valentin	--		
HARTMANN	Friedrich	--	Hamburg	1362/061
HEINE	Carl	businessman	Schlieben	1366/062
HEISSE	J. C. G.	brewer	Angstedt, Sc-Ru	1364/062
HERZ	Sara	--	Muehleslow, Pr	1361/061
	Ernestine	--		
	Dorchen?	--		
HESS	August	peasant	Dalang	1367/062
HEUER	Wilhelm	shoemaker	Goldberg	1368/062
	Friederike	wife		
HEYMANN	Isador	tailor	Straszburg	1360/061
	Dora	--		
HOEVERMANN	G.	beer brewer	Dannenberg, Ha	1365/062
	Maria	wife		
HOFFMANN	F. G.	peasant	Ziegelrode	1363/061
	Henriette	--		
	Charlotte	--		
JACOBSON	Peter	soldier	Norge [Norway?]	1562/070
JEGELBARDT	M.	mechanic	Krotoschin	1563/070
JORDANS? [JORDAN?]	Emil	manager	Buhren	1564/070
JOSEPH	Gerson	tailor	Krotoschin	1561/070
JUST	Andreas	brewer	Bussleben	1565/070
KALMUCK	Auguste	--	Kozmin	1828/082

List 39 (continued)

KANGER	Franz	weaver	Schildberg	1832/082
KAPPELN	Elias	tailor	Muhlerslow	1825/082
	Israel	--		
KERNER	Hermann	cabinetmaker	Grueneberg	1835/082
	Heinrich	cabinetmaker		
KLUEVER?	Johann	peasant	Friedrichsthal	1833/082
[KLIWER?]	--	wife		
	--	3 children, 12-24 y		
KNIPPER	Wilhelm	--	Geppersdorf	1831/082
KOCH	Carl	--	Friedrichsthal	1834/082
	Sophie	wife		
KOCH	Otto Fried-	--	Rendsburg	1840/082
	rich			
KOEPCKE	Heinrich	manager	Mestlin	1836/082
	Maria	wife		
KOZMINSKY	Paul	--	Krotoschin	1826/082
KRAMM	Carl	sculptor	Cassel	1829/082
KRAMM	Heinrich	basketmaker	Cassel	1830/082
KREBS	Hermann	dyer	Naumburg	1838/082
KRUEGER	G. A.	shoemaker	Guben	1839/082
KRUEGER	Johann	laborer	Goldberg	1837/082
	Sophie	wife		
KUHN	Emma?	--	Kozmin	1827/082
LEUTLOFF	Emilia	--	Grueneberg	2099/094
LIENOW	Wilhelm	manager	Goldberg	2100/094
LIENOW	Jacob	shoemaker	Goldberg	2101/094
	Maria	wife		
LIENOW	Ernst	shoemaker	Goldberg	2102/094
MARCUS	Samuel	soldier	Golupp	2397/108
	Saul?	--		
MARTENS	Lisette	--	Preetz	2400/108
MICHAEL	Johann	manager	Defahr, Mk	2399/108
	Ernestine?	wife		
	--	son, 3/4 y		
MITTAG	Catharina	--	Breitungen, Sa	2398/108
	Louise	--		

List 39 (continued)

NAGELSCHMIDT	Henriette	--	Breslau	2569/115
	--	5 children, 2-12 y		
NEUBAUER	Johann	butcher	Steuermark, Pr	2568/115
NOACK	Carl	--	Damitsch	2570/115
	Sophie?	wife		
NOACK	August	--	Dammitzsch	2571/115
	Sophie?	--		
	Amalia	--		
NOACK	Carl	--	Dammitzsch	2572/115
	Louise	4 y		
PARTHEY	Friederike	--	Delibzsch	2751/124
PETERS	Carolina	--	Vollbuettel	2748/124
	Fritz	son, 7 y		
PETERS	Johann	tailor	Wustrow	2749/124
	--	wife		
PREYMANN	Johann	houseboy	Amtoia? Ha	2746/123
PROBSTHAM?	A.	manager	Alt Strelitz	2745/123
PULVERMANN	Sophia?	--	Krotoschin, Pr	2747/124
PUSTOW	H.	painter	Schwerin	2750/124
RAETHER	C. A.	tailor	Potsdam	2966/134
	Friederike	wife		
RAMBACH	Johann	--	Gustrow	2964/134
REINHOLD	August	cabinetmaker	Cassel	2965/134
RIECK	Friedrich	wheelwright	Plauhagen? [Plan- hagen?]	2968/134
ROSENTHAL	Julius	high school stu- dent	Eain? [Exin?]	2967/134
SAMUEL	Hermann	shoemaker	Birnbaum	3400/152
SCHATZ	Friedrich	--	Goldberg	3409/152
SCHMIDT	Carl	--	Robel	3397/152
SCHROEDER	J. C. F.	mason	Dresden	3404/152
	Johanna	wife		
SCHULTZ	Friedrich	soldier	Namslau	3403/152
SCHULTZ	Theodor	15 y	Hannover	3405/152
	Eduard	13 y		
	Adolph	12 y		

List 39 (continued)

SCHULTZ	Friedrich	cabinetmaker	Grueneberg	3406/152
SCHULTZ	Auguste	--	Grueneberg	3407/152
SCHULTZ	Johann	manager	Wessentin	3408/152
SCHUMACHER	Heinrich	musician	Mosean	3398/152
SCHUMACHER	Julius	peasant	Mosean	3399/152
SCUBINSKY? [SEUBINSKY?]	A.	tailor	Bromberg	3402/152
SELIG	Dorothea	--	Krotoschin	3401/152
TEGGE	Adolph	wood turner	Friedland	3677/164
WEEGMANN	Johanna	--	Striege	3947/177
WIENER	Bertha	--	Krotoschin	3946/177
WOLF	Johann	weaver	Goldberg	3948/177
	--	wife		
	--	2 children, 3/4 & 4 y		

List 40

Ship *Leontine*, Captain G. Thormann
Departing Hamburg 15 Jun 1850 for New York (Direct)

ACKERMANN	Gotth[ilf?]	manager	Tauthewalde? Pr	0056/004
ADLER	Helmuth	--	Friedland	0057/004
ANDING	Christian?	--	Berka	0058/004
BACKER	F. A.	miller	Micheln	0317/015
BARANOWSKI	Julius	soldier	Lippno, Ps?	0318/015
BAYENS	M.	pharmacist	Eiderstadt	0314/015
BEDHEIM	Ferdinand	blacksmith	Baltimore	0319/015
BENECKE	P. A.	manager	Christiansand	0311/014
BITTERMANN	Magdalena	--	Wien	0313/015
	Magdalena	daughter, 1? y		
BLUMER	Rudolph	businessman	Christiansand	0320/015
BOENECK	J.	music teacher	Berlin	0310/014
BONDEWITZ? [BANDEWITZ?]	Fritz	--	Glueckstadt	0316/015

List 40 (continued)

BRASCH	Julius	tailor	Zircke	0315/015
BUDE	Valentin?	architect	Tauthewalde?	0312/014
DAGELOW	Ludwig	--?	Schwerin	0627/029
DAVIDSOHN	Hartwig	soldier	Posen	0626/029
DEGENER	Wilhelm	laborer	Friedland	0624/029
DIRK	H. J.	laborer	Neuhof	0625/029
DIRKS	Peter	book dealer	Tondern	0623/029
EBEL	Otto	--? industrialist	Werben, Pr	0735/034
EHLE	Rosalia	--	Meuselbach	0736/035
ERNST	Otto	--	Breslau	0734/034
FRENZEL	Ernst	manager	Kleinstathen, Sa	0873/040
FRIEDRICH	Carl Andreas	painter	Gera	0874/040
GALEPP	Wilhelm Maria	shoemaker wife	Friedland	1068/049
GLUECK	J. F.	beer brewer	Suelz, Wu	1067/049
GYSENDOERFFER	C. J. L.	--	Hamburg	1069/049
HAAG	Friedrich	businessman	Stuttgart	1331/060
HACKER	Heinrich Anna Catharina Friedrich	manager -- manager	Soldin, Pr	1330/060
HALLAS	Carl	tanner	Bruenn	1329/060
HARTWIG	Friedrich	nailsmith	Friedland	1326/060
HENSEL	Carl	businessman	Beyersdorf	1332/060
HETSCHEL	Robert	brewer	Oetze	1327/060
HOME	Gustav	manager	Raigern	1328/060
JACOB	Ernestine	--	Exin? Pr	1550/070
JAHN	Nicolas --	carpenter wife	Meuselbach	1548/070
JOHANNSEN	Doris? [David?]	--	Harburg	1549/070
JUNGMANN	F. A.	tailor	Leipzig	1551/070
KADOW	Hans	master weaver	Friedland	1789/080
KNUDTZEN	N. C.	businessman	Norway	1791/080

List 40 (continued)

KOEHLER	Joachim	clothmaker	Friedland	1790/080
KURTH	Hermann	baker	Micheln, Sa	1792/080
LAMILA	Joseph	dyer	Ratibor	2080/093
LESSER	Alexander	businessman	Berlin	2081/093
MARCUSE	H? C.	--?	Wriezen	2357/106
MATZ	Wilhelmine	--	Meuselbach	2356/106
MEISER	Gustav	tailor	Brieg	2354/106
MEYEN? [MEYER?]	Hermann	laborer	Friedland	2355/106
MUELLER	Carl	cabinetmaker	Namslam? Si?	2358/106
MUELLER	Johann? -- --	manager wife 3 children, 6-14 y	Holzhammer, Ba	2359/106
MUELLER	Barbara	--	Holzhammer	2360/106
MUELLER	C.	miller	Perleberg	2361/106
NABRA	Samuel	soldier	Inowraslav, Ps	2560/114
NEUMANN	Carl Christine	carpenter --	Friedland	2557/114
NEUMANN	Friedrich -- --	shoemaker wife son, 7¼ y	Friedland	2558/114
NILSEN	T.	soldier	Mandel	2556/114
NILSEN	H.	tobacco manufacturer	Weilen, Denmark	2559/114
OSTDAHL	Nicolas	cabinetmaker	Christiania	2637/118
PIETSCH	Carl	businessman	Namslam, Pr	2729/123
REISE	Anhalt?	--	Ostrowo, Pr	2932/132
RETTSCHLAG	Kuepia?	--	Guestrow	2933/132
ROCHEL	Carl Robert	soldier	Creuznach	2931/132
ROSENBERG	Maria Gustav Traugott	-- son, 13 y son, 10 y	Langenberg	2935/132
ROSLER	Carl	cabinetmaker	Friedland	2930/132
RUHL	___	clothmaker	Guestrow	2934/132

List 40 (continued)

SALOMON	Lewin	cigarmaker	Zircke, Pr	3336/149
SAUER	Heinrich	manager	Eckstedt, Pr	3339/149
SCHAEPPE	Johann	weaver	Stone? Ps	3340/149
	Regina	--		
SCHALLAU	Ferdinand	shoemaker	Friedland	3331/149
	Theresa	--		
SCHMIDT	W.	shoemaker	Prtizwald	3334/149
SCHMUL	Samuel H.	--	Ostrowo, Pr?	3335/149
	--	wife		
	--	3 children, 3/4-7 y		
SCHOEN	Gustav	painter	Berlin	3330/149
SCHOEPPE	Emilia	--	Berlin	3333/149
	Auguste	--		
	Maria	--		
SCHROEDER	Hermann	carpenter	Pancka	3337/149
SCHROEDER	Carl	miller	Gera	3341/149
STAHL	Carl	cabinetmaker	Friedland	3332/149
STANGE	Albrecht	tailor	Spandau	3338/149
TONNESEN	T.	laborer	Mandel	3662/163
TROEPPER	Friedrich	manager	Soldin, Pr	3663/163
	--	wife		
	--	4 children, 5-14 y		
UMBACH	Philipp	bookseller	Cassel	3720/166
VOIGT	--	blacksmith	Guestrow	3765/168
VOSS	C. T.	miller	Friedland	3764/168
WADRIG	Johann	manager	Bassow	3920/176
WENIGER	Friedrich	--	Koenigsee	3921/176

List 41

Ship *Leibnitz* (Hamburg flag) Captain H. K. S. Joergensen
Departing Hamburg 15 Mar 1850 for New York (Direct)

ABEL	Therese	--	Posen	0007/002
ABRAHAMCZYK	Samuel	businessman	Wreschen, Ps	0004/002
ABRAHAMCZYK	Pauline	--	Wreschen, Ps	0005/002
	Lenschen?	--		
	Ernestine	--		
	Roeschen?	--		
	Isac	--		
	Louis	--		
	Johanna	--		
ARNOLD	Johann Caspar	shoemaker	Erlangen	0006/002
BERLS	Johann Fried-rich	baker	Noda, Pr	0129/007
BIERMANN	Wilhelm	cabinetmaker	Schwerin	0126/007
BOELSING	Friedrich	machinist	Berlin	0130/007
BOLLOW	Christ[ophe]r?	tailor	Suelsdorf	0127/007
BORCK	Albert	painer	Camin, Pr	0128/007
BREHM	Sigm[und?]	painter	Koenigsberg, Ba?	0125/007
DAEBELOW	Friederike Georgine?	--	Goldberg, Mk	0571/027
	Friederike	--		
DANNENBERG	H.	plumber	Koenigsberg	0570/027
	--	wife		
	--	son		
DASSAN	Hans Peter	laborer	Langeloe, Ho	0568/027
DICKO	Johann	cigarmaker	Lindau	0569/027
DRUSCHEL	Eduard	nailsmith	Drossen, Sa	0567/027
EBERT	Heinrich	--	Dreyluetzow, Mk	0691/033
ENGEL	Wilhelm	shoemaker	Wieselbach, Ba	0690/033
FLETH	Anna Elisabeth	--	Ralma	0807/038
FRANCK	J.	businessman	Baiersdorf	0804/038
FRANKE	Johann	brickmaker	Zilz, Si	0805/038
FROEHLICH	Maria	--	Hamburg	0806/038
GROTH	J.	tailor	Robel, Mk	0961/045

List 41 (continued)

GRUENBERG	Marcus	businessman	Gollop, Pr	0960/045
HANSEN	Christian	tailor	Marne	1179/054
HAUSMANN	H.	cabinetmaker	Waldeck	1180/054
HELLMING	Hermann	machinist	Langensalza	1177/054
HERZOG	H. Eduard	weaver	Wieselbach	1181/054
HEYN	C. L.	--	Neumuehle	1183/054
HEYNE	G. F.	clothmaker	Neudam	1178/054
HOEPFFNER	Otto	mason	Langensalza, Th	1182/054
	Friedrich	--		
HORNER	Joseph	music master?	Koenigswerte, Bo	1184/054
JACOBSOHN	S?	cigarmaker	Potsdam	1499/068
JODEL	F. J.	--	Wangen, Wu	1498/068
KLAUS	Gottfr[ied]	--?	Erfurt	1606/073
KNACKE? [KNAEKE?]	Wilhelm	shoemaker	Nienburg	1603/073
KOCH	J. C. C.	--?	Sondershausen	1608/073
KOCH	Carl Ernst	--	Sondershausen	1609/073
	Friederike			
	Louise			
	Emilie	--		
KRAUSE	C. H.	tailor	Wieselbach	1607/073
KROHNFELD	Regina	--	Budisleben	1605/073
KRUSE	E. F. C.	cabinetmaker	Neustadt, Ho	1612/073
KUNKEL	Ludwig	carpenter	Robel, Mk	1610/073
	--	wife		
KUNKEL	Wilhelm	--	Robel, Mk	1611/073
	Lisette	--		
KUSCHKE	Wilhelm	peasant	Zonndorf, Pr	1602/073
	--	wife		
	--	children		
KUTZ	Simon	tailor	Sandomierz, Russia	1604/073
	--	family		
LAAKE	August	cabinetmaker	Werber, Pr	1978/089
	--	wife		
LAAKE	Maria	--	Werber, Pr	1979/089
	Jette	--		
	Wilhelm	--		

List 41 (continued)

LAMPE	Wilhelm	--	Wittenberg	1972/089
LANG	Christian	machinist	Wunsiedel	1971/089
LEPKE	Samuel	--	Zarrentin, Mk	1973/089
LESSER	Jette	--	Posen	1976/089
LEUTHMER	Maria	girl	Wien	1968/089
LEUTHMER	--	Fraeulein	Wien	1969/089
LIMPERT*	Melchior	peasant [*So spelled]	Diedorf, Mn	1974/089
LIMPER*	C. H.	-- -- [*So spelled]	Diedorf, Mn	1975/089
LUERSCH	Carl	machinist	Berlin	1977/089
LYTZER	Eduard	glazier	Wiesselbach	1970/089
MAACK	Nicholas	journeyman baker	Ronner	2213/100
MAHNKE	Ludwig	journeman cabi- netmaker	Robel? Mk	2212/100
MOSCHE	F. W.	gardener	Camenz, Sa	2215/100
MUELLER	Carl	tailor	Cleden	2214/100
NICOLAI	J? H.	weaver	Zimern, Sa	2515/113
OERTEL	Philipp	tailor	Berlin	2605/117
OPPENHEIMER	E.	painter	Breslau	2606/117
OTTO	Johann Hein- rich	peasant	Grossmolzen	2602/117
OTTO	G. F.	weaver	Grossmolzen	2603/117
OTTO	Ernst	peasant	Grossmolzen	2604/117
RINALDY	Josephina	girl	Wien	2821/128
RINALDY	Ferdinand	--	Wien	2822/128
RODECK	Wilhelm	cigarmaker	Berlin	2825/128
ROTH	Johann	--	Sandomiss, Ps	2823/128
RUCKDESCHEL	Friedrich	cabinetmaker	Wunsiedel	2824/128
SALOMON	Abraham	businessman	Gollup, Pr	3063/138
SCHEIDLER	J. M.	--	Hellmershausen	3064/138
SCHILDKNECHT	Dorothea	--	Waldeck	3065/138
SCHMIDT	Lisette	--	Robel, Mk	3075/138

List 41 (continued)

SCHNEIDER	Barbara	--	Wunsiedel, Ba	3069/138
SCHNELL	F.	laborer	Werle	3074/138
SCHROEDER	Dorothea --	Mad[am?] daughter	Wiesselbach, Ba	3068/138
SCHROEDER	Wilhelm	cabinetmaker	Werle	3073/138
SCHROEDER	Christina	Mad[am?]	Goldberg, Mk	3076/138
SCHROEDER	Carl Fritz Heinrich	-- -- --	Goldberg, Mk	3077/138
SCHUPFERLING	Georg	baker	Erlangen, Ba	3072/138
SIMON	Eisick [Isaac]	tailor	Sandomiss	3066/138
SONDERMANN	Chr[istine?] --	Mad[am?] child	Noda, Pr	3067/138
STARK	Johann M.	baker --	Erlangen, Ba	3071/138
SUEHN	F.	--	Colzin	3070/138
THEDE	Fritz	journeyman baker	Robel, Mk	3620/162
THOM	F. W.	tailor	Marienwerder	3621/162
WALTER	Nicolas	gardener	Worms	3793/170
WATKE	P. A.	mason	Krockau, Ho	3795/170
WENDE	Georg	tailor	Waldeck	3789/170
WIEDEWITZ	F. C.	laborer	Beiersberg	3791/170
WIEDEWITZ	Carl Sophia	laborer --	Beiersberg	3792/170
WIENECKE	J. D. L.	laborer	Altona	3796/170
WINTERMANTEL	Ulrich	--	Muenchweiler, Bd	3797/170
WITTENBURG	Maria	--	Steinbeck	3794/170
WOLFF	Rudolph Ludwig	physician	Goerltzow? [Gaeltzow?] Pr	3790/170
ZABEL? [ZAABEL?]	Eugen Robert	master carpenter	Danzig	4022/181
ZAKSEZEWSKI	T. T.	shoemaker	Berlin	4023/181

List 42

Ship *Leibnitz* (Hamburg flag) Captain H. K. S. Joergensen
Departing Hamburg 31 Aug 1850 for Galveston and New Orleans (Direct)

AHLF	H.	cabinetmaker	Neuhaus, Pr	0086/005
ASCHENBRAND	J. Conrad	waiter	Cassel	0087/005
BAUER	Friedrich	farmhand	Burow	0440/020
BECKER	Wilhelm	cabinetmaker	Altona	0439/020
BERGMANN	C.	plumber	Greifswald	0434/020
BEWIN	M.	tailor	Schmiede	0438/020
	Michaelis	tailor		
	Dorothea	--		
BEY	Heinz Peter	--?	New Orleans	0437/020
	Matta?	wife		
BEYLAND	C. F.	--?	Hamburg	0435/020
BEYLAND	D. G.	coppersmith	Gadelegen	0436/020
	--	wife		
	--	4 children, 3-7-3/4 y		
BOSTEN	Maria	--	Buetzow	0443/020
BOSTIAN	Johann	manager	Krackow	0441/020
BUCHTIEN	Christian	glazier	Buetzow	0442/020
	--	wife		
	--	4 children		
BUER	D.	--?	Althagen	0444/020
CHODOROWSKY	Meyer	shoemaker	Racky	0548/025
DEPPERIOM?	W.	cabinetmaker	Heinebach	0662/031
FRAENKEL	S.	--	Posen	0919/042
FRENZ? [FRANZ?]	Louise	--	Gewitzen	0920/042
	--	son, 3 y		
	--	daughter, ¼ y		
GELHMANN	J. G.	potter?	Warin	1137/052
GLANZ	L. C. F.	cabinetmaker	Penzlin	1136/052
HENNINGS	Friedrich	laborer	Brackow	1413/064
	--	wife		
	--	4 children, 3-19 y		
HENRICHSEN	H. C.	seaman	Foehr	1411/063
HEYDE	Christian	baker	Berlin	1412/063
	Otto	baker		
	Heinrich	baker		

List 42 (continued)

KLOPMANN	H.	tai or	Granzin	1900/085
KOEHNCKE	Johann	manager	Krabow	1901/085
	--	wife		
	--	2 children, ½-2 y		
KOENIG	L.	tailor	Althagen	1902/085
	--	wife		
	--	2 daughters, 3/4- 4 y		
KOEPKE	Friedrich	--?	Burow	1899/085
	--	wife		
	--	2 children, 9-16 y		
KRUEGER	Ferdinand	cigarmaker	Hamburg	1898/085
LADENDORF	Friederike	--	Penzlin	2146/096
LANGER	Adolph	tailor	Tarnowitz	2149/096
LIEBENOW	E.	baker	Greifwald	2147/096
LUCKFIL?	Johann	tailor	Kieritz	2148/096
LUETZENBARGER	C. W.	tailor	Grossenberkel?	2150/096
MAEDEL	Heinrich Helene	green grocer? --	New Orleans Glueckstadt	2443/109
MARTZAHN	Christian	--	Karbow	2445/109
	--	wife		
	--	4 children, 12-20 y		
MELHAUSE	H.	bricklayer	Klabow [so spelled]	2450/110
MINGEGRAMM	Friedrich	tailor	Ballenstaedt	2444/109
MOELLER	Heinrich	farmhand	Krabow	2447/110
MOELLER	Johann	wheelwright	Krabow	2448/110
MOELLER	Wilhelm	--	Krabow	2449/110
	--	boy, 3 y		
MUELLER	J. C. F.	brewer	Hohenzientz	2442/109
MUELLER	Gotth[ilf?]	wheelwright	Krabow	2446/110
PETERS	P. C.	seaman	Foehr	2775/125
PIMBACH	J. J.	tailor	Modlich	2776/125
QUISDORF	L? A.	weaver	Neudorf	2818/127
	--	4 children, 7-3/4 to 15 y		
REIMERS	E. G.	blacksmith	Oldenburg	3003/135

List 42 (continued)

RHODE	Heinrich	mason	Penzlin	3001/135
RIX	Daniel F.	--	Altona	3002/135
	--	wife		
	--	son, 3/4 y?		
	--	daughter		
ROEHL	J. F. H.	--	Sternberg	3004/135
ROETTCHER	J. C.	tinsmith	Pritzwalk	3006/135
	--	wife		
	--	2 children, 18 & 19 y		
ROSSBULT	Elise	--	Krabow	3005/135
SCHLIMM	J. H.	cabinetmaker	Zerrnin	3502/156
	--	wife		
	--	4 children, 7-18 y		
SCHMIDT	J? M. T.	laborer	Gevezin	3500/156
SCHROEDER	C.	cabinetmaker	Altona	3499/156
SCHROEDER	H.	cabinetmaker	Dulow	3504/156
SCHULZ	J. H. F.	laborer	Gevezin	3501/156
SELTRECHT	A. T. F.	cabinetmaker	Mollenstorf	3498/156
STERNBERG	--	blacksmith	Ruhn	3503/156
	--	wife		
	--	2 children		
TELTZ	Andreas Friedrich	journeyman tailor	Friedland	3692/165
THEY	Friedrich Maria	butcher wife	Celle	3694/165
THORNGREL	J.	baker	Copenhagen	3693/165
VELSCH	Carl	butcher?	Graepelin	3777/168
WASSMANN	J.	laborer	Gewitzin	3979/179
WEGNER	Catharina Julia	-- --	Altona	3978/179
	--	2 children, 2½-4½ y		
WESTPHAL	Maria	--	Krabow	3980/179
WOLFF	Sophia	--	Krabow	3981/179
ZIERIAKS	Ludwig	blacksmith	Buetzow	4068/182

DEGENER, 40

DEICKE, 26

DEIMEL, 30

DELFF, 38

DEMPE, 39

DENNER, 36

DENNING, 37

DEPPERIOM, 42

DESSAUER, 39

DETHJENS, 29

DETLOF, 31

DETLOFF, 36

DEUERLING, 37

DICKO, 41

DIETRICH, 31

DIETRICHS, 29

DIRCKS, 36

DIRK, 40

DIRKS, 40

DISSEN, 26, 37

DITTMAR, 27

DOELTZ, 29

DOERR, 29

DOHR, 29

DOHRN, 33

DONNER, 33

DRAPPIEL, 36

DREGE, 26

DREHBAUM, 39

DREIER, 33

DRESDNER, 26

DREYER, 36, 39

DROEGE, 31

DROESEN, 28

DRUSCHEL, 41

DRUT, 32

DUEBEL, 38

DUESENBERG, 39

DUPONT, 31

EBEL, 40

EBENSPERGER, 37

EBERHARD, 38

EBERLE, 33

EBERLEIN, 29

EBERT, 41

EBNER, 30

ECKERT, 27, 28

EFFNER, 26

EGGERS, 26

EGGERT, 39

EHEMANN, 36

EHLE, 40

EHLERS, 30, 33

EHRENDRICH, 36

EHRLICH, 29

EICHACKER, 34

EICHHORST, 37

EICHLER, 35

EISICH, 37

ELBLEIN, 37

ELDER, 30

ELITT, 26

ELKUS, 36

ELLERBUSCH, 38

ELLERT, 28

ENGEL, 26, 41

ENGELHARDS, 36

ERBE, 28

ERDMANN, 31

ERNST, 36, 40

ERPENSTEIN, 33

ESBACH, 29

EULE, 38

EURICH, 33

EVERS, 27, 28, 33

EWALD, 36

EWERS, 39

EWERT, 28

FABER, 37

FAHRENHOLZ, 27

FALKENHAGEN, 38

FALLER, 26

FARBACH, 33

FASS, 29

FEDERLEIN, 36

FELLNER, 29

FELTEN, 33

FESKY, 39

FEYBUSCH, 36

FICKE, 31

FIEDLER, 29

FIEDLUND, 33

FINGER, 27

FINN, 32

FISCHEL, 26, 31

FISCHER, 28, 30, 32, 37

FLETH, 41

FLOEDER, 26, 36

FOERSTER, 28, 30

FRAENKEL, 26, 42

FRANCK, 29, 41

FRANCKEL, 28

FRANK, 28, 29

FRANKE, 29, 30, 37, 41

FREITAG, 37

FRENZ, 42

FRENZEL, 40

FRESSDORF, 27

FREUND, 27, 29

FREWERT, 31

FRICK, 31

FRICKE, 26

FRIEDEMANN, 32

FRIEDLAENDER, 36

FRIEDRICH, 28, 29, 36, 40

FRIEDSAM, 28

FRIESE, 39

FROEHLICH, 41

FROST, 38

FUCHS, 37, 38

FUERGANG, 33

FUERSTE, 33

FUTH, 29

GABEL, 39

GABELIN, 27

GABLER, 31

GALEPP, 40

GANS, 36.

GARBING, 28

GARMSEN, 31

GASPARI. See CASPARI

GEBHARDT, 26, 29

GEHLE, 37

GEHLMANN. See GELHMANN

GEHRMANN, 26

GEIERSHOFER, 28

GEISSEL, 36

GELHMANN, 42

GEORG, 29

GERHARDT, 34

GERSON, 39

GIESE, 26, 27

GIESECKE, 34

GILLWALD, 39

GLANDER, 34

GLANZ, 42

GLAS, 29

GLISSMANN, 37

GLUECK, 40

GOELDNER, 39

GOERS, 37

GOGE, 29

GOLDSCHMIDT, 36

GOMPERTZ, 28

GOSSOW, 29

GOTTHOLD, 28

GRAEFE, 39

GRAEFNER, 27

GRAETZER, 28

GRAGERT, 33

GRAMANN, 32

GRENA, 26

GRIEPENKIEL, 39

GRIMM, 35, 36

GRISCHOW, 33

GROFELMANN, 34

GROH, 33

GROLLPFEIFER, 26

GROOTH, 33

GROSSE, 31

GROSSMANN, 28

GROTH, 41

GROTHHUSEN, 29

GRUENBEIN, 38

GRUENBERG, 41

GRUMSEN, 29

GRUNAR, 39

GRUNDMANN, 28

GRUNERT, 31

GUDEMANN, 30

GUENTHER, 26, 33, 39

GUINSCHE, 30

GULICHSRUD, 33

GURKER, 37

GUSTLOFF, 29

GUTKIND, 27

GUTMANN, 31

GYSENDOERFFER, 40

KNIPPER, 39

KNOBLOCH, 30

KNOCH, 30

KNORDTS, 37

KNUDTZEN, 40

KNUEBBEL, 36

KNUTH, 27

KOCH, 26, 28, 29, 37, 38, 39, 41

KOCK, 36

KOCKERT, 37

KODOROWSKY. See CHODOR- OWSKY

KOECKRITZ, 29

KOEHLER, 27, 29, 36, 40

KOEHLER. See also KOLLER

KOEHN. See COEHN

KOEHNCKE, 42

KOELBL, 30

KOENIG, 42

KOEPCKE, 27, 39

KOEPKE, 42

KOERNER, 35

KOERNER. See also KERNER

KOHN, 29, 38

KOHN. See also COHN

KOJETZKY, 26

KOLB, 26, 32

KOLBOW, 38

KOLLER, 36

KOLLER. See also KOEHLER

KONRAD. See CONRAD

KOPH, 36

KOPITZ, 27

KORALL, 28

KORCK, 37

KOTH, 29

KOTTEK, 26

KOTTLOW, 36

KOWITZ. See COWITZ

KOZMINSKY, 39

KRAKOWIZER, 28

KRAMM, 39

KRAUSE, 26, 32, 41

KREBS, 39

KREFFT, 33

KRETSCHMANN, 31

KREUTZFELD, 31

KRICK, 26

KROEGER, 26, 34

KROG, 36

KROGICK, 34

KROHNFELD, 41

KRUEGER, 26, 27, 30, 31, 36, 39, 42

KRUG, 30

KRULL. See CRULL

KRUMBUS, 31

KRUSCHKE, 26

KRUSE, 29, 41

KRUSEMARCK, 33

KSCHINKA, 35

KUEBER, 36

KUECKHOEFEL, 31

KUEHN, 33

KUFMANN, 33

KUH, 28

KUHL, 33

KUHN, 39

KUMMERT, 28

KUNDE, 38

KUNKEL, 41

KUNSTMANN, 35

KUNZHALS, 31

KURTH, 31. 40

KURTZ, 29

KURZHALS, 31

KUSCHKE, 41

KUTZ, 41

LAAKE, 41

LADENDORF, 27, 42

LAFIN, 38

LAMILA, 40

LAMPE, 41

LANDSCHUTZ, 29

LANE, 29

LANG, 41

LANGBEIN, 29

LANGE, 35, 36, 38

LANGER, 42

LANGHALS, 31

LASCH, 27

LAU, 27, 33

LAUBNER, 33

LAUENROTH, 33

LECHERT, 26

LEDERGERW, 29

LEHMANN, 28, 33, 36

LEHNERT, 27, 28

LEHRNITZ, 37

LEINE, 27

LEISE, 36

LEITZER. See LYTZER

LEMBCKE, 33, 37

LEMCKE, 31,

LEMKE, 26, 33

LEMM, 31

LEMPKE, 26

LENAU, 31

LENTH, 38

LENTZING, 27

LEOPOLD, 36

LEPKE, 41

LERCHE, 26, 33

LESCHINSKA, 26

LESCHNISKY, 37

LESSER, 28, 40, 41

LEUSCHOW, 36

LEUTHMER, 41

LEUTLOFF, 39

LEVIN, 28, 36

LEVISON, 29

LEVY, 26, 28, 36

LICHEWSKY, 27

LICHTENHEIM, 30

LICHTENSTERN, 26

LIEBENOW, 42

LIEBSCHNER, 28

LIENOW, 39

LILIENTHAL. See LINIENTHAL

LIMPER, 41

LIMPERT, 41

LINCK, 35

LINDENAU, 30

LINDENBAUM, 32

LINDNER, 28, 37

LINDOW, 31

LINIENTHAL, 26

LINKE, 29

LIPINSKI, 26

LIPPMANN, 29

LISTICH, 38

LITHAUER, 28

LITTMANN, 33

LITTNER, 37

LOEPER, 36

LOHFING, 37

LOHGERBER, 26

LOLL, 30

LORENTZ, 27

LORENZ, 27

LOW, 29

LOY, 27

LUBAN, 33

LUBENSKY, 36

LUCKFIL, 42

LUDWIG, 28, 32

LUEBKE, 31

LUECK, 29

LUERSCH, 41

LUETZENBARGER, 42

LUTZ, 30

LUX, 36

LYTZER, 41

MAACK, 41

MAAS, 30, 31

MACHEL, 36

MAEDEL, 42

MAERZ, 28

MAGAWITZ, 36

MAHN, 32, 33

MAHNERT, 37

MAHNKE, 41

MAIER, 30

MAITAG, 28

von MALIGNON, MALIGNAN, 37

MALLEIS, 27, 34

MAMEROW, 27

MAMMEN, 28

MANASSE, 26

MANDELBAUM, 28

MANHEIMER, 36

MANN, 31

MARCKUSY, 36

MARCUS, 36, 39

MARCUSE, 40

MARKIEWITZ, 31

MARTENS, 28, 39

MARTHON, 31

MARTIES, 27

MARTIN, 29, 33

MARTZAHN, 42

MARWEDEL, 36

MASUR, 38

MATERNE, 31

MATSCHINSKI, 28

MATTHIAS, 27

MATTWICH, 26

MATZ, 40

MAYER, 28, 33

MAZZUCKI, 29

MEDANS, 37

MEISER, 40

MEISSNER, 28

MELCHES, 29

MELHAUSE, 42

MELZNER, 28

MENDEL, 27, 28

MENDHEIM, 29

MENGE, 31

MENTZEL, 29

MENZEL, 35

METZDORF, 35

MEUSEL, 28

MEYEN, MEYER, 40

MEYER, 26, 27, 28, 29,
  30, 31, 37, 40

MEYERFELD, 28

MEYNCKE, 28

MICHAEL, 39

MICHAELIS, 28

MICHEL, 29

MINGEGRAMM, 42

MINKE, 38

MISSELHARN, 28

MITTAG, 39

MOCK, 26

MOELLER, 33, 36, 37, 42

MOERER, 38

MOORES, 36

MORGENSTERN, 36

MOSCHE, 41

MOSER, 35

MOSES, 26

MOSESCHEYER, 36

MOTHs, 26

MUCKE, 26

MUECK, 28

MUEHLENDORF, 29

MUELLER, 26, 28, 29, 31,
  33, 37, 40, 41, 42

MUHLMEISTER, 33

MUHSFELD, 33

MUNTEN, 32

MUSIKER, 26

NABRA, 40

NADLER, 36

NAGELSCHMIDT, 39

NATHANN, 36

NAUMANN, 27

NEITHARDT, 33

NELSEN, 30

NEUBAUER, 39

NEUDECK, 36

NEUDORF, 36

NEUMANN, 29, 34, 40

NEUMEISTER, 29

NIBBE, 34

NICKELSEN, 37

NICOLAI, 35, 41

NIELANDT, 26

NIEMANN, 29, 36

NIENBURG, 29

NILSEN, 40

NOACK, 35, 39

NOELKE, 29

NOLL, 36

NOLT, 37

NOWACK, 30, 36

NUERNBERGER, 28

OBERFELD, 29

OBERNFELD, 29

OBST, 26

OEHME, 28

OELZE, 37

OERTEL, 37, 41

OLDACH, 36

OPPENHEIM, 37

OPPENHEIMER, 28, 41

OSTBYE, 33

OSTDAHL, 40

OTTENBURG, 30

OTTO, 26, 41

PARISER, 26

PARTHEY, 39

PAUER, 35

PAULANGER, 37

PAULS, 31

PAUSEWEIN, 37

PEECK, 29

PEIN, 28

PEMUELLER, 30

PESCHKE, 28

PESCHKY, 36

PESTER, 36

PETER, 28

PETERS, 39, 42

PETRAM, 32

PETSCH, 36

PETTER, 37

PEWESDORF, 31

PFAFF, 28

PFAFFENSCHLAGER, 26

PFEFFER, 34

PFEIFER, 27

PFEIFFER, 29

PFOTENHAUER, 37

PHILIPP, 29

PIEPERS, 31

PIETSCH, 40

PIMBACH, 42

PINK, 33

PINKUS, 29

PITSCH, 26, 31

PITTER. See PETTER

PITTINS, PITTIUS, 36

PLESS, 31

POEHL, 33

POHERT, 37n

POHLMANN, 26, 33, 36

POLCHOW, 33

POLL, 38

POLTER, 27

POMPEJUS, 30

POSPSCHILL, 29

PRACHT, 26

PRAHL, 37

PRALOW, 37

PRESINSKY, 36

PREYMANN, 39

PRIESTER, 27

PRILL, 38

PRITZLAFF, 31

PRIWE, 31

PROBSTHAM, 39

PROSCH, 26

PUDER, 30

PUFF, 36

PULS, 26, 27

PULVERMANN, 39

PURUCKER, 26

PUSTOW, 39

PUTZ, 32

QUAST, 29

QUISDORF, 42

RAABE, 32

RAEBEL, 28

RAETHER, 39

RAMBACH, 39

RAMPENDAHL, 32

RASCHKE, 26

RATH, 33

RATHJENS, 30

RATZE, 36

RATZEL, 27

RAUCHFASS, 26

RAWOHL, 27

RECHENBACH, 28

REICHARDT, 30

REICHERT, 28

REIMERS, 42

REINCKE, 29

REINHARD, 28, 36

REINHARDT, 36

REINHOLD, 39

REISE, 31, 40

REMER, 27

REMMIN, 38

RESER, 36

RETTSCHLAG, 40

REUTER, 35

REWALD, 35

RHODE, 42

RIBBECK, 35

RICHTER, 26, 27, 28, 29, 30,
  35

RICKHOF, 29

RIECK, 39

RIEDEL, 28

RIEGELMANN, 28

INDEX TO BIRTHPLACES

This is a temporary index. At the end of Part 3 geographical notes have been appended which should be consulted by the researcher.

BARTENSTEIN, Pr, 30

BASSOW, 40

BAUTZEN, Sa, 38

BECKADEL, 37

BEIERSBERG, 41

BELGARD, 29

BELOW, 29

BENTZIN, 26

BERG, Mk, 26

BERGEN, 26

BERKA, 40

BERLIN, 26, 27, 28, 29, 30, 31, 32, 33, 34, 35, 36, 37, 39, 40, 41, 42

BEVERANGEN, BEVERUNGEN, 28,

BEVENSEN, Pr, 36

BEYERSDORF, 40

BEYERSDORF. See also BAIERSDORF

BIRCKICHT, 31

BIRNBAUM, 26, 39

BISCHOFSWERDER, 31

BISPERODE, 29

BITTERFELD, Gr, 28

BITZFLETH, 36

BLANKENHAIN, 31

BLANKENSTEIN, 31

BOCHZOFF, 27

BOEHLEN, 31

BOETZOW, 38

BOHRSCHUETZ, 34

BOIONOCOW, Mk, 26

BOITZENBURG, Mk, 27

BOLTENHAGEN, 29

BOSDORF, Pr, 26

BOSSEBORN, Ol, 30

BOTSCHOW, Pr, 37

BOTTENDORF, 26

BRACK, 37

BRACKENSDORF, 37

BRACKOW, 42

BRAUNSBERG, 26

BRAUNSCHWEIG, 26, 28, 37

BREITUNGEN, Sa, 39

BRESLAU, Sa, 30

BRESLAU, 30, 36, 40, 41

BRIEG, Pr, 30, 40

BRINKUM, Ol, 39

BROCK, 26

BROCK, Mk, 37

BROCK. See also BRACK

BROMBERG, 39

BROSSBUETTEL, 28

BRUELL, 26

BRUENN, 40

BRUN, 27

BRUNSTADT, 36

BUDISLEBEN, 41

BUECKEBURG, 33

BUETZOW, 42

BUHREN, 39

BUNDE, 29

BURGKANDSTEDT, 37

BURGKUNSTADT, 28

BURKERSDORFF, 28

BUROW, 42

BURSINGHAUSEN, Ha, 34

BUSSLEBEN, 39

BUTZOW, Mk, 37

BUTZOW. See also BUETZOW

BUXTEHUDE, 26

CALAU, Lausitz, 35

CALAU. See also COLAU

CAMENZ, 28, 41

CAMMIN, Pr, 31, 41

CAMMIN. See also COMMIN, KAMIN

CARLSHAFEN, Pr, 28

CARLSRUHE, 36

CASSEL, 28, 31, 39, 40, 42

CELLE, 28, 42

CHODZIESEN, Pr, 27

CHRISTIANSAND, 40

CHRISTIANIA, 40

CHRISTIANI, No, 27

CINCINNATI, 30

CISMAR, 26

CLEDEN, 41

COBLENZ, 30, 34

COBURG, 29, 33

COHLENFELD, 37

COLAU, 35

COLAU. See also CALAU

COLZIN, 41

COMMIN, Pr, 31

COMMIN. See also CAMMIN, KAMIN

CONSTANZ, 28

COPENHAGEN, 28, 29, 30, 33, 42

COPENHAGEN. See also KOPENHAGEN

CORNECK, Pr, 26

CRAILSHEIM, 29

CREUZNACH, 40

CREWITZ, Mk, 26, 37

CRIVITZ, 29

CUESTRIN, Pr, 29

CUNERN, 26

DABLERSTEIN, 33

DALANG, 39

DALLBERG, Mk, 31

DAMITSCH, DAMMITZSCH, 39

DANKERODE, 29

DANNDORF, 31

DANNDORF. See also DONNDORF

DANNENBERG, Ha, 32, 39

DANZIG, 37, 41

DASSE, 39

DEFAHR, Mk, 39

DEGRITZ, 28

DELIBZSCH, 39

DERMISDORF, Th, 26

DERMSDORF, Th, 26

DETMOLD, 30

DEUTSCH CRONE, Pr, 26

DEUZ, 33

DEWITZ, 36

DIEDORF, Mn, 41

DIEMERSDORF, 26

DINKLAN, DINKLAU, 29

DITHMAR, 28

DITMANNSRIETH, Ba, 30

DOBBERTIN, Mk, 27, 29, 35

DOBBIN, 37

DOBRAWITZ, Bo, 34

DOEBEL, Sa, 28

DOEBELN, 28, 29

DOEMITZ, 39

DOERFLAS, 26

DOHREN, 36

DONNDORF, 31

DONNDORF. See also DANNDORF

DRABISCHAU, 32

DRAEMEN, No, 27

DRANSFELD, Han, 31

DRESDEN, 31, 32, 35, 39

DREYLUETZOW, Mk, 41

DROBISCHAU. See DRABISCHAU

DROGDERSEN, 33

DROSSEN, Sa, 41

DUESSELDORF, 38

DULOW, 42

EBELEBEN, 32

EBERSDORF, 29

ECKSTEDT, Pr, 40

ECKZIN, Pr, 36

EGELSDORF, 32

EHLERSTORF, 33

EICHENHAUSEN, 36

EIDERSTADT, 40

EISENACH, 26

EISENBERG, 31

EISLEBEN, 26

ELBOGEN, Bo, 28

ELDAGSEN, Han, 30

ELMSHORN, 30

ENGELLADE, 28

ERBACH, 29

ERFURT, 28, 41

ERLANGEN, 28, 41

ERLAU, 32

ERLBACH, Sa, 28

ERXLEBEN, 29

EUTHHAUSEN, 29

EXIN, 36, 39, 40

FAHRENRODE, Sa, 26

FALKENHAGEN, Mk, 27

FALKENWALDE, Pr, 31

FASSELDORF, Ba, 26, 36

FASSOLDSHOF, 28

FAURNIDAU, Wu, 35

FEKFH TO? 35

FERNOSFELD, Pr, 36

FILEHNE, 26, 29, 37

FLENSBURG, 31

FOEHR, 37, 42

German and Central European Emigration
Monograph Number 1, Part 3

RECONSTRUCTED PASSENGER LISTS FOR 1850:

HAMBURG TO AUSTRALIA, BRAZIL, CANADA, CHILE,

AND THE UNITED STATES

Part 3: Passenger Lists 43 through 60

Clifford Neal Smith

Reprint, 1983
Reprint, 1984
Reprint, 1989   qz
Reprint, January 1996   u

CONTENTS

INTRODUCTION

The passenger lists preserved in the files of the Hamburg police authorities are the single most important genealogical research link between the Old and New Worlds, for they record the birthplaces and the destinations of millions of central European emigrants. Neither the naturalization files nor the port of entry records in lands of settlement consistently contain this information in such detail.[1] It must be noted with regret that similar files maintained by Bremen police authorities were destroyed in the *Feuersturm* of 1945, when the city itself went up in flames. The Bremen files probably were considerably larger than those of Hamburg and contained the names of most of the emigrants from western Germany and Switzerland.[2] Consequently, the reconstruction of nineteenth-century western German emigration records can only be approached by analysis of the files of each *Gemeinde* (community) in the country, a formidable task which proceeds at a slow and opportunistic pace.[3]

The Hamburg police lists are divided into two series, Direct and Indirect. The Direct series, in 399 volumes, begins in 1850 and includes all ships leaving Hamburg (and associated minor ports) without stopping at other European ports to take on emigrant passengers. The Indirect series, in 118 volumes, beginning in 1855, includes ships which made intermediate European and British ports of call. For purposes of genealogical research, the distinction does not seem to be significant, excepting that some emigrants may have been taken aboard at other ports and, therefore, are unlisted in these passenger lists. Consequently, the lists for each year of both series will be presented together in these monographs.

During the first years in which names of emigrants were recorded, the actual passenger lists apparently were not preserved. Instead, the police clerks entered the data from these original lists into large bound registers in a quasi-alphabetical fashion. This makes it difficult for researchers to determine who among the emigrants may have accompanied the subject of research. Extended family or support groups and coreligionists frequently emigrated together, a matter of significance to the researcher. To remedy this defect, the 1850 passenger lists have been reconstructed from the quasi-alphabetical entries to be found in the registers.

All the reconstructed lists for 1850 have been abstracted from microfilm roll number 1 (Library of Congress, Manuscript Division, shelf number 10,897) made of the following archival materials:

Hamburg. Staatsarchiv. Bestand Auswandereramt. Auswanderer Listen, Direkt, 1850.

The Library of Congress has microfilms of both the Direct and Indirect volumes for the period 1850-1873. The Genealogical Society of Utah, Salt Lake City, has the entire 517 volumes on microfilm, from 1850 to 1913, when the series was discontinued.

There are a total of 4,074 entries in the Direct series for 1850. Some entries record only one emigrant, other entries list entire families. It seems likely that the total number of individuals emigrating via Hamburg in 1850 may have been about 7,000 (of which almost 2,500 are listed in this monograph). Later passenger lists contain more information than do those of 1850, notably the names and ages of all family members. For the 1850 entries, the information hereinafter is as follows:

Column

1 Surname
2 Given names
3 Occupation. Some of the terms used are those of Hamburg dialect, rather than modern *Hochdeutsch*, and may not be correctly translated. For example a commonly reported occupation is that of *Oeconom*. This means farmer or manager. In these monographs the term has been uniformly translated as manager.
4 Birthplace. See the section at the end of Part 3 for notes thereon.
5 Reference number/Page number in register. The reference number has been assigned by this compiler and is not to be found in the registers. The number will probably have little use to researchers, other than indicating place on the register page relative to nearby names.

Having found a surname of interest, researchers should consider all other emigrants on the ship for possible accompanying extended-family members and coreligionists. These relationships may occasionally be inferred by considering also the birthplaces common to a number of passengers. The Index to Birthplaces can also be used to identify persons from the same birthplaces who have traveled on different ships. Occasionally, names listed herein may supplement data missing in other emigrant lists. For example, in the monograph entitled *Nineteenth-Century Emigration of "Old Lutherans"* . . .[4] it is reported that the names of 98 emigrants to Australia had not been found in German administrative files. Some of these persons may be included among the passengers of the three ships which sailed from Hamburg to Australia in 1850.

---

1. A detailed description of the Hamburg emigration files will be found in Clifford Neal Smith and Anna Piszczan-Czaja Smith, *Encyclopedia of German-American Genealogical Research* (New York: R. R. Bowker, 1976), pp. 199-200. Additional information on supplementary research materials in the Hamburg Staatsarchiv can be found in Smith & Smith, *American Genealogical Resources in German Archives* (Munich: Verlag Dokumentation, 1977), p. 227, et seq.

2. Of the nearly 79,000 persons emigrating from Germany to the United States in 1850, only about 7,000 passed through the port of Hamburg. Thus the great majority of Germans must have emigrated via the ports of Bremen and LeHavre. U.S. Bureau of the Census, *Historical Statistics of the United States: Colonial Times to 1957* (Washington, D.C.: Government Printing Office, 1960), p. 57.

3. See the back cover of this monograph for a listing of monographs in the German-American Genealogical Research series having to do with communal records on emigration.

---

4. Clifford Neal Smith, *Nineteenth-Century Emigration of "Old Lutherans" from Eastern Germany (Mainly Pomerania and Lower Silesia) to Australia, Canada, and the United States.* German-American Genealogical Research Monograph 7 (McNeal, AZ: Westland Publications, 1980), p. 46.

ABBREVIATIONS USED

Am America; usually meaning the United States

Au Austria

b born (maiden name)

Ba Bavaria, a state now in West Germany; formerly included lands in Rheinland-Pfalz

Bd Baden; now part of the state of Baden-Wuerttemberg in West Germany

Bi Birkenfeld, a former principality which in 1850 belonged to Oldenburg; territory now in Rheinland-Pfalz, West Germany

Bo Bohemia, former kingdom, now part of Czechoslovakia

c child, children

Ca Cassel (now Kassel); Hessen-Cassel was a principality, also called Electoral Hesse, now in the state of Hessen, West Germany

d daughter

De Detmold; Lippe-Detmold, a former principality, now in Nordrhein-Westfalen, West Germany

Di Ditmarschen, a region in the present state of Schleswig-Holstein, West Germany

Dk Denmark

Ds Dessau, formerly a political unit of Saxony, now in East Germany

Ha Hannover, a sovereign territory, now in Niedersachsen, West Germany

He Hessen, a former principality, now in the state of Hessen, West Germany

Ho Holstein, now in Schleswig-Holstein, West Germany

Hu Hungary; in 1850 a part of the Austro-Hungarian Empire

La Lauenburg, a former principality, now a part of the state of Schleswig-Holstein, West Germany

Li Lippe; Lippe-Detmold, a former principality, now in Nordrhein-Westfalen, West Germany

Mk Mecklenburg, a former principality, now in East Germany

Mn Meiningen; Sachsen-Meiningen, a former principality, now in East Germany

No Norway

Ol Oldenburg, a former principality, now in Niedersachsen, West Germany

Pm Pomerania, a former Prussian province, now in Poland

Po Poland

Pr Prussia; in 1850 a kingdom with lands now in East and West Germany and Poland

Ps Posen; in 1850 a Prussian province, now in Poland

Ru   Rudolstadt; Schwarzburg-Rudolstadt, a former principality,
now in East Germany

s   son, sons

Sa   Saxony, a former kingdom, now
mainly in East Germany

Sb   Swabia, a region, now in Baden-
Wuerttemberg, West Germany

Sc   Schwartzburg. *See* Rudolstadt
and Sondershausen

Si   Silesia, a Prussian province
in 1850, now part of Poland

Sl   Schleswig, a former province,
now in Schleswig-Holstein,
West Germany

Sn   Sondershausen; Schwarzburg-
Sondershausen, a former prin-
cipality in Thuringia, now in
East Germany

St   Strelitz; Mecklenburg-Strelitz,
a former principality, now in
East Germany

Sw   Sweden

Sz   Switzerland

Th   Thuringia, a region, now in East
Germany

Ty   Tyrol, a region in Austria

We   Weimar; Sachsen-Weimar-Eisenach,
a former principality, now in
East Germany

Wu   Wuerttemberg, a former kingdom,
now in Baden-Wuerttemberg, West
Germany

y   year, years

List 43

Ship *Louise*, Captain J. Hildebrand
Departing Hamburg 1 May 1850 for Quebec (Direct)

BERGMANN	Martha	--	Walsleben	0231/011
BLUMENNAGEL	Margaretha	--	Gotha	0230/011
BOESE	G.	cabinetmaker	Lueben	0232/011
BRANDUS	August	peasant	Grube	0229/011
BUSKE	J. G.	blacksmith	Scharpenorth	0233/011
ERHARDT	Caspar	butcher	Gotha	0715/034
GENTSCHOW	J. Doris	baker wife	Schwerin	1024/047
GUTTMANN	B.	soldier	Wuerzburg	1025/047
HAUNN	Carolina	--	Grafendora	1271/058
HAUNN	Christian Eduard	cabinetmaker	Grafendora	1270/058
HAUNN	Friedrich	baker	Grafendora, Pr	1269/058
HERZOG	Christian	weaver	Seehausen	1274/058
HUEBNER	Carl Lisette	child child	Penzlin	1273/058
HUEBNER	C. T. Th.	shoemaker	Penzlin	1272/058
KEPPNER	Franz	miller	Blumberg	1702/077
KLAMB	Wilhelm Friederike	laborer wife	Hakenwalde	1704/077
KLAMB	Anton Wilhelmine Bertha	child child child	Hakenwalde	1705/077
KOPPIN	Gustav	carpenter	Klewitz	1701/077
KREIBERG	Theodor	soldier	Stavenhagen	1706/077
KREUTER	J. Friederike	baker wife	Guestrow	1699/077
KREUTER	Ferdinand Louise Ludwig Lina	child child child child	Guestrow	1700/077
KRUSEN	Friedrich	--	Penzlin	1703/077

List 43 (continued)

LANGKLAR	C. C.	cabinetmaker	Malchin	2032/091
MAHRT	F.	laborer	Friedrichsthal, Ho	2278/103
MAHRT	Hans Juergen	child	Friedrichsthal, Ho	2279/103
MATHIAS	I? [J?]	soldier	Posen	2281/103
MERBACH	Friedrich	--	Weilheim? [Werl-heim?]	2280/103
SCHUETZ	Mathias Anna Maria	peasant wife	Probfeld	3212/144
SCHUETZ	Thomas Elise Margaretha	-- -- --	Probfeld	3213/144
SELCHOW	Carl	businessman	Bremen	3214/144
SERRIN	J. L. F.	carpenter	Bolz, Mk	3215/144
THIELMANN	Volkmar	peasant [two entries for same person]	Guntersleben	3648/163
TROIDL	Caspar	butcher	Unterbernrieth, Ba	3645/163
WAGENER	Johann	shoemaker	Kofpoldwitz	3852/172
WANDERER	F. A. H.	shoemaker	Neuhaus	3853/172
WANDERER	Rosina Louise Salmon? Lina?	wife child child child	Neuhaus	3854/172
ZWETZ	Elisabeth Catharina* Louise Emil	-- -- child [*may be two persons]	Walsleben	4038/181

List 44

Ship *Maria Frederike*, Captain N. T. Schmidt
Departing Hamburg 18 April 1850 for Quebec (Direct)

AHRENDS	J. J. C.	shoemaker	Glashage	0034/003
BARTELS	Carl	weaver	Langenhagen	0195/010

6

List 44 (continued)

BEYERLEIN	Heinrich	miller	Gorkwitz	0194/010
	Adolph	child		
BOLTZE	Louise	--	Wusend?	0193/010
BURMEISTER	Joachim	machinist?	Warnow	0192/009
	--	wife		
	--	child, ½ y		
ECKHARDT	August	--	Bordenhagen	0707/033
ECKHARDT	Carolina	--	Holstein	0704/033
EICHELBERG	Maria	--	Goldberg, Mk	0705/033
	Louis	child		
	Heinrich	child		
	Fritz	child		
ENDMANN	Friedrich	blacksmith	Croplin	0706/033
	--	wife		
FRANCKE	Wilhelm	shoemaker	Altenburg	0828/039
GERTH	Michael	shoemaker	Monstab, Sa-Go	1006/047
GREUFENHEIR	Julius	manager	Gotha	1005/046
HACKE	Elise	maid	Nossenstein	1236/056
HACKE	Johann	laborer	Waren	1235/056
	Elise	wife		
HEIDTMANN	Carl	laborer	Gramboe	1234/056
	--	wife		
	Hermann	child		
HOMANN	Ludwig	laborer	Wenzen	1233/056
JAEGER	Joachim	blacksmith	Croplin	1517/068
	--	wife		
JAHNS	Heinrich	laborer	Wenzen	1516/068
KALLENBACH	Anna	--	Molschleben	1667/075
	Martha	--		
	Martha Elisa-beth	--		
KALLENBACH	Maria Doro-thea	--	Buffleben	1669/075
	--	2 children		
KAUFMANN	A. E.	cabinetmaker	Kleinfahne, Sa-Go	1664/075
KAVEL	Johann Ga-briel	shoemaker	Parchim	1665/075
	--	wife		
	--	3 children		

List 44 (continued)

KOEHLER	Regina	--	Schmalkalden	1666/075
	Elisabeth	--		
KOEHN	Friedrich	laborer	Goldberg, Mk	1662/075
	--	wife		
	--	baby		
KOESTER	Heinrich	cabinetmaker	Goldberg, Mk	1662/075
	--	wife		
	--	child, 3 y		
KRAUSE	August Hein-rich	blacksmith	Thomasbrueck	1668/075
KUESTER	Christian	blacksmith	Bordenhagen	1670/075
LANGULA	Johann Fried-rich	mason	Thomasbrueck	2012/090
	--	wife		
LANGULA	Christian Gottlieb?	--	Thomasbrueck	2013/090
	--	wife		
LEIFHEIT	Friedrich	manager	Arendshausen	2011/090
	--	wife		
	Andreas	--		
	Georg	child		
	Johann	child		
MERTENS	Christoph?	manager	Nordling, Pr	2262/102
	--	wife		
	--	3 children		
NIEMEYER	Friedrich	blacksmith	Wilershausen, Ha	2533/113
NITZLER	Caspar	carpenter	Wegman, Go	2534/113
PAPE	Heinrich	--	Arendshausen	2670/120
PAUL	Friedrich	blacksmith	Seeberge	2673/120
PFAU	Georg Hein-rich	shoemaker	Marburg	2674/120
PRIEN	H. C.	journeyman black-smith	Keetz	2669/120
PROETZ	Julius Aug-ust	laborer	Seeberge	2671/120
PROETZ	Friedrich Wilhelm	laborer	Seeberge	2672/120
REITH	Friederike	bride of G. H. Pfau	Marburg	2860/129

8

List 44 (continued)

SCHMID? [SCHMEEL?]	Christian	shepherd	Goldbeck	3165/142
SCHMID	Johann Christian	laborer	Krautauf	3172/142
SCHUMACHER	Lisette	--	Parchim	3174/142
SCHUMANN	Theodor	pharmacist	Wormbrusen? [Warmbrusen?]	3176/142
SCHWARZ	Gerhard	dyer	Heyde, Ho	3177/142
SEYFFERST	Johanne Christiane	-- --	Tuettleben	3173/142
SIEGFRIED	Carl	manager	Grosfahne, Sa-Go	3170/142
SIEGFRIED	Heinrich Christian Christina Wilhelm --	-- -- -- 3 small children	Grosfahne, Sa-Go	3171/142
STAACK	Friedrich Lisette	--? wife	Backhorst, Ho	3166/142
STAACK	Friedrich Maria Margaretha	child? child child	Backhorst, Ho	3167/142
STOLLE	F. E. T. -- Christian Heinrich	manager wife child child	Backhorst, Ho	3168/142
STOLLE	Johanna Maria --	-- 4 children	Thomasbrueck	3175/142
SYBOLD	Johann Jacob	manager	Grosfahne, Sa-Go	3169/142
VOSS	Friedrich	laborer	Kosbade? [Kasbade?]	3747/167
WAGNER	Johann Heinrich Maria Dorothea? Wilhelm	manager wife 10 months old	Molschleben	3824/171
WEIDEL	Friedrich -- Emilia Pauline	tailor wife small child small child	Tarau, Sa	3825/171

List 44 (continued)

WITT	Maria	--	Grapenstietz? [Grafenstietz?]	3823/171
ZANGE	Heinrich Louis	carpenter	Guenthersleben	4035/181

List 45
Ship *Der 27 May* (Hamburg flag) Captain P. Lafrenz
Departing Hamburg 15 Apr 1850 for New Orleans (Direct)

ALLERS	Paul	tailor	Helmste	0025/003
ARPOLD	Albert	wheelwright	Thuesdorf	0024/002
BARTELS	F. --	cabinetmaker wife	Hildesheim	0172/009
BECK	Friedrich	wheelwright	Burgkesler	0173/009
BECK	Friedrich	--	Tatun, Pr	0175/009
BIERDEMANN	G. F. C.	cabinetmaker	Lueneburg, Br	0169/009
BILLING	Wilhelm	--?	Laucha	0174/009
BRUECKNER	Ludwig	--?	Neuendorf	0170/009
BURMEISTER	Leopold	painter	Zechlin	0171/009
CYLIAX	Carl August Christian Lud- wig Carl Albert	--	Obermoellern	0518/024
CYLIAX	Christian? Gottlieb? --	manager wife	Obermoellern	0517/024
DEMMER	Anna Johanne? Anna Hermann	-- -- -- --	Stettin	0584/027
DEMMER	G. A. --	businessman wife	Stettin	0583/027
DEMPWOLFF	August	--	Stade	0586/027
DERLET*	Sebastian	tailor	Saal, Ba	0581/027
DERRET*	Eustach	coachman [*so spelled]	Saal, Ba	0582/027
DUSENDSCHOEN	Carl	cake baker	Hamburg	0585/027

10

EXNER	Catharine	--	Wien	0700/033
	Maria	--		
EXNER	Johann	ribbon maker?	Wien	0699/033
	--	wife		
FERBER	J. C.	manager	Naumburg	0819/038
	--	wife		
	Franz	--		
	Johanna	--		
FERLER	Kunig[unde]	--	Oberleiterbach, Ba	0820/038
GOTTEL	Wilhelm Adolph	manager	Elbing	0988/046
GRAEBENER	Rudolph	--	Wilsnack	0996/046
	Dorothea	--		
GRAEFE	August	--	Roque Island, America [Rock Island, Illinois?]	0997/046
GREINER	Henriette	--	Obermoellern	0994/046
	Louise	--		
GREINER	J. J.	shoemaker	Obermoellern	0993/046
	--	wife		
GROBER	Friedrich August	manager	Obermoellern	0989/046
	--	wife		
GROBER	Emilia Pauline	--	Obermoellern	0990/046
	Friederike	--		
	Carl August	--		
GROBER	Johann Carl	manager	Obermoellern	0991/046
	--	wife		
GROBER	Amalia Friederike	--	Obermoellern	0992/046
	Carl	--		
	Hanna?	--		
	Henriette	--		
	Charlotte	--		
	Johann	--		
GROBER	Hanna Rose	--	Obermoellern	0995/046
HALLE	Adolph	businessman	Hamburg	1217/055
HALLER	Carl	butcher	Wettin	1213/055
	--	wife		

List 45 (continued)

HALLER	Friederike	--	Wettin	1214/055
	Albert	--		
	Auguste	--		
	Hermann	--		
	Pauline	--		
	Wilhelm	--		
HALLER	Friedrich	--	Wettin	1215/055
	Otto	--		
	Ida	--		
HEYNEKAMP	Conrad	--?	Hagen, Li	1212/055
HUDZIETZ	Christian	miller	Groschuetz	1216/055
KAMPF	Heinrich	soldier	Neuhaus, Pr	1645/074
KAPPMEIER	H.	miner	Lauthenthal	1647/074
	--	wife		
	Christiana	--		
	Maria	--		
	Louise	--		
	Auguste	--		
KATHER	Wilhelm	dyer	Hildesheim	1646/074
KNAPPE	Ferdinand	mechanic	Wettin	1648/074
	Carl			
KOEHL	Wilhelm	miller	Groschuetz	1649/075
KOOP	Peter	pastry baker	Hamburg	1650/075
LEITCHTWEISS	Josepha	girl [unmarried?]	Wien	2001/090
	Wilhelm	--		
	Josephine	--		
LEMM	H.	manager	Luhme	2002/090
MOLDENHAUER	Carl	peasant	Laucha	2253/101
NERGER	S? [L?] G.	soldier	Parchim	2524/113
OHMS	Carl	--	Stade	2614/117
PANNENSCHMIDT	Wilhelm	butcher	Morl	2663/120
PANSE	F. W.	peasant	Obermoellern	2664/120
PIRL	Wilhelm	cabinetmaker	Wettin	2662/120
PUPKE	Andreas	cabinetmaker	Quassel, Mk	2665/120
PUPKE	Fritz	--	Quassel	2666/120
	Sophia	--		
	Heinrich	--		
	Wilhelm	--		
	Martin	--		

12

List 45 (continued)

ROTTELSDORFER	Georg	--	Oberleiterbach	2852/129
RUDEL	Eduard	tailor	Burghesler	2851/129
	Christian	tailor		
	--	wife		
SCHLUMES	Joseph	blacksmith	Gurtsch	3135/141
SCHMIDT	Johann Chris-tian	laborer	Scharmbeck, Ho	3133/141
SCHOPPE	Johanna Sophia*	--	Laucha	3136/141
	Bernhard	--		
	Alexander?	--		
	[*may be 2 persons]			
SCHOPPE	Friedrich	--	Laucha	3137/141
	Magdalena	--		
SCHROEDER	G. F.	businessman	Dargun	3134/141
SCHULTZ	Sophia	--	Hamburg	3138/141
TOLLERT	Christian? Friedrich	butcher	Laucha	3629/162
TOLLERT	Friedrich	butcher	Laucha	3630/162
TROST	Albert	confectioner	Hamburg	3628/162
VOGEL	Eduard	assistant cook?	Berlin	3739/167
	Amalia	--		

List 46
Ship *Miles*, Captain J. J. Ariansen
Departing Hamburg 31 May 1850 for New York (Direct)

ALLGEIER	G.	cabinetmaker	Gebbingen, Pr	0051/004
BARTELS	J.	tailor	Heithof	0298/014
BARTELS	Christine	--	Heithof	0299/014
	Friedrich	½ y		
BENING	Theodor	carpenter	Wendorf	0297/014
BIRKE	Carl	blacksmith	Landau, Sa	0294/014
	--	wife		
	--	2 children, 2 & 8 y		
BIRKE	J.	blacksmith	Breslau	0295/014

List 46 (continued)

BROCKMANN	J.	peasant	Rewisenhof	0296/014
	--	wife		
	--	2 children, 5 & 9 y		
DIEDRICH	Anna	--	Salzwedel	0620/029
	--	3 children, 3/4 to 7½ y		
FEIKE	J.	peasant	Setzdorf	0861/040
FEIKE	Stephan	--	Setzdorf	0862/040
FRANK	Babette	--	Schondra	0863/040
FREUNDT	J.	glazier	Goldberg	0865/040
FREUNDT	Christian	shoemaker	Goldberg	0866/040
FREUNDT	Heinrich	businessman	Goldberg	0867/040
	Doris	--		
FRIEDRICKA	--	--	Krackow	0864/040
GEORGI	Friedrich	plumber	Breslau	1058/049
	Therese	--		
GERLACH	H.	shoemaker	Plankenberg	1059/049
GLASSMANN	Carl	cabinetmaker	Krackow	1057/049
	Friederike	--		
GOLDBERG	Jacob	weaver	Ober Walbrungen	1056/049
HACKENBERG	F.	baker	Friedeberg	1319/060
HANSEN	Friedrich	--	Rewisenhof	1318/060
	--	wife		
	--	child, 8 y		
HAUCKE	Victoria	--	Setzdorf	1317/060
KAECKE	Gottfried	businessman	Segeberg	1773/080
KAROWSKI	J.	--	Birnbaum	1774/080
KAUER	Josef	weaver	Lebau	1768/079
KLEH	A.	blacksmith	Frankenstein, Pr	1770/080
KNEISSEL	J. F. C.	peasant	Utestadt, Pr	1771/080
	--	wife		
	--	child, 2½ y		
KOCH	Nicolaus	peasant	Roemhild, Th	1769/080
KOHLMANN	C. J. W.	machinist	Kranichfeld	1772/080
	August	--		
	Auguste	--		
	Mina?	3/4 y		

List 46 (continued)

LANGENBUCHER	Friedrich	baker	Stuttgart	2069/093
LIEBAS	Dorothea --	-- 4 children, ½ to 7½ y	Salzwedel	2070/093
MICHI	Carl	peasant	Utestadt? [Ilte- stadt?]	2342/105
MUELLER	F. H. Carolina	-- --	Hamburg	2341/105
MUELLER	G.	cabinetmaker	Grueneberg	2340/105
MUELLER	Theodor	surgeon	Neu Strelitz	2343/105
NUSSBAUM	Esther? Babette	-- --	Weimarschminde?	2550/114
OFFENBORN	H.	peasant	Oismar	2635/118
PETERSEN	Carolina	--	Rewisenhof	2721/122
PETERSEN	Dorothea	--	Rewisenhof	2722/122
PROBST	Carl	confectioner	Berlin	2720/122
RICHTER	Christian? Lisette?	chemist wife	Dessau	2915/131
SABIN	W.	soldier	Muehlrose, Pr	3316/148
SAENGER	Johann Cas- par Johanna	manager --	Mittelhausen	3314/148
SCHOBER	Dorothea	--	Rewisenhof	3318/148
SCHRADER	Johanna? --	-- child, ¼ y	Hamburg	3317/148
SCHUELER	Gustav	wallpaper hanger	Berlin	3320/148
SITTIG	Eleanore Theodor	-- businessman	Segeberg	3319/148
STEPHAN	E. T. G. Wilhelmine	wheelwright wife	Eckersberg	3313/148
STOEHR	Eugen	wax pourer	Altstadt	3315/148
VANDAL	J. J. H.	horse worker	Boitzenburg	3761/168
WALTHER	Carl -- --	buther wife 3 children, 1½ to 8 y	Ichtershausen	3914/176

List 46 (continued)

WEIDNER	Moritz	cabinetmaker	Segeberg, Ho	3912/176
	Clara	--		
WEIDNER	Julius	--	Segeberg, Ho	3913/176
WINDSCHEFFEL	G.	surgeon	Neustrelitz	3915/176
WOLF	Joseph	--	Friedeberg, Au?	3911/176
	--	wife		
	Ferdinand	8½ y		
ZEBERNICK	Carl	butcher	Hagenow	4052/182
ZEDLER	August	cabinetmaker	Gnadenfrey, Pr	4053/182
	--	wife		
	--	child, 3/4 y		

List 47
Ship *Miles*, Captain J. J. Ariansen
Departing Hamburg 16 Oct 1850 for New York (Direct)

ASCHER	Hermann? [Her-mine?]	--	Buck, Pr	0102/006
	--	2 children, 1½ & 3 y		
DANKER	Carl	--?	Jabel	0675/031
DANKER	Louise?	--	Malchow	0676/031
	Rinka	--		
DEHN	F.	businessman	Hamburg	0677/031
ECKHOFF	Johann	journeyman carpenter	Jabel, Mk	0790/037
EHRICH	Eleanor	--	Waldbach, Sa	0789/037
FUERSTENOW	J. C. F.	journeyman tailor	Buetzow	0946/043
GERTZ	Johann	footman?	Malchow	1154/053
GOHLMANN	Carl	shoemaker	Waldbach, Sa	1153/053
GUENTHER	Heinrich	weaver	Malchow	1155/053
HARTWIG	J.	cabinetmaker	Schwerin	1463/066
	Friederike	daughter		
HINNEMANN	Johann	shepherd	Ruhethat, Mk	1462/066
HINRICHS	Hans	peasant	Schirp, Di	1461/066

16

List 47 (continued)

KOCH	Rieka	--	Malchow	1946/087
KUHN	Heinrich W.	cigarmaker?	Hamburg	1945/087
LAMM	Michaelis	shoemaker	Graetz, Pr	2190/098
LEIBNITZ	Leopold	businessman	Neustadt, Pr	2192/098
LEWIN	Paulina	--	Buck? [Buk?] Pr	2191/098
MARCUSE	Theodor	--	Berlin	2485/111
MUELLER	Friedrich	businessman	Meusselbach, Th	2486/111
	--	wife		
	--	3 children, 3/4 to 4½ y		
PAUL	Friederike	--	Malchow	2799/126
PIEHL	Johann	laborer	Granzin, Mk	2800/126
PULS	Elisabeth	Frau	Jabel	2798/126
	--	4 children, 17-24 y		
RADDER	Ferdinand	clothmaker	Malchow	3034/136
RUSER? [RIESER?]	J. D.	soldier	Futterkam	3036/137
RISSLAND	H. C.	peasant	Benewitz, Th	3038/137
	--	wife		
	--	2 children, 3/4 & 7 y		
ROEBKE	Sophia	--	Malchow	3035/136
ROOS	J. F.	soldier	Copenhagen	3037/137
SCHAFFT	Carl T. Emil?	12 y	Berlin	3574/159
SCHROEDER	Wilhelm	manager	Penckow	3573/159
STUCKEN	Elise	--	Bergedorf	3572/159
SYDOW	J. A. F.	potter	Altbrandenburg	3571/159
WAGNER	Christian	tailor	Oberhain	4006/180
WALTHER	C. C.	pastor	Winsen, Ha	4004/180
	--	wife		
	--	4? [6?] children, 12-20 y		
WENZEL	Friedrich	farmhand	Kleekamp, Mk	4003/180
WILD	Carl Conrad	gold worker	Frankfurt	4001/180
WOEDECKE	Auguste	--	Berlin	4002/180

List 47 (continued)

| WOLFAWITZ | Lewin | merchant | Tiekotschin, Po | 4005/180 |
| ZIRCKEL | Meyer | merchant | Makowo, Po | 4074/183 |

List 48
Ship *Nordamerica* (Hamburg flag) Captain C. P. Rathje
Departing Hamburg 16 Mar 1850 for New York (Direct)

ALLARDT	Eduard --	music teacher family	Breslau	0014/002
ALTWEIN	J. C. --	laborer family	Weissensee	0013/002
BADEN	J. B.	glovemaker	Weimar	0350/016
BAEHR	Louis Eva	book printer wife	Weimar	0342/016
BAETZEL	Louis	tailor	Strassburg	0139/007
BAHLMANN	Johannes	peasant	Kl[ein] Colmar, Ho	0137/007
BAHRT	Johann Friedrich	--	Obervitz, Th	0340/016
BARFKNECHT	W. --	mason wife	Hohenschoenau	0144/007
BAUER	Julius	businessman	Berlin	0145/008
BAUER	--	pharmacist	Hohenlinde	0140/007
BAYE? [BOYE?]	Friedrich --	cabinetmaker wife	Parchim	0346/016
BECKER	Hermann	painter	Schwerin	0339/016
BECKHOLDT	Wilhelm	hatmaker	Chemnitz	0352/016
BEHR	Caroline	--	Kups, Ba	0138/007
BERGER	J. D.	miller	Teuditz	0141/007
BIELER	Wilhelm	--?	Eisleben	0143/007
BLUMEL	D.	book printer	Darmstadt	0348/016
BLUMENFELD	David	printer	Schwerin	0341/016
BOHL	Ernst	cabinetmaker	Braunsberg	0344/016
BOLLMUELLER	Adolph	baker	Berlin	0351/016
BRAND	J. C. F.	shoemaker	Weimar	0349/016

18

BREUN	Zacharias	tailor	Xiams	0345/016
BRINCKMANN	Friedrich -- --	milk dealer wife 4 children, 2 to 7-3/4 y	Schwerin	0337/016
BRINCKMANN	Maria	--	Schwerin	0338/016
BUCHHOP	Heinrich	cabinetmaker	Braunsberg	0343/016
BUERGEL	W. --	shoemaker wife	Striegau	0347/016
BURCKHARDT	Abraham	tailor	Strassburg	0142/007
DIERKS	Hr.	peasant	Klein Colmar, Ho	0574/027
DENCKER	Fritz	--	--	0575/027
ENGELBRECHT	--	--	Berlin	0695/033
FOELSCHEN	C. F. M.	gardener	Puttbus	0811/038
FRANCKE	Andreas	cigar salesman?	Otterhausen	0810/038
FRIEDEL	Sophia --	-- daughter	Eisenach	0809/038
GOTTFRIEDEN	A. E.	watchmaker?	Riepe	0965/045
HANDMANN	Hugo	brewer	Saalfeld	1353/061
HARTUNG	Johann	laborer	Lenzen	1193/054
HASSMANN	Georg	weaver	Levitzhufen	1350/061
HECHT	Ludwig -- Friedrich	laborer wife laborer	Fiehlbaum	1194/054
HOFFMANN	C. F. --	mason family	Guenstedt	1192/054
HOFFMANN	C.	businessman	Oberg	1351/061
HOPPE	Johann Friedrich Maria	shoemaker wife	Cammin	1352/061
JEZKOWITSCH	Moses?	--	Inohatschewo? Po	1503/068
JOHMANN? [JOBMANN?]	Christine	--	Hamburg	1504/068
JUNGST	Albert	sadler	Cassel	1505/068
KLOSE	Ernst	businessman	Neisse	1628/074

List 48 (continued)

KNOLL	Johann Eph- raim?	peasant	Guenstedt	1622/073
	--	family		
KOCH	H. W.	peasant	Gunstedt	1625/074
	--	family		
KOESLER	L.	*See* WALTHER, Auguste		
KRUEGER	C. F.	cabinetmaker	Stargard	1623/073
KUECHLING	J. F.	baker	Tungenhausen	1624/073
LAUENSTEIN	N? D.	--	Hamburg	1981/089
MAERZ	H. C.	miller	Otterhausen	2222/100
MAURATH	L. F.	businessman	Berlin	2228/100
MERL	August	hand laborer	Reinsdorf	2224/100
	--	wife		
MEYER	Wilhelm	peasant	Stettin	2226/100
	--	family		
MOEHE	Sophia	--	Schleswig	2225/100
MUELLER	F. G.	weaver	Gelwitz	2223/100
	--	family?		
MUENSTER	Johann	seaman	Flensburg	2227/100
NOLTE	A. F. W.	landscape gardener	Goettingen	2518/113
OESAU	Catharina	--	Hamburg	2638/118
	Anna	--		
PUELHOFER	Barbara	--	Kropfersricht?	2654/120
	Andreas	mason		
REIMSCH	A.	cabinetmaker	Coeslin	2831/128
	--	family		
REINSTEIN	T. C.	--?	Kindelbruch	2832/128
RICHTER	C. F.	--	Clamzschwitz? [Clanzschwitz?]	2833/128
RISCHMUELLER	G. W.	manager	Rheinhausen	2828/128
ROESSLER	G. Alfried?	construction worker?	Halle am Saale	2830/128
ROWEDDER	T. T.	laborer	Eddelbuck? [Eddel- bock?]	2829/128
SANDHOP	Christian	butcher	Stralsund	3082/138
SCHNEEMANN	W.	manager	Rheinhausen	3081/138

List 48 (continued)

SCHWENDLER	C. W.	--?	Weissenschirmbach	3080/138
	--	family		
SUDER	Carl	soapmaker	Lobau? [Labau?]	3083/138
THEISSEN	H. H.	--	Rotenhagen bei Luebeck	3624/162
THILO	August	manager	Doberan	3625/162
WALTHER	Auguste	--	Schwerin	3928/177
	--	baby (L. Koesler)		
WANFRIED	Maria	--	Otterhausen	3801/170
	--	baby		
WEIL	Moses	merchant	Duttweiler	3932/177
WENDEROTH	R.	official	Cassel	3930/177
WIEGRAFF	Johanna	--	Hamburg	3802/170
WILDING	Johann Christian	shoemaker	Hamburg	3929/177
WOLFF	Andreas	master tailor	Oberweimar	3931/177
ZACHER	Johann Heinrich	mason	Otterhausen	4025/181
ZORNOW	G. C.	manager	Coeslin	4029/181
	--	family		
ZUGBAUM	Georg	sadler	Cassel	4028/181
ZUNCKEL	Eld.?	laborer	Guenzstedt	4027/181
ZWEIG	Joseph Ephraim	cabinetmaker	Guenzstedt	4026/181

List 49
Ship *Nordamerica* (Hamburg flag) Captain C. P. Rathje
Departing Hamburg 29 Jun 1850 for New York (Direct)

ADAM	Carolina	--	Chodziehew?	0068/004
ADLER	Albrecht	--?	Schwerin	0067/004
	--	wife		
	--	3 children, 0 to 5 y		
CARLSEN	Lisetta?	--	Hamburg	0539/025
CASSEL	Benjamin	--	Chodziesen	0540/025
DEF	Carl	manager	Koetzberg	0632/029

List 49 (continued)

DITTMER	J. E. C. -- --	laborer wife 3 sons, 12 to 17 y	Hamburg	0630/029
DOEBERREYNER	Philip	book dealer	Altona	0633/029
DOERING	H. A.	--?	Braunsberg	0631/029
EBERT	Wilhelm	coachman	Schwerin	0741/035
EHNSEN	Lisette	--	Parchim	0742/035
EHRLICH	E. H.	mason	Leipzig	0743/035
FRAASCH	Friedrich -- --	--? wife baby	Ludwigslust	0881/041
FRAASCH	Sophia	--	Ludwigslust	0882/041
FISCHER	Carl	shoemaker	Niederwildungen	0884/041
FLEISCHHUT	Georg	manager	Hornberg	0883/041
FRANZ	Barbara	--	Ahlfeld	0880/041
GESCHNITZER	Joseph -- --	hoofsmith [horse- shoer?] wife 4 children, 0 to 9 y	Bruch	1082/050
GESSLER	J. A.	gold worker	S[axony] Weimar	1080/050
GIESEMANN	Christian	shoemaker	Hamburg	1083/050
GLOH	Christina	--	Hamburg	1084/050
GRACK	Wilhelmine	--	Schwerin	1079/050
GUENTSCH	Rosina? Fr.	--	Weimar	1081/050
JAECKEL	August	clock? maker	Neisse	1554/070
KLENOW	Heinrich	painter	Luebeck	1810/081
KNOCH	Joseph -- --	manager wife 4 children, 14 to 25 y	Treba, Th	1807/081
KOESTER	Ludolph Auguste WAL- THER --	coachman wife baby	Schwerin	1806/081
KRAUSE	W. P. -- --	shoemaker wife baby	Stettin	1808/081

22

KROHNE	Heinrich	shoemaker	Hamburg	1809/081
	--	wife		
KUECHENMEISTER	J. T.	mason	Rheinfelden	1811/081
	--	wife		
	--	son, 5 y		
LAGER	Johann	soldier	Jassow	2086/093
LAUHE	Gottlieb	printer	Cospeda	2085/093
LEHMANN	J. C.	manager	Pratau?	2088/094
LELL	J. A. A.	--?	Berlin	2087/094
MALCHOW	Carl	hired hand	Stettin	2374/107
MANNEBACH	Julius	cabinetmaker	Schaedenrinkel	2371/106
MARX	Isaac	--?	Altdorf	2376/107
MENZEL	David	clothmaker	Sagan	2372/106
MEYER	Christoph	cabinetmaker	Bendingersbastel? [Bendingersbai-stel]	2373/107
MEYER	Heinrich	beer brewer? barber?	Hamburg	2375/107
MIRUS	G.	Doctor [M.D.?]	Dobeln?	2377/107
NETTENDORF	Emilia	--	Freiburg	2565/115
NIEMANN	Maria	--	Hamburg	2563/115
	--	2 children, small		
NOACK	G. A.	butcher	Dresden	2564/115
PAPHOLTZ	Wilhelmina	Frau	Braunsberg	2738/123
	--	3 children, 0 to 6 y		
PHILIPPSON	David	--?	Hayn	2737/123
POETSCH	J. C. F.	businessman	Leipzig	2739/123
POETSCH	C. H. R.	waiter	Leipzig	2739a/123
RATZENBERGER	J. F.	manager	Garnsdorf	2950/133
RIEGEL	G. A. T.	master tailor	Stettin	2952/133
	--	wife		
	Wilhelmine	daughter		
RINGLEB	August	tailor	Laucha	2954/133
	--	wife		
	--	4 children, 4 to 20 y		

List 49 (continued)

ROETHER	Eduard	businessman	Neisse	2951/133
ROMAN	Barbara --	Frau 3 children, to 5 y	Braunsberg	2955/133
ROSENBAUM	Valentin -- --	businessman wife 4 children, to 17 y	Sternberg	2953/133
ROSENBAUM	Ernestine	--	Sternberg	2956/133
SCHEEL	Carl Carl	tailor --	Schwerin	3364/150
SCHEEL	Henriette	--	Schwerin	3365/150
SCHLICHTING	H. A.	--	Wiederstrich	3366/150
SCHMIDT	Anna --	Frau 2 children, 2 & 3 y	Luebeck	3362/150
SCHMIDT	F. C. E.	laborer	Schwerin	3363/150
SCHMIDT	G. A. -- --	barber wife 3 children, 1½ to 7 y	Stettin	3367/150
SCHMIDT	Friedrich	weaver	Niedersimmern	3369/151
SEIDEL	Margaretha	--	Kotzersricht	3361/150
SELIGMANN	Aron	--?	Aldorf	3371/151
SIEDE	Julius*	musician [*listed twice]	Hamburg	3370/151
SPOERELL	K. T.	student	Ilmenau	3368/150
STRELL	Ignatz	--	Garrendorf, Ba	3360/150
THIESSEN	Carl	cabinetmaker	Neustadt	3669/164
THIESSEN	Ludwig	tanner	Neustadt	3670/164
TOEPFER	C. B. --	--? daughter, 15 y	Weimar	3668/164
ZUHM	A. Friedrich -- --	--? wife 3 children, 6 to 10 y	Stettin	4056/182

List 50

Ship *Nordamerica* (Hamburg flag) Captain C. P. Rathje
Departing Hamburg 26 Oct 1850 for New York (Direct)

ABEND	C. L?	mason	Berlin	0119/006
AHLERS	Johann	laborer	Jabel	0118/006
ALBRECHT	Christopher?	shoemaker	Plassig?	0120/006
BAERLING	--	--	Greifwald	0509/023
BUGE?	Gottlieb?	peasant	--?	0510/023
BUGE	--?	shepherd?	--?	0511/023
CMETHI?	L. J.	physician	Wuerzburg	0563/026
CUSELLE	Johann	businessman	Cincin[n]ati	0564/026
DALL	Andreas Peter	--?	Kistrup	0686/032
DEUTSCH	Eduard	businessman	Pesth	0687/032
DEUTSCHER	Babatj?	--	Aldorf	0685/032
	--	2 children, to 2½ y		
GERHARDT	Wilhelm	mechanic	Herrnstadt	1171/053
GNADENORT? [GNADENORF?]	Johanna	--	Altona	1170/053
HELLMER	F. Theodor	businessman	Leipzig	1495/067
HOFFMANN	Maria Rosina?	-- [name at bottom of list]	--	1496/067
KALZ	August	--	Cirkwitz	1965/088
KAPTER	Dominicus	weaver	Oberluetzow	1966/088
KRECHINKA	Mathias	school teacher	Cirkwitz	1964/088
KROMBACH	Victor --	--? wife	Posen	1962/088
KUNKEL	Maria --?	-- --	Schwerin	1963/088
MARCUS	Elias -- --	-- wife 2 children, to 6 y	Landau	2511/112
MAX	Meyer	physician	Weimar	2513/112
MIERZEWSKY	-- --	-- wife	Czernina?	2510/112

List 50 (continued)

MOELLER	C. H. F.	manager	Jabel	2507/112
	--	wife		
	--	3 children, to 6 y		
MUELLER	J. F.	painter	Segeberg	2509/112
MUNCKEL	E. L?	businessman	Alberg	2508/112
	--	wife		
	--	2 children		
NAGEL	Mathilde	--	Hamburg	2600/116
POHL	J. Friedrich	--	Radegosz	2816/126
	--	wife		
	--	5 children, 2-16 y		
RIESS	Johann	manager	Jabel	3059/137
	--	wife		
	--	10 children, 4 to 26 y		
SCHULER	Johann	shoemaker	Meldorf	3617/161
SCHROEDER	Adolph	tailor	Stove	3612/161
	--	wife		
SCHROEDER	Maria	--	Stove	3618/161
SCHUCK	--	manufacturer	Mainz	3614/161
	--	wife		
	--	3 children		
STARCKE	Carl Adolph	--	Ziegenrueck	3616/161
STEFFEN	J. H. W.*	--	Jabel	3613/161
	[*"14 year Ado[l]ph's son = TIEDGE and wife, see 7 (meaning unknown)]			
STEINER	Johann?	--?	Hamburg	3619/161
STRASSINE	Alexander Alerat? [Albert?]	shoemaker tailor	Gresen?	3615/161
THOMPSON	Thomas	merchant?	Apenrade	3712/165
TREDGE	C. F.	--	Jabel	3711/165
	--	wife		
	Adolphus?	son		

List 51

Ship *Perseverance* (English flag) Captain Edward White
Departing Hamburg 2 Apr 1850 for New York (Direct)

ABEL	J. F?	wheelwright	Bobzin	0021/002
ABEND	Ernst Louis	factory worker	Goerlitz	0020/002
BACH	Maria Sophie	--	Gruenstadt	0159/008
BORMANN	H.	technician	Northeim	0157/008
	--	wife		
BRAGER	Julius	tailor	Zadelsdorf	0158/008
BRANDT	Johann	peasant	Gribitz	0160/008
	--	wife		
	--	family		
BRANDT	Johann	--	Gribitz	0161/008
	Maria	--		
BRANDT	Carl	butcher	Hagenow	0162/008
EVERT	Carl	--	Gribitz	0698/033
	Heinrich	--		
	Lina	--		
EVERT	Johann Christian	tailor	Gribitz	0697/033
	--	wife		
	--	family		
FESTGE	Wilhelmine	--	Langensalza	0815/038
GEBERT	J.	plumber	Berlin	0983/046
GEISSLER	Friedrich Heinrich	businessman	Eulenburg, Ho	0984/046
GNIFFKE	F. A.	soldier	Neufahrwasser, Pr	0980/045
GOARN	Johann	peasant	Mittelkirchen	0985/046
GRABOW	Johann	servant [*dienst-knecht*]	Bolitz	0976/045
GRUELLMEYER	F. R.	--?	Gera	0978/045
GRUELLMEYER	Ernestine	--	Gera	0979/045
	Maria	--		
GRUNOW	Carl	--?	Berlin	0981/045
	--	wife		
	--	son		
GRUNOW	Wilhelm	--	Berlin	0982/046
	Pauline	--		
	Ottilia	--		

List 51 (continued)

GUTTENBERG	W. H. C.	businessman?	Kirchlies, Ba	0977/045
HAGEN	F.	--?	Granzin	1202/055
HAGEN	J. C. C.	--	Granzin	1203/055
HEINSMANN	Theodor	--?	Berlin	1200/055
HEINSMANN	Mathilde	--	Berlin	1201/-55
	Mathilde	--		
	Anna	--		
	Carl	--		
	Maria	--		
KOETKE	J. C.	servant	Pruenemuhle, Mk	1640/074
KUERSTEN	G. Albrecht	blacksmith	Langensalza	1641/074
LEMKE	Joachim	peasant	Rochberg	1988/089
LEMKE	C.	--?	Grabow	1991/090
LEMKE	J.	tailor	Grabow	1992/090
LEVERS	Ludwig	shoemaker	Hackendorf	1990/089
LUTH	Johann Fried-rich	blacksmith	Frethorst	1989/089
MASCH	Joachim	shoemaker	Hackendorf	2244/101
MATTHISEN	Nicolaus Cas-par	soldier	Husum	2245/101
MERTENS	Augusta	--	Berlin	2243/101
NICKELS	Oscar	bookbinder	Gruenberg	2521/113
NORDMANN	P. J?	peasant	Meldorf	2520/113
PENZIG	F. W.	butcher	Lomasch? [Lomatch?]	2657/120
	--	wife		
	--	family		
PENZIG	G. Adolph?	--	Lomasch? [Lomatch?]	2658/120
	L. C.	--		
RECHBERG	Friedrich?	peasant	Kieve	2843/128
RIES	H.	peasant	Eutin	2845/129
ROEMCKE	Carl	tailor	Roebnitz	2844/129
RUSSEGGER	Albert	gold worker	Salzburg	2846/129
SCHLEEF	Christian	shoemaker	Burghausen	3113/140
SCHLEICHHARDT	Johann Lud-wig	gardener	Gruenstadt	3114/140

List 51 (continued)

SCHLEICHHARDT	Eleanore Friederike	--	Gruenstadt	3115/140
SCHMIDT	Carl August	--?	Langensalza	3118/140
SCHNEIDER	Wilhelmine	Mad[am?]	Berlin	3116/140
	Rudolph	child		
	Anna	child		
	Max	child		
	Thomas?	child		
SCHULTZ	Heinrich	sadler	Gribitz	3117/140
SCHUMACHER	Hermann	tinsmith	Schaefstaedt	3121/140
STADLER	A.	butcher	Karlsbad	3120/140
STEINFELD	Sophia	--	Eutin	3119/140
VOGEL	Johanna Chr[istine?]	--	Marklissa	3738/167
	--	son		
WALDOW? [WALDON?]	Christian	peasant	Kieve	3812/171
	--	wife		
	--	family		
WALDOW	Friedrich Johann	--	Kieve	3813/171
WEISS	Franz	--	Hungary	3811/171
	--	wife		
	Nujar?*	--		
	Komorn*	--		
	[Could these be geographic names?]			
WILCKE*	Christian	--	Gribitz	3815/171
	Maria	--		
	Henriette	--		
	Wilhelm	--		
WILKE*	Carl	shoemaker	Gribitz	3814/171
	--	wife		
	--	family		
	[*so spelled]			

List 52

Ship *Rhein* (Hamburg flag) Captain H. Ehlers
Departing Hamburg 6 Apr 1850 for New York (Direct)

ANDERSON	Erich	tailor	Stockholm	0022/002
ANDERSON	Osk[ar?]	furrier	Ripen	0023/002
BALCK	Mathias	tailor	Ornbau	0165/008
BARNIECK	Jacob	--?	Beerwalde	0163/008
	Henriette	wife		
	--	4 children, female		
	--	1 child, male		
BAUER	J. Friedrich	sculptor	Wittenberge	0166/008
BISCHOFF	Georg	soldier	Nuernberg	0164/008
BOETTGER	Friedrich	tailor	Hamburg	0168/008
BRABAND	Elisabeth	--	Komlosen	0167/008
CLAUS	Carl Adolph	miller	Meissen	0516/024
DIETRICH	Wilhelm	--	Kopenhagen	0580/027
	Christine	wife		
	Ferdinand	baby		
DIETZEN	Henriette	--	Lauchau	0579/027
FISCHER	Leonhard	cabinetmaker	Herieden	0816/038
FRIEDRICH	Albert August	pharmacist	Meschlitz	0818/038
FROEHLICH	C. G. E.	--	Dresden	0817/038
GROSSKOPF	J. J.	tailor	Bickenbach	0986/046
GROSSKOPF	Anna Barbara	unmarried	Bickenbach	0987/046
HANSEN	Johann	shoemaker	Kopenhagen	1209/055
	Catharine	wife		
	Heinrich	son		
HELLRIEGEL	F. L.	miller	Hayn, Sa	1207/055
HELLWAGE	H. S.	--	Culm	1205/055
HOFFER	Jonas	teacher	Wien	1210/055
HOFFMANN*	Heinrich	mechanic	Breslau	1208/055
HOFMANN*	Ernst	carpenter [*so spelled]	Chodziesen	1211/055
HOLTZEY	Carl	--	Unterwelleborn	1204/055
HORN	Elise	--	Heinamof in Ronn-hild	1206/055

List 52 (continued)

JAUCHE	F. W.	--	Ziegenrueck	1510/068
	F. C. W.	--		
	Julius Wilhelm	--		
JAUCHE	Paul Wilhelm	--	Ziegenrueck	1511/068
	Henriette?	baby		
KIRCHHOF	Hermann	peasant	St. Louis	1643/074
	Hermann	boy		
	Maria	child		
	Franz	child		
KLAHRE	G. H.	gardener	Naumburg	1642/074
KRUEGER	G. J. W.	miller	Guelitz	1644/074
LACHMANN	Carl	peasant	Bertelsdorf	1997/090
LANG	Johann	mason	Breslau	1999/090
LAUSEN	P. Friedrich	tailor	Kopenhagen	1998/090
LESSER	Martin	businessman	Stettin	2000/090
LEETSCH	Wilhelm	tailor	Neu Strelitz	2145/096
LIEBMANN	August	--	Reichmansdorf	1993/090
LINDSTEDT	Doris	--	Bordelsholm	1996/090
LIPMANN	G. F.	--	Grossnendorf	1994/090
	Catharine Elisabeth	wife		
	Georg Heinrich	child		
LIPMANN	Johann Carl	child	Grossnendorf	1995/090
	Henriette Georgi?	child		
	--	baby		
MAHNCKE	Louise	--	Wittenburg	2247/101
MAYER	Dominick?	surgeon	Frankenthal	2251/101
MICHAELIS	C. F. G.	gardener	Lestin	2246/101
MOEHNER	Michaelis	furrier	Lissa	2249/101
MOELLER	Hans Petersen	helmsman	Hamburg	2250/101
MOEVES	Friedrich	businessman	Berlin	2252/101
MORTELL	Carl	sugar refiner	Schoenberg	2248/101
NOETHLICH	Carl	blacksmith	Bucha	2522/113

List 52 (continued)

NUEN? [NUN?]	Carl Johann	baker	Parchim	2523/113
OERTEL	Christian	--	Culm	2613/117
PATZER	Friedrich	--	Bucha	2659/120
	Heinrich	--		
	Mathilde	--		
POTSDAMMER	Michaelis	furrier	Lissa	2661/120
PRINZLER	Ernst	--	Schreibersdorf	2660/120
	Caroline	wife		
	--	2 boys		
	--	baby		
RASMUSSEN	Hansing?	Frau	Kopenhagen	2848/129
	--	baby		
REINHARDT	August	manager	Altenburg	2847/129
RIEGLOR?	Anton	--	Wien	2850/129
[RIEGLAR?]	--	wife		
ROESE	Gustav	beltmaker?	Zeitz	2849/129
SAND	Joseph	peasant	Missouri	3125/140
	--	wife		
SCHELLHORN	Eduard	manager	Graefinau	3129/140
SCHMIDT	Friederike	--	Kaulsdorf	3122/140
SCHMIDT	August Gott-lieb?	weaver	Wangerin	3126/140
SCHMIDT	Heinrich	weaver	Wangerin	3130/140
SCHMIDT	Wilhelmine	wife of [Hein-rich?]	Wangerin	3131/141
	--	baby		
SCHWARTZ	Amalia	Frau	Rogowa	3132/141
	Jacob	child		
	Anna	child		
	David	child		
	Salosch?	child		
	Maria	baby		
STELLER	Franziska	--	Magdeburg	3124/140
STELLER	Albertine	--	Magdeburg	3127/140
STRAAGE	--	butcher	Beerwalde	3123/140
SVENSON	Oll.	tailor	Ripen, Dk	3128/140

List 52 (continued)

THIEMANN	Wilhelm	cabinetmaker	Wuenschendorf	3627/162
WIEFEL	J. C.	--	Unterwellnborn	3816/171
WIRTH	Anton	peasant	Onnbau? [Ornbau?]	3817/171
WULFF	Franciska Maria	--	Ottensen	3818/171
ZABEL	Gottfried	--	Dresden	4033/181
ZIMMERMANN	C. F.	peasant	Gniefkowo? [Gutef- kowo?]	4032/181

List 53

Ship *Rhein* (Hamburg flag) Captain H. Ehlers
Departing Hamburg 24 Aug 1850 for New York (Direct)

ACKERMANN	C. J. F.	day laborer	Kelle	0085/005
ACKERMANN	F? C.	15 y	Grussow	0084/005
	W. F. C.	11 y		
AUERBACH	Elise	--	Meiningen	0083/005
	--	4 children, to 9-3/4 y		
BERG	D. J. F.	day laborer	Wahlow	0429/019
	--	wife		
	--	baby		
BIESTERFELD	J. C.	tailor	Wunstorf	0433/019
BILLERBECK	Henriette?	wet-nurse	Baerwalde	0430/019
BODENSCHATZ	Gustav	--	Zella bei Gotha	0431/019
BORMANN	Henriette	--	Freiburg	0432/019
DEMMIN	Johann	peasant	Tergentin	0660/030
	--	wife		
	--	3 children, 3 to 7 y		
DOLL	Sophie Chris- tine	--	Gruessow	0658/030
DRECKMANN	Heinrich	--	Grabow	0659/030
DUTSCHMANN	Auguste Naethania?	-- --	Dresden	0661/031

List 53 (continued)

EICHSTEDT	Bertha [child]	-- 2½ y	Parchim	0772/036
EICHSTEDT	Carl -- --	cabinetmaker wife 4 children, 16 to 28 y (1 son a miller; 1 son a baker)	Parchim	0771/036
FISCHER	Carl	manager	Weimar	0918/042
FITZNER	C. H. -- --	carpenter wife 2 children, 9 & 10 y	Else	0917/042
FUHRSBERG	Christian	plumber	Braunschweig	0916/042
GEIST	Theodor	manager	Guestrow	1132/052
GOLTZSCH	Christian Friedrich	hatter	Altona	1130/052
GOLTZSCH	Sophia	--	Altona	1135/052
GRASELER	Hermann	--	Wien	1133/052
GRAVENHORST	E. August	shoemaker	Lauenburg	1134/052
GRELL	Wilhelm	ropemaker?	Guestrow	1131/052
HAESSNER	C. F. J.	painter	Berlin	1406/063
HEICKER	Elisabeth	--	Luebtheen	1409/063
HEYNSEN	Sophia	--	Tergentin	1408/063
HOFFMANN	J. E? C.	highschool student	Arnstadt	1410/063
HUELTNER	Johanna	--	Nuernberg	1407/063
IHDE	Joachim	hired hand	Lembzin	1577/071
KLAAR	August --	painter wife	Zellin	1892/085
KLEIN	Caroline	--	Weimar	1896/085
KOSTROZINER	Caecilia?	--	Kurnick	1895/085
KOTZ	Wilhelm Jesratt?	-- --	Roedelheim	1897/085
KREMPIN*	Anna Marian [Surname could be KREMP.]	-- --	Schwerin	1894/085
KREPLIN	Maria Franz- isca	--	Hamburg	1893/085

List 53 (continued)

LEICHARD?	Hermann	businessman	Berlin	2138/096
LESSLAFT?	H. A. R.	--	Berlin	2142/096
LEVIN	Kaschia? Alex?	--	Kurnick?	2143/096
LEWERENTZ*	C. C.	tanner	Parchim	2144/096
LEWERENZ*	Dorothea	servant [*so spelled]	Silz	2137/096
LORENZEN	P. -- --	lawyer wife 4 children, 10-20 y	Bredstedt	2141/096
LOTZE	Catharine Elisabeth	--* -- [*Did not arrive]	Koenigsee	2139/096
LUEBKE	Christian	tailor	Hamburg	2140/096
MAHNCKE	L?	tailor	Neustadt	2439/109
MARTIN	Carl Friedrich	weaponsmaker?	Weimar	2440/109
MARTIN	Otto	7 y [with Carl Friedrich Martin #2440/109]	Weimar	2441/109
MAYER	Heinrich	peasant	Ranis	2438/109
MOELLER	Albert Christian Johann	farmhand farmhand	Satow	2437/109
MUELLER	F. W. A. -- --	day laborer wife baby	Wahlow	2436/109
NEBE	August	sadler	Altona	2588/116
OTTO	J. H. -- --	tailor wife 3 children, 12-17 y	Lanckow? [Lauckow?]	2645/118
PASCHEN	A. J. W?	servant?	Grussau? [Grussow?]	2769/124
PAUL	Carl Siegmund	cablemaker	Strigau?	2774/125
PETER	F. W. L?	shepherd boy	Stuer	2768/124
PFEFFERKORN	Valentin	-- ("Did not arrive")	Kreutzburg	2773/125

List 53 (continued)

POMMEREHN	Friedrich	--	Ludwigslust	2772/125
	--	wife		
	--	son, 11 y		
PULS	Wilhelmine? Maria	21 y	Grussow	2770/125
PULS	C. F. H.	farmhand	Grussow	2771/125
RAABE	Christian	--	Tergentin	2997/135
RADDEN	Friedrich	cabinetmaker	Altona	2996/135
RAUMANN	Anna Margaretha	-- --	Schaffhausen	2992/135
RIPPEL	Traugott	shoemaker	Meiningen	2989/135
ROMANOW?	--	--	Koblin	2998/135
ROMMEL	Augusta	--	Weimar	2999/135
	--	baby		
ROMMEL	F. A. W.	watchmaker	Weimar	3000/135
	--	wife		
ROSENBOHM	C. D. H.	coachman	Tharow? [Sharow?]	2990/135
RUFF	Henriette	--	Koenigsee	2993/135
RUSS	Eduard	book dealer	Hamburg	2994/135
RUSS	August	machinist	Berlin	2995/135
SCHAEFER	Rudolph	weaponsmaker	Zella bei Gotha	3481/155
SCHAU	J. F.	carpenter	Ranis	3485/155
	--	wife		
	--	3 children, to 19 y		
SCHIRMER	Wilhelmine	Frau	Saalfeld	3482/155
	--	5 children, 3-20 y		
SCHLUETER	W. Christian	--	Neustadt	3490/156
SCHMIDT	Henriette	--	Meiningen	3478/155
SCHNEIDER	Johann Peter	coppersmith	Bredstedt	3492/156
	--	wife		
	--	3 children		
SCHNEIDER	Wilhelmine?	--	Roedelheim	3497/156
SCHOBERT	Friederike	--	Tesdorff [Tesdorpf?]	3495/156
SCHROEDER	J. C. P.	farmhand	Petersdorf	3479/155

List 53 (continued)

SCHROEDER	J. J. H.	shepherd	Gruessow	3480/155
SCHROETER	F. J.	laborer	Berlin	3491/156
	--	wife		
SCHULTZ	Friedrich	--	Goldberg	3488/156
	--	wife		
	--	child or children		
SCHUMANN	F. E.	butcher	Rosthal	3494/156
SOSSAU	Johann	peasant	Altorf	3493/156
SPANJOR?	Johann	baker	S[ank]t Margar-ethen	3487/155
SPECK	Carl Julius	tailor	Krempe	3486/155
SPIECKERMANN	Henry	seaman	New York	3489/156
STRATTMANN	J.	--	Luebz	3496/156
	--	3 persons		
SUHR	Eduard	18 y	Ludwigslust	3483/155
SUHR	Charlotte	--	Ludwigslust	3484/155
TAEGER	Heinrich	tailor	Legerde	3690/165
TEUBNER	Eduard	baker	Weimar	3691/165
THIEME	Richard	--?	Zella bei Gotha	3685/164
THROMM	Johann[a?]	--	Eschwege	3689/164
	--	baby		
TUNELL	Johann	manager	Garleben? [Gor-leben?]	3686/164
TUNELL	Heinrich	manager	Garleben? [Gor-leben?]	3686a/164
TUNELL	Charlotte Sophia	Fraeulein Frau	Garleben? [Gor-leben?]	3687/164
TUNELL	Maria	Fraeulein	Garleben? [Gor-leben?]	3688/164
UHLMANN	Julius	tailor	Lauban? [Lanban?]	3727/166
ULLRICH	O. H. A.	--	Berlin	3726/166
VERBENIUS	Clara	--	Weimar	3776/168
VOSS	C. H. C.	day laborer	Gruessow	3772/168
	--	wife		
VOSS	Maria? F. J.	maid	Gruessow	3773/168
	Ludwig J. H.	13 y		

List 53 (continued)

VOSS	J. F. C.	servant boy, 15 y	Gruessow	3774/168
VOSS	J. F. J.	boy, 11 y	Gruessow	3775/168
WACHTER	Carl	tailor	Weimar	3977/179
WINGE	Johann	horseshoer	Baerwalde	3976/179

List 54

Ship *Romanow* (Hamburg flag) Captain J. H. Nieman
Departing Hamburg 2 Mar 1850 for New York (Direct)

AHLERS	G. L.	businessman	Hamburg	0001/002
ALBRECHT	Johanna?	girl	Fichtenwerde	0003/002
ASCH	Rosalia Moritz	-- --	Posen	0002/002
BACHMANN	Georg	waiter	Posen	0122/007
BAUER	J. C. W.	laborer	Hadersleben	0123/007
BRAUN	H.	candidate [for an academic degree]	Hildburghausen	0124/007
BYCK	Ernestine	--	Posen	0121/007
CAMPE	Conrad	baker	Eschershausen	0513/024
CHARPENTIER	Louis	--?	Stadt Ilm, formerly? Rudolstadt	0512/024
DEICKMANN	C.	peasant	Schwerin, Mk	0566/027
DRUCKER	Philipp	--	Posen	0565/027
EGGERT	W. E.	chairmaker?	Stralsund	0689/033
ERBE	Emilia	--	Malchow, Mk	0688/033
FRANZ	B. --	-- wife	Wien	0803/038
GAEDE	A.	shoemaker	Prenzlau	0958/045
GEHLMANN	Elise	--	Malchow, Mk	0959/045
HAGEDORN	J. F.	shoemaker	Luechow	1173/054

38

List 54 (continued)

HANNEWALD	A.	shepherd?	Meissen	1175/054
HEILIGENORT? [HEILIGENORF?]	J. E. F.	baker --	Stralsund	1174/054
HENNINGSEN	H.	baker	Schwerin	1176/054
HIRSCH	Abraham	tailor	Strassburg	1172/054
JESSEL	Gutthilf?	child	Posen	1497/068
KOENIG	Adolph	gold worker	Dresden	1601/073
LEVISOHN	Rieke	--	Posen	1967/089
MANHEIMER	Heinrich	--?	Posen	2208/100
MARTINI	Ja. --	Mad[am?] son	Meissen	2210/100
MEYER	Christian	peasant	Glueckstadt	2211/100
MOLCK	C. F?	cabinetmaker	Kiel	2207/100
MONSON	Carl	laborer	Sconning, Sw	2206/100
MOYER	H.	--?	Hamburg	2209/100
NEUGEDACH	leonore?	girl	Corneck, Ps	2514/113
OHSCHUTZ? [OFSCHUTZ?]	Maria*	-- (*--? RICHTER)	Winzbach	2601/117
PANCER	Franz	businessman	Kirohschlach	2652/120
ROSENTHAL	L.	cabinetmaker	Lehbuss	2820/128
SOLTAU	Wilhelm	book printer	Hamburg	3060/138
STEIN	Carl	peasant	Dambach	3062/138
STOLCH	Carl Oswald	--?	Cottbus, Pr	3061/138
UCKROW	A.	waiter	Cuestrin, Pr	3713/166
VOIGT	C. C. Fried-	shoemaker	Stadt Ilm, Principality of Rudolstadt	3733/167
WALDMANN	H.	weaver	Neustadt	3784/170
WALLIS	G. E.	peasant	Greifswald	3786/170
WASSERMANN	Hanchee?	--	Chrim, Ps	3782/170
WENCK	Wilhelm	tailor	Langensalza, Pr	3783/170
van der WICK	--?	--	Emden	3788/170
WIESE	Hinrich	sailor	Elmshorn	3787/170

List 54 (continued)

| WIESER | Ferdinand | businessman | Freudenberg | 3785/170 |
| ZIRKE | Bertha | Mad[am?] | Posen | 4021/181 |

List 55

Ship *San Francisco*, Captain C. L. Kramer
Departing Hamburg 15 Jun 1850 for Port Adelaide and Sydney (Direct)

AHRENSTEIN	Adolph	businessman	Lipstadt	0053/004
	--	wife		
	Levy	--		
	David	--		
	Franz	--		
	--?	--		
AHRENSTEIN	Friedrich?	businessman	Hamburg	0054/004
	Auguste	--		
AMSBERG	Johann	businessman	Hamburg	0055/004
BANDHOLZ	Friedrich	carpenter	Kiel	0307/014
BECKER	Friedrich A.	wheelwright	Leipzig	0306/014
BINDER	August	mason	Grenitz	0308/014
BRAUNACK	Friedrich	clothmaker	Torschtiegel	0309/014
	--	wife		
	--	2 sons, 19 & 30 y		
ERICKSEN	Johanne	--	Altona	0733/034
FINDERSEN	C. C.	baker	Mark Kleberg	0870/040
FISCHER	Christian	shepherd	Osteritz	0871/040
	--	wife		
	--	3 children, 3-6 y		
FROMM	Gottlieb?	tailor	Milloslowe	0872/040
GASSAN	J.	peasant	Tarnow	1064/049
	Maria	--		
	Elisabeth	child		
GOMALLA	Mathes	peasant	Gonrow?	1063/049
GORMANN	Johann	peasant	Tarnow	1065/049
	--	wife		
	--	3 children, to 15 y		
GRABASCH	Louise	--	Muschten	1066/049

40

HANEL	Carl	sadler	Libau	1325/060
HEMMERLING	J. F.	peasant	Muschten	1323/060
	--	wife		
	--	3 children, 3-10 y		
HUBENER	Gottlieb?	peasant	Zirchaw	1324/060
	Anna	wife		
HUPPATZ	Johann	shoemaker	Tauer	1322/060
	--	wife		
	--	4 children, 2-11 y		
IRMLER	Georg	peasant	Sawade, Pr	1546/070
	Anna	wife		
IRMLER	Friedrich	peasant	Sawade, Pr	1547/070
	--	wife		
	--	3 children, to 9 y		
KALCKWITZ	Wilhelm	peasant	Schmoelen	1787/080
	--	wife		
	--	daughter, 17 y		
KILIAN	Christian	peasant	Tauer	1783/080
	--	wife		
	--	4 children, 3-7 y		
KLAKE	Gottlieb	wheelwright	Kay, Pr	1784/080
	--	wife		
	--	2 children, to 5 y		
KOCH	Michael	shoemaker	Kracau	1788/080
KOOPMANN	Gottlieb	tailor	Wismar	1782/080
KURTZE	Samuel	carpenter	Brausendorf?	1785/080
	--	wife	[Bransendorf?]	
	--	child, 5 y		
	--	2? babies		
KURTZE	Wilhelm	peasant	Brausendorf?	1786/080
	--	wife	[Bransendorf?]	
	--	small child		
LEHMANN	Gottlob	peasant	Muschten?	2079/093
	--	wife		
	--	small child		
LEWELS	Carl Johann	distiller	Hamburg	2078/093
MATISKE	Samuel	peasant	Schmoelew?	2352/106
	--	wife	[Schmoelen?]	
	--	3 children, 7-11 y		

List 55 (continued)

MATHIES	Catharina?	--	Hamburg	2353/106
MATTNER? [MALTNER?]	Gottfried -- --	peasant wife children [partly illegible] to 7 y	Kay	2350/106
MEINEKE	Johann	peasant	Boitzenburg	2348/105
MEINJE	August	peasant	Meullerhausen	2351/106
MEYER	Wilhelm	cabinetmaker	Zagajewitzky? Pr [Zagrajewitzky?]	2347/105
MIETHKE	C. G. A. -- --	peasant wife 3 children, 9-17 y	Stargard	2346/105
MUELLER	Johann Julia Rosina --	tailor -- -- 3 children, 7-17 y	Forschtiegel? [Torschtiegel?]	2349/106
NAGEL	Heinrich Louise	tailor --	Bowitz	2555/114
NOACK	Anna Anna	-- --	Raben	2551/114
NOACK	Johann Anna Maria	peasant -- 12 y	Tauer	2552/114
NOACK	Elisabeth -- Martin	-- child, 2 y peasant	Tauer	2553/114
NOACK	Gottfried Gottlieb Anna	-- -- 6 y	Tauer	2554/114
PAETZEL	Gottlob Anna Rosine	shepherd wife	Jany	2724/123
PAETZEL	Carl August Wilhelm Ernst	peasant peasant	Jany	2725/123
PAETZEL	Anna Johanna? Anna Dorothea Christiana	18 y 16 y 13 y	Jany	2726/123
PARDE	August	wheelwright	Muschten	2727/123

List 55 (continued)

POECK	Gottlieb?	peasant	Kay	2728/123
	--	wife		
	--	2 children		
RAGL?	Christian	shoemaker	Muschten	2922/132
	--	wife		
	--	son, 14 y		
RECIMANN	Gottlob	shepherd	Muschten	2921/132
	--	wife		
	--	3 children, 18-26 y		
RICHSTEIG	Georg	peasant	Coschten	2923/132
	--	wife		
	--	4 children, ? to 13 y		
RICHTER	E. C.	shepherd	Cottbus	2926/132
RICHTER	Sophia	--	Hamburg	2929/132
ROEDINGER	Friederike	--	Berlin	2927/132
	--	5 children, 10-21 y		
ROESSLER	Wilhelm	peasant	Neubauroh	2924/132
	--	wife		
	--	6 children, ? to 12 y		
ROI	Ferdinand	shoemaker	Tirschtiegel	2925/132
	--	wife		
	--	child, 3 y		
ROMM	Daniel	peasant	Gutabschied	2920/132
	--	wife		
	--	4 children, 2-11 y		
RUETHNING	F. L.	manufacturer	Paderborn	2928/132
	--	wife		
	--	2 children, 7 & 12 y		
SAEGEN-SCHMITTER	Gottlieb?	peasant	Scharky	3328/149
SCHAEPE	Christian	peasant	Sawade	3323/149
	--	wife		
	--	4 children		
SCHMERL	Gottfried	peasant	Deutsch Kessel	3322/148
	--	wife		
	--	child		
SCHROEDER	J. G.	cabinetmaker	Moeckern	3321/148
	--	wife		
	--	4 children		

List 55 (continued)

SCHUETZ	Mathias	peasant	Babitz	3325/149
SCHULTZ	Friedrich	peasant	Muschten	3326/149
	--	wife		
	--	small child		
SCHULTZ	Gottlob	shepherd	Muschten	3326a/149
	--	wife		
	--	son, 13 y		
SEMLER	George	peasant	Heirde	3324/149
	--	wife		
	--	4 children		
STENKE	Gottfried	miller	Kay	3327/149
	Wilhelm	miller		
	Anna Rosina	--		
	--	4 children, to 15 y		
STENKE	Louise	--	Kay	3327a/149
	--?	--		
STURZEL	Carl	peasant	Schmoellen	3329/149
TILEMANN	C. H.	businessman	Neustadt	3661/163
UPLEGGER	J. E. G.	peasant	Neu Teschow	3719/166
VOIGT	Robert O.	carpenter	Ehrenberg	3762/168
VORWERK	Gottfried	shoemaker	Langheinersdorf	3763/168
	--	wife		
	--	5 children, to 13 y		
WENSKE	Gottlob	peasant	Muschten	3919/176
	--	wife		
	--	3 children, to 2 y		
WOLFF	Christian	shepherd	Osteritz, Pr	3917/176
	--	wife		
	--	3 children, 6-17 y		
WUNDERSITZ	Carl	peasant	Ritschuetz	3918/176
	--	wife		
	--	3 children, 6-14 y		
ZAHNLEITER	Philipp	mason	Kaeferthal	4054/182
ZIRCK	Dorothea	--	Hamburg	4055/182
	James	--		

List 56

Ship *Sir Isaac Newton*, Captain J. G. Niemann
Departing Hamburg 27 Jul 1850 for New York (Direct)

ABRAHAM	Levy	nailsmith	Ragazin	0074/005
AHLERT	Christ-[ophe]r?	--	Hagenow	0077/005
AHRENS	Carl	laborer	Buelow	0076/005
AMON	Martin Emil	--? butcher	Hildburgshausen	0075/005
BOHS	Lisette?	--	Luebthausen	0393/018
BREMER	H. Otto --	peasant wife	Frensdorf	0392/018
BUSACKER	Johann	laborer	Neudorf	0391/018
BASCH	Heymann	tailor	Posen	0390/018
DOSE	C.	economist? [manager?]	Steinfeld	0648/030
EGGERT	Sophia	--	Krug, Mk	0762/036
ELLERN? [ELTERN?]	Sophia	--	Buelow	0761/036
ETZ	Heinrich --	tailor wife	Nassau	0758/035
EVERS	Carl Friedrich	butcher	Lueneburg	0760/035
EVERS	Heinrich August	businessman	Hamburg	0759/035
FRUEHLING	Itzig Rosalia	tailor --	Graetz	0902/042
GARLING	Friedrich --	shoemaker wife	Lohmen, Mk	1108/051
GERTZ	Josephine	--	Goldberg	1109/051
GOLDBERG	Christian	laborer	Niendorf	1110/051
HARMS	Charlotte	--	Uetersen, Ho	1384/062
HEINS	Maria	--	Krakow	1385/062
HEINS	Johann	cabinetmaker	Hagenow? [Hagenau?]	1386/062
HERSCH	Gumpel	tailor	Hinterslaw?	1383/062
IHDE	Friedrich	tailor	Uelitz	1570/071

List 56 (continued)

JAMNICK	Moritz	shoemaker	Muelerslaw	1569/071
KAEHLER	Johann	master forester	Geppersdorf	1854/083
	--	wife		
	--	3 children, 3/4- 10 y		
KNUTTEL	Wilhelm	laborer	Ruest	1857/084
KOCH	Friedrich	mill builder	Hagenow	1859/083
	--	wife		
	--	3 children, 4- 7-3/4 y		
KOSCHEMINSKY	Abraham	tailor	Mulerslaw	1855/083
KRAKOW	Wilhelm	shoemaker	Hagenow	1860/083
KRAKOW	Lisette?	--	Hagenow	1861/083
KRUSE	H.	tailor	Wamkow	1858/083
KUHLES	N? [M?] B.	plumber	Coburg	1856/083
LADIG	Friedrich	shepherd	Badresch	2117/095
LEMME	Ferdinand	soldier	Braunschweig	2118/095
LICHTENFELD	Israel	butcher	Dobrzin	2116/095
MAN	Joachim	laborer	Niendorf	2409/108
MICHAELS	August	tailor	Damwalde, Pr	2410/108
	--	wife		
	--	5 children, ¼-14 y		
NEUMANN	Friedrich	soapmaker	Hagenow	2577/115
NICKLAS	Johann	manager	Klein Pritz	2575/115
	--	wife		
	--	daughter, 2½ y		
NICKLAS	Wilhelm	shepherd	Klein Pritz	2576/115
NIEKEL	Friedrich	shepherd	Woeten, Mk	2578/115
PAULY	C. F.	mason	Lutschene	2752/124
REICH	Mathilde	--	Holstein	2976/134
REIMERS	J. J. D.	soldier	Schwartau	2977/134
RESCH	W.	tailor	Salgan	2975/134
RICHTER	Heinrich	mechanic	Posen	2979/134
ROESE	Christian	cabinetmaker	Kosbade?	2978/134
	--	wife		
	--	3 children, 4½- 7-3/4 y		

List 56 (continued)

SCHEWE	Mina	--	Langenheide	3431/153
SCHILLING	Carl	furrier	Hagenow	3432/153
	--	wife		
	--	son, 3/4 y		
SCHILLING	Gustav	--	Hagenow	3433/153
SCHLUNDT	Johann	wheelwright	Basedow	3421/153
	Doris	--		
SCHMIDT	G. G.	gardener	Delitz	3437/153
SCHRAMM	Christian	journeyman brick burner	Damwalde	3436/153
SCHROEDER	Carl	tailor	Schwerin	3434/153
SCHULTZ	Joachim	wheelwright	Kosbade	3426/153
	--	wife		
	--	4 children, 3-7-3/4 y		
SCHULTZ	Johann	wheelwright	Kosbade	3427/153
SCHULTZ	J. C.	laborer	Buelow	3428/153
SCHULZE	Friedrich	peasant	Rechenzien	3430/153
	Dorothea	wife		
	--	4 children, 11-21 y		
SCHUMACHER	C.	blacksmith	Brobergen	3425/153
SENEL	Joachim	wood turner	Uetersen	3422/153
	--	wife		
	--	8 children, 7½-24 y		
SENEL	Claus	--	Uetersen	3423/153
SILBERBERG	Nathan	furrier	Zduly	3420/153
SOHN	Georg	laborer	Wustertherofen, Mk	3438/153
	--	wife		
	--	6 children, 3-15 y		
STAMANN	Sophia	--	Ruest	3429/153
STAUDE	Heinrich	student	Goldberg	3424/153
STEIN	Anna	--	Woeten	3435/153
THORMANN	Friedrich	laborer	Dambeck	3681/164
TOPP	Johann	laborer	Bulow	3680/164
ULRICH	W. H.	businessman	Grimmen	3724/166
	H.	cabinetmaker		

List 56 (continued)

WALLENBERG	Johann	laborer	Rostock	3953/178
WANDSCHNEIDER	J.	manager	Darze	3955/178
WIESE	Wilhelm	--?	Hamburg	3954/178
	Johanna	daughter, 17 y		
	Simon	son, 14 y		
WOLFF	G. Th.	tailor	Neudam	3952/178
	Carolina	--		
	--	son, ½ y		
ZAEPERECK	Carolina	--	Hagenow	4059/182
ZERCK	Christian	laborer	Neuhof, Mk	4058/182
ZIEMANN	Friedrich	cabinetmaker	Damwalde? [Damwald?] Pr	4060/182

List 57

Ship *Sophie* (Hamburg flag) Captain Matthias Wilcken
Departing Hamburg 25 Apr 1850 for Port Adelaide & Melbourne (Direct)

AHRENS	F. W. A.	peasant	Grabow	0035/003
BAHLE? [BUHLE?]	Adolph	mason	Hamburg	0202/010
BAISELER	Christiane	--	Schmiegel	0203/010
BANDT	Louis	miller	Pomerania	0200/010
	Adelheit	--		
	Richard	--		
	Anna	--		
BERGMANN	Bertha	--	Neukirk, Pr	0205/010
BISSE	Georg	peasant	Gernschwald	0196/010
	Eva	--		
	Hans	--		
BISSE	Maria	--	Gernschwald	0197/010
	Elisabeth	--		
	Anna	--		
BLOCK	Carl Joachim	cabinetmaker	Hamburg	0201/010
BOHM	J. C.	shoemaker	Hamburg	0198/010
BOHNSACK	Johann J.	peasant	Neuhof, Mk	0204/010

48

BOSTELMANN	O. H.	coachman	Hamburg	0199/010
CLASOHM	Elisabeth	--	Schlagsdorf, Mk	0523/024
	Johann*	--		
	Joachim*	--		
		[*might be 1 person]		
CLASOHM	Joachim H.	--	Schlagsdorf, Mk	0522/024
CLASS	Eugen	peasant	Metzdorf	0521/024
COURVOISIER	Georg	--	Preilack	0520/024
DAMCKE	Anna	Frau	Bobersberg, Pr	0590/028
	Anna	child		
DAMCKE	Carl	shepherd	Bobersberg, Pr	0589/028
DEGNER	Johann	peasant	Wismar	0592/028
	Wilhelmine	--		
	Carl	child		
DOMANN	Martin	peasant	Dradhausen	0591/028
FIEDLER	Ernst	forester	Zittitz	0829/039
	Wilhelmine	--		
FIEDLER	Friedrich Ernst	child	Zittitz	0830/039
	Maria	child		
	Carl	child		
	Rudolph	child		
FROEDE	Georg	baker	Firschtiegel? [Tirschtiegel?]	0831/039
FUNCK	Georg	cabinetmaker	Hamburg	0832/039
GASSAU	J. G.	peasant	Tawnow? [Taurnow?]	1010/047
GASSAU	Maria	--?	Tawnow? [Taurnow?]	1011/047
	Elise	--		
	Friedrich	child		
GEBERT	Johann	peasant	Wismar	1013/047
	Elisabeth	--		
	--	4 children		
GERDTS	Johann	shoe repairman	Kiel	1008/047
	Friederike	--		
GERDTS	Carl	--	Kiel	1009/047
	Sophia	--		
	Friedrich	--		
	Johann	--		
GROCK	Elise	--	Preilacke	1007/047

List 57 (continued)

GROTH	Carl	businessman	Damshagen	1012/047
HAESELER	Dorothea S? [L?]	--	Hamburg	1244/057
HANNEMANN	Catherine Maria	-- child	Hamburg	1243/056
HARMSEN	H. A.	--	Oldenburg, Ol	1246/057
HIRDES*	Elisabeth	--	Cassel	1245/057
HIRDESS*	Johannes	cigarmaker [*so spelled]	Cassel	1238/056
HIRDESS	Amalia	--	Cassel	1239/056
HIRSCHBERG	Abraham	businessman	Nanau, Pr	1242/056
HOFFMANN	Carl	businessman	Brandenburg	1241/056
HOFFMANN	Johanna	--	Bilau	1237/056
HOFRICHTER	Joseph	mason	Kanth? [Kauth?]	1240/056
JAHNCKE	Ludwig	goatherd?	Zurow	1518/068
KLEES	Anna	--	Oldenburg, La	1677/076
KOCH	Friedrich	businessman	Drachtersen	1673/076
KOKEGEI	J. C. Maria Elisa- beth	shepherd --	Robersberg	1671/075
KOKEGEI	Johann Gott- lieb? Caroline Louise	-- --	Robersberg	1672/075
KREISLER	Wilhelm	peasant	Brilon, Pr	1675/076
KREISLER	S--? Laura Lina?	-- -- --	Brilon, Pr	1676/076
KURTZE	Oswald	businessman	Schwiebus	1674/076
MOUZON	C. F. G.	painter?	Berlin	2263/102
MUELLER	Johanna Bertha Clothilde	-- child child	Sommerfeld	2264/102
PETATZ	Martin Johann[a?]	peasant --	Tauer	2675/120
PETOW	Jacob	butcher	Luebecke	2676/121
PILZ	Emilia	--	Crossin, Pr	2680/121

50

PONDS	Heinrich	shoemaker	Hamburg	2677/121
	Wilhelmine	--		
PONDS	Johannes	child	Hamburg	2678/121
	Louise	child		
von PUTTKAMER	--	military	Kiel	2679/121
RACKOWSKY	Franz	shoemaker	Wien	2864/129
REINCKE	Carl	mason	Doberan, Mk	2866/129
	Maria	--		
REINHOLZ	Joachim	mason	Rostocke	2867/129
	Juliana	[wife?]		
	Franziska?	child		
	Juliana	child		
	Emma	child		
	Fritz	child		
	Hermann	child		
	Gustav	child		
RING	August	coppersmith	Schwerin	2865/129
ROTHER	Louise	--	Bilau	2861/129
	Hermann	child		
	August	child		
ROTHER	Carl	mason	Protschkenhayn	2862/129
	Carolina	--		
ROTHER	August	child	Protschkenhayn	2863/129
	Anna	child		
	Maria	child		
	Carl	child		
SCHILLER	Heinrich	butcher	Rostock	3181/143
SCHNEIDER	Carolina	--	Schmiegel	3180/143
	Paulina	--		
von SEE	Christian	blacksmith	Croeplin, Pr	3179/143
SEHER	Johanna	--	Bilau? [Bilaw?]	3178/142
TACKMANN	Joachim	laborer	Brilon	3639/162
	--	wife		
	--	child, ½ y		
WEGER	Ernst	blacksmith	Dresden	3828/171
WEHLACK	August	--	Bobersberg	3826/171
	Sophia	--		

List 57 (continued)

WEHLACK	Maria Doro- thea	--	Bobersberg	3827/171
	Maria Pauline	--		
	Johann Gottlob?	--		
WEISER	Louise Auguste	--	Dresden	3831/172
WENDT	H. L? [S?]	peasant	Rostock	3829/171
	Catharina	--		
	Louise	child		
WULFF	Peter Hein- rich	businessman	Neumuehlen, Ho	3830/172

List 58

Ship *Sankt Pauly*, Captain L. Eckmann
Departing Hamburg 26 Oct 1850 for Valdivia and Valparaiso (Direct)

ANDREAS	Hermann	physician	Braunschweig	0105/006
BANNHOLZER	Matthias	businessman	Stuttgart	0483/022
BJOERNSON	Friedrich August	tailor	Stockholm	0482/022
DECHER	Joseph	machinist	Speyer, Ba	0681/031
	--	wife		
	--	9 children, 2-26 y		
FOLTZ	Jacob	manager	Speyer, Ba	0954/044
HEINRICH	L.	manager	Berlin	1475/066
HERBST	Adolph	businessman	Luebeck	1476/066
HESPE	C. P.	shoemaker	Stockholm	1477/066
JETSCHMANN	F. W.	manager	Berlin	1592/071
KOESTER	Wilhelm	physician	Braunschweig	1955/087
LUNGERBECK	Julius	gold worker	Greifenhagen, Pr	2197/098
MEYER	Christian	businessman	Luebecke	2490/111
POHL	Johann Thomas	peasant	Radegast, Pr	2804/126
	--	wife		
	--	5 children, 3-19 y		
SAEDLINJ? [SOEDLING?]	E. E.	businessman	Stockholm	3585/160

52

SCHMIDT	Hermann	businessman	Luebeck	3586/160
SCHOEBITZ	Gottlieb	peasant	Maltsch an O[der]	3588/160
	--	wife	Pr	
	--	5 children, 5-22 y		
SCHULZ	August	book dealer	Breslau	3587/160
	--	wife		
	--	4 children, 5-19 y		
TEICHELMANN	F.	manager	Berlin	3705/165

List 59

Ship *Susanne*, Captain -- Amueller
Departing Hamburg 15 Aug 1850 for Valdivia (Direct)

ANSORGE	Carl Heinrich	master tailor	Hirschfelde	0079/005
BEUERLEIN	E.	lawyer	Rosenfeld	0412/019
BOHMWALD	C. G.	mason	Gr[oss] Schoenau	0410/019
	--	wife		
	--	3 children, 3½-8½ y		
BUCK	Fidel? [Eitel?]	peasant	Mengen	0411/019
	--	wife		
	--	son, 11 y		
DEMPFLIN	Carl	student	Laupheim	0655/030
DOELL	Ferdinand	businessman	Witzenhausen	0656/030
	Catharina	--		
FLUESTER	Julius	manager	Reichenau	0913/042
FRIEDRICH	C. G.	weaver	Gross Schoenau	0912/042
	--	wife		
	--	7 children, 11-27 y		
GERSTER	Paul	hunter	Haelzingen?	1122/051
GIESSEN	Carl	--?	Rumpenhain	1119/051
GOLDBERG	Christiane	--	Gross Schoenau	1120/051
	--	daughter, 5 y		
GRUENEWALD	Gottlieb?	weaver	Gross Schoenau	1121/051
	--	wife		
	--	2 children, 10 & 18 y		

List 59 (continued)

HAEBLER	Carl Gottlieb?	manufacturer	Gross Schoenau	1396/063
HAEBLER	C. Benjamin	weaver	Gross Schoenau	1397/063
HAENSCHEL	F. August	peasant	Witgensdorf	1398/063
HELT	Emilia	--	Glogau	1399/063
ISRAEL	C. B.	mason	Gross Schoenau	1574/071
	--	wife		
	--	child, 1-3/4 y		
KIESLING	Moritz	soldier	Johnsdorf	1877/084
KLOTZ	Martin	fisherman?	Trochtelfingen	1879/084
KOHLER	J. N.	cabinetmaker	Trochtelfingen	1878/084
KNOCHENHAUER	Carl	businessman	Cassel	1874/084
KOTHER	J. G.	tailor	Keibersdorf	1875/084
	--	wife		
	--	4 children, ¼-8½ y		
KRAUSE	Auguste	--	Gross Schoenau	1876/084
KRUG	Heinrich	peasant	Breslau	1880/084
LINCKE	Johann Friedrich	weaver	Gross Schoenau	2128/095
	Carl Gottlob	--		
LOCHER	Joseph	brewer	Betzgenweiler	2130/095
LORENZ	Ernst Gotthilf?	carpenter	Hirschfelda	2129/095
	--	son, 5 y		
MAETTIG	J. F.	weaver	Gross Schoenau	2424/109
	--	wife		
	--	2 children, 2 & 5 y		
MUELLER	Johann Gottlob	welldigger?	Gross Schoenau	2423/109
von MUSCHGAY	C. Otto	forester	Zwiefalten	2425/109
NEUMANN	Julius	blacksmith	Ostnitz	2584/115
NEUMANN	C. G.	carpenter	Bertsdorf	2585/115
	--	wife		
	--	child, 1½ y		
RIEDEL	Julius	farmer	Pfuhl	2985/134
SCHILLING	Carl	businessman	Cassel	3451/154
SCHLEGEL	Hermann	needle maker?	Glogau	3454/154

List 59 (continued)

SCHMID	Joseph	weaver	Trachtelfingen	3453/154
STAEHLE	Anton	miller	Grossenzugen?	3452/154
WAENTIG	Carl Gottlieb	weaver	Gross Schoenau	3961/178
WAHL	Anton	wagoner	Zwiefalten	3964/178
WEDEKIND	August	businessman	Hammeln	3965/178
WEDER	Johann Fried-rich	miller	Ruppersdorf	3961/178
WEIDELINER	Jacob	carpenter	Betzgenweiler? [Betzgenweiter?]	3963/178
WINKEL	Carl	businessman	Cassel	3960/178
ZEIDLER	J. G.	weaver	Gross Schoenau	4063/182
	--	wife		
	--	child, 1½ months		
ZEIDLER	Johann Gott-lieb?	weaver	Gross Schoenau	4064/182
	Johanna? Chris-tine	wife		

List 60

Ship *Veitis (Vectis)* Captain W. Tase
Departing Hamburg 15 Jun 1850 for Quebec (Direct)

BERNER	Carl	miller	Edena	0323/015
BESE	Carl	mason	Krackow	0324/015
	--	wife		
	--	4 children, 3/4-7¼ y		
BOBZIEN	Heinrich	laborer	Beutz	0321/015
	--	wife		
	--	son, 3½ y		
BOCKHOLT	C. H.	--?	Charlottenthal	0322/015
BULL	Hans	--	Schwerin	0325/015
EEDING	E. V. W.	soldier	Copenhagen	0737/035
FRAEDERICH	Joachim	--	Kreien	0878/041

List 60 (continued)

FREUCK	Friedrich	peasant	Altsammt	0875/041
FREUDE	August	cabinetmaker	Parchim	0876/041
FREUDE	August	4 y	Parchim	0877/041
	Lisette	¼ y		
GLAEVCKE	Gustav	peasant	Ahrenhagen	1070/049
HABERKORN	Catharine	--	Mitterteich, Ba	1334/060
HAMEISTER	C. F. T. M.	manager	Gerdeshagen	1333/060
HOFFMANN	Friederike	--	Kelbra	1335/060
JAHR	Ernst	--	Helberungen, Th	1553/070
JOHN	J. H.	peasant	Elxleben	1552/070
KOSSEL	Ludwig	tailor	Charlottenthal	1793/081
	--	wife		
	--	2 children, 3/4- 7-3/4 y		
PABST	Johann Chris- tian?	manager	Straussfurth, Bd	2730/123
PROTSCHKI	Andreas	miller	Mitterteich	2731/123
RABE	Albert	businessman	Bucha	2937/132
RETHWISCH	W.	blacksmith	Parchim	2936/132
SEIDEL	Christian	shoemaker	Berlin	3343/149
	--	wife		
	--	2 children, 1 & 15 y		
SEIDEL	Ernst Alex- ander	--	Berlin	3344/149
SOLLEMANN	Henriette	--	Parchim	3342/149
THALACKER	E. A.	manager	Andisleben	3664/163
	--	wife		
	--	4 children, 1-7½ y		
TRAEGERIN*	Magdalene	--	Fuchsmuehle	3665/163
		[*surname may be TRAEGER]		

SURNAME INDEX
By Ship-List Number

INDEX TO BIRTHPLACES

This is a partial index. The geographical notes herein will be of assistance to researchers.

German and Central European Emigration
Monograph Number 1, Part 4

RECONSTRUCTED PASSENGER LISTS FOR 1850:

HAMBURG TO AUSTRALIA, BRAZIL, CANADA, CHILE,

AND THE UNITED STATES

Part 4: Supplemental Notes on Emigrants' Places of Origin

Clifford Neal Smith

Reprint, 1983
Reprint, 1984
 Reprint, April 1991   qz

INTRODUCTION

Analysis of the entries in the Hamburg police records discloses that emigrants came from about 1,750 places of origin in central Europe. These geographic locations are indexed herein with notes as to latitude and longitude, thus making it possible for researchers readily to find them on detailed maps of the region. Unfortunately, however, the Hamburg officials were frequently imprecise as to which of several villages of the same name the emigrants came; when lucky, researchers have only the kingdom, province, or region as clues. As a consequence, these notes list all occurrences of the village name throughout Germany, Poland, and Czechoslovakia on modern maps. The official standard names approved by the U.S. Board on Geographic Names have been used;[1] many of the spellings are slightly different from those which were used in the 1850 Hamburg records. In addition, the valuable work by Fritz Verdenhalven on the name changes for former Prussian communities[2] has been consulted. Meyer's *Lexikon*[3] has not been used herein (because latitude and longitude are not given therein), but it should be consulted to determine the emigrants' likely religious affiliation and the *Kreisverwaltung*[4] to which the village belonged. The purpose of listing all occurrences of a village name throughout Germany, Poland, and Czechoslovakia is to make certain the researcher checks all the possibilities when searching for linking church and civil records. With some frequency, however, the number of villages and farms is too great for listing, in which case the researcher is told how many occurrences there are in the U.S. geographic lists (see under BERG, for example). The names of "farms" (estates) have also been listed, because many of these estates belonged to nobles who may still have maintained ancillary governmental records in 1850.

How, then, is the researcher to determine which of a number of villages of the same name is the place of origin of the listed emigrant? In many cases the question can only be resolved by laboriously checking the records of each village; in other cases there may be outside clues--an old passport handed down among descendants; the evidence of a naturalization in the New World giving the kingdom from whence the immigrant came;[5] the immigrant's religious affiliation;[6] or family traditions which otherwise identify the village.[7] Most importantly, the researcher should attempt to determine whether the emigrant traveled aboard ship with others from the same region, a common practice. By determining that the voyagers came from neighboring villages the researcher is most likely to establish not only geographic locality but also the circles of friends and relatives forming the nuclei of new settlements and religious congregations in the New World.

A glance at the map of Germany will make apparent the fact that most emigrants through the port of Hamburg would have been from eastern and central Germany, Poland, and Czechoslovakia, Austria, and Hungary; emigrants through the port of Bremen-Bremerhaven would have been from western and southwestern Germany and Switzerland. This rule of thumb is not iron-clad, of course, as some larger groups of emigrants leased ships sailing from other ports. As a consequence, the geographic location of villages has been listed herein in the following order: (1) those of modern East Germany (DDR); (2) those of Polish-occupied Germany and Poland; and (3) those of West Germany (BRD).

Most of the West German emigrants through the port of Hamburg were probably from the neighboring (modern) states of Niedersachsen and Schleswig-Holstein.

There are a few place names in the following index in which the monograph on "Old Lutheran" emigrants has been cited.[8] However, many more place names are listed in that monograph, and it should be consulted automatically for all emigrants because an unknown number of the emigrants of 1850 were probably of this religious persuasion. In this manner the Hamburg police records can be compared with religious and civil records in areas for which access is currently difficult.

Explanation of the Entries

```
KLEIN TREPPOW, Mecklenburg,   2
  1.  53-18N, 13-05E, Klein Trebbow, Neubrandenburg,
                                     DDR
  2.  53-42N, 11-23E, Klein Trebbow, Schwerin, DDR
```

The name of the village in the above example is given as it appears in the Hamburg police records. Following the village name is shown the monograph part in which the name appears--1, 2, or 3. Researchers should refer to the indexes to each monograph part to determine the ship list in which the place name is given. Thereafter, are shown the latitudes and longitudes of two villages of this or similar names. In this case the modern spelling appears to have changed slightly from that given in the Hamburg record of 1850. Since the Hamburg record specifies Mecklenburg, the first choice for investigation would be the village in Schwerin (number 2 above). Meyer's *Lexikon* will give the *Kreis* name as of 1912, which probably is the same as it was in 1850, and possibly the parish name as well. Thereafter, the researcher will find it useful to enter the catalog of the Genealogical Society of Utah--either via the microfilms available in stake libraries of the Church of Jesus Christ of Latter Day Saints (the Mormons) or in the printed volume by Ronald Smelser.[9] In either event the researcher will be able to determine whether there is a relevant microfilm of the village church register by entering under the *modern* political designation, in this example, Schwerin. Although the village itself may not be listed, the parish record, under another name,[10] may have been microfilmed.

Abbreviations Used in the Entries

DDR (Deutsche Demokratische Republik) is the designation used herein for the post-1945 area known as East Germany. The modern *Regierungsbezirke* [governmental districts] of the DDR are as follows:

East Berlin	Potsdam	Suhl
Rostock	Frankfurt/Oder	Gera
Schwerin	Halle	Leipzig
Neubrandenburg	Cottbus	Dresden
Magdeburg	Erfurt	Karl-Marx-Stadt

Polish-occupied Germany, meaning Pomerania, Upper and Lower Silesia, is the area east of the Oder River which belonged to Germany from 1919 to 1945.

Poland includes much of what in 1850 was known as West and East Prussia, part of which was called Province Posen.

1

2

BRD (Bundesrepublik Deutschland) is the designation used herein for the post-1945 area known as West Germany. The modern states of West Germany are:

Schleswig-Holstein	Baden-Wuerttemberg
Niedersachsen	Bavaria (Bayern)
Nordrhein-Westfalen	Hamburg
Hessen	Bremen
Rheinland-Pfalz	West Berlin
Saar	

1. U.S. Department of the Interior. Office of Geography. *[Gazetteer for the] Deutsche Demokratische Republik; [Gazetteer for] Poland; [Gazetteer for the] Bundesrepublik Deutschland; [Gazetteer for] Czechoslovakia.* All published in Washington, D.C. by the Government Printing Office, 1955-1960.

2. Fritz Verdenhalven, *Namensaenderungen ehemals preussischer Gemeinden von 1850 bis 1942* (Neustadt/Aisch, Bavaria: Verlag Degener, 1971).

3. *Meyers Orts- und Verkehrs-Lexikon des Deutschen Reichs.* Fifth edition (Leipzig & Wien: Bibliographisches Institut, 1912) in 4 volumes.

4. The *Kreisverwaltung* roughly corresponds to county-level governmental organization in the United States. Records are most likely to contain the details of individual migration. *See also* Clifford Neal Smith, *American Genealogical Resources in German Archives* (Munich: Verlag Dokumentation; available in the United States through R. R. Bowker Co., 1977).

5. American naturalization records, to be found among county court records before 1906, usually list only the kingdom, whereas the corresponding Hamburg record is likely to list only the village of origin.

6. Most villages supported only one church, either Catholic or Lutheran and Reformed, so that by knowing the religious affiliation of the emigrant one can usually eliminate villages having churches of the opposite persuasion. This observation does not hold for the larger towns and cities which had churches of both sects.

7. Some useful clues might be traditions that the village was near a river; had a castle on the hill; belonged to a known noble family; spoke a certain dialect; men of the village fought in such-and-such army and war.

8. Clifford Neal Smith, *Nineteenth-Century Emigration of "Old Lutherans" from Eastern Germany (Mainly Pomerania and Lower Silesia) to Australia, Canada, and the United States.* German-American Genealogical Research Monograph Number 7 (McNeal, AZ: Westland Publications, 1980).

9. Ronald Smelser, Thomas Dullien, and Heribert Hinrichs, *Preliminary Survey of the German Collection.* Finding Aids to the Microfilmed Manuscript Collection of the Genealogical Society of Utah, Number 2 (Salt Lake City, Utah: University of Utah Press, 1979).

10. Maralyn A. Wellauer, 3239 North 58th Street, Milwaukee, Wisconsin 53216, has compiled several lists of Evangelical (Lutheran) congregations in East Germany and Poland as they existed before World War I. They should be consulted by the researcher to determine which parish a given village belonged.

AALESUND, 1
Community in Norway

ABBENDRODE, 1 [probably Abbenrode]
1. 51° 55' N, 10° 37' E, Magdeburg, DDR
2. 52° 15' N, 10° 44' E, Niedersachsen, BRD

ABENDORF, 2 [probably Abbendorf]
1. 52° 45' N, 10° 55' E, Magdeburg, DDR
2. 52° 54' N, 11° 54' E, Schwerin, DDR
3. 52° 50' N, 10° 42' E, Niedersachsen, BRD
4. 53° 12' N, 9° 23' E, Niedersachsen, BRD

ADELEBSEN, 1
1. 51° 35' N, 9° 45' E, Niedersachsen, BRD

ADELSDORF, 1
1. 51° 19' N, 13° 35' E, now Dorf der Jugend, Dresden, DDR
2. 49° 29' N, 10° 41' E, Bavaria, BRD
3. 49° 43' N, 10° 54' E, Bavaria, BRD

AETIGEN, Switzerland, 1

AHLE, 1
1. 52° 06' N, 7° 03' E, Nordrhein-Westfalen, BRD
2. 52° 12' N, 8° 31' E, Nordrhein-Westfalen, BRD

AHLFELD, 3 [probably Ahlefeld]
1. 51° 00' N, 7° 33' E, Nordrhein-Westfalen, BRD
2. 54° 24' N, 9° 40' E, Schleswig-Holstein, BRD

AHRENDSEE, Thuringia, 1
1. 54° 13' N, 13° 08' E, Rostock, DDR

AHRENHAGEN, 3 [probably Ahrenshagen]
1. 53° 41' N, 12° 19' E, Shwerin, DDR
2. 54° 15' N, 12° 36' E, Rostock, DDR

AHRENSFELDE, 1
1. 52° 35' N, 13° 35' E, Frankfurt/Oder, DDR
2. 53° 39' N, 10° 15' E, Schleswig-Holstein, BRD
3. 53° 46' N, 10° 30' E, Schleswig-Holstein, BRD

AIDHAUSEN, 2
1. 50° 09' N, 10° 26' E, Bavaria, BRD

ALBANY AM SEE, 1
Not found

ALBERG, 3 [probably Ahlberg]
1. 51° 27' N, 9° 31' E, Hessen, BRD

ALBERTSDORF, 2
1. 54° 07' N, 12° 14' E, Rostock, DDR
2. 54° 26' N, 11° 06' E, Schleswig-Holstein, BRD

ALDORF, 2, 3
1. 52° 44'N, 08° 30' E, Niedersachsen, BRD

ALLSTEDT, 2
1. 51° 24' N, 11° 23' E, Halle, DDR
2. 52° 08' N, 06° 55' E, Alstaette, Nordrhein-Westfalen, BRD
3. 52° 17' N, 07° 46' E, Alstedde, Nordrhein-Westfalen, BRD

ALSHOFF, 2
A village of this name not found; a farm by this name at 51° 04' N, 06° 42' E, Nordrhein-Westfalen, BRD. Another farm, listed by Meyer's *Lexikon*, in Kreis Reuss, Frixheim-Anstel [not found].

ALT BATKOP
Not found.

ALTBRANDENBURG, 3
1. 52° 25' N, 12° 33' E, City of Brandenburg, Potsdam, DDR
2. There is a forest called Altstadt-Brandenburger Forst.

ALTDORF, 3
1. 51° 03' N, 12° 41' E, Leipzig, DDR
2. 47° 49' N, 10° 38' E, Bavaria, BDR
3. 48° 06' N, 07° 53' E, Baden-Wuerttemberg, BDR
4. 48° 16' N, 07° 49' E, Baden-Wuerttemberg, BDR
5. 48° 09' N, 12° 11' E, Bavaria, BDR
6. 48° 34' N, 12° 07' E, Bavaria, BDR
7. 48° 35' N, 09° 16' E, Baden-Wuerttemberg, BDR
8. 48° 38' N, 09° 00' E, Baden-Wuerttemberg, BDR
9. 48° 59' N, 11° 17' E, Bavaria, BDR
10. 49° 17' N, 08° 13' E, Rheinland-Pfalz, BDR
11. 49° 21' N, 09° 37' E, Baden-Wuerttemberg, BDR
12. 49° 23' N, 11° 21' E, Bavaria, BDR
13. 50° 53' N, 06° 22' E, Nordrhein-Westfalen, BDR
14. 54° 14' N, 10° 54' E, Schleswig-Holstein, BDR

ALTENBURG, 1, 2, 3
1. 50° 59' N, 12° 27' E, Leipzig, DDR
2. 51° 09' N, 11° 46' E, Halle, DDR
3. 51° 49' N, 11° 45' E, Halle, DDR
In the BRD there are at least 15 villages, hills, and farms of this name, plus many more at ALTENBERG.

ALTENKUNDSTADT, 2 [correctly spelled ALTENKUNSTADT]
1. 50° 08' N, 11° 15' E, Bavaria, BRD

ALTENLATOW, Prussia, 2
Not found. Might be Altenplathow at 52° 25' N, 12° 09' E, Magdeburg, DDR

ALTENLOHM, 1 [Polish = Lislau]
Village in Silesia, Liegnitz administrative region, Kreis Goldberg-Haynau; village coordinates not found:
Goldberg 51° 07' N, 15° 55' E, Polish-occupied Germany
Haynau 51° 16' N, 15° 56' E, Polish-occupied Germany

ALTFRACKNICK, Prussia, 2
Not found

ALTHAGEN, 2
1. 54° 22' N, 12° 25' E, Rostock, DDR

ALTHOFF, 2
1. 54° 05' N, 11° 56' E, Rostock, DDR
2. 53° 57' N, 20° 26' E, Althof, now called Stary Dwor, Poland
3. 49° 41' N, 07° 53' E, Rheinland-Pfalz, BRD
4. In the BRD there are eight farms of this name.

ALT HUETTE, 1
1. 54° 13' N, 18° 17' E, now called Stara Huta, Poland
2. 47° 47' N, 08° 09' E, Baden-Wuerttemberg, BRD
3. 48° 55' N, 09° 34' E, Baden-Wuerttemberg, BRD
4. 48° 57' N, 13° 19' E, Bavaria, BRD
5. 48° 59' N, 13° 17' E, Bavaria, BRD
6. 49° 03' N, 13° 11' E, Bavaria, BRD
7. 49° 20' N, 12° 46' E, Bavaria, BRD

ALTONA, 1, 2, 3
1. 53° 33' N, 09° 56' E, Now a part of Hamburg
In the BRD there are also numerous farms of this
name, for which Meyer's *Lexikon*.

ALTSAMMT, 3 [probably ALT SAMMIT or ALT SAMITZ]
1. 53° 39' N, 12° 13' E, Schwerin, DDR

ALTSHEIM, 1
Not found.

ALTSTADT, 3
In the DDR there are four villages of this name.
In Polish-occupied Germany and Poland there are
three villages of this name.
In the BRD there are seven villages of this name.

ALT STRELITZ, 2
1. 53° 20' N, 13° 06' E, City of Strelitz, Neubrandenburg, DDR

AMTOIA, 2 [probably Amt Hoya is meant]
1. 52° 48' N, 09° 09' E, Niedersachsen, BRD

ANDENHAUSEN, Bavaria, 2
1. 50° 40' N, 10° 04' E, Suhl, DDR

ANDISLEBEN, 3
1. 51° 05' N, 10° 55' E, Erfurt, DDR

ANDORF, Holstein
1. 52° 51' N, 11° 00' E, Magdeburg, DDR
2. 48° 32' N, 11° 51' E, Bavaria, BRD
3. 49° 25' N, 10° 37' E, Bavaria, BRD
4. 52° 40' n, 07° 49' E, Niedersachsen, BRD
[Of the four villages described, #4 appears the
most likely.]

ANGSTEDT, Schwarzburg-Rudolstadt, 2
1. 50° 42' N, 11° 01' E, also called Angstedt am
Ilm; postal address was
Graefinau/Ilm

ANKER, AUKER, Lauenburg, 2
1. 51° 22' N, 10° 11' E, a farm in Erfurt, DDR
2. 53° 55' N, 19° 37' E, now Wielki Dwor, Poland
3. 47° 46' N, 12° 10' E, Bavaria, BRD
4. 48° 32' N, 08° 24' E, Baden-Wuerttemberg, BRD
5. 53° 41' N, 10° 38' E, Schleswig-Holstein, BRD
[Of the five villages described, #5 appears the
most likely.]

ANKUM, Oldenburg, 1
1. 52° 33' N, 07° 53' E, Niedersachsen, BRD

ANNABERG, Saxony, 1, 2
1. 50° 34' N, 13° 00' E, Annaberg-Buchholz, Karl-
Marx-Stadt, DDR
2. 49° 56' N, 18° 18' E, Polish-occupied Germany
3. 50° 28' N, 18° 10' E, Sankt Annaberg, Polish-
occupied Germany

ANSBACH, 2
1. 49° 18' N, 10° 35' E, Bavaria, BRD
2. 49° 55' N, 09° 37' E, Bavaria, BRD

APENRADE, 2, 3
1. 51° 34' N, 10° 44' E, Erfurt, DDR
2. 50° 45' N, 09° 03' E, Appenrod, Hessen, BRD

APOLDA, 1
1. 51° 01' N, 11° 30' E, Erfurt, DDR

APPELHAGEN, 1
1. 53° 49' N, 12° 32' E, Neubrandenburg, DDR

ARENDSHAUSEN, 3 [probably ARENSHAUSEN]
1. `51° 23' N, 09° 58' E, Erfurt, DDR

ARNDORF, 2 [probably ARNSDORF]
1. In the DDR there are eight villages of this
name.
2. In Polish-occupied Germany and Poland there are
two villages of this name.
3. In the BRD there are three villages, spelled
ARNDORF, all in Bavaria.

ARNSGRUEN, 2
1. 50° 19' N, 12° 14' E, Karl-Marx Stadt, DDR
2. 50° 35' N, 12° 04' E, Gera, DDR

ARNSTADT, 2, 3
1. 50° 50' N, 10° 57' E, Erfurt, DDR
2. 51° 41' N, 11° 30' E, Arnstedt, Halle, DDR

AROLDSEN, 1 [probably AROLSEN]
1. 51° 22' N, 09° 01' E

ASSEL AM STADE, KEDINGEN, 1
1. 53° 41' N, 09° 26' E, Niedersachsen, BRD
[formerly Stade administration region, Kreis
Kedingen, Hannover]

ASTADKARGET, 1
In Norway?

ASTRONOW, Prussia, 2
Not found

AUMA, Saxony-Weimar, 1
1. 50° 42' N, 11° 56' E, Gera, DDR

AUSSIG, 2
1. 51° 24' N, 13° 11' E, Leipzig, DDR

BABITZ, 3
1. 53° 10' N, 12° 32' E, Potsdam, DDR

BACKHORST, Holstein, 3 [probably BOCKHORST]
1. 52° 05' N, 08 12' E, Nordrhein-Westfalen, BRD
2. 52° 14' N, 08° 47' E, Nordrhein-Westfalen, BRD
3. 53° 02' N, 07° 35' E, Niedersachsen, BRD
4. 53° 04' N, 09° 02' E, Niedersachsen, BRD
5. 53° 21' N, 09° 34' E, Niedersachsen, BRD

BADENHAUSEN, 3
1. 51° 48' N, 10° 13' E, Niedersachsen, BRD

BADRESCH, 3
1. 53° 33' N, 13° 37' E, Neubrandenburg, DDR

BAELINGEN, 2 [possibly Belingen]
1. 49° 59' N, 06° 56' E, Rheinland-Pfalz, BRD

BAERENRIETH, Bavaria, 1
1. 47° 40 N, 09° 41' E, Bernried, Baden-Wuerttemberg, BRD
2. 47° 52' N, 11° 18' E, Bavaria, BRD
3. 48° 55' N, 12° 53' E, Bavaria, BRD
4. 49° 19' N, 12° 33' E, Bavaria, BRD
5. 49° 34' N, 12° 17' E, Bernrieth, Bavaria, BRD
6. 48° 42' N, 13° 34' E, Baernreuth, Bavaria, BRD
7. 48° 51' N, 13° 18' E, Baernreuth, Bavaria, BRD

BAERENRIETH, Bavaria [continued]
8. 49-52N, 11-29E, Baernreuth, Bavaria, BRD
9. 50-03N, 11-41E, Baernreuth, Bavaria, BRD

BAERWALDE, 3 [probably Beerwalde]
1. 50-53N, 12-14E, Liepzig, DDR
2. 51-03N, 12-59E, Karl-Marx-Stadt, DDR
3. 50-34N, 12-32E, Baerenwalde, Karl-Marx-Stadt, DDR
4. 54-12N, 12-47E, Behrenwalde, Rostock, DDR
5. See also Beerwalde

BAGNOLS, France, 2

BAIERSDORF, 2
1. 48-58N, 11-45E, Bavaria, BRD
2. 49-40N, 11-02E, Bavaria, BRD
3. 50-06N, 11-16E, Bavaria, BRD

BALINGEN, 1
1. 48-17N, 08-51E, Baden-Wuerttemberg, BRD

BALLAM, BALLUM, 1
1. There was a Ballum, Schleswig-Holstein, Kreis Tondern (coordinates not shown)
2. 53-27N, 13-26E, Ballin, Neubrandenburg, DDR
3. 50-11N, 19-23E, Balin, Poland
4. 51-56N, 18-49E, Balin, Poland
5. 53-03N, 19-23E, Balin, Poland

BALLENSTAEDT, 2
1. 51-43N, 11-14E, Halle, DDR

BALLINGEN, 2
Not found. Might now be Bałąg, Poland, at 53-50N, 20-14E.

BALTENHAGEN, 2
Not found.

BALTIMORE, 2
No doubt, Baltimore, Maryland, is meant.

BANROW, Mecklenburg, 1
Not found. There is a Bansow, 53-43N, 12-22E, Schwerin, DDR

BARBECKE, 1
1. 52-11N, 10-17E, Niedersachsen, BRD

BARCKOW, 2
1. 53-42N, 13-11E, Neubrandenburg, DDR
2. 52-31N, 21-39E, Barchow, Poland
3. 54-18N, 22-12E, Barukau, now Barkowo, Poland

BARECK, 2
Not found.

BARINGAU, Thuringia, 2 [probably Barigau]
1. 50-38N, 11-06E, Gera, DDR

BARINGEN, 2
Not found. In East Prussia the village of Bareisch-kehmen was renamed Baringen in 1938; it might have been called Baringen by 1850. This town was in Kreis Ebenrode, formerly called Stallupoenen.

BARMBECK BEI HAMBURG, 1
1. 53-35N, 10-03E, Now part of City of Hamburg

BARMEN, 1
1. 50-57N, 06-18E, Nordrhein-Westfalen, BRD
2. 51-17N, 07-13E, Nordrhein-Westfalen, BRD

BARNINGEN, 2
Not found.

BARONOW, 1
Not found. There was the following:
(a) Baronen, Kreis Crossen, Posen administrative district. Now Polish-occupied Germany.
(b) Baronie, Kreis Militsch (now Strebizko)
(c) Baronie, Kreis Rubnik (now Czuchow)

BARTELSDORF, 2
1. 53-08N, 09-29E, Niedersachsen, BRD
2. 53-29N, 10-32E, Schleswig-Holstein, BRD

BARTENHAUSEN, 1
1. 54-06N, 11-58E, Rostock, DDR

BARETENSTEIN, 2
1. 49-21N, 09-53E, Baden-Wuerttemberg, BRD

BASEDOW, 3
1. 53-20N, 13-48E, Neubrandenburg, DDR
2. 53-42N, 12-41E, Neubrandenburg, DDR
3. 53-25N, 10-35E, Schleswig-Holstein, BRD

BASSOW, 2
1. 53-37N, 13-27E, Neubrandenburg, DDR

BAUTZEN, Saxony, 1, 2
1. 51-11N, 14-26E, Dresden, DDR

BAYERSDORF, 1
Not found. Possibly Beiersdorf, of which eight villages in DDR; also Baiersdorf, of which 3 villages in BRD.

BECKADEL, 2
Not found.

BEERWALDE, 3
1. 50-53N, 12-14E, Leipzig, DDR
2. 51-03N, 12-59E, Karl-Marx-Stadt, DDR
See also Baerwalde

BEIERSBERG, 2
Not found. There was a domain called Beyerberg, near Wassertruedingen, Franconia, Bavaria, BRD.

BEILWITZ, 1
Not found.

BELGARD, 2
1. 54-00N, 16-00E, Polish-occupied Germany
2. 54-40N, 17-39E, Polish-occupied Germany

BELITZ, Prussia, 1
1. 53-54N, 12-30E, Neubrandenburg, DDR
2. 53-00N, 11-04E, Niedersachsen, BRD

BELOW, 2
1. 53-16N, 12-28E, Neubrandenburg, DDR
2. 53-18N, 13-01E, Neubrandenburg, DDR
3. 53-37N, 11-59E, Schwerin, DDR

BENDINGERSBASTEL? 3 [probably Bendingbostel]
1. 52-57N, 09-25E, Niedersachsen, BRD

BENEWITZ, Thuringia, 3 [correctly Bennewitz]
1. 51-07N, 12-16E, Leipzig, DDR
2. 51-11N, 13-02E, Leipzig, DDR
3. 51-22N, 12-43E, Leipzig, DDR
4. 51-26N, 12-06E, Halle, DDR
5. 51-31N, 13-02E, Leipzig, DDR
Also two villages spelled Binnewitz.

BENNDORF, BENNSDORF, 1
1. 51-04N, 12-32E, Leipzig, DDR
2. 51-08N, 11-38E, Halle, DDR
3. 51-18N, 11-53E, Halle, DDR
4. 51-33N, 12-20E, Leipzig, DDR
5. 51-34N, 11-29E, Halle, DDR

BENTWISCH, 1
1. 54-07N, 12-12E, Rostock, DDR
2. 53-45N, 09-10E, Niedersachsen, BRD

BENTZIN, 2
1. 53-57N, 13-17E, Neubrandenburg, DDR
2. 52-50N, 09-34E, Benzen, Niedersachsen, BRD

BERG, Mecklenburg, 1, 2
1. 51-27N, 12-37E, Leipzig, DDR
2. 51-33N, 14-43E, Cottbus, DDR
3. 52-51N, 13-31E, Frankfurt/Oder, DDR
4. 53-06N, 13-37E, Neubrandenburg, DDR
There are also over 85 villages of this name in BRD.

BERGEDORF, 3
1. 53-05N, 08-28E, Niedersachsen, BRD
2. 53-13N, 08-57E, Niedersachsen, BRD
3. 53-29N, 10-14E, Hamburg suburb, BRD

BERGEN, 2
1. 50-20N, 12-12E, Karl-Marx-Stadt, DDR
2. 50-28N, 12-17E, Karl-Marx-Stadt, DDR
3. 51-28N, 14-15E, Cottbus, DDR
4. 51-46N, 13-45E, Cottbus, DDR
5. 52-06N, 11-22E, Magdeburg, DDR
6. 54-25N, 13-26E, Rostock, DDR
There are an additional 12 villages of this name in
the BRD.

BERKA, 2
1. 50-57N, 10-05E, Erfurt, DDR
2. 51-03N, 10-23E, Erfurt, DDR
3. 51-21N, 10-56E, Erfurt, DDR
4. 51-41N, 10-07E, Niedersachsen, BRD

BERLIN, 1, 2, 3
1. 52-31N, 13-24E, City of Berlin, DDR & BRD
2. 54-02N, 10-27E, Schleswig-Holstein, BRD

BERTELSDORF, BERTHELSDORF, 1, 3
1. 50-46N, 12-30E, Karl-Marx-Stadt, DDR
2. 50-52N, 13-22E, Karl-Marx-Stadt, DDR
3. 50-52N, 13-50E, Dresden, DDR
4. 50-57N, 12-48E, Karl-Marx-Stadt, DDR
5. 50-57N, 13-07E, Karl-Marx-Stadt, DDR
6. 51-01N, 14-45E, Dresden, DDR
7. 51-03N, 14-13E, Dresden, DDR
8. 49-23N, 10-59E, Bavaria, BRD
9. 50-17N, 10-58E, Bavaria, BRD

BERTSDORF, 3
1. 50-53N, 14-44E, Dresden, DDR

BETZENWEILER, 3 [probably BETZENWEILER]
1. 48-07N, 09-34E, Baden-Wuerttemberg, BRD

BEUTHEN, Prussia, 1 [Polish = BYTOM]
1. 50-21N, 18-58E, Polish-occupied Germany
2. 51-44N, 15-50E, Polish-occupied Germany

BEUTZ, 3
Not found. Possibly Beutzen, Landkreis Celle,
Niedersachsen, BRD

BEVENSDORF, 1
Not found.

BEVENSEN, Prussia, 2
1. 52-37N, 09-29E, Niedersachsen, BRD
2. 53-05N, 10-35E, Niedersachsen, BRD

BEVERANGEN, BEVERUNGEN, 2 [probably BEVERINGEN]
1. 53-09N, 12-13E, Potsdam, DDR
2. 51-40N, 09-22E, Nordrhein-Westfalen, BRD

BAYERSDORF, 2
1. 51-36N, 12-11E, Halle, DDR
2. 52-45N, 15-06E, Polish-occupied Germany

BICKENBACH, 3
1. 49-45N, 08-37E, Hessen, BRD
2. 50-07N, 07-32E, Rheinland-Pfalz, BRD
3. 51-00N, 07-26E, Nordrhein-Westfalen, BRD

BIEBER, Hessen-Cassel, 1
1. 50-05N, 08-48E, Hessen, BRD
2. 50-09N, 09-19E, Hessen, BRD
3. 50-38N, 08-35E, Hessen, BRD

BIES, Holstein, 1
Not found. There was a farm called Bies in Landkreis Duesseldorf (near Hasselbeck-Krumbach), Nordrhein-Westfalen, BRD

BILAU, BILAW, 3 [possibly Biehla]
1. 51-19N, 14-06E, Dresden, DDR
2. 51-28N, 13-30E, Cottbus, DDR
3. 53-17N, 20-27E, Billau (Polish=Zbyluty) Poland
There was also a village called Langenbielau in
Lower Silesia (Polish=Bielawa).

BINDE, 1
1. 52-51N, 11-23E, Magdeburg, DDR

BINNLAU, 1 [possibly Binau]
1. 49-22N, 09-03E, Baden-Wuerttemberg, BRD

BIRCKICHT, 2
1. 50-17N, 11-07E, Birkig, Bavaria, BRD.
2. 50-17N, 11-19E, Birkach, Bavaria, BRD
Might also be Birkigt, of which four villages in
the DDR.

BIRNBAUM, 2, 3
1. 50-51N, 10-44E, Erfurt, DDR
2. 47-39N, 10-50E, Bavaria, BRD
3. 48-07N, 12-42E, Bavaria, BRD
4. 49-38N, 10-43E, Bavaria, BRD
5. 50-20N, 11-26E, Bavaria, BRD

BISCHOFSWERDER, 2 [probably BISCHOFSWERDA]
1. 51-07N, 14-11E, Dresden, DDR
There was also a farm called Bischofswerder at
52-54N, 13-23E, Potsdam, DDR

BISPERODE, 2
1. 52-05N, 09-30E, Niedersachsen, BRD

BISSENDORF, 1
1. 52-14N, 08-10E, Niedersachsen, BRD
2. 52-31N, 09-46E, Niedersachsen, BRD

BITAN, BITOW, 1
Not found

BITTERFELD, 2
1. 51-37N, 12-19E, Halle, DDR

BITZFLETH, 2 [probably BUETZFLETH]
1. 53-40N, 09-29E, Niedersachsen, BRD

BLANKENBURG, 1
1. 51-12N, 10-45E, Erfurt, DDR
2. 51-47N, 10-57E, Magdeburg, DDR
3. 52-36N, 13-27E, East Berlin, DDR
4. 53-13N, 13-56E, Neubrandenburg, DDR
5. 48-35N, 10-49E, Bavaria, BRD
There are also 3 villages spelled Blankenberg in
the DDR and one in Poland (Polish=Gołagora).

BLANKENHAIN, 2
1. 50-48N, 12-17E, Karl-Marx-Stadt, DDR
2. 50-51N, 11-21E, Erfurt, DDR

BLANKENSTEIN, 2
1. 50-24N, 11-42E, Gera, DDR
2. 51-02N, 13-26E, Dresden, DDR
3. 51-24N, 07-14E, Nordrhein-Westfalen, BRD

BLUMBERG, 3
1. 51-31N, 13-11E, Leipzig, DDR
2. 52-36N, 13-37E, Frankfurt/Oder, DDR
3. 53-12N, 14-09E, Frankfurt/Oder, DDR
4. 54-19N, 20-01E, (Polish=Mikolajewo) Poland
5. 47-50N, 08-32E, Baden-Wuerttemberg, BRD
6. 48-33N, 12-17E, Bavaria, BRD

BOBERSBERG, Prussia, 3
1. 51-17N, 13-33E, Dresden, DDR
2. 51-57N, 15-05E, Polish-occupied Germany

BOBZIN, 3
1. 53-29N, 12-05E, Schwerin, DDR
2. 53-29N, 11-09E, Schwerin, DDR

BOCHOW, Rochow, 1 [probably BOCHOW]
1. 51-57N, 13-6E, Potsdam, DDR
2. 52-23N, 12-48E, Potsdam, DDR

BOCHZOFF, 2
Not found. There was a Bochzowe in Oranienburg,
Bezirk Potsdam, 52-45N, 13-14E, Potsdam, DDR

BOCKHORST. See BACKHORST

BOEHLEN, 2
1. 50-36N, 11-03E, Suhl, DDR
2. 51-11N, 12-52E, Leipzig, DDR
3. 51-12N, 12-23E, Leipzig, DDR
4. 51-15N, 12-45E, Leipzig, DDR
5. 51-16N, 13-18E, Dresden, DDR
6. 52-20N, 08-45E, Bohlen, Nordrhein-Westfalen,
BRD

BOETZOW, 1, 2
1. 52-38N, 13-8E, Potsdam, DDR

BOHNSLAEN, BOHUSLAEN, Sweden, 1

BOHRSCHUETZ, 2
Not found.

BOIONOCOW, Mecklenburg, 2
Not found. Possibly one of the following villages:
1. 53-34N, 10-58E, Boissow, Schwerin, DDR
2. 52-21N, 16-53E, Bocianowo, Poland
3. 53-57N, 21-02E, Bocianowo, Poland

BOITZENBURG, Mecklenburg, 2, 3
1. 53-23N, 10-43E, Schwerin, DDR

BOLITZ, 3
Not found. Might be the following village:
1. 53-59N, 20-03E, Bolity (German=Bolitten) Poland
It also might refer to Boelitzer Mark, an area at
51-48N, 11-33E, Magdeburg, DDR

BOLTENHAGEN, 2
1. 54-05N, 13-05E, Rostock, DDR

BOLZ, Mecklenburg, 2, 3
1. 53-41N, 12-00E, Schwerin, DDR

BORDELSHOLM, BORDESHOLM, 1, 3
1. 54-11N, 10-01E, Schleswig-Holstein, BRD

BORDENHAGEN, 3
Not found.

BOSDORF, Prussia, 2
1. 51-15N, 12-18E, Boesdorf, Leipzig, DDR
2. 52-25N, 11-05E, Boesdorf, Magdeburg, DDR
3. 51-38N, 14-32E, Bohsdorf, Cottbus, DDR
4. 51-59N, 12-41E, Bossdorf, Halle, DDR
5. 54-09N, 10-29E, Boesdorf, Schleswig-Holstein,
BRD

BOSSEBORN, Oldenburg, 2
There was a village of this name southeast of
Hoexter, 51-46N, 09-23E, Nordrhein-Westfalen, BRD
(mentioned in Meyer's *Lexikon*)

BOTSCHOW, Prussia, 2 [probably BOTTSCHOW]
1. 52-19N, 14-56E, Polish-occupied Germany
2. 52-38N, 13-08E, Potsdam, DDR

BOTTENDORF, 2
1. 51-18N, 11-24E, Halle, DDR
2. 49-51N, 06-22E, Rheinland-Pfalz, BRD (also
called Bollendorf)
3. 51-01N, 08-48E, Hessen, BRD
4. 52-46N, 10-35E, Niedersachsen, BRD

BOWITZ, 3
Not found. Might be BOWYCZYN (also called BOWYE-
ZYNY) or BOWYCZYN TOWARYSTWO, 52-13N, 19-04E, Poland

BRACK, 2
1. 51-00N, 09-42E, Braach, Hessen, BRD
2. 51-51N, 09-37E, Braak, Niedersachsen, BRD
3. 53-37N, 10-15E, Schleswig-Holstein, BRD
4. 54-00N, 10-06E, Schleswig-Holstein, BRD
5. 54-07N, 10-35E, Braak, Schleswig-Holstein, BRD
A village called Braak was merged into Latendorf,
Kreis Segeburg, in 1939. *See also* Brake, Brock

BRACKENSDORF, 2
Not found.

BRACKOW, 2
Not found.

BRAKE, 1
1. 52-04N, 08-36E, Nordrhein-Westfalen, BRD
2. 53-00N, 08-24E, Niedersachsen, BRD
3. 53-20N, 08-29E, Niedersachsen, BRD
4. 53-21N, 09-23E, Niedersachsen, BRD
5. 52-01N, 08-55E, Brake im Lippe, Nordrhein-Westfalen, BRD
6. 53-08N, 08-38E, Braake, Niedersachsen, BRD
See also Brack, Broke, Bruch

8

BRAMBERG, 1
  1. 50-06N, 10-40E, Bavaria, BRD
  2. 53-35N, 07-35E, Niedersachsen, BRD

BRAMSCHE, Oldenburg, 1
  1. 52-24N, 07-59E, Niedersachsen, BRD
  2. 52-27N, 07-21E, Niedersachsen, BRD

BRANDENBURG, 3
  1. 52-25N, 12-33E, Potsdam, DDR
  2. 48-14N, 10-04E, Baden-Wuerttemberg, BRD
  3. 50-42N, 06-09E, Nordrhein-Westfalen, BRD

BRANDIS, 1
  1. 51-20N, 12-36E, Leipzig, DDR
  2. 51-48N, 13-10E, Cottbus, DDR

BRANSENDORF? 3
  Not found.

BRAUNSBERG, 1, 2, 3
  1. 53-03N, 12-50E, Potsdam, DDR
  2. 53-03N, 12-50E, Schwerin, DDR
  3. 54-23N, 19-50E, (Polish=Braniewo) Poland
  4. 48-16N, 12-55E, Bavaria, BRD
  5. 48-21N, 12-40E, Bavaria, BRD
  6. 50-59N, 07-11E, Nordrhein-Westfalen, BRD
  7. 51-07N, 07-12E, Nordrhein-Westfalen, BRD

BRAUNSCHWEIG, 1, 2, 3
  1. 52-16N, 10-32E, Niedersachsen, BRD
  2. 51-46N, 14-20E, Brunschwig, merged with Cottbus
     in 1903

BRAUSENDORF? 3
  Not found. There was an estate of this name in
  Prussia, Posen administrative district, Kreis
  Meseritz, about 7 kilometers from Golzen.

BREDSTADT, BREDSTEDT, 1, 3
  1. 54-37N, 08-59E, Schleswig-Holstein, BRD

BREITENBACH, 1
  1. 50-33N, 10-46E, Suhl, DDR
  2. 50-41N, 10-30E, Suhl, DDR
  3. 50-52N, 12-31E, Karl-Marx-Stadt, DDR
  4. 51-00N, 12-04E, Halle, DDR
  5. 51-01N, 13-19E, Karl-Marx-Stadt, DDR
  6. 51-24N, 10-20E, Erfurt, DDR
  7. 51-32N, 11-07E, Halle, DDR
  There are also eleven villages of this name in BRD.

BREITUNGEN, Saxony, 2 [possibly Regis-Breitingen]
  1. 51-05N, 12-26E, Regis-Breitingen, Leipzig, DDR
  2. 48-31N, 10-00E, Breitingen, Baden-Wuerttemberg,
     BRD

BREMEN, 1, 3
  1. 47-44N, 09-56E, Baden-Wuerttemberg, BRD
  2. 48-02N, 09-22E, Baden-Wuerttemberg, BRD
  3. 51-30N, 07-57E, Nordrhein-Westfalen, BRD
  4. 53-05N, 08-48E, City of Bremen, BRD

BRESLAU, 1, 2, 3 [Polish=Wrocław]
  1. 51-06N, 17-02E, Polish-occupied Germany

BRESLAU, Saxony, 2
  Not found.

BRETERNITZ, 1
  1. 50-37N, 11-25E, Gera, DDR

BRIEG, Prussia, 1, 2
  1. 50-51N, 17-28E, Polish-occupied Germany

BRILON, Prussia, 3
  1. 51-24N, 08-35E, Nordrhein-Westfalen, BRD

BRINKUM, Oldenburg, 2
  1. 53-01N, 08-48E, Niedersachsen, BRD
  2. 53-16N, 07-34E, Niedersachsen, BRD

BROBERGEN, 3
  1. 53-36N, 09-11E, Niedersachsen, BRD

BROCK, Mecklenburg, 2
  1. 52-03N, 07-12E, Nordrhein-Westfalen, BRD
  2. 52-04N, 07-52E, Nordrhein-Westfalen, BRD
  There is a Brock area in Niedersachsen, BRD
  See also Brack, Brake, Bruch

BROMBERG, 1, 2 (Polish=Bydgoszcz)
  1. 53-09N, 18-00E, Poland

BROSSBUETTEL, 2
  Not found.

BRUCH, 3
  Not found. There are nine villages, plus many
  farms, of this name in BRD. A village Bruch
  existed before 1909, when it was merged with neighboring village to make Reinerbeckerhorst; in turn,
  the combined village was renamed Reinerbeck after
  1932. The village was in Kreis Hameln-Pyrmont, BRD
  See also Brack, Brake, Brock,

BRUEHEIM, BRUHEIM, Saxony-Gotha, 1
  1. 51-00N, 10-35E, Erfurt, DDR

BRUELL, 2
  1. 53-44N, 11-43E, Bruel, Schwerin, DDR
  2. 54-46N, 09-04E, Bruell, a farm, Schleswig-Hol-
     stein, BRD

BRUENN, BRUN, 2 [probably BRUNN]
  1. 50-30N, 12-26E, Karl-Marx-Stadt, DDR
  2. 50-39N, 12-20E, Gera, DDR
  3. 52-55N, 12-30E, Potsdam, DDR
  4. 53-40N, 13-22E, Neubrandenburg, DDR
  5. 52-46N, 12-44E, Brunne, Potsdam, DDR
  6. 50-58N, 07-49E, Bruen, Nordrhein-Westfalen, BRD
  7. 51-17N, 06-16E, Bruen, Nordrhein-Westfalen, BRD
  8. 48-37N, 12-28E, Brunn, Bavaria, BRD

BRUNSTADT, 2
  Not found. There was a Brunstatt in Alsace-Lorrain
  Kanton Muehlhausen-Sued.

BRUSOW, 1
  1. 54-04N, 11-49E, Brusow, Rostock, DDR
  2. 53-24N, 14-08E, Bruessow, Neubrandenburg, DDR
  3. 54-00N, 13-37E, Bruessow, Rostock, DDR
  4. 51-39N, 22-02E, Poland

BUCHA, 3
  1. 50-38N, 11-30E, Gera, DDR
  2. 50-38N, 11-42E, Gera, DDR
  3. 50-53N, 11-31E, Gera, DDR
  4. 51-13N, 11-30E, Halle, DDR
  5. 51-23N, 13-02E, Leipzig, DDR
  Two farms of this name in Bavaria, BRD.

BUCHHOLZ, 1
  There are 23 villages of this name in DDR and 20
  more in BRD.

BUCK, BUK, Prussia, 3
1. 52-00N, 13-50E, Bugk, Cottbus, DDR
2. 52-12N, 13-55E, Frankfurt/Oder, DDR
3. 49-15N, 22-24E, Buk, Poland
4. 50-21N, 19-51E, Buk, Poland
5. 52-21N, 16-32E, Buk, Poland
6. 53-25N, 19-10E, Buk, Poland
7. 53-25N, 19-14E, Buk Goralski, Poland

BUDISLEBEN, 2
Not found.

BUECKEBURG, 1, 2
1. 52-16N, 09-03E, Niedersachsen, BRD

BUEHREN, BUHREN, Oldenburg, 1, 2
1. 51-03N, 07-48E, Nordrhein-Westfalen, BRD
2. 51-29N, 09-41E, Niedersachsen, BRD
3. 52-25N, 07-59E, Niedersachsen, BRD
4. 52-38N, 09-09E, Niedersachsen, BRD
5. 52-48N, 08-12E, Niedersachsen, BRD
6. 52-51N, 08-01E, Niedersachsen, BRD
7. 52-51N, 08-28E, Niedersachsen, BRD
8. 53-19N, 07-47E, Niedersachsen, BRD

BUETZOW, 2
1. 52-29N, 12-36E, Butzow, Potsdam, DDR
2. 53-50N, 13-39E, Butzow, Neubrandenburg, DDR
3. 53-51N, 11-59E, Buetzow, Schwerin, DDR

BULOW, 3
1. 53-35N, 11-46E, Buelow, Schwerin, DDR
2. 53-42N, 12-36E, Buelow, Neubrandenburg, DDR
3. 53-46N, 11-02E, Buelow, Schwerin, DDR
4. 53-46N, 12-06E, Buelow, Schwerin, DDR
5. 51-26N, 18-07E, Bulowe, Poland

BUNDE, 2
1. 53-11N, 07-16E, Niedersachsen, BRD
2. 52-12N, 08-35E, Buende, Nordrhein-Westfalen, BRD
3. 54-08N, 19-43E, Bunden (Polish=Bady) Poland

BURDESHOLM, 1
See Bordesholm

BURG, Prussia, 1
1. 50-31N, 12-14E, Karl-Marx-Stadt, DDR
2. 51-25N, 12-00E, Halle, DDR
3. 51-28N, 14-21E, Cottbus, DDR
4. 51-50N, 14-07E, Cottbus, DDR
5. 51-50N, 14-09E, Cottbus, DDR
6. 52-16N, 11-51E, Magdeburg, DDR
There are an additional 28 villages of this name in the BRD.

BURGHAUSEN, 3
1. 51-21N, 12-16E, Leipzig, DDR
2. 58-10N, 11-40E, Bavaria, BRD
3. 48-56N, 12-50E, Bavaria, BRD
4. 48-26N, 11-40E, Bavaria, BRD
5. 49-24N, 10-21E, Bavaria, BRD
6. 50-03N, 10-00E, Bavaria, BRD
7. 50-15N, 10-10E, Burghausen bei Muennerstadt, Bavaria, BRD

BURGHESLER, BURG-KESLER, 3 [probably BURGHESSLER]
1. 51-09N, 11-39E, Halle, DDR

BURGKANDSTEDT, BURGKUNSTADT, 2
1. 50-08N, 11-15E, Bavaria, BRD
The latter spelling is correct.

BURGLEMNITZ, 1
1. 50-32N, 11-31E, Gera, DDR

BURKERSDORFF, 2
1. 50-10N, 11-17E, Bavaria, BRD
There are 9 villages of this name in the DDR, plus 2 farms.

BURKHASLACH, Prussia, 1 [probably BURGHASLACH]
1. 49-44N, 10-36E, Bavaria, BRD

BUROW, 2
1. 53-07N, 13-06E, Potsdam, DDR
2. 53-13N, 11-56E, Schwerin, DDR
3. 53-24N, 12-01E, Schwerin, DDR
4. 53-47N, 13-16E, Neubrandenburg, DDR
5. 50-06N, 19-46E, Poland

BURSINGHAUSEN, Hannover, 2 [probably BARSINGHAUSEN]
1. 52-18N, 09-27E, Niedersachsen, BRD

BUSSLEBEN, 2 [probably BUESSLEBEN]
1. 50-58N, 11-07E, Erfurt, DDR

BUTIGHEIM, Wuerttemberg, 1 [probably BIETIGHEIM]
1. 48-55N, 08-15E, Baden-Wuerttemberg, BRD
2. 48-57N, 09-07E, Baden-Wuerttemberg, BRD

BUTTERSTIEG, Holstein, 1
1. 53-56N, 1032E, Schleswig-Holstein, BRD

BUTZOW, Mecklenburg, 2
1. 52-29N, 12-36E, Potsdam, DDR
2. 53-50N, 13-39E, Neubrandenburg, DDR
3. 53-51N, 11-59E, Buetzow, Schwerin, DDR
Probably #3 is correct.

BUXTEHUDE, 1, 2
1. 53-27N, 09-42N, Niedersachsen, BRD

CALAU, Lausitz, 2
1. 51-45N, 13-56E, Calau, Cottbus, DDR
2. 50-33N, 12-35E, Kohlau, Karl-Marx-Stadt, DDR

CAMENZ, 1, 2
1. 51-16N, 14-06E, Dresden, DDR
2. 50-31N, 16-52E, Polish-occupied Germany
Modern spelling Kamenz in both cases.

CAMMIN, COMMIN, Prussia, 3
1. 53-26N, 13-18E, Neubrandenburg, DDR
2. 53-59N, 12-21E, Rostock, DDR
3. 53-35N, 13-20E, Rostock, DDR
4. 53-59N, 13-24E, Kammin, Rostock, DDR
5. 53-58N, 14-47E, Cammin, Pommern, Polish-occupied Germany
In addition, there are 21 villages called Kamien in Poland.

CANHAVEN, CANHUSEN, 1
1. 53-37N, 07-13E, Niedersachsen, BRD
Canhusen is the correct spelling.

CAPPELN, Oldenburg, 1
1. 52-49N, 08-07E, Niedersachsen, BRD

CARLSBURG, 1
1. 51-06N, 14-28E, Carlsberg, Dresden, DDR
2. 53-58N, 13-37E, Karlsburg, Rostock, DDR
3. 54-09N, 15-35E, Karlsberg, Polish-occupied Germany
4. 49-30N, 08-02E, Carlsberg, Rheinland-Pfalz, BRD

CARLSHAFEN, Prussia, 2
1. 54-07N, 13-50E, Carlshagen, Rostock, DDR
2. 51-38N, 09-27E, Carlshafen (or Karlshafen) Hessen, BRD

CARLSRUHE, 2
1. 51-02N, 14-28E, Dresden, DDR
2. 54-09N, 12-28E, Rostock, DDR
3. 52-42N, 13-06E, Karlsruh, Potsdam, DDR
4. 52-55N, 12-11E, Karlsruhe, Schwerin, DDR
5. 53-39N, 12-48E, Karlsruhe, Neubrandenburg, DDR
6. 50-55N, 17-50E, Carlsruhe, Polish-occupied Germany
7. 49-01N, 08-24E, Carlsruhe (or Karlsruhe) Baden-Wuerttemberg, BRD

CAROW, 1
1. 52-21N, 12-19E, Karow, Magdeburg, DDR
2. 52-37N, 13-28E, Karow, East Berlin, section of
3. 53-32N, 12-16E, Karow, Schwerin, DDR
4. 53-51N, 11-28E, Karow, Rostock, DDR
5. 53-51N, 12-11E, Karow, Schwerin, DDR
6. 54-24N, 13-30E, Karow, Rostock, DDR

CASLIN, COSLIN, 1
1. 53-48N, 13-03E, Kaslin, Neubrandenburg, DDR

CASSEL, 1, 2, 3
1. 51-19N, 09-30E, Cassel (Kassel), Hessen, BRD

CELLE, Hannover, 1, 2
1. 52-37N, 10-05E, Niedersachsen, BRD

CHARLOTTENTHAL, 3
1. 53-41N, 12-16E, Schwerin, DDR
2. 49-29N, 12-38E, Bavaria, BRD
3. 54-20N, 10-22E, Schleswig-Holstein, BRD
Also 2 farms of this name in the DDR.

CHEMNITZ, 3
1. 50-50N, 12-55E, Karl-Marx-Stadt, DDR
2. 53-35N, 13-09E, Neubrandenburg, DDR

CHODZIEHEW, 3
1. 52-59N, 16-55E, Chodziez, Poland, a possibility
There was a village Choszewen, Kreis Sensburg, Ostpreussen [East Prussia] which was merged with Hohensee in 1936.

CHODZIESEN, Prussia, 1, 2, 3
1. 52-59N, 16-55E, Poland
Kolmar (Polish=Chodzicz), a town ceded to Poland in 1919-1921.

CHR. ALB. KOOG, Holstein, 1
1. 54-47N, 08-44E, Schleswig-Holstein, BRD
Should read Christian-Albrechts-Koog.

CHRIM, Posen, 3
Not found. There is a farm called Krim in the DDR.

CHRISTIANI, CHRISTIANIA, Norway, 2

CHRISTIANSAND, 2

CHRISTIANSTAT, Sweden, 1

CHRISTIANSTHAL, Sweden, 1

CILLI, Styria [Steiermark] Austria, 1

CINCINNATI, Ohio, 2, 3

CIRKWITZ, 3
Not found.

CISMAR, 2
1. 54-11N, 10-59E, Schleswig-Holstein, BRD

CLAMSCHWITZ, CLANSCHWITZ, 3
1. 51-13N, 13-10E, Leipzig, DDR
Clanzschwitz and Clanschwitz are the usual spellings.

CLEDEN, 2
1. 51-52N, 13-56E, Kleeden, Cottbus, DDR

COBLENTZ, 1, 2
1. 51-12N, 14-17E, Dresden, DDR
2. 53-32N, 14-08E, Koblentz, Neubrandenburg, DDR
3. 51-23N, 14-20E, Koblenz, Cottbus, DDR
4. 50-21N, 07-36E, Koblenz, Rheinland-Pfalz, BRD

COBURG, 2, 3
1. 50-15N, 10-58E, Bavaria, BRD

COELN, 1
1. 51-10N, 13-30E, Coelln, Dresden, DDR
2. 51-14N, 14-23E, Coelln, Dresden, DDR
3. 53-43N, 12-17E, Koelln, Schwerin, DDR
4. 53-46N, 13-21E, Koelln, Neubrandenburg, DDR
5. 50-56N, 06-57E, Koeln, Nordrhein-Westfalen, BRD

COESLIN, 1, 3
1. 51-39N, 11-59E, Koesseln, Halle, DDR
2. 51-09N, 12-03E, Koessuln, Halle, DDR
See also CASLIN, COSLIN

COETHEN, 1
1. 51-45N, 11-58E, Koetthen, Halle, DDR
2. 52-48N, 13-56E, Koethen, Frankfurt/Oder, DDR

COHLENFELD, 2
Not found.

COLAU, 2
1. 51-26N, 12-40E, Kollau, Leipzig, DDR
2. 51-50N, 14-47E, Kohlo, Polish-occupied Germany

COLMAR, Holstein, 3
1. 53-20N, 08-20E, Colmar-Moor, Niedersachsen, BRD

COLZIN, 2
1. 53-31N, 10-57E, Koelzin, Schwerin, DDR
2. 53-58N, 13-27E, Koelzin, Rostock, DDR

COMMIN. See CAMMIN

CONSTANZ, 2
1. 47-40N, 09-11E, Baden-Wuerttemberg, BRD
Modern spelling is Konstanz.

COPENHAGEN, Denmark, 1, 2, 3

CORNECK, Prussia, 2, 3
Not found.

COSCHTEN, 3
Not found.

COSLIN. See CASLIN, COESLIN

COSPEDA, 3
1. 50-57N, 11-33E, Gera, DDR
2. 50-43N, 11-45E, Kospoda, Gera, DDR

COTTBUS, 1, 3
1. 51-46N, 14-20E, Cottbus, DDR

CRAILSHEIM, 2
1. 49-09N, 10-05E, Baden-Wuerttemberg, BRD

CRAMOW, 1
1. 53-36N, 12-27E, Neubrandenburg, DDR
2. 53-43N, 11-17E, Schwerin, DDR

CREUZNACH, 2
1. 49-50N, 07-52E, Rheinland-Pfalz, BRD
Now called Bade Kreuznach.

CREWITZ, Mecklenburg, 2
1. 53-18N, 13-34E, Krewitz, Neubrandenburg, DDR

CRIMITZSCHAU, 1
1. 50-49N, 12-23E, Crimmitschau, Karl-Marx-Stadt,
DDR
2. 51-04N, 12-14E, Krimmitzschen, Halle, DDR (in
1938 merged with Rehmsdorf,
Kreis Zeitz

CRIVITZ, 2
1. 53-35N, 11-39E, Crivitz, Schwerin, DDR
2. 51-44N, 13-46E, Crinitz, Cottbus, DDR
3. 52-54N, 11-17E, Kriwitz, Niedersachsen, BRD
There is also a farm called Krievitz in the DDR.

CROEPLIN, Prussia, 3
1. 54-04N, 11-48E, Kroepelin, Rostock, DDR

CROSSEN AM ODER, 1
1. 51-02N, 12-56E, Karl-Marx-Stadt, DDR
2. 50-58N, 11-59E, Krossen, Rostock, DDR
3. 52-03N, 15-09E, Crossen, Polish-occupied Germany
(Polish=Krosno Odrzanskie)
Probably #3 is meant herein; there are several villages called Krossen in Poland.

CROSSIN, Prussia, 3
Not found. Probably Crossen is meant, but there is
a Crossinsee [lake] in the DDR. *See also* Crossen
am Oder.

CUESTRIN, Prussia, 2, 3
1. 52-34N, 14-37E, Kuestrin-Kietz, Frankfurt/Oder,
DDR
2. 52-35N, 14-39E, Kuestrin, Polish-occupied Germany

CULM, 3
1. 50-25N, 12-05E, Kulm, Karl-Marx-Stadt, DDR
2. 50-30N, 11-45E, Kulm, Gera, DDR

CUNERN, 2
Not found.

CUXHAVEN, 1
1. 53-53N, 08-42E, Niedersachsen, BRD

CZERNINA? 3
1. 50-46N, 21-48E, Czernin, Poland
2. 53-54N, 19-04E, Czernin, Poland
3. 51-44N, 16-38E, Czernina (also called Lesten),
Polish-occupied Germany
4. 52-51N, 19-26E, Czernino, Poland

CZRIKHOF, 1
Not found.

DABLERSTEIN, 2
Not found.

DADERSHEIM, 1
Not found.

DALANG, 2
1. 52-15N, 12-42E, Damelang, Potsdam, DDR (possible)

DALLBERG, Mecklenburg, 2
1. 53-44N, 11-17E, Dalberg, Schwerin, DDR

DAMBACH, DAMBECK, 3
1. 52-48N, 11-10E, Magdeburg, DDR
2. 53-15N, 11-46E, Schwerin, DDR
3. 53-22N, 12-30E, Neubrandenburg, DDR
4. 53-27N, 12-56E, Neubrandenburg, DDR
5. 53-47N, 11-22E, Rostock, DDR
6. 53-58N, 13-29E, Rostock, DDR
7. 52-47N, 11-10E, Magdeburg, DDR (called Dambeck
Dorf or Amt Dambeck)
All DDR villages spelled Dambeck. There are an additional seven villages of this name in BRD, but
all spelled Dambach.

DAMGARTEN, 1
1. 54-15N, 12-28E, Damgarten, or Ribnitz-Damgarten,
Rostock, DDR

DAMITSCH, DAMMITZSCH, 2
There was a Dammratsch, called Dammfelde after 1938,
in Kreis Oppeln, Upper Silesia (now Polish-occupied
Germany). Also a Damitz an der Elbe, correctly
spelled Doemitz. *See* Domitz *herein*

DAMSHAGEN, 3
1. 53-56N, 11-09E, Rostock, DDR

DAMWALDE, Prussia, 3
1. 53-20N, 12-22E, Dammwolde, Neubrandenburg, DDR

DANKERODE, 2
1. 51-35N, 09-46E, Neubrandenburg, DDR

DANNDORF, 2
1. 51-58N, 13-26E, Damsdorf, Cottbus, DDR
2. 52-18N, 13-16E, Damsdorf, Potsdam, DDR
3. 50-09N, 11-22E, Danndorf, Bavaria, BRD
4. 52-26N, 10-55E, Danndorf, Niedersachsen, BRD

DANNENBERG, Hannover, 2
1. 51-04N, 07-36E, Nordrhein-Westfalen, BRD
2. 53-06N, 11-06E, Niedersachsen, BRD
3. 53-09N, 08-59E, Niedersachsen, BRD

DANZIG, 1, 2
1. 54-21N, 18-40E (Polish=Gdansk) Poland

DARGUN, 3
1. 53-54N, 12-51E, Dargun, Neubrandenburg, DDR
2. 53-53N, 14-04E, Dargen, Rostock, DDR

DARKEHMEN, Prussia, 1
Darkehmen (also Dargekyem) is the same as Angerapp
in East Prussia.

DARMSTADT, 3
1. 49-52N, 08-39E, Hessen, BRD

DARZE, DASSE, DASZE, 2, 3
1. 53-22N, 12-23E, Neubrandenburg, DDR
2. 53-29N, 11-54E, Schwerin, DDR
3. 52-33N, 23-15E, (also called Dasze), Poland

DEFAHR, Mecklenburg, 2
Not found.

DEGRITZ, 2
Not found.

DELIBZSCH, 2
1. 51-32N, 12-21E, Delitzsch, Leipzig, DDR

DELITZ, 3
1. 51-25N, 11-54E, Delitz am Berge, Halle, DDR

DENSTORF, 1
1. 52-15N, 10-25E, Niedersachsen, BRD

DERENTHAL, 1
1. 51-42N, 09-26E, Niedersachsen, BRD
Now spelled Derental.

DERMISDORF, Thuringia, 2
1. 51-12N, 11-12E, Dermsdorf, Erfurt, DDR

DESSAU, 3
1. 51-50N, 12-15E, Halle, DDR
1. 52-49N, 11-29E, Magdeburg, DDR

DETMOLD, 2
1. 51-56N, 08-53E, Nordrhein-Westfalen, BRD

DEUTSCH CRONE, Prussia, 1, 2
1. 53-16N, 16-28E, Deutsch Krone, Polish-occupied
Germany (Polish=Walcz)

DEUTSCH KESSEL, 3
1. 5019-N, 12-18E, Kessel, Karl-Marx-Stadt, DDR

DEUTSCHKRONE. *See* DEUTSCH CRONE

DEUZ, 2
1. 50-56N, 06-59E, Deutz, Nordrhein-Westfalen, BRD
2. 50-53N, 08-09E, Deutz, Nordrhein-Westfalen, BRD

DEWITZ, 2
1. 51-23N, 12-32E, Leipzig, DDR
2. 52-50N, 11-37E, Magdeburg, DDR
3. 53-30N, 13-23E, Neubrandenburg, DDR

DIEDORF, Meiningen, 2
1. 50-40N, 10-08E, East Berlin, DDR
2. 51-11N, 10-17E, Erfurt, DDR
3. 48-21N, 10-46E, Bavaria, BRD

DIEMERSDORF, 2
1. 54-21N, 11-01E, Schleswig-Holstein, BRD

DIETERSDORF, 1
1. 51-32N, 11-02E, Halle, DDR
2. 52-04N, 12-49E, Potsdam, DDR
There are an additional nine villages of this name
in the BRD.

DIETRICHSHUETTE, 1
Not found.

DINGELSTEDT, 1
1. 51-19N, 10-19E, Digelstaedt, Erfurt, DDR
2. 51-59N, 10-59E, Dingelstedt, Magdeburg, DDR

DINKLAN, DINKLAU, 2
1. 52-10N, 10-04E, Dinklar, Niedersachsen, BRD

DITHMAR, 2
Not found. There is an area called Dithmarschen in
Schleswig-Holstein, BRD.

DITTERSBACH, 1
1. 50-41N, 13-27E, Karl-Marx-Stadt, DDR
2. 50-48N, 13-29E, Karl-Marx-Stadt, DDR
3. 50-56N, 13-29E, Karl-Marx-Stadt, DDR
4. 51-03N, 13-59E, Dresden, DDR
5. 51-01N, 14-52E, Dittersbach auf dem Eigen, Dresden, DDR
6. 50-45N, 16-18E, Polish-occupied Germany

DOBBERTIN, DOPPERTIN, Mecklenburg, 1, 2
1. 53-38N, 12-04E, Magdeburg, DDR
2. 53-01N, 14-02E, Dobberzin, Frankfurt/Oder, DDR

DOBBIN, 2
1. 53-37N, 12-02E, Schwerin, DDR
2. t3-37N, 12-20E, Schwerin, DDR

DOBELN? 3
1. 51-07N, 13-07E, Doebeln, Leipzig, DDR
2. 52-07N, 10-54E, Dobbeln, Niedersachsen, BRD

DOBERAN, Mecklenburg, 3
1. 54-06N, 11-54E, Bad Doberan, Rostock, DDR

DOBRAWITZ, Bohemia, 2

DOBRZIN, 3
1. 50-45N, 17-52E, Dobrzen, Polish-occupied Germany
(also called Klein Doebern and
Gross Doebern)
2. 53-26N, 20-23E, Cobrzienen (or Dobrzyn) Poland
3. 51-26N, 14-58E, Dobrzyn (or Dobers) Polish-occupied Germany
4. 52-39N, 19-20E, Dobrzyn nad Wisla, Poland

DOEBEL, Saxony, 2
1. 51-07N, 13-07E, Doebeln, Leipzig, DDR
2. 48-12N, 09-35E, Dobel, Baden-Wuerttemberg, BRD
3. 48-21N, 08-33E, Dobel, Baden=Wuerttemberg, BRD
4. 48-48N, 08-30E, Dobel, Baden-Wuerttemberg, BRD
In addition, there are six villages called Dobl in
the BRD. #1 is probably correct here.

DOENITZ, 2
1. 53-08N, 11-15E, Schwerin, DDR

DOERFLAS, 2
1. 49-35N, 10-49E, Bavaria, BRD
2. 49-59N, 11-35E, Bavaria, BRD
3. 50-00N, 12-05E, Doerflas bei Marktredwitz, Bavaria, BRD

DOESCHNITZ, 1
1. 50-37N, 11-14E, Gera, DDR

DOESTRUP, 1
Not found.

DOHREN, 2
1. 52-20N, 11-01E, Doehren, Magdeburg, DDR
2. 53-18N, 09-42E, Dohren, Niedersachsen, BRD
3. 53-28N, 08-47E, Dohren, Niedersachsen, BRD
4. 52-10N, 08-25E, Doehren, Niedersachsen, BRD
5. 52-09N, 08-35E, Doehren, Nordrhein-Westfalen,
BRD
6. 52-20N, 09-46E, Doehren, Niedersachsen, BRD
7. 52-26N, 09-02E, Doehren, Nordrhein-Westfalen,
BRD
8. 52-53N, 08-44E, Doehren, Niedersachsen, BRD

DOMITZ, 1
1. 53-06N, 11-15E, Doemitz, Schwerin, DDR
2. 51-39N, 12-53E, Dommitzsch, Leipzig, DDR
3. 51-36N, 11-50E, Domnitz, Potsdam, DDR

DOMSUEHL, DOMSUHL, 1
1. 53-29N, 11-46E, Schwerin, DDR
Domsuehl is the correct spelling.

DONNDORF, 2
1. 51-18N, 11-22E, Halle, DDR
2. 49-56N, 11-30E, Bavaria, BRD

DOPPERTIN. See DOBBERTIN

DORNFELD, 1
1. 50-40N, 11-04E, Doernfeld an der Heide, Gera,
DDR
2. 50-44N, 11-02E, Doernfeld an der Ilm, Erfurt,
DDR

DRABISCHAU, DROBISCHAU, 2
1. 50-38N, 11-04E, Droebischau, Gera, DDR

DRACHTERSEN. See DROGDERSEN

DRACKENBURG, Hannover, 1
1. 52-41N, 09-13E, Niedersachsen, BRD

DRADHAUSEN, 3
1. 51-54N, 14-19E, Drachhausen, Cottbus, DDR

DRAEMEN, Norway, 2

DRANSFELD, Hannover, 2
1. 51-30N, 09-46E, Niedersachsen, BRD

DRAUTHEIM, DRENTHEIM, 1
Not found.

DRESDEN, 1, 2, 3
1. 51-03N, 13-45E, Dresden, DDR

DREYLEUTZOW, Mecklenburg, 2
1. 53-32N, 11-07E, Dreiluetzow, Schwerin, DDR

DROBISCHAU. See DRABISCHAU

DROGDERSEN, 2, 3
1. 53-42N, 09-23E, Drochtersen, Niedersachsen, BRD

DRONSHEIM. See DRAUTHEIM

DROSSEN, Saxony, 2
1. 50-54N, 12-15E, Drosen, Leipzig, DDR

DUDENHAUSEN, Lippe-Detmold, 1
1. 52-48N, 09-05E, Duddenhausen, Niedersachsen,
BRD

DUEMERHUETTE, 1
1. 53-34N, 11-14E, Dummerhuette (or Duemmerhuette)
Schwerin, DDR

DUENPFL, 1
1. 49-07N, 12-51E, Dumpf, Bavaria, BRD

DUESSELDORF, 2
1. 51-13N, 06-46E, Nordrhein-Westfalen, BRD

DULOW, 2
1. 50-09N, 19-31E, Dulowa, Poland

DUHRNLEISS, 1
Not found.

DUTTWEILER, 3
1. 49-18N, 08-13E, Rheinland-Pfalz, BRD

EBELEBEN, 2
1. 51-17N, 10-44E, Erfurt, DDR

EBERSDORF, 2
1. 50-29N, 11-40E, Gera, DDR
2. 50-53N, 12-59E, Karl-Marx-Stadt, DDR
3. 51-05N, 14-41E, Dresden, DDR
4. 50-13N, 16-41E, Polish-administered Germany
There are additional villages of this name in BRD.

ECKERSBERG, 3
1. 50-55N, 14-48E, Eckertsberg, Dresden, DDR
2. 51-07N, 11-33E, Eckartsberga, Halle, DDR
3. 51-02N, 12-37E, Eckersberg, Leipzig, DDR
4. 53-49N, 21-51E, Eckersberg (Polish=Okartowo),
Poland
5. 47-48N, 11-57E, Eckersberg, Bavaria, BRD
6. 48-34N, 11-30E, Eckersberg, Bavaria, BRD

ECKSTEDT, Prussia, 2
1. 51-04N, 11-08E, Erfurt, DDR

ECKZIN, Prussia. See Exin

EDDELBOCK, EDDELBUCK, 3
1. 53-57N, 09-09E, Eddelak, Schleswig-Holstein, BRD
2. 50-07N, 09-18E, Edelbach, Schleswig-Holstein, BRD

EDENA, 3
1. 48-26N, 13-15E, Eden, Schleswig-Holstein, BRD

EGELSDORF, 2
1. 50-38N, 11-05E, Gera, DDR

EGER, Bohemia, 1

EHLERSTORF, 2
1. 54-21N, 09-47E, Ehlersdorf, Schleswig-Holstein,
BRD
2. 54-17N, 10-50E, Ehlerstorf (farm), Schleswig-
Holstein, BRD

EHRENBERG, 3
1. 50-29N, 10-39E, Suhl, DDR
2. 50-58N, 12-28E, Leipzig, DDR
3. 50-59N, 14-10E, Dresden, DDR
4. 48-34N, 11-28E, Bavaria, BRD
5. 50-38N, 07-25E, Rheinland-Pfalz, BRD
6. 51-16N, 07-16E, Nordrhein-Westfalen, BRD

EHRENFRIEDERSDORF, 1
1. 50-39N, 12-57E, Karl-Marx-Stadt, DDR

EICHENHAUSEN, 2
1. 47-57N, 11-36E, (township) Bavaria, BRD
2. 50-19N, 10-18E, Bavaria, BRD

EICHFELD, 1
1. 50-43N, 11-16E, Gera, DDR
2. 52-56N, 11-47E, Magdeburg, DDR
3. 49-50N, 10-18E, Bavaria, BRD

EIDERSTADT, 2
1. 54-20N, 08-45E, Eiderstedt (peninsula), Schleswig-Holstein, BRD

EISENACH, 1, 2, 3
1. 50-59N, 10-19E, Erfurt, DDR
2. 53-44N, 21-19E, Eisenack (Polish=Czaszkowo),
Poland
3. 49-51N, 06-31E, Eisenach, Rheinland-Pfalz, BRD
#1 is almost certainly correct.

14

EISENBERG, 2
1. 50-58N, 11-54E, Gera, DDR
2. 54-23N, 20-03E, (Polish=Zelazna Gora), Poland
3. 47-36N, 10-36E, (township) Bavaria, BRD
4. 49-33N, 08-06E, Rheinland-Pfalz, BRD

EISLEBEN, 1, 2, 3
1. 51-32N, 11-33E, Halle, DDR

ELBING, 1, 3
1. 54-10N, 19-23E, (Polish=Elblag), Poland
2. 50-32N, 07-55E, Elbingen, Rheinland-Pfalz, BRD
3. 51-37N, 10-14E, Elbingen, Niedersachsen, BRD

ELBOGEN, Bohemia, 2

ELDAGSEN, Hannover, 2
1. 52-10N, 09-39E, Niedersachsen, BRD
2. 52-23N, 08-56E, Nordrhein-Westfalen, BRD

ELEXLEBEN. *See* ELXLEBEN

ELFBARGSLAEN, Sweden, 1

ELMSHORN, 2, 3
1. 53-45N, 09-39E, Schleswig-Holstein, BRD

ELSE, 3
1. 53-59N, 20-47E, Elsau (Polish=Olszewnik) Poland
2. 51-11N, 07-46E, Elsen, Nordrhein-Westfalen, BRD
3. 51-05N, 06-46E, Elsen, Nordrhein-Westfalen, BRD
4. 51-44N, 08-41E, Elsen, Nordrhein-Westfalen, BRD
5. 52-03N, 08-04E, Elve (farming community), Nord-
                   rhein-Westfalen, BRD
6. 50-25N, 08-02E, Elz, Hessen, BRD
7. 52-07N, 09-44E, Elze, Niedersachsen, BRD
8. 52-35N, 09-45E, Elze, Niedersachsen, BRD

ELXLEBEN, 1, 3
1. 50-52N, 11-03E, Erfurt, DDR
2. 51-03N, 10-57E, Erfurt, DDR

EMDEN, 3
1. 52-14N, 11-16E, Magdeburg, DDR
2. 53-22N, 07-13E, Niedersachsen, BRD

ENGELLADE, 2
Not found.

EPE, Oldenburg, 1
1. 52-11N, 07-02E, Nordrhein-Westfalen, BRD
2. 52-26N, 08-01E, Niedersachsen, BRD

ERBACH, 2
1. 50-50N, 10-17E, Suhl, DDR
2. 48-20N, 09-53E, Baden-Wuerttemberg, BRD
3. 49-38N, 08-40E, Hessen, BRD
4. 49-39N, 09-00E, Hessen, BRD
5. 50-01N, 08-05E, Hessen, BRD
6. 50-02N, 07-41E, Rheinland-Pfalz, BRD

ERFURT, 1, 2
1. 50-59N, 11-02E, Erfurt, DDR

ERLANGEN, 1, 2
1. 49-36N, 11-01E, Bavaria, BRD

ERLAU, 2
1. 50-32N, 10-45E, Erlau, Suhl, DDR
2. 51-01N, 12-56E, Erlau, Karl-Marx-Stadt, DDR
3. 50-31N, 12-48E, Erla, Karl-Marx-Stadt, DDR
4. 48-27N, 11-46E, Erlau, Bavaria, BRD

5. 48-34N, 13-35E, Erlau, Bavaria, BRD
6. 48-50N, 10-07E, Erlau, Baden-Wuerttemberg, BRD
7. 49-51N, 10-48E, Erlau, Bavaria

ERLBACH, Saxony, 2
1. 50-19N, 12-22E, Karl-Marx-Stadt, DDR
2. 50-46N, 12-44E, Karl-Marx-Stadt, DDR
3. 51-07N, 12-53E, Karl-Marx-Stadt, DDR
4. 50-15N, 10-47E, Erlebach, Suhl, DDR
5. 51-01N, 13-02E, Erlebach, Karl-Marx-Stadt, DDR
There are additional villages of this name in BRD.

ERLENBACH, 1
There are 13 villages of this name in BRD.

ERXLEBEN, 2
1. 52-45N, 11-46E, Magdeburg, DDR

ESCHERSHAUSEN, 3
1. 51-41N, 09-38E, Niedersachsen, BRD
2. 51-55N, 09-39E, Niedersachsen, BRD

ESCHWEGE, 1, 3
1. 51-11N, 10-04E, Hessen, BRD

ETZEBACH, 1
1. 50-44N, 11-26E, Etaelbach, Gera, DDR
2. 50-47N, 07-41E, Etzbach, Rheinland-Pfalz, BRD
3. 50-32N, 07-52E, Etzelbach, Rheinland-Pfalz, BRD

EULENBURG, Holstein, 3
1. 53-22N, 10-51E, Schwerin, DDR
2. 50-36N, 07-28E, Eulenberg, Rheinland-Pfalz, BRD
3. 50-43N, 07-21E, Eulenberg, Nordrhein-Westfalen,
                   BRD

EUPERN, 1
1. 51-54N, 12-42E, Euper, Halle, DDR
2. 50-47N, 07-47E, Eupel or Eupeln, Rheinland-Pfalz
                   BRD

EUTHAUSEN, 2
1. 47-56N, 11-52E, Eutenhausen, Bavaria, BRD
2. 47-55N, 10-26E, Eutenhausen, Bavaria, BRD

EUTIN, 3
1. 54-08N, 10-37E, Schleswig-Holstein, BRD

EXIN, 2
1. 54-10N, 12-43E, Eixen, Erfurt, DDR
2. 52-54N, 13-21E, Exin (forester's lodge), Pots-
                   dam, DDR
3. 48-38N, 12-47E, Exing, Bavaria, BRD

FAHRENRODE, Saxony, 2
1. 50-57N, 10-24E, Farnroda, Erfurt, DDR

FALKENBURG, 1
1. 51-35N, 13-15E, Cottbus, DDR
2. 54-33N, 13-37E, Rostock, DDR
3. 53-32N, 16-00E, Polish-occupied Germany
4. 53-03N, 08-29E, Niedersachsen, BRD
There are 8 villages called Falkenberg in DDR;
three more in Polish-occupied Germany; nine in BRD.

FALKENHAGEN, Mecklenburg, 2
1. 52-26N, 14-19E, Frankfurt/Oder, DDR
2. 53-12N, 12-12E, Potsdam, DDR
3. 53-22N, 13-46E, Neubrandenburg, DDR
4. 53-33N, 12-42E, Neubrandenburg, DDR
[continued next page]

FALKENHAGEN, Mecklenburg [continued]
5. 53-48N, 10-57E, Rostock, DDR
6. 54-13N, 13-16E, Rostock, DDR
7. 51-31N, 10-06E, Niedersachsen, BRD

FALKENWALDE, Prussia, 2
1. 53-16N, 14-00E, Neubrandenburg, DDR

FASSELDORF, Bavaria, 2
Not found.

FAURNIDAU, Wuerttemberg, 2
1. 48-42N, 09-37E, Faurndau, Baden-Wuerttemberg,
BRD

FEHMARN, 1
1. 54-28N, 11-08E (island) Schleswig-Holstein, BRD

FEINSBERG, Silesia, 1
Not found.

FEKFH TO? 2
Not found (obviously garbled).

FELDSBERG, 1
1. 53-20N, 13-27E, Feldberg, Neubrandenburg, DDR
2. 47-52N, 08-04E, Feldberg (township) Baden-Wuerttemberg, BRD
3. 47-46N, 07-39E, Feldberg, Baden-Wuerttemberg,
BRD
4. 48-34N, 13-25E, Feldsberg (farm) Bavaria, BRD

FERNOSFELD, Prussia, 2
Not found. There is a Fernowsfelde, Kreis Usedom-
Wollin, mentioned in "Nineteenth-Century Emigration
of "Old Lutherans" from Eastern Germany (Mainly Pomerania and Lower Silesia) to Australia, Canada, and
the United States," German-American Genealogical Research Monograph No. 7 (McNeal, AZ: Westland Publications, 1980).

FICHTENWERDE, 3
Not found.

FIEHLBAUM, 3
Not found.

FILEHNE, FILENE, 1, 2
Not found.

FILSEN, Hannover, 1
1. 50-14N, 07-35E, Rheinland-Pfalz, BRD
No village of this name was found in Niedersachsen,
BRD (former Hannoverian territory).

FINKWAERDER, 1
1. 53-32N, 09-52E, Finkenwerder (section of city)
Hamburg, BRD

FINSTERWALDE, 1
1. 51-38N, 13-43E, Cottbus, DDR
2. 53-53N, 22-45E, (Polish=Stare Cimochy) Poland
3. 47-45N, 11-43E, Bavaria, BRD

FIRSCHTIEGEL. See Tirschtiegel

FISCHBACH, 1
1. 50-32N, 10-44E, Suhl, DDR
2. 50-39N, 10-09E, Suhl, DDR
3. 50-53N, 10-28E, Erfurt, DDR
4. 50-58N, 10-22E, Erfurt, DDR
5. 51-05N, 14-01E, Dresden, DDR
There are 26 villages of this name in BRD.

FLENSBURG, Schleswig, 1, 2, 3
1. 54-47N, 09-26E, Schleswig-Holstein, BRD

FLOTOW, Prussia, 1
1. 53-24N, 13-20E, Flatow, Neubrandenburg, DDR
2. 52-44N, 12-57E, Flatow, Potsdam, DDR
3. 53-21N, 17-03E, Flatow, Polish-occupied Germany

FOEHR, 1, 2
1. 54-43N, 08-30E, (island) Schleswig-Holstein, BRD

FORCHHEIM, 2
1. 50-43N, 13-16E, Karl-Marx-Stadt, DDR
2. 51-07N, 13-04E, Leipzig, DDR
3. 48-10N, 07-42E, Baden-Wuerttemberg, BRD
4. 48-50N, 11-41E, Bavaria, BRD
5. 48-50N, 08-19E, Baden-Wuerttemberg, BRD
6. 49-10N, 11-20E, Bavaria, BRD
7. 49-43N, 11-04E, Bavaria, BRD

FORDAU, 1
1. 53-09N, 18-11E, Fordon, Poland

FORSCHTIEGEL? See TIRSCHTIEGEL

FRANDKE, 2
Not found.

FRANITZ, 2
Not found.

FRANKENHAUSEN, 2
1. 50-50N, 11-06E, Karl-Marx-Stadt, DDR
2. 51-21N, 11-06E, Bad Frankenhausen, Halle, DDR
3. 49-47N, 08-43E, Hessen, BRD
4. 51-25N, 09-26E, Hessen, BRD

FRANKENSTEIN, Prussia, 1, 2, 3
1. 50-54N, 13-13E, Karl-Marx-Stadt, DDR
2. 50-35N, 16-48E, Polish-occupied Germany
3. 49-26N, 07-59E, Rheinland-Pfalz, BRD

FRANKENTHAL, 3
1. 50-53N, 12-01E, Gera, DDR
2. 51-08N, 14-07E, Dresden, DDR
3. 54-20N, 13-17E, Rostock, DDR
4. 49-22N, 12-27E, Bavaria, BRD
5. 49-32N, 08-21E, Rheinland-Pfalz, BRD

FRANKFURT/ODER/MAIN? 1, 2, 3
1. 52-21N, 14-33E, Frankfurt/Oder, DDR
2. 50-07N, 08-41E, Frankfurt/Main, BRD
3. 49-41N, 10-32E, Bavaria, BRD

FRANZBURG, 1
1. 54-11N, 12-53E, Rostock, DDR
2. 52-21N, 12-58E, Franzenberg, Potsdam, DDR
3. 52-18N, 09-36E, (farm) Niedersachsen, BRD

FRAUENANNA, Bavaria, 2
1. 48-59N, 13-18E, Frauenau (township) Bavaria, BRD

FRAUENBURG, 2
1. 54-22N, 19-41E (Polish=Frombork) Poland
There are nine villages named Frauenberg in Bavaria,
BRD.

FRAUENFELD, Switzerland, 1

FRAUSTADT, Prussia, 1
1. 51-48N, 16-19E, Polish-occupied Germany

FREDENHAGEN, 1
1. 51-43N, 09-46E, Fredelshagen (forester's lodge)
Niedersachsen, BRD

FREDENWALDE, 2
Not found.

FREIBERG, 1, 3
1. 50-20N, 12-14E, Karl-Marx-Stadt, DDR
2. 50-55N, 13-22E, Karl-Marx-Stadt, DDR
3. 50-52N, 16-20E, Freiburg, Silesia, Polish-occupied Germany
4. 48-07N, 12-16E, Bavaria, BRD
5. 50-06N, 10-54E, Bavaria, BRD
6. 51-30N, 07-37E, Nordrhein-Westfalen, BRD

FRENSDORF, 3
1. 52-16N, 13-05E, Fresdorf, Potsdam, DDR
2. 49-49N, 10-52E, Bavaria, BRD
3. 52-26N, 07-04E, Niedersachsen, BRD

FRETHORST, 3
1. 53-04N, 12-33E, Fretzdorf, Potsdam, DDR
2. 52-04N, 07-08E, Frettholt, Nordrhein-Westfalen,
BRD

FREUDENBERG, 3
1. 52-42N, 13-49E, Frankfurt/Oder, DDR
2. 54-14N, 12-30E, Rostock, DDR
3. 54-13N, 21-19E, (Polish=Radosze) Poland
4. 49-29N, 11-59E, Bavaria, BRD
5. 49-45N, 09-19E, Baden-Wuerttemberg, BRD
6. 50-54N, 07-52E, Nordrhein-Westfalen, BRD
7. 54-01N, 10-21E, Schleswig-Holstein, BRD

FRICKENHAUSEN, Bavaria, 2
1. 48-04N, 10-19E, Bavaria, BRD
2. 48-36N, 09-22E, Baden-Wuerttemberg, BRD
3. 49-40N, 10-05E, Bavaria, BRD
4. 50-24N, 10-14E, Bavaria, BRD

FRIEDEBERG, 3
1. 51-37N, 11-44E, Friedeburg, Halle, DDR
2. 52-52N, 15-32E, Friedeberg in Neumark, Polish-
occupied Germany
3. 50-58N, 15-23E, Friedeberg am Queis, Polish-
occupied Germany
4. 53-27N, 07-50E, Friedeburg, Niedersachsen, BRD
There are three villages named Friedberg in BRD.

FRIEDEBERG, Austria? 3

FRIEDENFELS, 1
1. 53-08N, 13-44E, Friedenfelde, Neubrandenburg,
DDR
2. 49-53N, 12-07E, Bavaria, BRD

FRIEDLAND, 1, 2
1. 52-06N, 14-16E, Frankfurt/Oder, DDR
2. 53-41N, 13-33E, Neubrandenburg, DDR
3. 50-29N, 17-36E, Friedland in Oberschlesien,
Polish-occupied Germany
4. 50-40N, 16-11E, Friedland in Schlesien, Polish-
occupied Germany
5. 51-25N, 09-56E, Niedersachsen, BRD

FRIEDRICHSBERG, 1
1. 52-31N, 13-28E, section of East Berlin, DDR
2. 50-06N, 11-19E, Bavaria, BRD
3. 54-18N, 10-08E, (section of city) Schleswig-
Holstein, BRD

FRIEDRICHSTHAL, Mecklenburg, 2, 3
1. 50-27N, 11-13E, Suhl, DDR
2. 50-40N, 12-36E, Karl-Marx-Stadt, DDR
3. 52-47N, 13-16E, Potsdam, DDR
4. 53-10N, 14-21E, Frankfurt/Oder, DDR
5. 53-39N, 11-19E, (section of city) Schwerin, DDR
6. 53-32N, 21-14E, (Polish=Cis) Polish-occupied
Germany
There are three additional villages of this name in
the BRD.

FRITZENHAUSEN, 2
1. 48-04N, 10-19E, Frickenhausen, Bavaria, BRD
2. 48-36N, 09-22E, Frickenhausen, Baden-Wuerttemberg,
BRD
3. 49-40N, 10-05E, Frickenhausen, Bavaria, BRD
4. 50-25N, 10-14E, Frickenhausen, Bavaria, BRD

FROEBEL, Prussia, 1
Not found.

FUCHSMUEHLE, 3
1. 49-55N, 12-09E, Fuchsmuehl, Bavaria, BRD
2. 49-23N, 10-10E, Fuchsmuehle, Bavaria, BRD

FUERSTENAU, Oldenburg, 1
1. 50-44N, 13-50E, Dresden, DDR
2. 53-20N, 13-32E, Neubrandenburg, DDR
3. 54-03N, 20-05E, (Polish=Ksiezno) Poland
4. 54-11N, 19-09E, (Polish=Kmiecin) Poland
5. 54-13N, 21-34E, (Polish=Lesniewo) Poland
6. 51-50N, 09-19E, Nordrhein-Westfalen, BRD
7. 52-18N, 10-20E, Niedersachsen, BRD
8. 52-31N, 07-43E, Niedersachsen, BRD

FUNFHAUS bei WIEN, Austria, 2

FUTTERCAMP, Holstein, 1
1. 54-17N, 10-39E (farm) Schleswig-Holstein, BRD
2. 54-21N, 10-33E (farm) Schleswig-Holstein, BRD

FUTTERKAM, 3
Possibly Futterkamp (Futtercamp) above.

GADEBUSCH, 1
1. 53-42N, 11-07E, Schwerin, DDR

GADELEGEN, 2
1. 52-32N, 11-22E, Gardelegen, Magdeburg, DDR

GAELTZOW, 2
See GOERLTZOW, GUELTZOW

GAIS, Switzerland, 1

GAMSTADT, 1
1. 50-57N, 10-52E, Gamstaedt, Erfurt, DDR

GANTERSLEBEN, 2
See GUENTHERSLEBEN

GARDELEN, 1
1. 52-32N, 11-22E, Gardelegen, Magdeburg, DDR

GARKOWO, 2
1. 53-02N, 20-06E, Garkowo Nowe, Poland
2. 53-02N, 20-05E, Garkowo Stary, Poland

GARLEBEN, 1, 3
1. 51-50N, 09-57E, Garlebsen, Niedersachsen, BRD
2. 53-03N, 11-22E, Gorleben, Niedersachsen, BRD

GARNSDORF, 1, 3
1. 50-38N, 11-21E, Gera, DDR
2. 50-55N, 12-55E, Karl-Marx-Stadt, DDR

GARRENDORF, Bavaria, 3
1. 49-26N, 11-54E, Gaermersdorf, Bavaria, BRD

GARSTOW, Prussia, 2
1. 52-59N, 11-46E, Garsedow, Schwerin, DDR

GARTOW, 2
1. 52-53N, 12-31E, Potsdam, DDR
2. 53-02N, 11-28E, Niedersachsen, BRD

GARWITZ, 2
1. 53-27N, 11-42E, Schwerin, DDR

GARZ, 1
1. 52-45N, 12-12E, Magdeburg, DDR
2. 52-51N, 12-38E, Potsdam, DDR
3. 53-02N, 12-05E, Potsdam, DDR
4. 53-53N, 14-10E, Rostock, DDR
5. 54-19N, 13-21E, Rostock, DDR

GAY, 2
1. 53-37N, 20-11E (Pol.=Gaj) Poland
2. 50-45N, 06-25E Gey, Nordrhein-Westfalen, BRD
There are about 25 villages named Gaj in Poland.

GEBBINGEN, Prussia, 3
Not found.

GEBERSDORF, 1, 2
1. 50-32N, 11-17E, Suhl, DDR
2. 51-54N, 13-25E, Cottbus, DDR
3. 48-31N, 11-02E, Bavaria, BRD
4. 48-45N, 12-06E, Bavaria, BRD
5. 49-05N, 11-14E, Bavaria, BRD
6. 49-20N, 10-38E, Bavaria, BRD
7. 49-25N, 11-01E, Bavaria, BRD
8. 50-57N, 09-18E, Hessen, BRD

GEBSTEDT, 1
1. 51-06N, 11-30E, Erfurt, DDR

GEHREN, 2
1. 50-39N, 11-00E, Suhl, DDR
2. 51-48N, 13-39E, Cottbus, DDR
3. 53-35N, 13-44E, Neubrandenburg, DDR
4. 47-47N, 10-43E, Bavaria, BRD
5. 53-18N, 08-23E, Niedersachsen, BRD
6. 53-43N, 09-17E, Niedersachsen, BRD

GEINSEN, 2
1. 49-18N, 08-15E, Geinsheim, Rheinland-Pfalz, BRD
2. 49-53N, 08-24E, Geinsheim, Hessen, BRD

GELWITZ, 3
Not found.

GENETSK, 2
Not found

GENT (GENEVA), Switzerland, 1

GENTHIEN, 1
1. 52-24N, 12-10E, Genthin, Magdeburg, DDR
2. 52-53N, 11-32E, Genzien, Magdeburg, DDR

GEPPERSDROF, 2, 3
Not found.

GERA, 1, 2, 3
1. 50-52N, 12-05E, Gera, DDR

GERDESHAGEN, 3
1. 53-15N, 12-12E, Gerdshagen, Potsdam, DDR
2. 53-42N, 12-06E, Gerdshagen, Schwerin, DDR
3. 53-43N, 12-05E, Gerdshagen, Schwerin, DDR
4. 54-00N, 11-50E, Gerdshagen, Rostock, DDR

GERNSCHWALD, 3
Not found.

GEROSCHIN, 1
Not found.

GEVEZIN, 2
1. 53-34N, 13-07E, Neubrandenburg, DDR

GEWITZEN, GEWITZIN, 2
See GEVEZIN

GIELOW, 2
1. 53-42N, 12-45E, Neubrandenburg, DDR

GIFFHORN, 1
1. 52-29N, 10-33E, Gifhorn, Niedersachsen, BRD

GILLERSDORF, 1
1. 50-37N, 11-01E, Suhl, DDR

GISPERSLEBEN, 1
1. 51-01N, 10-59E, (section of city) Erfurt, DDR

GLASHAGE, GLASHAGEN, 3
1. 53-47N, 11-25E, Rostock, DDR
2. 54-05N, 11-52E, Rostock, DDR
3. 54-10N, 13-03E, Rostock, DDR

GLATZ, Hungary, 2

GLEICHENWIESSEN, Thuringia, 2
1. 50-22N, 10-38E, Gleicherwiesen, Suhl, DDR

GLEIMA, 1
1. 50-32N, 11-32E, Gera, DDR
There are six villages named Gleina in DDR.

GLOETZ, Mecklenburg, 2
Not found.

GLOGAU, 2, 3
1. 52-35N, 22-28E, Poland

GLUECKSTADT, 1, 2, 3
1. 53-47N, 09-25E, Schleswig-Holstein, BRD
2. 47-47N, 11-57E, Glueckstatt, Bavaria, BRD

GNADENFELD, 2
1. 48-43N, 11-10E, Bavaria, BRD

GNADENFREY, Prussia, 1, 3
Not found.

GNANZIEN, 2
1. 53-50N, 13-45E, Genvezin, Neubrandenburg, DDR

GNESEN, 1, 2
1. 53-26N, 13-42E, Gneisenau, Neubrandenburg, DDR

GNIEFKOWO? 3
1. 52-54N, 12-50E, Gnewikow, Potsdam, DDR
2. 52-33N, 17-15E, Gniewkowo, Poland
3. 52-53N, 18-26E, Gniewkowo, Poland

GNOSEN, 2
Not found.

GOBITZ, 1
1. 51-05N, 12-11E, Goebitz, Halle, DDR

GOELMGEN, 2
1. 52-02N, 12-20E, Golmenglin, Magdeburg, DDR

GOERLITZ, 2, 3
1. 51-10N, 15-00E, Dresden, DDR
2. 51-13N, 13-04E, Leipzig, DDR
3. 50-50N, 12-02E, Gorlitzsch, Gera, DDR
4. 54-05N, 21-29E, (Pol.=Gierloz) Poland

GOERLTZOW, Prussia, 2
1. 51-39N, 12-05E, Goelzau, Halle, DDR
See also Gueltzow

GOETTINGEN, 2, 3
1. 48-28N, 10-05E, Baden-Wuerttemberg, BRD
2. 50-53N, 08-46E, Hessen, BRD
3. 51-32N, 09-56E, Niedersachsen, BRD
4. 51-40N, 08-14E, Nordrhein-Westfalen, BRD

GOHLAU, Prussia, 1
1. 51-05N, 13-20E, Gohla, Dresden, DDR
1. 53-01N, 10-56E, Niedersachsen, BRD
There are five villages named Gola in Poland.

GOLDBECK, 3
1. 52-43N, 11-51E, Magdeburg, DDR
2. 52-51N, 12-23E, Neubrandenburg, DDR
3. 53-08N, 12-31E, Potsdam, DDR
4. 53-57N, 11-07E, Rostock, DDR
5. 52-06N, 09-09E, Niedersachsen, DDR
6. 53-24N, 09-38E, Niedersachsen, DDR

GOLDBERG, Mecklenburg, 1, 2, 3
1. 53-35N, 12-05E, Schwerin, DDR
2. 53-57N, 11-47E, Rostock, DDR
3. 54-31N, 13-34E, Rostock, DDR
4. 51-07N, 15-55E, Goldberg in Schlesien, Polish-occupied Germany
5. 50-01N, 11-43E, Bavaria, BRD
6. 52-56N, 08-22E, Niedersachsen, BRD
7. 53-06N, 08-27E, Niedersachsen, BRD

GOLDENITZ, 2
1. 53-22N, 11-07E, Schwerin, DDR
2. 53-55N, 12-09E, Goeldenitz, Schwerin, DDR
3. 54-01N, 12-18E, Goeldenitz, Rostock, DDR
4. 51-12N, 13-03E, Goeldnitz, Leipzig, DDR

GOLDLANDER, 2
Not found.

GOLDLAUTER, 2
1. 51-12N, 13-03E, Leipzig, DDR

GOLDSCHIN, 2
1. 50-57N, 12-22E, Goeldschen, Leipzig, DDR

GOLIN, Prussia, 2
1. 51-08N, 14-20E, Golenz, Dresden, DDR
2. 53-54N, 22-32E, Gollen (Pol.=Golubie) Poland

GOLKOWKO, 2
1. 53-12N, 19-34E, Golkowo, Poland

GOLLOP, GOLLUP, GOLUPP, Prussia, 2
1. 53-52N, 22-32E, Gollupken (Pol.=Golubka) Poland
2. 54-10N, 22-18E, Gollubien (Pol.=Golubie Wezewskie) Poland
3. 54-18N, 22-44E, Gollubien (Pol.=Golubie) Poland

GOMMATSHAUSEN, 1
Not found.

GONROW? 3
Not found.

GORKWITZ, 3
1. 50-35N, 11-47E, Goerkwitz, Gera, DDR

GORLEBEN? 3
1. 53-03N, 11-22E, Niedersachsen, BRD

GOSCHUETZ, 2
1. 50-38N, 11-52E, Goeschitz, Gera, DDR

GOSEWIT, 1
1. 54-46N, 09-36E, Gosewatt (farm), Schleswig-Holstein, BRD

GOSSDORF, 1
1. 50-57N, 14-10E, Dresden, DDR

GOSSITZ, 1
1. 50-37N, 11-35E, Goessitz, Gera, DDR

GOTHA, 1, 3
1. 50-57N, 10-43E, Erfurt, DDR
2. 51-25N, 12-36E, Leipzig, DDR

GOTHENBURG, 1

GRABEN, 1
1. 52-14N, 12-26E, Graeben, Potsdam, DDR
There are 16 villages of this name in BRD.

GRABOW, 1, 2, 3
1. 51-46N, 12-56E, Grabo, Cottbus, DDR
2. 51-57N, 12-39E, Grabo, Halle, DDR
3. 52-07N, 12-45E, Grabow, Potsdam, DDR
4. 52-15N, 11-57E, Grabow, Magdeburg, DDR
5. 52-29N, 12-39E, Grabow, Potsdam, DDR
6. 53-05N, 12-24E, Grabow, Potsdam, DDR
7. 53-16N, 12-10E, Grabow, Potsdam, DDR
8. 53-17N, 11-34E, Grabow, Schwerin, DDR
9. 53-17N, 12-27E, Grabow, Neubrandenburg, DDR
10. 54-03N, 13-04E, Grabow, Rostock, DDR
11. 54-14N, 13-24E, Grabow, Rostock, DDR
12. 53-01N, 11-06E, Brabow, Niedersachsen, BRD
In addition, there are seven villages of this name in Poland and Polish-occupied Germany.

GRADEN, 2
Not found.

GRAEFENBERG, Prussia, 2
1. 49-01N, 11-17E, Grafenberg, Bavaria, BRD
2. 51-14N, 06-50E (section of city) Nordrhein-Westfalen, BRD
3. 49-39N, 11-15E, Graefenberg, Bavaria, BRD
4. 57-37N, 10-17E, Greifenberg, Bavaria, BRD
5. 48-04N, 11-05E, Greifenberg, Bavaria, BRD

GRAEFENTHAL, 1, 2
  1. 50-32N, 11-18E, Suhl, DDR

GRAEFINAU, 3
  1. 50-42N, 11-01E, Graefinau Angstedt, Suhl, DDR
  2. 48-51N, 13-24E, Grafinau, Bavaria, BRD

GRAEPELIN, 2
  1. 53-34N, 09-11E, Graepel, Niedersachsen, BRD

GRAET, 2
  1. 47-36N, 09-43E, Greit, Bavaria, BRD

GRAETZ, Prussia, 1, 3
  1. 50-38N, 11-28E, Gera, DDR
  2. 52-14N, 16-22E, (Pol.=Grodzisk Wielkopolski)
    Poland

GRAFENDORA, Prussia, 3
  1. 50-40N, 11-32E, Graefendorf, Gera, DDR
  2. 50-51N, 10-15E, Graefendorf, Suhl, DDR
  3. 51-18N, 11-53E, Graefendorf, Halle, DDR
  4. 51-32N, 12-52E, Graefendorf, Leipzig, DDR
  5. 51-40N, 13-13E, Graefendorf, Cottbus, DDR
  6. 51-55N, 13-12E, Graefendorf, Potsdam, DDR
  7. 50-10N, 11-26E, Grafendobrach, Bavaria, BRD
  8. 48-35N, 11-50E, Grafendorf, Bavaria, BRD
  9. 50-07N, 09-45E, Graefendorf, Bavaria, BRD

GRAFENHAGEN, Prussia, 2, 3
  1. 51-38N, 11-25E, Greifenhagen, Halle, DDR
  2. 53-15N, 14-29E, Greifenhagen, Polish-occupied
    Germany

GRAFENSTIETZ? 3
  1. 51-37N, 11-25E, Graefenstuhl, Halle, DDR

GRAFENTHAL, Prussia, 2
  See GRAEFENTHAL

GRAJEWO, 1
  1. 53-39N, 22-27E, Poland

GRAMBOE, 3
  Not found.

GRAMBOW, 2, 3
  1. 53-25N, 14-20E, Neubrandenburg, DDR
  2. 53-33N, 12-03E, Schwerin, DDR
  3. 53-37N, 11-17E, Schwerin, DDR
  4. 53-44N, 12-34E, Neubrandenburg, DDR

GRAMSTAEDT, 2
  Not found.

GRAMZOW, 2
  1. 53-07N, 13-10E, Potsdam, DDR
  2. 53-08N, 11-55E, Schwerin, DDR
  3. 53-13N, 14-00E, Neubrandenburg, DDR
  4. 53-51N, 13-23E, Neubrandenburg, DDR

GRANZIN, Mecklenburg, 2, 3
  1. 53-21N, 11-44E, Schwerin, DDR
  2. 53-25N, 12-54E, Neubrandenburg, DDR
  3. 53-27N, 11-09E, Schwerin, DDR
  4. 53-28N, 10-51E, Schwerin, DDR
  5. 53-30N, 11-57E, Schwerin, DDR

GRAPENSTIETZ, 3
  See GRAFENSTIETZ?

GRASSLEBEN, 1
  1. 52-19N, 11-01E, Grasleben, Niedersachsen, BRD

GRAUDENZ, Prussia, 2
  Not found.

GREBBIN, 1
  1. 53-31N, 11-52E, Schwerin, DDR
  2. 51-03N, 06-08E, Grebben, Nordrhein-Westfalen,
    BRD

GREIBURG, 2
  Not found.

GREIFENHAGEN, Prussia, 2, 3
  1. 51-38N, 11-25E, Halle, DDR
  2. 53-15N, 14-29E, Polish-occupied Germany

GREIFFENAU, 2
  See GRAEFINAU

GREIFSWALD, 2, 3
  1. 54-06N, 13-23E, Rostock, DDR

GREISENBERG, 1
  Not found.

GRENITZ, 3
  Not found.

GRESEN, 3
  Not found.

GRIBITZ, 3
  Not found.

GRIMEN, GRIMMEN, 1, 3
  1. 54-06N, 13-03E, Grimmen, Rostock, DDR
  2. 53-37N, 20-51E, Grammen (Pol.=Grom) Poland
  3. 53-41N, 07-56E, Grimmens, Niedersachsen, BRD

GROCKOW, 1
  Not found.

GROSCHUETZ, 3
  Not found.

GROSFAHNE, Saxony-Gotha, 3
  Not found.

GROSS BREITENBACH, 2
  1. 50-35N, 11-02E, Grossbreitenbach, Suhl, DDR

GROSS GLOGAU, Silesia, 1, 2
  1. 51-40N, 16-06E, Glogau, Polish-occupied Germany

GROSS GOELITZ, 1
  1. 50-42N, 11-13E, Grossgoelitz, Gera, DDR

GROSS NORDENDE, 1
  1. 53-42N, 09-39E, Schleswig-Holstein, BRD

GROSS OERNER, 1
  1. 51-37N, 11-30E, Grossoerner, Halle, DDR

GROSS SCHOENAU, 3
  1. 50-54N, 14-41E, Grossschoenau, Dresden, DDR

GROSSBAMMSDORF, 2
  1. 50-16N, 10-22E, Grossbardorf, Bavaria, BRD

GROSSENBERKEL, 2
  1. 52-16N, 08-44E, Grossenberken, Nordrhein-West-
    falen, BRD

GROSSENHAYN, 2
1. 51-17N, 13-33E, Grossenhain, Dresden, DDR
2. 53-34N, 08-58E, Grossenhain, Niedersachsen, BRD

GROSSENZUGEN? 3
Not found.

GROSSGLOGAU, 2
1. 51-40N, 16-06E, Glogau, Polish-occupied Germany

GROSSLANDORF, 1
Not found.

GROSSMANDERN, Prussia, 1
Not found.

GROSSMELZEN, GROSSMOLZEN, 1, 2
1. 51-02N, 11-08E, Grossmoelsen, Erfurt, DDR
2. 54-18N, 19-54E, Gross Maulen (Pol.=Muly) Poland
3. 53-21N, 15-38E, Grossmellen, Polish-occupied
   Germany
4. 54-16N, 16-03E, Grossmoellen, Polish-occupied
   Germany

GROSSNENDORF, GROSSNENNDORF, 1, 3
1. 52-42N, 14-25E, Grossneuendorf, Frankfurt/Oder,
   DDR
2. 50-32N, 11-18E, Grossneundorf, Suhl, DDR
3. 52-20N, 09-23E, Gross Nenndorf, Niedersachsen,
   BRD

GROSSNOSSEN, 1
Not found.

GROSSRETBACH, 1
1. 50-56N, 10-52E, Grossrettbach, Erfurt, DDR

GROSSWICH, GROSSWITZ, 2
1. 51-34N, 12-53E, Grosswig, Leipzig, DDR
2. 51-41N, 12-42E, Grosswig, Halle, DDR
3. 53-51N, 09-27E, Gross Wisch, Schleswig-Holstein,
   BRD
4. 53-51N, 09-22E, Grosswisch, Schleswig-Holstein,
   BRD

GRUBE, 3
1. 51-10N, 14-40E, Dresden, DDR
2. 52-26N, 12-57E, Potsdam, DDR
3. 52-40N, 14-14E, Frankfurt/Oder, DDR
4. 53-00N, 12-00E, Schwerin, DDR
5. 53-43N, 12-35E, Neubrandenburg, DDR
6. 54-14N, 11-02E, Schleswig-Holstein, BRD

GRUENAU, 1
1. 50-32N, 11-29E, Gera, DDR
2. 50-39N, 12-37E, Karl-Marx-Stadt, DDR
3. 50-41N, 13-04E, Karl-Marx-Stadt, DDR
4. 52-25N, 13-35E, (section of city) Soviet Zone
   (Berlin?) DDR
5. 54-18N, 12-39E, Rostock, DDR
6. 49-56N, 11-37E, Grunau, Bavaria, BRD
7. 49-34E, 12-08E, Gruenau, Bavaria, BRD
There are other villages named Grunau, Grunaue, in
DDR; an additional 8 villages of these names (Pol.=
Gronowo, Zieleniak, Pieczonki) in Polish-occupied
Germany and Poland.

GRUENBERG, 2, 3
1. 50-50N, 13-07E, Karl-Marx-Stadt, DDR
2. 50-51N, 12-24E, Schwerin, DDR
3. 51-10N, 13-51E, Magdeburg, DDR
4. 51-22N, 14-04E, Magdeburg, DDR

5. 53-21N, 14-09E, Neubrandenburg, DDR
6. 51-56N, 15-30E, Polish-occupied Germany
There are five villages of this name in BRD.

GRUENEBERG, Prussia, 2, 3
1. 52-52N, 13-14E, Potsdam, DDR
2. 50-58N, 13-22E, Grueneburg, Neubrandenburg, DDR
3. 54-19N, 19-52E, Grunenberg (Pol.=Gronkowo) Poland

GRUENENPLAU, GRUENENPLAN, 2
1. 53-11N, 12-53E, Gruenplan, Neubrandenburg, DDR
2. 51-58N, 09-44E, Gruenenplan, Niedersachsen, BRD

GRUENHOFF, Mecklenburg, 2
1. 53-26N, 11-06E, Gruenhof, Schwerin, DDR
2. 53-26N, 10-26E, Gruenhof, Schleswig-Holstein,
   BRD
3. 48-23N, 10-21E, Gruenhoefe, Bavaria, BRD

GRUENSTADT, 3
1. 50-32N, 12-50E, Gruenstaedtel, Karl-Marx-Stadt,
   DDR
2. 49-34N, 08-10E, Rheinland-Pfalz, BRD
3. 49-02N, 10-19E, Baden-Wuerttemberg, BRD

GRUESSOW, 3
1. 53-27N, 12-26E, Neubrandenburg, DDR
2. 53-59N, 13-58E, Rostock, DDR
3. 50-44N, 16-04E, Gruessau, Polish-occupied Germany

GRUETZENDORF, 2
1. 52-08N, 12-32E, Gruetzdorf (farm), Potsdam, DDR

GRUMBACH, Prussia, 1
1. 50-26N, 11-30E, Gera, DDR
2. 50-33N, 13-06E, Karl-Marx-Stadt, DDR
3. 50-42N, 10-27E, Suhl, DDR
4. 50-46N, 10-19E, Suhl, DDR
5. 50-50N, 12-38E, Karl-Marx-Stadt, DDR
6. 51-02N, 13-33E, Dresden, DDR
7. 51-04N, 10-37E, Erfurt, DDR
8. 49-39N, 07-34E, Rheinland-Pfalz, BRD

GRUNOW, 2
1. 52-09N, 14-24E, Grunow, Frankfurt/Oder, DDR
2. 52-36N, 14-02E, Grunow, Frankfurt/Oder, DDR
3. 53-08N, 14-04E, Gruenow, Frankfurt/Oder, DDR
4. 53-19N, 13-57E, Gruenow, Neubrandenburg, DDR
5. 53-21N, 13-19E, Gruenow, Neubrandenburg, DDR

GRUSSAU? GRUSSOW, 2, 3
See GRUESSOW

GUBEN, Prussia, 2
1. 51-57N, 14-43E, Cottbus, DDR

GUCHEN, Prussia, 2
1. 51-33N, 19-15E, Gucin, Poland
2. 51-47N, 21-04E, Gucin, Poland
3. 52-43N, 20-36E, Gucin, Poland
4. 48-41N, 08-09E, Gucken (farm) Baden-Wuerttemberg
   BRD

GUELITZ, 3
1. 53-12N, 11-59E, Schwerin, DDR
2. 53-47N, 12-46E, Neubrandenburg, DDR

GUELTZOW, 1
1. 53-42N, 12-51E, Guelzow, Neubrandenburg, DDR
2. 53-49N, 12-04E, Guelzow, Schwerin, DDR
3. 54-02N, 13-07E, Guelzow, Rostock, DDR
4. 50-29N, 19-38E, Gulzow, Poland
5. 53-49N, 14-59E, Guelzow, Polish-occupied Germany
6. 53-27N, 10-30E, Guelzow, Schleswig-Holstein, BRD

GUENSTEDT, 3
1. 51-13N, 11-04E, Erfurt, DDR

GUENTHERSLEBEN, 1, 3
1. 51-18N, 10-46E, Gundersleben, Erfurt, DDR
2. 49-52N, 09-54E, Guentersleben, Bavaria, BRD

GUENZERODE, 2
1. 51-25N, 10-10E, Guenterode, Erfurt, DDR
2. 51-31N, 10-40E, Guenzerode, Erfurt, DDR

GUENZSTEDT, 3
See GUENSTEDT

GUESTROW, 1, 2, 3
1. 53-48N, 12-10E, Schwerin, DDR

GUNSTEDT, 3
See GUENSTEDT

GUNTERSLEBEN, Saxony-Gotha, 1, 3
See GUENTHERSLEBEN

GUNZERODE, 2
See GUENZERODE

GURTSCH, 3
1. 50-15N, 12-16E, Guerth, Karl-Marx-Stadt, DDR
2. 53-49N, 18-55E, Gurcz, Poland

GUSTROW, 1, 2, 3
See GUESTROW

GUTABSCHIED, 3
Not found.

GUTEFKOWO? 3
1. 52-44N, 20-38E, Gutkowo, Poland
2. 52-50N, 20-07E, Gutkowo, Poland
3. 53-48N, 20-24E, Gutkowo, Poland

GUTENDORF, 2
1. 51-33N, 11-58E, Halle, DDR
2. 48-06N, 12-38E, Bavaria, BRD
3. 49-09N, 12-57E, Bavaria, BRD

GUTWITZ, 1
Not found.

HACKENDORF, 3
1. 54-10N, 19-16E, Hakendorf (Pol.=Zawadka) Poland
2. 48-41N, 11-59E, Bavaria

HADEFINEN? 1
Not found.

HADERSLEBEN, 3
1. 51-33N, 11-39E, Hedersleben, Halle, DDR
2. 51-52N, 11-16E, Hedersleben, Halle, DDR
3. 51-59N, 11-18E, Hadmersleben, Magdeburg, DDR

HAELZINGEN? 3
1. 47-37N, 07-37E, Haltingen, Baden-Wuerttemberg,
BRD

HAGEN, Lippe, 3
1. 52-24N, 12-06E, Magdeburg, DDR
2. 52-45N, 11-10E, Magdeburg, DDR
3. 54-24N, 13-34E, Rostock, DDR
4. 54-34N, 13-37E, Rostock, DDR
There are 25 villages of this name in BRD; however,
the city in Nordrhein-Westfalen, BRD, is probably
meant herein.

HAGENAU? 3
1. 52-46N, 11-32E, Magdeburg, DDR
2. 53-58N, 19-48E, (Pol.=Chojnik) Poland
3. 47-48N, 12-57E, Bavaria, BRD
4. 48-24N, 11-36E, Bavaria, BRD
5. 48-43N, 12-21E, Bavaria, BRD
6. 49-00N, 10-55E, Bavaria, BRD
7. 49-07N, 12-29E, Bavaria, BRD
8. 49-09N, 12-07E, Bavaria, BRD
9. 49-19N, 10-19E, Bavaria, BRD

HAGENOW, 1, 2, 3
1. 53-26N, 11-12E, Schwerin, DDR
2. 53-34N, 12-33E, Neubrandenburg, DDR

HAKENWALDE, 3
1. 50-58N, 12-10E, Heuckenwalde, Heuckewalde,
Halle, DDR
There is a Hackenwalde, about 5 kilometers north-
west of Gollnow (53-54N, 22-32E, Poland) but the
village is not shown on postwar Polish maps. *See*
also Clifford Neal Smith, *Nineteenth-Century Emi-*
gration of "Old Lutherans" from Eastern Germany
(Mainly Pomerania and Lower Silesia) to Australia,
Canada, and the United States. German-American
Genealogical Research monograph no. 7 (McNeal, AZ:
Westland Publications, 1980).

HALLE, HALLE AM SAALE, 1, 3
1. 51-30N, 12-00E, Halle, DDR
2. 50-54N, 07-45E, Nordrhein-Westfalen, BRD
3. 51-12N, 07-17E, Nordrhein-Westfalen, BRD
4. 51-59N, 09-34E, Niedersachsen, BRD
5. 52-04N, 08-22E, Nordrhein-Westfalen, BRD
6. 52-26N, 08-55E, Niedersachsen, BRD

HALLUND, Sweden, 1

HAM BEI HAMBURG, 2
Now part of the city.

HAMBURG, 1, 2, 3
1. 53-33N, 10-00E, Hamburg, BRD

HAMELN, HAMMELN, 2, 3
1. 52-06N, 09-21E, Niedersachsen, BRD

HAMMERSPRING, 2
Not found.

HANNOVER, 1, 2
1. 52-22N, 09-43E, Niedersachsen, BRD
2. 53-11N, 08-31E, Hannoever, Niedersachsen, BRD

HANSHEIM, 1
Not found.

HARBURG, 1, 2
1. 53-28N, 10-00E, Now part of the city of Hamburg,
BRD

HARTENBERG, 2
1. 51-47N, 10-49E, (forester's lodge) Magdeburg,
DDR

[continued]

HARTENBERG [continued]
2. 50-24N, 10-34E, Hartenburg (hill) Suhl, DDR
3. 49-27N, 11-29E, Bavaria, BRD

HARTHAN, Saxony, 1
1. 50-47N, 12-55E, Harthau, Karl-Marx-Stadt, DDR
2. 50-54N, 12-31E, Harthau, Karl-Marx-Stadt, DDR
3. 51-38N, 15-35E, Hartau, Polish-occupied Germany

HASELDORF, 1
1. 51-00N, 14-56E, (forester's lodge) Dresden, DDR
2. 53-45N, 13-02E, Hasseldorf, Neubrandenburg, DDR
3. 53-37N, 09-36E, Schleswig-Holstein, BRD

HASENMOOR, 2
1. 53-54N, 09-59E, Schleswig-Holstein, BRD

HASSLOW, Holstein, 1
1. 54-15N, 19-34E, Haselau (Pol.=Zajaczkowo) Poland
2. 52-49N, 10-20E, Hassloh (forest), Niedersachsen, BRD

HATTORF, Hannover, 2
1. 51-39N, 10-14E, Niedersachsen, BRD
2. 52-21N, 10-45E, Niedersachsen, BRD

HAYNE, Saxony, 3
1. 51-26N, 12-19E, Hayna, Leipzig, DDR
2. 51-16N, 15-56E, Haynau, Polish-occupied Germany
3. 49-07N, 08-12E, Hayna, Rheinland-Pfalz, BRD

HEIDESBACH, 1
1. 50-38N, 10-44E, Heidersbach, Suhl, DDR
2. 48-32N, 08-09E, Heidenbach (farm community), Baden-Wuerttemberg, BRD
3. 50-48N, 09-15E, Heidelbach, Hessen, BRD
4. 52-07N, 09-00E, Heidelbeck, Nordrhein-Westfalen, BRD

HEILBRONN, Wuerttemberg, 1, 2
1. 49-08N, 09-13E, Baden-Wuerttemberg, BRD
2. 49-10N, 10-22E, Bavaria, BRD
3. 49-03N, 12-34E, Heilbruenn, Bavaria, BRD

HEILIGENSTADT, 1
1. 51-23N, 10-08E, Erfurt, DDR
2. 48-13N, 12-37E, Bavaria, BRD
3. 48-49N, 11-48E, Bavaria, BRD
4. 49-52N, 11-10E, Bavaria, BRD
5. 53-56N, 09-28E, Heiligenstedten, Schleswig-Holstein, BRD

HEINA, Thuringia, 1
1. 51-16N, 15-56E, Haynau, Polish-occupied Germany
2. 51-26N, 12-19E, Hayna, Leipzig, DDR
3. 50-25N, 10-32E, Haina, Suhl, DDR
4. 50-59N, 10-32E, Haina, Erfurt, DDR
5. 51-06N, 09-35E, Hessen, BRD

HEINAMOF IN RONNHILD, 3
See HEINA; ROEMHILD: RONNHILD

HEINEBACH, 2
1. 51-03N, 09-40E, Hessen, BRD

HEINERICHS, Prussia, 2
1. 50-36N, 10-39E, Heinrichs, Suhl, DDR

HEINRICHAU, 2
1. 52-46N, 12-22E, Heinrichsaue, Potsdam, DDR
2. 50-39N, 17-00E, Polish-occupied Germany
3. 53-36N, 19-22E, (Pol.=Jedrychowo), Poland

HEINROTHA, 1
1. 53-55N, 19-07E, Heinrode (Pol.=Mleczewo) Poland

HEINSBERG, 1
1. 51-02N, 08-09E, Nordrhein-Westfalen, BRD
2. 51-04N, 06-05E, Nordrhein-Westfalen, BRD

HEIRDE, 3
1. 50-57N, 10-06E, Herda, Erfurt, DDR

HEITHAUSEN, 1
1. 52-48N, 09-02E, Heitheusen, Niedersachsen, BRD
2. 52-48N, 09-15E, Heithuesen, Niedersachsen, BRD

HEITHOF, 3
1. 52-21N, 08-26E, Heithoefen, Niedersachsen, BRD
2. 52-17N, 08-40E, Heithoefen (farm), Nordrhein-Westfalen, BRD

HELBERUNGEN, Thuringia, 3
1. 51-18N, 11-13E, Heldrungen, Halle, DDR

HELGOLAND, 2
1. 54-12N, 07-53E, (island) Schleswig-Holstein, BRD

HELLBECK, 1
Not found.

HELLMERSHAUSEN, 2
Not found.

HELM, 2
1. 53-28N, 11-06E, Schwerin, DDR

HELMSDORF, 2
1. 50-46N, 12-27E, Karl-Marx-Stadt, DDR
2. 51-02N, 14-03E, Dresden, DDR
3. 51-18N, 10-21E, Erfurt, DDR
4. 51-36N, 11-37E, Halle, DDR
5. 48-30N, 12-20E, Bavaria, BRD

HELMSTADT, 1
1. 49-19N, 08-59E, Baden-Wuerttemberg, BRD
2. 49-46N, 09-43E, Bavaria, BRD
3. 52-14N, 11-00E, Helmstedt, Niedersachsen, BRD

HELMSTE, 3
1. 53-31N, 09-29E, Niedersachsen, BRD

HEMERRICHS, 2
Not found.

HENRICHSBERG, 2
1. 52-16N, 11-44E, Heinrichsberg, Magdeburg, DDR

HERFORD, 1
52-08N, 08-41N, Nordrhein-Westfalen, BRD

HERIEDEN, 3
1. 51-31N, 10-44E, Herreden, Erfurt, DDR
2. 49-14N, 10-31E, Herrieden, Bavaria, BRD

HERMANNSDORF, HERMANNSTORF, 1
1. 50-34N, 12-54E, Hermannsdorf (train stop) Karl-Marx-Stadt, DDR
2. 49-28N, 11-42E, Hermannsdorf, Bavaria, BRD
3. 49-10N, 12-25E, Hermannsdorf (farm), Bavaria, BRD
4. 54-32N, 09-27E, Hermannsort (farm), Schleswig-Holstein, BRD
5. 48-00N, 11-54E, Herrmannsdorf, Bavaria, BRD
6. 48-16N, 09-05E, Herrmannsdorf, Baden-Wuerttemberg, BRD
7. 48-54N, 12-42E, Herrmannsdorf, Bavaria, BRD

HERNSTEINFELD, 2
Not found.

HERRENBERG, 2
1. 53-50N, 10-46E, Herrnburg, Rostock, DDR
2. 53-43N, 19-49E, Hernsberg (Pol.=Rogowo) Poland
3. 48-36N, 08-52E, Baden-Wuerttemberg, BRD

HERRENHAUSEN, 1
1. 52-23N, 09-41E, (section of town) Niedersachsen, BRD
2. 53-19N, 08-06E, (farm community) Niedersachsen, BRD

HERRNHUTH, 3
1. 51-01N, 14-45, Dresden, DDR*
2. 49-29N, 11-06E, Herrnhuette (section of town) Bavaria, BRD
*Headquarters in Germany of the Unitas Fratrum (Moravian Brethren or Moravian Church) which was prominent in North America as a missionary group. *See* Clifford Neal Smith and Anna Piszczan-Czaja Smith, *Encyclopedia of German-American Genealogical Research* (New York: R. R. Bowker, 1976), p. 53.

HERRNSTADT, 3
1. 51-33N, 16-42E, Polish-occupied, Germany

HERSEGEHOEFEL, 1
Not found.

HERZOGSWALDE, 1
1. 51-01N, 13-30E, Dresden, DDR
2. 53-58N, 20-05E, (Pol.=Ksiaznik) Poland

HESEPE, Oldenburg, 1
1. 52-25N, 07-07E, Niedersachsen, BRD
2. 52-26N, 07-59E, Niedersachsen, BRD

HETTSTADT, 1
1. 51-39N, 11-30E, Hettstedt, Halle, DDR
2. 49-48N, 09-49E, Bavaria, BRD

HEYDE, Holstein, 3
1. 54-12N, 26-11E, Schleswig-Holstein, BRD
There are 33 villages named Heide in BRD.

HEYDEFRIED, 1
Not found.

HILDBURGSHAUSEN, 1, 3
1. 50-25N, 10-45E, Hildburghausen, Suhl, DDR

HILDESHEIM, 3
1. 52-09N, 09-58E, Niedersachsen, BRD

HIMMEL, Prussia, 2
Not found.

HINTERSLAW? 3
Not found.

HIRSCHFELDA, HIRSCHFELDE, 3
1. 50-57N, 14-54E, Hirschfelde, Dresden, DDR
2. 52-38N, 13-48E, Hirschfelde, Frankfurt/Oder, DDR
there are five villages named Hirschfeld in DDR; one in Poland; three in BRD, plus two named Hirschfelden.

HIRSCHHEIM, 1
1. 48=05N, 12-29E, Hirchham, Bavaria, BRD
2. 48-22N, 12-46E, Hirschhorn, Bavaria, BRD

3. 49-27N, 08-54E, Hirschhorn, Hessen, BRD
4. 49-31N, 07-41E, Hirschhorn, Rheinland-Pfalz, BRD

HIRZBACH, 1
1. 50-34N, 11-25E, Gera, DDR
2. 50-41N, 07-28E, Rheinland-Pfalz, BRD

HOCHHEIM, 1
1. 50-57N, 11-00E, Erfurt, DDR
2. 51-01N, 10-40E, Erfurt, DDR
3. 53-14N, 12-04E, Potsdam, DDR
4. 49-39N, 08-20E, (section of town) Rheinland-Pfalz, BRD
5. 50-01N, 08-21E, Hochheim am Main, Hessen, BRD
6. 50-22N, 10-27E, Hoechheim, Bavaria, BRD

HOF, 2
1. 51-14N, 13-11E, Leipzig, DDR
There are 28 villages of this name in BRD.

HOFGEISMAR, 1
1. 51-29N, 09-24E, Hessen, BRD

HOFGRABAU, 1
1. 53-33N, 11-50E, Hof Grabow, Schwerin, DDR

HOFHAGEN, 2
Not found.

HOHENEBE, 2
1. 51-18N, 10-49E, Hohenebra, Erfurt, DDR

HOHENLINDE, 3
1. 48-47N, 09-41E, (farm) Baden-Wuerttemberg, BRD
2. 48-09N, 12-00E, Hohenlinden, Bavaria, BRD

HOHENMASCH, 2
1. 49-57N, 12-04E, Masch*, Bavaria, BRD
2. 52-10N, 08-37E, Masch*, Nordrhein-Westfalen, BRD
3. 52019N, 08-39E, Masch*, Nordrhein-Westfalen, BRD
*No village named Hohenmasch was found, but it is possible the prefix (Hohen-) has been dropped in modern times.

HOHENSCHOENAU, 1, 3
1. 53-35N, 15-09E, Polish-occupied Germany

HOHENZIENTZ, 2
1. 52-11N, 12-03E, Hohenziatz, Magdeburg, DDR

HOHENZIERITZ, 2
1. 53-27N, 13-06E, Neubrandenburg, DDR

HOLSTEIN, 3
1. 54-41N, 09-29E, (farm) Schleswig-Holstein, BRD
2. 51-04N, 09-58E, (hill) Hessen, BRD
3. 52-19N, 07-23E, Holsten, Niedersachsen, BRD
4. 52-33N, 07-51E, Holsten, Niedersachsen, BRD
5. 52-52N, 09-08E, Holsten, Niedersachsen, BRD
6. 52-13N, 08-08E, Holsten (farm community), Niedersachsen, BRD

HOLZHAMMER, Bavaria, 2
1. 48-54N, 13-20E, Bavaria, BRD
2. 49-33N, 12-04E, Bavaria, BRD
3. 48-33N, 13-17E, (farm), Bavaria, BRD

HOLZMINDEN, 2
1. 51-49N, 09-27E, Niedersachsen, BRD

HONINGSLEBEN, 1
1. 49-38N, 11-06E, Honings, Bavaria, BRD

HORB, 2
1. 48-26N, 08-41E, Baden-Wuerttemberg, BRD
2. 50-09N, 11-12E, Bavaria, BRD
3. 50-17N, 11-08E, Bavaria, BRD

HORNBERG, 3
1. 51-27N, 11-35E, Hornburg, Halle, DDR
2. 47-40N, 07-57E, Baden-Wuerttemberg, BRD
3. 48-13N, 08-14E, Baden-Wuerttemberg, BRD
4. 48-37N, 08-34E, Baden-Wuerttemberg, BRD
5. 48-58N, 09-40E, Baden-Wuerttemberg, BRD
6. 49-12N, 09-32E, Baden-Wuerttemberg, BRD

HOSELDORF, 1
See Haseldorf

HOTZENPLUTZ, 2
1. 50-15N, 17-43E, Hotzenplotz (stream), (Czech=
Osoblaha) Polish-occupied Ger-
many

HOWISCH, 1
1. 52-52N, 11-37E, Hoewisch, Magdeburg, DDR

HUNGARY, 3

HUNTEBURG, 2
1. 54-24N, 19-47E, Huntenberg (Pol.=Podgorze) Poland
2. 52-26N, 08-17E, Niedersachsen, BRD

HUSUM, 2, 3
1. 52-34N, 09-15E, Niedersachsen, BRD
2. 52-48N, 08-14E, Niedersachsen, BRD
3. 52-59N, 08-18E, Niedersachsen, BRD
4. 53-33N, 08-27E, Niedersachsen, BRD
5. 54-28N, 09-03E, Schleswig-Holstein, BRD

ICHTERSHAUSEN, 3
1. 50-53N, 10-58E, Erfurt, DDR

ILLFELD, 2
1. 51-35N, 10-47E, Ilfeld, Erfurt, DDR
2. 49-03N, 09-15E, Ilsfeld, Baden-Wuerttemberg,
BRD

ILM STADT, Rudolstadt, 3
1. 51-07N, 11-40E, (stream) Erfurt, DDR

ILMENAU, 3
1. 50-41N, 10-54E, Suhl, DDR
2. 49-48N, 10-31E, Bavaria, BRD

ILSENBURG, Prussia, 1
1. 51-52N, 10-41E, Magdeburg, DDR
2. 50-54N, 08-19E, (forester's lodge) Nordrhein-
Westfalen, BRD

ILTESTADT? 3
1. 48-35N, 13-29E, Ilzstadt (section of town),
Bavaria, BRD

IMENHAUSEN, 2
1. 48-29N, 09-06E, Immenhausen, Baden-Wuerttemburg,
BRD
2. 51-25N, 09-30E, Immenhausen, Hessen, BRD

IMMENRODE, 1
1. 51-22N, 10-44E, Erfurt, DDR
2. 51-30N, 10-38E, Erfurt, DDR
3. 51-57N, 10-29E, Niedersachsen, BRD

INNERWEGGITHAL, Switzerland, 1

INOHATSCHEWO? Poland, 3
Not found.

INOWRACLAW, INOWROSLAV, 2
1. 52-48N, 18-16E, Poland

ISERLOHN, 1
1. 51-22N, 07-42E, Nordrhein-Westfalen, BRD

ITZEHOE, 2
1. 53-55N, 09-31E, Schleswig-Holstein, BRD

JABEL, Mecklenburg, 3
1. 53-10N, 12-26E, Potsdam, DDR
2. 53-33N, 12-33E, Neubrandenburg, DDR
3. 52-57N, 11-05E, Niedersachsen, BRD

JANISCHWALDE, 1
1. 51-52N, 14-30E, Jaenschwalde, Cottbus, DDR

JANOVA, Poland, 2
1. 53-47N, 13-24E, Janow, Neubrandenburg, DDR
2. 50-55N, 21-46E, Janowa, Poland
There are 35 villages named Janow and 25 villages
named Janowo in Poland. There is a Janov bei Boeh-
misch Kamnitz and Janov bei Oberleutensdorf, both
in Czechoslovakia.

JANY, 3
1. 54-16N, 22-10E, Poland

JARWIN, 1
1. 53-55N, 13-21E, Jarmen, Neubrandenburg, DDR

JASSOW, 3
1. 49-45N, 21-28E, Jaslo, Poland
There was a Jassow, Pomerania, about 5 kilometers
south of Wollin (53-51N, 14-37E, Polish-occupied
Germany) along the east coast of Stettiner Bucht
(bay). It is not shown on modern Polish maps.
See also Clifford Neal Smith, *Nineteenth-Century
Emigration of "Old Lutherans" from Eastern Germany
(Mainly Pomerania and Lower Silesia) to Australia,
Canada, and the United States.* German-American
Genealogical Research Monograph No. 7 (McNeal, AZ:
Westland Publications, 1980).

JASTADT, JOSTADT, 2
1. 50-31N, 13-06E, Joehstadt, Karl-Marx-Stadt, DDR

JAUER, 2
1. 51-14N, 14-11E, Dresden, DDR
2. 50-57N, 12-23E, Jauern, Leipzig, DDR
3. 50-41N, 20-33E, Jawor, Poland
4. 50-56N, 18-38E, Jawor, Poland
5. 51-03N, 16-11E, Jawor (Ger.=Jauer) Poland
6. 51-22N, 17-52E, Jawor, Poland

JAVORIN, Prussia, 1
Not found.

JENA, 1
1. 50-56N, 11-35E, Gera, DDR

JENER, TENER, 1
Not found.

JOEKOEPINGSLAEN, Sweden, 1

JOHENREITH, Bavaria, 1
    Not found.

JOHNSDORF, 3
    1. 50-51N, 14-42E, *also called* Kurort Jonsdorf,
            Dresden, DDR
    2. 51-18N, 14-22E, Dresden, DDR
    3. 52-18N, 13-23E, Juehnsdorf, Potsdam, DDR
    There is a Johnsdorf bei Boehmisch Kamnitz and a
    Johnsdorf bei Oberleutensdorf, both in Czechoslo-
    vakia.

JOSTADT. *See* JASTADT

JULIUSBURG, 1
    1. 51-16N, 17-20E, Polish-occupied Germany
    2. 53-25N, 10-30E, Schleswig-Holstein, BRD
    3. 51-48N, 09-41E, (farm) Niedersachsen, BRD

JUNIEN, 1
    1. 53-57N, 22-05E, (Pol.=Junie) Poland

JUSTROW, 2
    Not found.

KAEFERTHAL, 3
    1. 49-31N, 08-31E, Kaefertal (section of city),
            Baden-Wuerttemberg, BRD

KALLENDA, 1
    See KOELEDA

KALTENLENGSFELD, Saxony-Meiningen, 2
    1. 50-39N, 10-12E, Suhl, DDR

KALWAY, Poland, 1
    1. 53-57N, 19-09E, Kalwa (or Kalwe), Poland
    2. 52-24N, 16-36E, Kalwy, Poland

KAMIN, 2
    1. 53-59N, 11-44E, Rostock, DDR
    2. 53-59N, 13-24E, Rostock, DDR
    3. 54-35N, 13-20E, (also spelled Cammin), Rostock,
            DDR
    There are 25 villages named Kamien in Poland. *See
    also* Clifford Neal Smith, *Nineteenth-Century Emi-
    gration of "Old Lutherans" from Eastern Germany
    (Mainly Pomerania & Lower Silesia) to Australia,
    Canada, and the United States.* German-American
    Genealogical Research Monograph No. 7 (McNeal, AZ:
    Westland Publications, 1980).

KAMPE, 2
    1. 54-34N, 13-32E, (also spelled Campe), Rostock,
            DDR
    2. 54-08N, 15-21E, Kamp (section of city), Polish-
            occupied Germany
    3. 53-05N, 07-50E, Niedersachsen, BRD
    There are four farms of this name in BRD.

KANGERSAGEN, Norway, 2

KANNSTADT, 2
    1. 48-48N, 09-12E, Cannstadt (or Bad Cannstadt,
            section of city), Baden-Wuert-
            temberg, BRD

KANTH, 2, 3
    1. 51-02N, 16-46E, Polish-occupied Germany

KARBACH, Bavaria, 1
    1. 47-42N, 09-48E, Baden-Wuerttemberg, BRD
    2. 49-52N, 09-38E, Bavaria, BRD
    3. 49-54N, 10-34E, Bavaria, BRD
    4. 50-09N, 07-37E, Rheinland-Pfalz, BRD

KARBO, KARBOW, 1, 2
    1. 53-20N, 12-35E, Karbow, Neubrandenburg, D
    2. 53-24N, 12-06E, Karbow, (also called Hof
            bow), Schwerin, DDR
    3. 53-24N, 12-07E, Karbow, Schwerin, DDR
    4. 54-03N, 13-36E, Karbow, Rostock, DDR
    5. 53-17N, 19-25E, Karbowo, Poland

KARCHOW, 2
    1. 53-21N, 12-31E, Neubrandenburg, DDR
    2. 51-54N, 16-50E, Karchowo, Poland

KARLSBAD, 3
    Probably CARLOVY VARY (Ger.=Karlsbad), Czech
            vakia

KASBADE? KASSBADE, 1, 3
    See KOSBADE

KAUGERSAGEN, Norway, 2

KAULSDORF, 1, 3
    1. 50-38N, 11-26E, Gera, DDR
    2. 52-38N, 13-35E, (section of city), East 1
            DDR

KAUTH? 2, 3
    A village of this name in Czechoslovakia, ab
    kilometers west of Klattau (Czech.=Klatovy) o
    road. *See also* KANTH

KAY, Prussia, 3
    1. 48-03N, 12-45E, Bavaria, BRD
    2. 48-52N, 12-30E, Bavaria, BRD
    3. 48-35N, 12-29E, Bavaria, BRD
    4. 48-34N, 08-55E, Kayh, Baden-Wuerttemberg
    There was also a Kay, Kreis Zuellichau, Bran
    not shown in recent maps. *See* Clifford Neal
    *Nineteenth-Century Emigration of "Old Luther
    from Eastern Germany (Mainly Pomerania and L
    Silesia) to Australia, Canada, and the Unite
    German-American Genealogical Research Monogr
    (McNeal, AZ: Westland Publications, 1980).

KAZMIN, 2
    Not found.

KEETZ, 3
    1. 53-44N, 11-38E, Keez, Schwerin, DDR

KEIBERSDORF, 3
    Not found.

KEIL, 3
    1. 53-29N, 11-36E, (forest, also called Tri
            Schwerin, DDR

KELBRA, Prussia, 1, 3
    1. 51-25N, 11-02E, Halle, DDR

KELLE, 3
    1. 51-14N, 10-05E, Kella, Erfurt, DDR
    2. 49-38N, 06-50E, Kell, Rheinland-Pfalz, B
    3. 50-27N, 07-19E, Kell, Rheinland-Pfalz, B

KELLINGHUSEN, Holstein, 2
1. 51-32N, 08-27E, Kellinghausen, Nordrhein-Westfalen, BRD
2. 52-31N, 07-44E, Kellinghausen, Niedersachsen,
BRD
3. 52-52N, 08-31E, Kellinghausen, Niedersachsen,
BRD
4. 53-57N, 09-43E, Schleswig-Holstein, BRD

KEMBERG, Prussia, 2
1. 51-47N, 12-38E, Halle, DDR

KEMEL, Prussia, 2
1. 50-10N, 08-01E, Hessen, BRD

KEMNITZ, 2
1. 52-50N, 11-07E, (community, also called Stein-
itz), Magdeburg, DDR
2. 50-26N, 11-59E, Karl-Marx-Stadt, DDR
3. 51-04N, 13-39E, Dresden, DDR
4. 51-04N, 14-48E, Dresden, DDR
5. 52-08N, 12-59E, Potsdam, DDR
6. 52-25N, 12-52E, Potsdam, DDR
7. 53-08N, 12-14E, Potsdam, DDR
8. 54-04N, 13-33E, Rostock, DDR

KEMPEN, 1, 2
1. 51-05N, 06-06E, Nordrhein-Westfalen, BRD
2. 51-07N, 07-03E, Nordrhein-Westfalen, BRD
3. 51-22N, 06-25E, Nordrhein-Westfalen, BRD
4. 51-48N, 08-57E, Nordrhein-Westfalen, BRD
5. 53-04N, 09-43E, Niedersachsen, BRD

KESSCHENDORF, KETSCHENDORF, 2
1. 52-21N, 14-05E, Ketschendorf (or Ketchendorf),
Frankfurt/Oder, DDR
2. 49-50N, 11-04E, Ketschendorf, Bavaria, BRD
3. 50-15N, 10-58E, Ketschendorf, Bavaria, BRD
4. 49-19N, 10-53E, Kitschendorf, Bavaria, BRD

KEUSCHBERG, 2
1. 51-18N, 12-04E, Halle, DDR

KIEL, 1, 2, 3
1. 48-35N, 07-49E, (also called Kehl), Baden-Wuerttemberg, BRD
2. 54-20N, 10-08E, Schleswig-Holstein, BRD
3. 54-33N, 09-10E, Schleswig-Holstein, BRD
4. 53-29N, 07-13E, (farm) Niedersachsen, BRD

KIERITZ, 2
1. 52-40N, 14-26E, Kienitz, Frankfurt/Oder, DDR
2. 51-10N, 12-23E, Kiertzsch, Leipzig, DDR
See also KYRITZ

KIETZ, Prussia, 1
1. 51-56N, 14-04E, Cottbus, DDR
2. 52-07N, 13-55E, (section of city), Cottbus, DDR
3. 52-10N, 14-15E, (section of city), Frankfurt/
Oder, DDR
4. 52-15N, 13-01E, Potsdam, DDR
5. 52-17N, 13-10E, Potsdam, DDR
6. 52-27N, 13-46E, Frankfurt/Oder, DDR
7. 52-34N, 14-37E, Frankfurt/Oder, DDR
8. 52-45N, 12-19E, Potsdam, DDR
9. 53-05N, 11-20E, (also kalled Kietz in der Len-
zer or Kietz ueber Lenzen),
Schwerin, DDR

KIEVE, 3
1. 53-17N, 12-36E, Neubrandenburg, DDR
2. 52-15N, 07-21E, Kiewe (farm), Nordrhein-Westfalen, BRD

KINDELBRUCH, 3
1. 51-16N, 11-05E, Kindelbrueck, Erfurt, DDR

KIRCHENLAMNITZ, 2
1. 50-09N, 11-57E, Kirchenlamitz, Bavaria, BRD

KIRCHHEIM, 1
1. 50-53N, 11-01E, Erfurt, DDR
There are 15 villages (and sections of cities) of
this name in BRD.

KIRCHHEIM, Wuerttemberg, 2
1. 48-39N, 09-27E, Kirchheim unter Teck, Baden-
Wuerttemberg, BRD
2. 48-53N, 10-24E, Kirchheim am Ries, Baden-Wuerttemberg, BRD
3. 49-03N, 09-10E, Kirchheim am Neckar, Baden-Wuerttemberg, BRD
4. 49-23N, 08-40E, (section of city), Baden-Wuerttemberg, BRD

KIRCHKOGEL, Holstein, 1
1. 53-39N, 12-10E, Kirch Kogel, Schwerin, DDR

KIRCHLIES, Bavaria, 3
1. 50-10N, 11-23E, Kirchleus, Bavaria, BRD
2. 50-09N, 11-18E, Kirchlein, Bavaria, BRD

KIRCHZELL, 2
1. 49-37N, 09-11E, Bavaria, BRD

KIRSCHENLAMNITZ, 2
See KIRCHENLAMNITZ

KIROHSCHLACH, 3
1. 48-24N, 08-12E, Kirchloch (farm), Baden-Wuerttemberg, BRD
Could be KIRCHSCHLAG (Czech.=Svetlik), about 5 kilometers east of Schwarzbach (Czech.=Cerna) near the
Aigen, Upper Austria, border crossing into Czechoslovakia.

KISTRINCHEN, 1
1. 53-13N, 13-23E, Kuestrinchen, Neubrandenburg,
DDR

KISTRUP, 3
Not found.

KITZ, 2
Not found. See KIETZ

KITZINGEN, 1
1. 49-44N, 10-10E, Bavaria, BRD

KLABOW, 2
1. 53-37N, 11-36E, Kladow, Schwerin, DDR
2. 52-27N, 13-08E, (section of city), West Berlin,
BRD

KLADRUM, 1
1. 53-34N, 11-48E, Schwerin, DDR

KLAPSCHEN, 1
See KLOPPSCHEN

KLEEFELD, 2
1. 53-42N, 11-34E, Schwerin, DDR
2. 54-12N, 20-07E, (Pol.=Glebisko), Poland
3. 52-22N, 09-47E, (section of city), Niedersachsen, BRD
4. 53-08N, 08-04E, Niedersachsen, BRD
5. 47-57N, 11-41E, Bavaria, BRD

KLEEKAMP, 3
1. 53-48N, 11-33E, Schwerin, DDR
2. 52-07N, 08-15E, Nordrhein-Westfalen, BRD
3. 52-04N, 08-09E, (farm), Nordrhein-Westfalen, BRD

KLEIN BEESEN, 2
1. 52-22N, 13-21E, Kleinbeeren, Potsdam, DDR
2. 52-14N, 13-38E, Kleinbesten, Potsdam, DDR
3. 48-24N, 10-22E, Kleinbeuren, Bavaria, BRD

KLEIN COLMAR, Holstein, 3
1. 53-45N, 09-30E, Kollmar, Schleswig-Holstein, BRD
2. 53-55N, 09-36E, Kollmoor, Schleswig-Holstein, BRD
There is a village called Klein Kollmar on the main road between Glueckstadt and Elmshorn in Schleswig-Holstein, BRD

KLEIN ENDERSDORF, 1
1. 49-09E, 10-55E, Enderndorf, Bavaria, BRD

KLEIN GOERLITZ, 1
1. 50-42N, 11-15E, Kleingoelitz, Gera, DDR
2. 50-25N, 12-14E, Kleingornitz, Karl-Marx-Stadt, DDR
See also GOERLITZ

KLEIN LUECHOW, 2
1. 53-34N, 13-50E, Klein Luckow, Neubrandenburg, DDR
2. 53-41N, 12-29E, Klein Luckow, Neubrandenburg, DDR
See also LUECHOW

KLEIN PETERWITZ, Thuringia, 2
1. 51-30N, 12-15E, Peterwitz, Leipzig, DDR
2. 51-31N, 14-11E, Klein Partwitz, Cottbus, DDR

KLEIN PRITZ, 3
1. 53-38N, 11-57E, Schwerin, DDR

KLEIN ROGAHN, 2
1. 53-36N, 11-21E, Schwerin, DDR
2. 53-40N, 22-21E, Klein Rogallen (Pol.=Rogale Maly), Poland

KLEIN ROSENTHAL, 2
1. 53-42N, 22-15E, Kleinrosen (Pol.=Rozynsk Maly), Poland
2. 54-15N, 22-10E, Klein Rosinsko (Pol.=Rozynsk Maly), Poland

KLEIN TREPPOW, Mecklenburg, 2
1. 53-18N, 13-05E, Klein Trebbow, Neubrandenburg, DDR
2. 53-42N, 11-23E, Klein Trebbow, Schwerin, DDR

KLEIN WELKE, 2
1. 51-13N, 14-24E, Kleinwelka, Dresden, DDR
2. 53-01N, 12-03E, Klein Welle, Schwerin, DDR

KLEINAU, Prussia, 1
1. 52-48N, 11-31E, Magdeburg, DDR
2. 54-25N, 19-47E, Klenau (Pol.=Klejnowo), Poland
3. 48-29N, 11-19E, Klenau, Bavaria, BRD
4. 54-15N, 11-01E, Klenau, Schleswig-Holstein, BRD

KLEINAU, Thuringia, 1
1. 52-48N, 11-31E, Magdeburg, DDR

KLEINBENEBECK, 1
1. 54-24N, 09-27E, Klein Bennebek, Schleswig-Holstein, BRD

KLEINFAHNEN, Sachsen-Gotha, 3
1. 51-02N, 10-51E, Kleinfahner, Erfurt, DDR

KLEINGESCHWINDA, Thuringia, 1
1. 50-35N, 11-30E, Kleingeschwenda, Gera, DDR
2. 50-36N, 11-19E, Kleingeschwenda, Gera, DDR

KLEINLOGISCH, Prussia, 1
Not found.

KLEINSTATHEN, Saxony, 2
1. 51-15N, 12-23E, Kleinstaedeln (section of city), Leipzig, DDR

KLENZE, Prussia, 2
1. 53-52N, 12-39E, Klenz, Neubrandenburg, DDR
2. 52-56N, 10-57E, (also Clenze), Niedersachsen, BRD

KLENZOW, 1
1. 54-05N, 10-35E, Klenzau, Schleswig-Holstein, BRD

KLESEBACH, KLESEBECK, 2
Not found.

KLETZKE, Prussia, 2
1. 53-00N, 12-03E, Schwerin, DDR

KLEWITZ, 3
1. 52-40N, 14-30E, Polish-occupied Germany

KLINGE, 2
1. 51-05N, 13-11E, Liepzig, DDR
2. 51-45N, 14-31E, Frankfurt/Oder, DDR
3. 53-10N, 07-29E, Niedersachsen, BRD
4. 53-35N, 07-49E, (farm), Niedersachsen, BRD

KLINGENTHAL, 2
1. 50-22N, 12-28E, Karl-Marx-Stadt, DDR

KLINKE, Mecklenburg, 2
1. 53-29N, 12-37E, Klink, Neubrandenburg, DDR
2. 52-36N, 11-37E, Magdeburg, DDR
3. 51-06N, 07-51E, (farm) Nordrhein-Westfalen, BRD

KLOPSCHEN, KLUPSCHEN, Prussia, 1
1. 54-20N, 19-53E, Klopchen (Pol.=Chlopki), Poland

KLUETZ, 2
1. 53-58N, 11-10E, Rostock, DDR
2. 51-58N, 08-53E, Kluet, Nordrhein-Westfalen, BRD

KLUPSCHEN, KLOPSCHEN, Prussia, 1
See Klopschen

KNAUTHEIM, 2
1. 51-16N, 12-18E, Knauthain (section of city), Leipzig, DDR

KOBAL, 1
1. 54-06N, 20-45E, Kobeln (Pol.=Kobiela), Poland
2. 47-57N, 12-09E, Kobel, Bavaria, BRD
3. 48-23N, 10-49E, Kobel, Bavaria, BRD
4. 48-31N, 12-21E, Kobel (farm), Bavaria, BRD
5. 48-24N, 12-13E, Kobl*, Bavaria, BRD
*Four farms of this name, all in Bavaria, BRD.

KOBLIN, 3
1. 51-15N, 13-20E, Kobeln, Dresden, DDR
2. 51-35N, 14-43E, Koebeln, Cottbus, DDR
3. 52-06E, 14-39E, Kobbeln, Frankfurt/Oder, DDR

KOEDITZ, 1
1. 50-40N, 11-08E, (community), Gera, DDR
2. 50-38N, 11-22E, Gera, DDR
3. 50-20N, 11-51E, Bavaria, BRD

KOELEDA, Rudolstadt, 1, 2
1. 51-11N, 11-14E, Koelleda, Erfurt, DDR

KOENIGSBACH, 2
1. 48-58N, 08-37E, Baden-Wuerttemberg, BRD
2. 49-23N, 08-09E, (also called Koenigsbach an der
Weinstrasse), Rheinland-Pfalz,
BRD
3. 50-19N, 07-35E, Rheinland-Pfalz, BRD
4. 54-19N, 09-33E, (farm), Schleswig-Holstein, BRD

KOENIGSBERG, Prussia, 1, 2
1. 52-17N, 12-35E, Potsdam, DDR
2. 53-04N, 12-26E, Potsdam, DDR
3. 52-58N, 14-26E, Koenigsberg in Neumark, Polish-
occupied Germany
4. 50-39N, 08-32E, Hessen, BRD
5. 52-15N, 08-52E, Nordrhein-Westfalen, BRD
There are also four farms of this name in BRD.

KOENIGSBERG, Bavaria, 2
1. 50-05N, 10-35E, Bavaria, BRD

KOENIGSEE, KOENIGSSEE, 1, 2, 3
1. 50-39N, 11-06E, Koenigsee, Gera, DDR
2. 47-36N, 13-00E, (community), Bavaria, BRD

KOENIGSHOFEN, 1
1. 51-44N, 10-46E, Koenigshof, Magdeburg, DDR
2. 51-00N, 11-55E, Gera, DDR
3. 49-09N, 10-32E, Koenigshofen auf der Heide,
Bavaria, BRD
4. 49-33N, 09-45E, Baden-Wuerttemberg, BRD
5. 50-04N, 09-12E, Bavaria, BRD
6. 50-10N, 08-18E, Hessen, BRD
7. 50-18N, 10-29E, Bavaria, BRD
8. 48-07N, 09-51E, (farm), Baden-Wuerttemberg, BRD

KOENIGSWERTE, 2
1. 51-19N, 14-20E, Koenigswartha, Dresden, DDR
2. 51-40N, 07-53E, Koenigswirth, Nordrhein-Westfalen, BRD
There is a village called Koenigswerth on the out-
skirts of Falkenau (Czech.=Sokolov) about 20 kilometers southwest of Karlsbad (Czech.=Karlovy Vary),
Czechoslovakia.

KOETZBERG, 3
Not found.

KOFPOLDWITZ, 3
Not found.

KOGEL, 2
1. 53-25N, 12-25E, Neubrandenburg, DDR
2. 53-30N, 10-56E, Schwerin, DDR
3. 53-39N, 10-49E, Schleswig-Holstein, BRD
4. 47-49N, 11-51E, (farm), Bavaria, BRD
5. 47-40N, 10-46E, Koegel*, Bavaria, BRD
*There are three farms of this name in Baden-Wuert-
temberg and Bavaria, BRD.

KOLBE, 1
1. 50-43N, 11-40E, Kolba, Gera, DDR
2. 52-04N, 21-29E, Kolbiel, Poland

KOLBERG, 1
1. 52-15N, 13-48E, Potsdam, DDR
2. 54-11N, 15-35E, Polish-occupied Germany
3. 47-53N, 12-04E, Bavaria, BRD

KOLLWEILER, Bavaria, 1
1. 49-31N, 07-35E, Rheinland-Pfalz, BRD

KOMLOSEN, 3
Not found.

KONGSBERG, 2
Not found.

KOPENHAGEN, Denmark, 1, 2, 3

KORNTHAL, Wuerttemberg, 1
1. 48-49N, 09-07E, Korntal, Baden-Wuerttemberg, BRD

KORTENHAGEN, 1
1. 53-47N, 09-43E, (farm), Schleswig-Holstein, BRD

KOSBADE? 3
1. 53-32N, 11-51E, Kossebade, Schwerin, DDR
2. 50-43N, 11-45E, Kospoda, Gera, DDR
3. 52-47N, 20-12E, Kossobudy, Poland

KOSEL, Prussia, 1
1. 51-21N, 14-47E, Magdeburg, DDR
2. 54-29N, 13-15E, Rostock, DDR
3. 50-20N, 18-10E, (also spelled Cosel), Polish-
occupied Germany
4. 54-30N, 09-46E, Schleswig-Holstein, BRD
There are also two villages in Czechoslovakia:
Kosel bei Boemisch Leipa and Kosel bei Bruex.

KOSIADEL, Prussia, 1
Not found.

KOSSMANNSDORF, 1
1. 49-48N, 10-58E, Koettmansdorf, Bavaria, BRD

KOTTSBERG, 2
Not found.

KOTZEMENSCHEL, 1
Not found.

KOTZERSRICHT, 3
1. 49-31N, 11-49E, Koetzersricht, Bavaria, BRD

KOZMIN, 2
1. 51-49N, 17-27E, Poland
2. 52-41N, 16-28E, Poland
3. 54-01N, 18-18E, Poland

KRABOW, 2
Not found.

KRACAU, 3
1. 50-52N, 11-21E, Krakau, Erfurt, DDR
2. 51-19N, 13-51E, Krakau, Dresden, DDR
3. 51-22N, 11-52E, Krakau, Halle, DDR
4. 51-59N, 12-18E, Krakau, Halle, DDR
5. 52-07E, 11-48E, Krakau (also Cracau), Mecklenburg, DDR
6. 50-05N, 19-55E, Krakau (Pol.=Krakow), Poland
7. 51-44N, 18-31E, Krakow, Poland

KRACKOW, Mecklenburg, 1, 2, 3
1. 53-21N, 14-16E, Neubrandenburg, DDR

KRAKOW, 1, 3
1. 53-39N, 12-16E, Schwerin, DDR
2. 53-55N, 13-37E, Neubrandenburg, DDR
3. 54-08N, 12-48E, Rostock, DDR
4. 54-24N, 13-26E, Rostock, DDR

KRANICHFELD, 1, 3
1. 50-51N, 11-12E, Erfurt, DDR

KRATOSCHIN, Poland, 1, 2
See KROTOSCHIN

KRAUSHEIM, 2
1. 49-23N, 09-38E, Krautheim, Baden-Wuerttemberg,
      BRD
2. 49-53N, 10-17E, Krautheim, Bavaria, BRD

KRAUTAUF, 3
1. 47-48N, 11-49E, Krauthof, Bavaria, BRD

KREIEN, 2, 3
53-24N, 12-03E, Schwerin, DDR

KREM, 2
Not found.

KREMPE, 3
1. 53-50N, 09-29E, Schleswig-Holstein, BRD

KRESSBAUCH, Wuerttemberg, 1
1. 49-17N, 09-19E, Kressbach, Baden-Wuerttemberg,
      BRD
2. 48-29N, 09-03E, (castle), Baden-Wuerttemberg,
      BRD

KREUTZBERG, Sachsen-Weimar, 1, 2
1. 52-52N, 13-13E, Kreuzberg, Potsdam, DDR
There are nine villages and five farms named Kreuzberg in BRD.

KREUTZBURG, 3
1. 53-07N, 11-59E, Schwerin, DDR
2. 50-59N, 18-13E, Polish-occupied Germany

KREYEN, 2, 3
See KREIEN

KREYLN, 2
Not found.

KROCKAU, Holstein, 2
1. 53-15N, 20-23E, (Pol.=Krokowo), Poland
2. 53-56N, 20-44E, (Pol.=Krokowo), Poland
3. 54-24N, 10-21E, Krokau, Schleswig-Holstein, BRD

KROGEN, 2
1. 51-07N, 13-23E, Kroegis, Dresden, DDR
2. 51-59N, 08-17E, Kroeger, Nordrhein-Westfalen,
      BRD
3. 54-01N, 10-37E, Kroegen (farm), Schleswig-Hol-
      stein, BRD

KRONSKAMP, 2
1. 53-24N, 11-35E, Schwerin, DDR
2. 53-56N, 12-19E, Schwerin, DDR

KROPFERSRICHT? 3
1. 49-29N, 11-45E, Bavaria, BRD

KROTOSCHIN, Prussia, 1, 2
1. 51-42N, 17-27E, (Pol.=Krotoszyn), Poland
2. 52-40N, 18-47E, Krotoszyn, Poland

3. 52-51N, 17-57E, Krotoszyn, Poland
4. 51-42N, 17-26E, Krotoszyn Stary, Poland
5. 53-30N, 19-24E, Krotoszyny (or Krotoszyny Pomor-
      skie), Poland

KRUG, Mecklenburg, 3
1. 52-12N, 12-23E, (farm), Potsdam, DDR

KUCKUCK, 1
1. 51-14N, 08-03E, (farm), Nordrhein-Westfalen, BRD
2. 51-46N, 06-09E, (farm), Nordrhein-Westfalen, BRD
3. 52-12N, 08-16E, (farm), Niedersachsen, BRD

KUESTRIN, 1
1. 52-34N, 14-37E, Frankfurt/Oder, DDR
2. 52-35N, 14-39E, Polish-occupied Germany

KUPS, Bavaria, 3
1. 50-12N, 11-17E, Kueps, Bavaria, BRD

KURNICK, 1
1. 49-51N, 10-02E, Kuernach, Bavaria, BRD

KUTLAU, Prussia, 1
1. 51-45N, 16-02E, Kittlau, Polish-occupied Germany

KYRITZ, Prussia, 2
1. 52-57N, 12-24E, Potsdam, DDR
2. 53-22N, 14-21E, (farm), Neubrandenburg, DDR
See also KIERITZ.

LAASCH, 1
1. 51-22N, 13-09E, Laas, Leipzig, DDR
2. 53-48N, 11-49E, Laase, Schwerin, DDR
3. 54-33N, 13-21E, Laase, Rostock, DDR
4. 53-12N, 12-03E, Laaske, Potsdam, DDR
5. 54-02N, 19-07E, Laase (Pol.=Lasy), Poland
6. 53-02N, 11-25E, Laasche, Niedersachsen, BRD
7. 53-04N, 11-18E, Laase, Niedersachsen, BRD
8. 51-05N, 06-34E, Laach, Nordrhein-Westfalen, BRD

LABAU, 3
Not found.

LAHRE, Ditmarschen, 2
1. 52-41N, 07-25E, Niedersachsen, BRD

LAIBACH, 1
1. 49-24N, 09-41E, Baden-Wuerttemberg, BRD
2. 48-30N, 08-50E, (farm), Baden-Wuerttemberg, BRD
3. 51-04N, 08-26E, (farm), Nordrhein-Westfalen,
      BRD

LALCHOW, 2
1. 53-27N, 12-12E, (farm), Schwerin, DDR
2. 53-36N, 20-31E, Lalkowy, Poland

LANBAN? 3
See Lauban

LANCKOW, 3
Not found.

LANDAU, 1, 3
1. 54-03N, 20-51E, (Pol.=Ladek), Poland
2. 54-17N, 18-45E, (Pol.=Ledowo), Poland
3. 48-41N, 12-41E, (also called Landau an der Isar)
      Bavaria, BRD
4. 49-12N, 08-07E, (also called Landau in der Pfalz)
      Rheinland-Pfalz, BRD
5. 51-21N, 09-05E, Hessen, BRD

LANDAU, Saxony, 3
Not found.

LANDECK, Tyrol, [Austria] 1
1. 50-21N, 16-53E, (also called Bad Landeck in
                    Schlesien), Polish-occupied
                    Germany
2. 53-32N, 16-57E, (also called Landeck in West-
                    preussen), Polish-occupied
                    Germany
3. 49-54N, 18-54E, Landek, Poland
4. 48-09N, 07-51E, Baden-Wuerttemberg, BRD

LANDEN, 2
Not found.

LANDESHUT, Silesia, 2
1. 50-47N, 16-02E, Polish-occupied Germany

LANDSBERG, 2
1. 51-31N, 12-10E, Landsberg bei Halle, Halle, DDR
2. 52-29N, 11-41E, (building), Magdeburg, DDR
3. 50-36N, 10-24E, (castle), Suhl, DDR
4. 51-02N, 18-26E, Polish-occupied Germany
5. 54-17N, 20-30E, (Pol.=Gorowo Iławeckie), Poland
6. 48-03N, 10-52E, Bavaria, BRD

LANDSBERG am W., 2
1. 52-44N, 15-14E, Landsberg an der Warthe, Polish-
                    occupied Germany

LANDSEEDORF, 1
Not found.

LANDSTREIT, Austria, 2
1. 51-00N, 10-21E, (also called Landstreif), Er-
                    furt, DDR

LANGELOE, 2
1. 53-04N, 09-47E, Langeloh, Niedersachsen, BRD
2. 53-16N, 09-47E, Langeloh, Niedersachsen, BRD
3. 53-36N, 10-16E, Langelohe, Schleswig-Holstein,
                    BRD
4. 53-45N, 09-41E, Langelohe, Schleswig-Holstein,
                    BRD

LANGENAU, 2
1. 50-50N, 13-18E, Karl-Marx-Stadt, DDR
2. 51-07N, 12-55E, Karl-Marx-Stadt, DDR
3. 53-38N, 19-19E, (Pol.=Legowo), Poland
4. 54-13N, 18-39E, (Pol.=Legowo), Poland
5. 47-40N, 07-48E, Baden-Wuerttemberg, BRD
6. 48-30N, 10-06E, Baden-Wuerttemberg, BRD
7. 50-26N, 09-32E, Hessen, BRD
8. 50-26N, 11-18E, Bavaria, BRD
9. 50-56N, 07-59E, Nordrhein-Westfalen, BRD

LANGENBERG, 2
1. 50-33N, 12-50E, Karl-Marx-Stadt, DDR
2. 50-50N, 12-43E, Karl-Marx-Stadt, DDR
3. 50-55N, 12-04E, (section of city), Gera, DDR
4. 51-19N, 13-23E, Dresden, DDR
5. 51-36N, 11-05E, (forester's lodge), Halle, DDR
6. 47-57N, 10-19E, Bavaria, BRD
7. 48-52N, 09-35E, Baden-Wuerttemberg, BRD
8. 49-46N, 10-29E, Bavaria, BRD
9. 50-36N, 09-54E, Hessen, BRD
10. 50-49N, 07-38E, Nordrhein-Westfalen, BRD
There are five other villages of this name in BRD.

LANGENBUELAU, 1
1. 50-41N, 16-37E, Langenbielau, Polish-occupied
                    Germany

LANGENFELDT, 2
1. 50-47N, 10-13E, Langenfeld, Suhl, DDR
2. 54-01N, 12-56E, Langenfelde, Rostock, DDR
3. 49-37N, 10-31E, Langenfeld, Bavaria, BRD
4. 50-23N, 07-06E, Langenfeld, Rheinland-Pfalz, BRD
5. 51-06N, 06-57E, Langenfeld, Nordrhein-Westfalen,
                    BRD
6. 51-22N, 07-42E, Langenfeld, Nordrhein-Westfalen,
                    BRD
7. 52-13N, 09-18E, Langenfeld, Niedersachsen, BRD
8. 48-06N, 07-38E, Langenfeld (farm), Nordrhein-
                    Westfalen, BRD

LANGENHAGEN, 2, 3
1. 53-34N, 12-02E, Schwerin, DDR
2. 51-32N, 10-19E, Niedersachsen, BRD
3. 51-41N, 08-32E, Nordrhein-Westfalen, BRD
4. 52-14N, 08-43E, Nordrhein-Westfalen, BRD
5. 52-27N, 09-45E, Niedersachsen, BRD
6. 54-13N, 10-46E, Schleswig-Holstein, BRD

LANGENHEIDE, 3
1. 53-21N, 11-01E, Schwerin, DDR
2. 52-04N, 08-51E, (farm), Nordrhein-Westfalen, BRD

LANGENSALZA, Prussia, 1, 3
Not found.

LANGENSALZA, Thuringia, 2
1. 51-06N, 10-39E, Erfurt, DDR

LANGENVILSEN, Sondershausen, 1
1. 48-27N, 12-08E, Langenvils, Bavaria, BRD

LANGERHAUSEN, LANGERSHAUSEN, 1
1. 53-24N, 09-02E, Langenhausen, Niedersachsen, BRD

LANGHEINERSDORF, 3
1. 50-57N, 13-15E, Langhennersdorf, Karl-Marx-Stadt
                    DDR

LAUBAN? 3
1. 51-05N, 14-34E, Lauba, Dresden, DDR
2. 51-07N, 15-17E, Polish-occupied Germany

LAUCHA, LAUCHAU, 3
1. 50-56N, 10-32E, Laucha, Erfurt, DDR
2. 51-07N, 14-39E, Laucha, Dresden, DDR
3. 51-13N, 11-41E, Laucha (also called Laucha an
                    der Unstrut), Halle, DDR

LAUCHSTADT, Prussia, 2
1. 51-23N, 11-51E, (also called Bad Lauchstaedt),
                    Halle, DDR

LAUCKOW? 3
Not found.

LAUENBURG, 1, 3
1. 54-33N, 17-46E, Lauenburg in Pommern, Polish-
                    occupied Germany
2. 51-46N, 09-45E, Lauenberg, Niedersachsen, BRD
3. 53-45N, 09-41E, Lauenberg, Schleswig-Holstein,
                    BRD
4. 53-22N, 10-34E, Schleswig-Holstein, BRD

LAUFFEN AM NECKAR, Wuerttemberg, 1
1. 49-04N, 09-09E, Baden-Wuerttemberg, BRD
2. 48-07N, 08-38E, Lauffen ob Rottweil, Baden-
                    Wuerttemberg, BRD

LAUPHEIM, 3
1. 48-14N, 09-53E, Baden-Wuerttemberg, BRD

LAUSSNITZ, 1
1. 50-40N, 11-30E, Lausnitz, Gera, DDR
2. 50-44N, 11-42E, Lausnitz, Gera, DDR
3. 51-15N, 13-53E, Dresden, DDR

LAUTERBERG, 1
1. 53-16N, 19-49E, Lautenburg (Pol.=Lidzbark), Poland
2. 51-39N, 10-28E, (also called Bad Lauterberg),
Niedersachsen, BRD

LAUTHENTHAL, 3
1. 51-52N, 10-18E, Lautenthal, Niedersachsen, BRD

LEBAU, 3
1. 51-44N, 11-48E, Leau, Halle, DDR
2. 54-45N, 17-33E, Leba, Polish-occupied Germany

LEBOW, 2
Not found.

LEBRA, 1
Not found.

LEGERDE, 3
1. 52-26N, 19-30E, Legarda, Poland
2. 54-47N, 08-51E, Legerade, Schleswig-Holstein,
BRD

LEHESDORF, 2
1. 49-31N, 11-34E, Lehendorf, Bavaria, BRD

LEHESTEN, Saxony, 1, 2
1. 50-28N, 11-27E, Gera, DDR
2. 50-45N, 11-47E, Gera, DDR
3. 50-59N, 11-35E, Gera, DDR

LEHSEN, Prussia, 2
1. 53-29N, 11-02E, Schwerin, DDR

LEHSTEN, Mecklenburg, 2
1. 53-34N, 12-55E, Neubrandenburg, DDR
2. 54-32N, 13-13E, Rostock, DDR
3. 50-07N, 11-55E, Bavaria, BRD
4. 50-15N, 11-39E, Bavaria, BRD

LEIBACH, Bavaria? 2
Not found.

LEIPE, Prussia, 1
1. 51-50N, 12-56E, Leipa, Cottbus, DDR
2. 51-51N, 14-03E, Cottbus, DDR
3. 53-36N, 19-50E, Leip (Pol.=Lipowo), Poland
4. 48-26N, 10-06E, Leibi, Bavaria, BRD

LEIPHEIM, 2
1. 48-26N, 10-12E, Bavaria, BRD

LEIPZIG, 1, 2, 3
1. 51-18N, 12-20E, Leipzig, DDR

LEMBACH, Bavaria, 2
1. 47-48N, 08-26E, Baden-Wuerttemberg, BRD
2. 48-46N, 13-24E, Bavaria, BRD
3. 49-56N, 10-42E, Bavaria, BRD
4. 51-02N, 09-21E, Hessen, BRD

LEMBZIN, 3
Not found.

LEMESRITH, 1
Not found.

LENGSFELD, 1
1. 50-43N, 13-12E, Lengefeld, Karl-Marx-Stadt, DDR
2. 50-50N, 11-20E, Lengefeld, Erfurt, DDR
3. 50-50N, 12-07E, Lengefeld (also called Poris-
Lengefeld), Gera, DDR
4. 51-07N, 11-43E, Lengefeld, Halle, DDR
5. 51-51N, 10-23E, Lengefeld, Erfurt, DDR
6. 51-30N, 11-16E, Lengefeld, Halle, DDR
7. 50-32N, 10-39E, Lengfeld, Suhl, DDR
8. 50-47N, 10-08E, (also called Stadtlengsfeld),
Suhl, DDR
There are twelve villages named Lengenfeld in BRD.

LENZEN, 1, 3
1. 53-05N, 11-29E, Schwerin, DDR
2. 53-43N, 12-01E, Schwerin, DDR
3. 53-34N, 14-17E, (farm) Neubrandenburg, DDR
4. 54-17N, 19-28E, (Pol.=Łecze), Poland
5. 53-05N, 11-01E, Niedersachsen, BRD
6. 47-27N, 10-07E, (farm), Bavaria, BRD

LESCHAU, 1
1. 53-47N, 20-53E, Leschnau (Pol.=Leszno), Poland
2. 51-51N, 16-35E, Leschno (Pol.=Leszno), Poland

LESEN, 1
1. 51-19N, 13-18E, Lessa, Dresden, DDR
2. 50-58N, 12-04E, Lessen, Gera, DDR
3. 52-34N, 10-48E, Lessien, Niedersachsen, BRD

LESTERMUEHL, 2
Not found.

LESTIN, 3
1. 51-32N, 11-55E, Lettin, Halle, DDR
2. 52-38N, 13-57E, Lettin (farm), Frankfurt/Oder,
DDR
3. 51-44N, 16-38E, Lesten, Polish-occupied Germany

LEUTENBERG, 2
1. 50-33N, 11-27E, Gera, DDR
2. 50-03N, 12-06E, Bavaria, BRD

LEUTKIRCH, 2
1. 47-45N, 09-19E, Baden-Wuerttemberg, BRD
2. 47-50N, 10-02E, Baden-Wuerttemberg, BRD

LEVITZHUFEN, 3
Not found.

LIBAU, 3
1. 50-43N, 16-00E, Liebau in Schlesien, Polish-
occupied Germany

LICHTENBERG, Grandduchy of, 1
1. 50-50N, 12-09E, Gera, DDR
2. 50-50N, 13-25E, Karl-Marx-Stadt, DDR
3. 50-50N, 13-53E, Dresden, DDR
4. 51-11N, 13-59E, Dresden, DDR
5. 52-19N, 14-27E, (section of city), Frankfurt/
Oder, DDR
6. 52-31N, 13-30E, (section of city), East Berlin,
DDR
7. 52-53N, 12-52E, Potsdam, DDR
8. 53-23N, 13-30E, Neubrandenburg, DDR
9. 51-02N, 13-04E, (farm), Karl-Marx-Stadt, DDR
10. 51-40N, 12-56E, Lichtenburg, Cottbus, DDR
11. 51-30N, 14-51E, Polish-occupied Germany
There are nine villages of this name in BRD. The
Grandduchy of Lichtenberg, or Hanau-Lichtenberg,
was in Kreis Dieburg, Hessen, BRD.

LICHTENHAIN, 1
1. 50-30N, 11-19E, Suhl, DDR
2. 50-36N, 11-08E, Suhl, DDR
3. 50-55N, 11-34E, Gera, DDR
4. 50-57N, 14-14E, Dresden, DDR
5. 53-14N, 13-36E, Neubrandenburg, DDR
6. 54-10N, 22-15E, (Pol.=Wierzbianka), Poland

LIEBENAU, 1
1. 50-47N, 13-52E, Dresden, DDR
2. 51-17N, 14-04E, Dresden, DDR
3. 52-18N, 15-26E, also called Liebenau bei Schwiebus, Polish-occupied Germany
4. 54-06N, 19-50E, (Pol.=Miłosna), Poland
5. 54-18N, 19-57E, (Pol.=Lubnowo), Poland
6. 47-43N, 09-36E, Baden-Wuerttemberg, BRD
7. 49-07N, 12-43E, Bavaria, BRD
8. 51-29N, 09-17E, Hessen, BRD
9. 52-36N, 09-06E, Niedersachsen, BRD

LIEDERSTADT, 1
1. 51-18N, 11-35E, Liederstaedt, Halle, DDR

LIEGNITZ, Prussia, 2
1. 51-12N, 16-12E, Polish-occupied Germany

LIENITZ, 2
1. 52-19N, 12-58E, Lienewitz, Potsdam, DDR

LINDA BEI FRIEDBERG, 1
1. 50-35N, 11-59E, Linda, Gera, DDR
2. 50-41N, 11-47E, Linda, Gera, DDR
3. 50-48N, 12-12E, Linda, Gera, DDR
4. 50-52N, 13-16E, Linda, Karl-Marx-Stadt, DDR
5. 50-55N, 11-24E, Linda, Erfurt, DDR
6. 51-00N, 12-37E, Linda, Leipzig, DDR
7. 51-54N, 13-07E, Linda, Cottbus, DDR
8. 50-41N, 11-46E, Linda-Kleina, Gera, DDR
9. 50-42N, 11-49E, Linda-Koethnitz, Gera, DDR
10. 50-42N, 11-46E, Linda-Steinbruecken, Gera, DDR

LINDAU, 2
1. 51-01N, 11-55E, Gera, DDR
2. 52-02N, 12-06E, Magdeburg, DDR
3. 47-33N, 09-41E, Baden-Wuerttemberg, BRD
4. 48-47N, 13-18E, Bavaria, BRD
5. 50-04N, 11-31E, Bavaria, BRD
6. 51-39N, 10-08E, Niedersachsen, BRD
7. 54-23N, 09-54E, Schleswig-Holstein, BRD
8. 54-36N, 09-48E, Schleswig-Holstein, BRD
There are five farms of this name in BRD.

LIPNA, Poland, 2
1. 49-28N, 21-21E, Poland
2. 51-42N, 20-38E, Poland
3. 50-16N, 20-03E, Lipna Wola, Poland
See also LIPPNO, Posen

LIPPELSDORF, Thuringia, 1
1. 50-32N, 11-15E, Suhl, DDR
2. 50-46N, 13-16E, Lippersdorf, Karl-Marx-Stadt,
   DDR

LIPPNO, Posen, 2
1. 50-47N, 20-07E, Lipno, Poland
2. 51-22N, 20-36E, Lipno, Poland
3. 51-27N, 18-42E, Lipno, Poland
4. 51-55N, 16-34E, Lipno, Poland
5. 52-20N, 22-50E, Lipno, Poland
6. 52-50N, 19-12E, Lipno, Poland

LIPSTADT, 3
1. 51-40N, 08-21E, Lippstadt, Nordrhein-Westfalen,
   BRD

LISSA, 1, 2, 3
1. 51-30N, 12-17E, (community), Leipzig, DDR
2. 51-10N, 16-51E, (also called Deutsch Lissa),
   Polish-occupied Germany
3. 51-14N, 15-02E, Polish-occupied Germany
4. 51-51N, 16-35E, (Pol.=Leszno), Poland

LOBAU, 1, 2, 3
See LOEBAU

LOBENSTEIN, 2
1. 50-27N, 11-39E, Gera, DDR
2. 48-46N, 13-31E, Bavaria, BRD

LOBURG, 1
1. 52-07N, 12-04E, Magdeburg, DDR
2. 52-03N, 07-53E, (farm community), Nordrhein-
   Westfalen, BRD

LOEBAU, Prussia, 1, 2, 3
1. 51-06N, 14-40E, Dresden, DDR

LOEHMA, 1
1. 50-53N, 12-17E, Lohma, Leipzig, DDR
2. 50-58N, 12-33E, Lohma, Leipzig, DDR
3. 50-37N, 11-51E, Gera, DDR
4. 50-35N, 11-28E, (farm), Gera, DDR
5. 54-35N, 13-37E, Lohme, Rostock, DDR
6. 52-38N, 13-40E, Loehme, Frankfurt/Oder, DDR
7. 49-37N, 12-26E, Lohma, Bavaria, BRD

LOEWENBERG, 1
1. 52-53N, 13-09E, Potsdam, DDR
2. 51-07N, 15-35E, Polish-occupied Germany
3. 51-02N, 09-05E, (forester's lodge), Nordrhein-
   Westfalen, BRD

LOHBURG, Prussia, 1
1. 54-13N, 19-43E, (Pol.=Płonne), Poland
See also LOBURG

LOHMEN, Mecklenburg, 3
1. 50-59N, 14-00E, Dresden, DDR
2. 53-41N, 12-06E, Schwerin, DDR

LOHR, Bavaria, 1
1. 49-06N, 10-08E, Baden-Wuerttemberg, BRD
2. 49-20N, 10-10E, Bavaria, BRD
3. 49-59N, 09-35E, Bavaria, BRD
4. 50-09N, 10-42E, Bavaria, BRD
5. 48-19N, 12-36E, (farm), Bavaria, BRD

LOMASCH? 3
1. 51-12N, 13-18E, Lommatzsch, Dresden, DDR
2. 51-54N, 23-10E, Łomazy, Poland

LOUISENHOFF, Mecklenburg, 1
1. 53-36N, 13-24E, (also spelled Luisenhof), Neubrandenburg, DDR
2. 53-40N, 12-10E, Schwerin, DDR
3. 53-42N, 13-54E, Neubrandenburg, DDR
4. 52-38N, 14-20E, (farm), Frankfurt/Oder, DDR
5. 53-00N, 13-54E, (farm), Frankfurt/Oder, DDR
6. 53-30N, 10-32E, (farm), Schleswig-Holstein, BRD
7. 53-39N, 07-16E, (farm), Niedersachsen, BRD
8. 54-34N, 09-26E, (farm), Schleswig-Holstein, BRD

LOUISVILLE [Kentucky? U.S.A.] 2

LUCKAU, 1
1. 51-51N, 13-43E, Cottbus, DDR
2. 53-26N, 21-10E, (Pol.=Łuka), Poland
3. 52-56N, 11-03E, Niedersachsen, BRD

LUDWIGSLUST, 2, 3
1. 53-19N, 11-30E, Schwerin, DDR
2. 52-31N, 14-25E, (farm), Frankfurt/Oder, DDR
3. 52-35N, 12-19E, (farm), Potsdam, DDR
4. 49-15N, 07-27E, Rheinland-Pfalz, BRD
5. 52-49N, 09-21E, Niedersachsen, BRD

LUEBBEN, 1, 2, 3
1. 51-57N, 13-54E, Cottbus, DDR
2. 54-09N, 17-13E, Lubben, Polish-occupied Germany

LUEBECK, 1, 2, 3
1. 53-52N, 10-42E, Schleswig-Holstein, BRD

LUEBECKE, 3
1. 50-42N, 18-39E, Lubecko, Poland
2. 52-18N, 08-37E, Luebbecke, Nordrhein-Westfalen,
     BRD

LUEBEN, 3
1. 51-24N, 16-12E, Polish-occupied Germany
2. 52-46N, 10-45E, Niedersachsen, BRD
3. 53-09N, 10-51E, Niedersachsen, BRD
See also LUEBBEN

LUEBLOW, Mecklenburg, 2
1. 53-25N, 11-28E, Schwerin, DDR

LUEBOW, 1
1. 53-51N, 11-31E, Rostock, DDR

LUEBS, LUEBZ, 1, 2, 3
1. 52-01N, 11-56E, Luebs, Magdeburg, DDR
2. 53-44N, 13-53E, Luebs, Neubrandenburg, DDR
3. 53-27N, 12-02E, Luebz, Schwerin, DDR
4. 52-41N, 17-41E, Lubcz, Poland

LUEBTHAUSEN, 3
Not found.

LUEBTHEEN, 3
1. 53-18N, 11-05E, Schwerin, DDR

LUECHOW, Mecklenburg, 2, 3
1. 53-54N, 12-42E, Neubrandenburg, DDR

LUECHOW, Prussia, 1
1. 50-19N, 22-38E, Luchow Dolny, Poland
2. 50-20N, 22-42E, Luchow Gorny, Poland
3. 52-58N, 11-09E, Niedersachsen, BRD
4. 53-41N, 10-32E, Schleswig-Holstein, BRD

LUEDA, Hannover, 2
1. 52-04N, 07-20E, Luedde (farm), Nordrhein-West-
     falen, BRD

LUENEBURG, 1, 2, 3
1. 53-15N, 10-24E, Niedersachsen, BRD

LUHME, 3
1. 53-11N, 12-50E, Potsdam, DDR

LUNA, Swabia, 1
Not found.

LUTJENBURG, Holstein, 2
1. 53-25N, 10-11E, Hamburg, BRD
2. 54-18N, 10-36E, Schleswig-Holstein, BRD

LUTSCHENE, 3
Not found.

LYON, [France?] 2

MAGDEBURG, 1, 2, 3
1. 52-10N, 11-40E, Magdeburg, DDR
2. 47-48N, 08-48E, Maegdeberg (farm), Baden-Wuert-
     temberg, BRD
3. 53-33N, 10-00E, Magdeburger Hafen (port), Ham-
     burg, BRD

MAINZ, 3
1. 52-25N, 11-28E, Mainz, Wuestemark (area), Mag-
     deburg, DDR
2. 47-50N, 11-58E, Bavaria, BRD
3. 50-00N, 08-15E, Rheinland-Pfalz, BRD

MAKOWO, Poland, 3
1. 53-05N, 22-40E, Poland
2. 53-42N, 19-40E, Poland

MALCHIN, Mecklenburg, 2, 3
1. 53-44N, 12-47E, Neubrandenburg, DDR
2. 49-47N, 08-37E, Malchen, Hessen, BRD
3. 48-19N, 13-12E, Malching, Bavaria, BRD

MALCHOW, Mecklenburg, 1, 2, 3
1. 52-35N, 13-29E, (section of city), East Berlin,
     DDR
2. 53-25N, 13-55E, Neubrandenburg, DDR
3. 53-27N, 11-46E, Schwerin, DDR
4. 53-29N, 12-11E, Schwerin, DDR
5. 53-29N, 12-26E, Neubrandenburg, DDR
6. 54-00N, 11-28E, Rostock, DDR
7. 52-17N, 14-31E, (farm), Frankfurt/Oder, DDR
There are three villages named Malkow in Poland.

MALKWITZ, Holstein, 2
1. 54-27N, 13-16E, Malkvitz, Rostock, DDR
2. 51-20N, 13-00E, Schwerin, DDR
3. 53-30N, 12-27E, Neubrandenburg, DDR

MALSDORF, 1
Not found.

MALTSCH AM ODER, Prussia, 3
1. 51-13N, 16-29E, (Pol.=Malczyce), Polish-occupied
     Germany

MANDEL, 2
1. 49-51N, 07-46E, Rheinland-Pfalz, BRD
2. 47-50N, 11-23E, Mandl, Bavaria, BRD

MANSFELD, 1
1. 51-35N, 11-28E, Halle, DDR
2. 53-13N, 12-02E, Potsdam, DDR
3. 51-36N, 11-27E, Mansfeld-Unterstadt (Leimbach),
     Halle, DDR

MANTEL, 1
1. 49-39N, 12-03E, Bavaria, BRD
2. 48-41N, 12-08E, (farm), Bavaria, BRD
3. 49-09N, 12-18E, (farm), Bavaria, BRD

MARBURG, 2, 3
1. 50-49N, 08-46E, Hessen, BRD

MARIENWERDER, 1, 2
1. 52-51N, 13-36E, Frankfurt/Oder, DDR
2. 53-44N, 18-55E, (Pol.=Kwidzyn), Poland
3. 52-24N, 09-38E, Niedersachsen, BRD

MARK KLEBURG, 3
1. 51-17N, 12-24E, Markkleeberg, Leipzig, DDR

MARKELITZ, 1
Not found.

MARKFIEBACH, 1
Not found.

MARKISCH, 1
There is a Markirch in France, west of Selestat
(Schlettstadt) and southwest of Strassburg.

MARKLISSA, 3
51-01N, 15-16E, Polish-occupied Germany

MARNE, 2
1. 53-57N, 09-00E, Schleswig-Holstein, BRD
2. 54-21N, 08-46E, Schleswig-Holstein, BRD
3. 53-47N, 09-06E, (farm), Niedersachsen, BRD

MARNITZ, 1
1. 53-19N, 11-56E, Schwerin, DDR

MARSLOW, 2
1. 54-09N, 12-35E, Marlow, Rostock, DDR
2. 54-32N, 13-33E, Marlow, Rostock, DDR

MARSOW, 2
1. 53-25N, 10-56E, Schwerin, DDR
2. 54-31N, 16-42E, Polish-occupied Germany

MARWITZ, 1
1. 52-41N, 13-09E, Potsdam, DDR
2. 51-39N, 06-30E, Marwick, Nordrhein-Westfalen,
BRD

MAS, 1
Not found.

MASS, Norway, 2

MECKERN, 2
See MOECKERN

MEINECK, 2
Not found.

MEININGEN, 1, 2, 3
1. 50-33N, 10-25E, Suhl, DDR
2. 51-31N, 08-30E, Meiningsen, Nordrhein-Westfalen,
BRD

MEISSEN, 1, 3
1. 51-09N, 13-29E, Dresden, DDR
2. 52-16N, 08-57E, Nordrhein-Westfalen, BRD

MELDORF, 3
1. 54-05N, 09-05E, Schleswig-Holstein, BRD

MELLINGEN, Thuringia, 1, 2
1. 50-56N, 11-24E, Erfurt, DDR

MEMEL, 2

MEMELSDORF, 2
1. 49-56N, 10-57E, Memmelsdorf, Bavaria, BRD
2. 50-09N, 10-52E, Memmelsdorf, Bavaria, BRD

MEMPSHIER, MERNPSHIER, 2
Not found.

MENDHAUSEN, 1
1. 50-23N, 10-28E, Suhl, DDR

MENGEN, 3
1. 47-57N, 07-43E, Baden-Wuerttemberg, BRD
2. 48-03N, 09-20E, Baden-Wuerttemberg, BRD

MENKHAGEN, 2
1. 51-12N, 08-13E, Menkhausen, Nordrhein-Westfalen,
BRD
2. 51-58N, 08-39E, Menkhausen (farm), Nordrhein-
Westfalen, BRD

MERSEBERG, 2
1. 51-22N, 12-00E, Merseburg, Halle, DDR

MESCHLITZ, 3
1. 51-09N, 14-32E, Meschwitz, Dresden, DDR

MESTLIN, Mecklenburg, 2
1. 53-35N, 11-56E, Schwerin, DDR

METTIN, 2
Not found.

METTKAN, 2
Not found.

METTLIN, Mecklenburg, 2
1. 47-40N, 07-55E, Mettlen (farm), Baden-Wuerttemberg, BRD

METZDORF, 3
1. 52-39N, 14-10E, Frankfurt/Oder, DDR
2. 49-15N, 09-34E, Baden-Wuerttemberg, BRD
3. 49-45N, 06-30E, Rheinland-Pfalz, BRD
4. 50-07N, 11-26E, Bavaria, BRD

MEULLERHAUSEN, 3
1. 50-53N, 11-22E, Muellershausen (forester's
lodge), Erfurt, DDR

MEUSELBACH, MEUSSELBACH, Thuringia, 1, 3
1. 50-34N, 11-05E, Meuselbach-Schwarzmuehle, Suhl,
DDR

MICHELN, 2
1. 51-48N, 11-58E, Halle, DDR

MICHELTONDERN, 2
Not found.

MIELBOCK, 2
Not found.

MILDENBERG, Bavaria, 2
1. 53-01N, 13-17E, Potsdam, DDR
2. 48-37N, 12-46E, (farm), Bavaria, BRD
3. 49-42N, 09-15E, Miltenberg, Bavaria, BRD

MILLOSLOWE, 3
1. 52-12N, 17-29E, Miłosław, Poland
2. 52-44N, 17-22E, Miłosławice, Poland
3. 52-31N, 16-04E, Miłostowo, Poland

MILLROWE, 2
1. 51-57N, 20-48E, Michrow, Poland

MILWAUKEE, [Wisconsin, U.S.A.] 1

MINDEN, 1
1. 49-50N, 06-28E, Rheinland-Pfalz, BRD
2. 52-17N, 08-55E, Nordrhein-Westfalen, BRD

MISSOURI, [U.S.A.] 3

MITTELHAUSEN, 3
1. 51-03N, 11-00E, Erfurt, DDR
2. 51-26N, 11-28E, Halle, DDR

MITTELHAUSEN [continued]
  3. 50-44N, 08-51E, Hessen, BRD
  4. 51-38N, 08-26E, (farm), Nordrhein-Westfalen,
    BRD

MITTELKIRCHEN, 3
  1. 48-21N, 12-44E, Mitterskirchen, Bavaria, BRD

MITTERTEICH, Bavaria, 3
  1. 49-57N, 12-15E, Bavaria, BRD

MITTWEIDA, MITTWEYDA, 2
  1. 50-32N, 12-52E, Mittweida, Karl-Marx-Stadt, DDR
  2. 50-59N, 12-59E, Mittweida, Karl-Marx-Stadt, DDR
  3. 52-04N, 14-09E, Mittweide, Frankfurt/Oder, DDR

MODLICH, 1, 2
  1. 51-38N, 19-33E, Modlica, Poland
  2. 52-08N, 17-40E, Modlica, Poland
  See also MOEDLICH

MOECKERN, 2, 3
  1. 50-57N, 12-26E, Mockern, Leipzig, DDR
  2. 50-51N, 11-46E, Gera, DDR
  3. 51-22N, 12-21E, Leipzig, DDR
  4. 52-08N, 11-57E, Magdeburg, DDR
  5. 52-45N, 11-46E, Magdeburg, DDR
  6. 53-07N, 12-49E, Potsdam, DDR
  7. 51-13N, 12-28E, Muckern, Leipzig, DDR
  8. 50-55N, 12-10E, Mueckern, Gera, DDR

MOEDLICH, Prussia, 1, 2
  1. 53-05N, 11-24E, Schwerin, DDR
  See also MODLICH

MOEHRENBACH, 2
  1. 50-38N, 11-00E, Suhl, DDR
  2. 50-55N, 07-45E, (forester's lodge), Rheinland-
    Pfalz, BRD

MOELLENBECK, Mecklenburg or Prussia, 2
  1. 52-43N, 11-37E, Magdeburg, DDR
  2. 53-17N, 11-44E, Schwerin, DDR
  3. 53-23N, 13-21E, Neubrandenburg, DDR
  4. 52-10N, 09-02E, Niedersachsen, BRD

MOELLN, 1
  1. 53-36N, 13-35E, Neubrandenburg, DDR
  2. 54-23N, 13-17E, Rostock, DDR
  3. 53-25N, 14-36E, (island), Polish-occupied Ger-
    many
  4. 53-38N, 10-41E, Schleswig-Holstein, BRD

MOLLENBECK, Mecklenburg or Prussia, 2
  See MOELLENBECK

MOLLENSTORF, 2
  1. 51-55N, 12-32E, Moellensdorf, Halle, DDR
  2. 53-30N, 13-01E, Neubrandenburg, DDR

MOLSCHLEBEN, Saxony-Gotha, 1, 3
  1. 51-00N, 10-47E, Erfurt, DDR

MOLSDORF, 1
  1. 50-54N, 10-58E, Erfurt, DDR

MONCKHAGEN, 1
  1. 54-09E, 12-13E, Moenchhagen, Rostock, DDR

MONSTAB, Saxony-Gotha, 3
  1. 51-00N, 12-21E, Leipzig, DDR

MORL, 3
  1. 51-33N, 11-55E, Halle, DDR
  2. 50-43N, 11-18E, Moerla, Gera, DDR

MOSEAN, 2
  1. 50-47N, 12-07E, Mosen, Gera, DDR

MUCHOW, 1
  1. 53-19N, 11-41E, Leipzig, DDR
  2. 52-23N, 19-47E, Muchowo, Poland

MUCHTEN, 2
  Not found.

MUEHLENBERG, 1
  1. 51-59N, 11-51E, (farm), Magdeburg, DDR
  2. 53-22N, 11-55E, (farm), Schwerin, DDR
  3. 48-58N, 09-52E, Baden-Wuerttemberg, BRD
  4. 50-14N, 06-17E, Rheinland-Pfalz, BRD
  5. 51-23N, 06-41E, Nordrhein-Westfalen, BRD
  6. 51-48N, 09-31E, Niedersachsen, BRD
  7. 52-59N, 07-37E, Niedersachsen, BRD
  8. 53-33N, 09-49E, Hamburg, BRD
  There are four farms of this name in BRD.

MUEHLESLOW, Prussia, 2
  Not found.

MUEHLHAUSEN, 2
  1. 50-18N, 12-16E, Karl-Marx-Stadt, DDR
  2. 51-13N, 10-27E, Erfurt, DDR
  3. 51-15N, 14-24E, Muehlhaeuser, Dresden, DDR
  There are 22 villages and one farm of this name in
  BRD.

MUEHLROSE, Prussia, 3
  1. 51-30N, 14-31E, Cottbus, DDR
  2. 53-46N, 12-13E, Muehl Rosin, Schwerin, DDR
  3. 52-15N, 14-25E, Muellrose, Frankfurt/Oder, DDR

MUELERSLAW, MULERSLAW, 2, 3
  1. 51-02N, 20-18E, Mularzow, Poland

MUELLERHAUSEN, 3
  1. 50-53N, 11-22E, Muellershausen (forester's
    lodge), Erfurt, DDR
  2. 51-47N, 09-57E, Muellershausen, Niedersachsen,
    BRD

MUENCHEN, 1, 2
  1. 51-37N, 13-19E, Cottbus, DDR
  2. 50-52N, 11-16E, (stopping place), Erfurt, DDR
  3. 48-42N, 13-28E, Bavaria, BRD
  4. 49-33N, 11-35E, Bavaria, BRD

MUENCHERHOLZEN, 2
  1. 51-12N, 12-47E, Muencherholz (forest), Leipzig,
    DDR

MUENCHWEILER, Baden, 2
  1. 48-15N, 07-52E, Muenweier, Baden-Wuerttemberg,
    BRD
  2. 49-09N, 07-58E, Muenchweiler am Klingbach,
    Rheinland-Pfalz, BRD
  3. 49-13N, 07-42E, Muenchweiler an der Rodalbe,
    Rheinland-Pfalz, BRD
  4. 49-28N, 07-26E, Glan-Muenchweiler, Rheinland-
    Pfalz, BRD
  5. 49-30N, 06-49E, Saar, BRD
  6. 49-33N, 07-53E, Muenchweiler an der Alsenz,
    Rheinland-Pfalz, BRD
  7. 49-13N, 07-42E, Muenchweilerhof (farm), Rhein-
    land-Pfalz, BRD

MUENDEN, 2
1. 51-09N, 08-45E, Hessen, BRD
2. 51-25N, 09-41E, Niedersachsen, BRD

MUENSTERBERG, 2
1. 51-50N, 12-24E, (farm), Halle, DDR
2. 50-36N, 17-02E, Polish-occupied Germany
3. 53-55N, 20-24E, (Pol.=Cerkiewnik), Poland

MUHLERSLOW, 2, 3
1. 51-02N, 20-18E, Mularzow, Poland

MUNSCHWITZ, Thuringia, 1
1. 50-35N, 11-28E, Gera, DDR

MUNSTERBERG, 2
See MUENSTERBERG

MUPTEN, 2
Not found.

MUSCHTEN, 3
1. 51-49N, 14-08E, Mueschen, Cottbus, DDR
2. 52-06N, 08-07E, Mueschen, Niedersachsen, BRD

NAGEL, 2
1. 49-59N, 11-55E, Bavaria, BRD
2. 50-11N, 11-15E, Bavaria, BRD
3. 52-11N, 08-42E, (farm), Nordrhein-Westfalen, BRD
4. 47-43N, 09-56E, Naegele (farm), Baden-Wuerttemberg, BRD
5. 48-02N, 09-53E, Naegele (farm), Baden-Wuerttemberg, BRD

NAMAY, 2
Not found.

NAMSLAM, Prussia or Silesia, 2
See NAMSLAU

NAMSLAU, 2
1. 51-05N, 17-43E, Polish-occupied Germany

NANAU, Prussia, 3
Not found.

NASSAU, 1, 3
1. 50-46N, 13-32E, Karl-Marx-Stadt, DDR
2. 51-10N, 13-31E, (farm), Dresden, DDR
3. 49-32N, 09-53E, Baden-Wuerttemberg, BRD
4. 50-19N, 07-48E, Rheinland-Pfalz, BRD
5. 48-53N, 12-52E, (farm community), Bavaria, BRD

NAUMBURG, 1, 2, 3
1. 51-09N, 11-49E, Halle, DDR
2. 51-48N, 15-15E, Naumburg am Bober, Polish-occupied Germany
3. 51-12N, 15-24E, Naumburg am Queis, Polish-occupied Germany
4. 51-15N, 09-10E, Hessen, BRD
5. 50-15N, 08-51E, (castle), Hessen, BRD

NEBELN, 1
1. 53-07N, 11-44E, Nebelin, Schwerin, DDR
2. 48-07N, 11-19E, Nebel, Bavaria, BRD
3. 54-39N, 08-22E, Nebel, Schleswig-Holstein, BRD

NEISSE, 1, 2, 3
1. 50-30N, 17-20E, (Pol.=Neisza), Polish-occupied Germany

NEKEWITZ, 1
1. 50-07N, 20-22E, Nekanowice, Poland

NEMDITZ, 1
1. 52-59N, 11-20E, Menitz, Niedersachsen, BRD

NETHRA, 1
1. 51-06N, 10-06E, Netra, Hessen, BRD

NETTKAN, 2
1. 53-17N, 08-09E, Nethen, Niedersachsen, BRD
2. 50-55N, 08-06E, Netphen, Nordrhein-Westfalen, BRD
3. 52-04N, 15-22E, now Deutsch Nettkow (or Strassberg), Polish-occupied Germany

NEU LUEBLOW, Mecklenburg, 2
1. 53-23N, 11-27E, Schwerin, DDR

NEU RUPPIN, 2
1. 52-56N, 12-48E, Neuruppin, Potsdam, DDR

NEU STRELITZ, 1, 3
1. 53-22N, 13-05E, Neustrelitz, Neubrandenburg, DDR

NEU TESCHOW, 3
1. 53-59N, 11-39E, Rostock, DDR
2. 54-04N, 19-50E, Neu Teschen (Pol.=Nowy Cieszyn) Poland

NEU ZACHNIN, Mecklenburg, 2
See NEU ZACHUM

NEU ZACHUEN, Mecklenburg, 2
See NEU ZACHUM

NEU ZACHUM, Mecklenburg, 2
1. 53-29N, 11-19E, Neu Zachun, Schwerin, DDR

NEUBAUROH, 3
Not found. There are numerous villages called Neubau in DDR and BRD.

NEUBRANDENBURG, Mecklenburg, 2
1. 53-34N, 13-16E, Neubrandenburg, DDR

NEUBUCKOW, 2
1. 54-02N, 11-40E, Neubukow, Rostock, DDR
2. 54-00N, 09-37E, Neu Buecken, Schleswig-Holstein, BRD

NEUDAM, 3
1. 52-01N, 11-05E, Neudamm, Magdeburg, DDR
2. 52-44N, 14-41E, Neudamm, Polish-occupied Germany
3. 54-25N, 09-57E, Neudamm (farm), Schleswig-Holstein, BRD
4. 54-53N, 08-44E, Neudamm (farm), Schleswig-Holstein, BRD

NEUDORF, 2, 3
There are 16 villages of this name in DDR; 7 in Polish-occupied Germany and Poland; 45 in BRD.

NEUENDORF, 3
There are 32 villages of this name in DDR; 10 in Poland; 6 in BRD.

NEUFAHRWASSER, Prussia, 3
1. 52-27N, 13-03E, Neu Fahrland, Potsdam, DDR
2. 54-24N, 18-40E, (Pol.=Nowy Port), Poland
3. 54-02N, 08-40E, (channel), Schleswig-Holstein, BRD

NEUHALDENSLEBEN, Prussia, 2
1. 52-18N, 11-25E, (also called Haldensleben),
Magdeburg, DDR
2. 47-40N, 09-36E, Neuhalden (farm), Baden-Wuerttemberg, BRD

NEUHAUS, 2
There are 12 villages of this name in DDR and about
65 in BRD.

NEUHAUS, Prussia, 3

NEUHAUS an der OSTSEE, 1

NEUHOF, Mecklenburg, 2, 3
There are 55 villages and farms of this name in
DDR; three in Polish-occupied Germany and Poland;
and about 75 in BRD.

NEUKIRCHEN, Pomerania, 1
There are eight villages of this name in DDR and
28 in BRD.

NEUKIRK, Prussia, 3
1. 51-06N, 14-19E, Neukirch, Dresden, DDR
2. 51-17N, 13-59E, Neukirch, Dresden, DDR
3. 54-11N, 18-54E, Neukirch (Pol.=Nowa Cerkiew),
Poland
4. 54-18N, 19-36E, Neukirch Hoehe (Pol.=Pogrodzie),
Poland
5. 47-40N, 09-42E, Neukirch, Baden-Wuerttemberg,
BRD
6. 48-01N, 08-11E, Neukirch, Baden-Wuerttemberg,
BRD
7. 48-12N, 08-42E, Neukirch, Baden-Wuerttemberg,
BRD
8. 50-41N, 08-03E, Neukirch (also called Stein-
Neukirch), Rheinland-Pfalz, BRD

NEUKLOSTER, 1
1. 53-52N, 11-42E, Rostock, DDR
2. 53-29N, 09-38E, Niedersachsen, DDR

NEULEVIN, 1
1. 52-43N, 14-17E, Neulewin, Frankfurt/Oder, DDR

NEUMARK, 1, 2
1. 50-40N, 12-21E, Karl-Marx-Stadt, DDR
2. 51-05N, 11-16E, Erfurt, DDR
3. 51-18N, 11-53E, Halle, DDR
4. 52-58N, 14-26E, (also called Koeningsberg in
Neumark), Polish-occupied Ger-
many
5. 53-17N, 14-47E, Polish-occupied Germany
6. 53-54N, 19-12E, (Pol.=Nowy Targ), Poland
7. 54-12N, 19-49E, (Pol.=Nowica), Poland
8. 51-10N, 16-36E, Neumarkt in Schlesien, Polish-
occupied Germany

NEUMASSOW, 2
1. 53-19N, 12-25E, Massow, Neubrandenburg, DDR

NEUMUEHLE, Prussia, 2
1. 50-40N, 12-38E, Karl-Marx-Stadt, DDR
2. 50-42N, 12-10E, Gera, DDR
3. 51-39N, 14-23E, Cottbus, DDR
4. 53-37N, 11-21E, (section of city), Schwerin, DDR
There are ten villages of this name in BRD.

NEUMUEHLEN, Holstein, 3
1. 49-15N, 12-46E, Bavaria, BRD
2. 52-15N, 09-06E, Niedersachsen, BRD
3. 52-53N, 07-57E, Niedersachsen, BRD

4. 52-57N, 09-15E, Niedersachsen, BRD
5. 53-33N, 09-55E, (section of city), Hamburg, BRD
6. 53-37N, 08-44E, (farm), Niedersachsen, BRD
7. 53-42N, 08-42E, (farm), Niedersachsen, BRD
8. 53-52N, 09-22E, (farm), Schleswig-Holstein, BRD
9. 53-54N, 10-32E, (farm), Schleswig-Holstein, BRD
10. 53-58N, 09-41E, (farm), Schleswig-Holstein, BRD
11. 54-03N, 09-28E, (farm), Schleswig-Holstein, BRD
12. 54-20N, 10-12E, (section of city), Schleswig-
Holstein, BRD

NEUNKIRCHEN, 1
1. 49-18N, 10-27E, Neunkirchen bei Leutershausen,
Bavaria, BRD
2. 49-21N, 07-11E, Saar, BRD
3. 49-23N, 09-01E, Baden-Wuerttemberg, BRD
4. 49-29N, 09-46E, Baden-Wuerttemberg, BRD
5. 49-30N, 07-29E, Neunkirchen am Potzberg, Rheinland-Pfalz, BRD
6. 49-31N, 11-19E, Neukirchen am Sand, Bavaria, BRD
7. 49-33N, 07-04E, Saar, BRD
8. 49-37N, 11-08E, Bavaria, BRD
9. 49-40N, 12-06E, Neunkirchen bei Weiden, Bavaria,
BRD
10. 49-44N, 08-47E, Hessen, BRD
There are eight additional villages of this name in
BRD.

NEUSALZ, 1
1. 51-48N, 15-43E, Polish-occupied Germany

NEUSALZA, 2
1. 51-03N, 14-32E, Neusalza-Spremberg, Dresden,
DDR

NEUSTAD LEBERSWALDE, 1
Not found.

NEUSTADT, 2, 3
There are 16 villages of this name in DDR; 2 in Poland; 36 in BRD.

NEUSTADT, Holstein, 1, 2
1. 54-06N, 10-49E, Schleswig-Holstein, BRD

NEUSTADT, Prussia, 2, 3
See NEUSTADT

NEUSTRELITZ, 2
1. 53-22N, 13-05E, Neubrandenburg, DDR

NEUZELLE, 2
1. 52-05N, 14-38E, Frankfurt/Oder, DDR
2. 49-00N, 11-29E, Neuzell, Bavaria, BRD

NEVERSHAUSEN, 1
1. 53-50N, 10-05E, Neverstaven (farm), Schleswig-
Holstein, BRD

NEW ORLEANS, [Louisiana, U. S. A.] 2

NEW YORK, [New York, U. S. A.] 1, 2, 3
1. 54-14N, 09-49E, (farm; also spelled Neujork),
Schleswig-Holstein, BRD

NIEDER ELDUNGEN, 2
1. 51-24N, 09-12E, Niederelsungen, Hessen, BRD

NIEDERNDORF, 2
1. 50-51N, 10-03E, Suhl, DDR
2. 50-53N, 11-58E, Gera, DDR
There are 16 villages of this name in BRD.

NIEDERSIMMERN, 1, 3
    See NIEDERZIMMERN

NIEDERWILDUNGEN, 3
    1. 51-07N, 09-07E, Bad Wildungen, Nordrhein-West-
                        falen, BRD

NIEDERZIMMER, NIEDERZIMMERN, 1, 3
    1. 51-00N, 11-11E, Niederzimmern, Erfurt, DDR

NIEHOF, 1
    1. 52-18N, ?   (farm), Niedersachsen, BRD
    2. 54-11N, 10-58E, (farm), Schleswig-Holstein, BRD
    3. 51-48N, 07-26E, Niehoff (farm), Nordrhein-West-
                        falen, BRD
    4. 52-01N, 07-02E, Niehoff (farm), Nordrhein-West-
                        falen, BRD
    5. 52-22N, 07-14E, Niehoff (farm), Niedersachsen,
                        BRD

NIENBURG, 2
    1. 51-50N, 11-45E, Halle, DDR
    2. 52-08N, 07-06E, Nienborg, Nordrhein-Westfalen,
                        BRD
    3. 52-02N, 07-49E, Nienborg (farm), Nordrhein-West-
                        falen, BRD
    4. 52-38N, 09-13E, Niedersachsen, BRD

NIENDORF, 1, 3
    There are 13 villages of this name in DDR; 14 in
    BRD.

NIESKY, Prussia, 2
    1. 51-26N, 13-22E, Nieska, Dresden, DDR
    2. 51-18N, 14-49E, Dresden, DDR

NODA, Prussia, 2
    1. 51-04N, 11-01E, Noeda, Erfurt, DDR

NORDHAUSEN, Prussia or Posen, 1, 2
    1. 50-20N, 12-21E, Karl-Marx-Stadt, DDR
    2. 51-31N, 10-48E, Erfurt, DDR
    3. 52-20N, 08-14E, (community), Niedersachsen, BRD
    4. 48-57N, 10-23E, Baden-Wuerttemberg, BRD
    5. 49-06N, 09-06E, Baden-Wuerttemberg, BRD
    6. 52-19N, 07-47E, Nordrhein-Westfalen, BRD
    7. 52-29N, 08-45E, Niedersachsen, BRD
    8. 51-26N, 07-39E, (farm), Nordrhein-Westfalen,
                        BRD

NORDHEIM, Prussia, 3
    1. 50-27N, 10-24E, Suhl, DDR

NORDLING, Prussia, 3
    1. 48-39N, 10-59E, Noerdling, Bavaria, BRD

NORGE, 2
    Perhaps Norway is meant.

NORTH LOEDER, 2
    1. 51-33N, 07-45E, Nordluenern, Nordrhein-West-
                        falen, BRD

NORTHEIM, 3
    1. 51-42N, 10-00E, Niedersachsen, BRD

NORTHEIM, Bavaria, 2
    1. 48-42N, 10-48E, Nordheim, Bavaria, BRD
    2. 49-06N, 09-08E, Nordheim, Baden-Wuerttemberg,
                        BRD
    3. 49-41N, 08-23E, Nordheim, Hessen, BRD
    4. 49-51N, 10-11E, Nordheim, Bavaria, BRD
    5. 50-29N, 10-11E, Nordheim vor der Rhoen, Bavaria,
                        BRD

NORWAY, 2
    1. 52-45N, 07-50E, Norwegen, Niedersachsen, BRD
    2. 54-41N, 09-41E, Norwegen (farm), Schleswig-
                        Holstein, BRD
    Probably the country is meant.

NOSSENSTEIN, 3
    1. 53-31N, 12-28E, Nossentin, Neubrandenburg, DDR

NUERNBERG, 1, 3
    1. 53-25N, 15-32E, Noerenberg, Polish-occupied
                        Germany
    2. 49-27N, 11-05E, Bavaria, BRD
    3. 50-04N, 08-10E, (also called Nuernberger Hof),
                        Hessen, BRD
    4. 48-22N, 12-55E, (farm), Bavaria, BRD

OBER LICHTENAU, 1
    1. 50-54N, 12-58E, Oberlichtenau, Karl-Marx-Stadt,
                        DDR
    2. 51-13N, 14-00E, Oberlichtenau, Dresden, DDR

OBER OPPURG, 2
    1. 50-42N, 11-41E, Gera, DDR

OBER OPPURGDOR, Thuringia, 2
    Not found.

OBER ROSSLAU, 2
    1. 51-00N, 13-05E, Oberrossau, Karl-Marx-Stadt,
                        DDR
    2. 51-01N, 12-29E, Oberrossla, Erfurt, DDR
    3. 50-05N, 11-58E, Oberroeslau, Bavaria, BRD

OBER WALBRUNGEN, 3
    1. 50-26N, 10-11E, Oberwaldbehrungen, Bavaria, BRD

OBERBILAU, 1
    Not found.

OBERG, 3
    1. 52-15N, 10-15E, Niedersachsen, BRD
    2. 51-42N, 07-55E, (farm), Nordrhein-Westfalen, BRD

OBERHAGN, OBERHAYN, 2, 3
    1. 50-38N, 11-08E, Oberhain, Gera, DDR
    2. 54-12N, 12-16E, Oberhagen, Rostock, DDR
    3. 51-17N, 07-17E, Ober Hagen (also written Ober-
                        hagen, a farm) Nordrhein-West-
                        falen, BRD
    4. 51-06N, 07-17E, Oberhagen, Nordrhein-Westfalen,
                        BRD
    5. 51-21N, 07-29E, Oberhagen, Nordrhein-Westfalen,
                        BRD
    There are five villages named Oberham in Bavaria, BR

OBERHOECHSTEDT, Bavaria, 1
    1. 49-14N, 08-12E, Oberhochstadt, Rheinland-Pfalz,
                        BRD
    2. 50-11N, 08-32E, Oberhoechstadt, Hessen, BRD
    3. 49-39N, 10-42E, Oberhoechstaedt, Bavaria, BRD
    4. 49-02N, 11-03E, Oberhochstatt, Bavaria, BRD
    5. 47-52N, 12-33E, Oberhochstaett, Bavaria, BRD

OBERLAURINGEN, Bavaria, 2
    1. 50-13N, 10-23E, Bavaria, BRD

OBERLEITERBACH, Bavaria, 3
    1. 47-47N, 11-17E, Oberlauterbach, Bavaria, BRD
    2. 48-21N, 12-46E, Oberleitenbach, Bavaria, BRD
    3. 50-02N, 10-58E, Bavaria, BRD

OBERLEUTERSDORF, 2
1. 50-58N, 14-39E, (farm), Dresden, DDR

OBERLUETZOW, 3
1. 47-57N, 09-56E, Oberluizen, Baden-Wuerttemberg,
BRD

OBERMOELLERN, 3
1. 51-10N, 11-41E, Halle, DDR

OBERSTEINACH, 1
1. 50-56N, 12-39E, Obersteinbach, Leipzig, DDR
2. 51-07N, 13-11E, Obersteinbach, Leipzig, DDR
3. 49-49N, 10-32E, Ober Steinach, Bavaria, BRD
There are 13 villages named Obersteinbach in BRD.

OBERSTROSSE, 2
1. 51-49N, 07-05E, Oberstrote, Nordheim-Westfalen,
BRD

OBERVITZ, Thuringia, 3
Not found.

OBERWEIMAR, 3
1. 50-58N, 11-21E, Erfurt, DDR
2. 50-45N, 08-42E, Hessen, BRD

OBERWEISBACH, OBERWEISSBACH, 1
1. 50-35N, 11-09E, Oberweissbach, Suhl, DDR
2. 48-55N, 09-30E, Oberweissach, Baden-Wuerttemberg, BRD
3. 49-36N, 11-45E, Oberweissenbach, Bavaria, BRD
4. 50-10N, 12-05E, Oberweissenbach, Bavaria, BRD
5. 50-14N, 11-42E, Oberweissenbach, Bavaria, BRD

OBERWELLNBORN, 1
1. 50-40N, 11-28E, Oberwellenborn, Gera, DDR

OBSENDORF, 1
Not found.

ODENHEIM, 1
1. 49-11N, 08-45E, Baden-Wuerttemberg, BRD

OELMITZ, 1
1. 49-36N, 17-15E, Olmuetz (Czech=Olomouc), Czechoslovakia

OELS, 1
1. 50-57N, 13-40E, Oelsa, Dresden, DDR
2. 51-06N, 14-38E, Oelsa, Dresden, DDR
3. 51-12N, 17-23E, (Pol.=Olesnica*), Polish-occupied Germany
*There are seven other villages named Olesnica in
Poland.

OETTINGEN, 1, 2
1. 52-58N, 09-37E, Ottingen, Niedersachsen, BRD
2. 48-57N, 10-36E, Bavaria, BRD

OETZE, 2
1. 48-04N, 12-07E, Oetz, Bavaria, BRD
2. 48-35N, 10-54E, Oetz, Bavaria, BRD
3. 52-29N, 10-01E, Otze, Niedersachsen, BRD

OLDENBURG, 2, 3
1. 53-57N, 13-33E, Rostock, DDR
2. 53-10N, 08-12E, Niedersachsen, BRD
3. 54-18N, 10-53E, Schleswig-Holstein, BRD
4. 51-51N, 09-13E, (farm), Nordrhein-Westfalen,
BRD
5. 52-37N, 08-54E, (farm, Niedersachsen, BRD

OLDISCHLEBEN, OLDISLEBEN, 2
1. 51-18N, 11-10E, Oldisleben, Halle, DDR

OLLESUND, Norway, 2

ONNBAU? 3
1. 50-50N, 06-40E, Onnau (farm), Nordrhein-Westfalen, BRD
See also ORNBAU

OPLAND, Hannover, 2
Not found.

OPPELN, Holstein, 1
1. 53-44N, 09-00E, Niedersachsen, BRD

OPPELN, 1
1. 51-08N, 14-42E, Dresden, DDR
2. 50-40N, 17-57E, (Pol.=Opole*), Polish-occupied
Germany
*There are five villages named Opole in Poland.

OPPURG, 1
1. 50-43N, 11-39E, Gera, DDR
See also OBER OPPURG

ORANIENBURG, Prussia, 2
1. 52-45N, 13-14E, Potsdam, DDR

ORNBAU, 3
1. 49-10N, 10-39E, Bavaria, BRD
2. 48-16N, 12-22E, Ornau, Bavaria, BRD
See also ONNBAU?

OSCHATZ, 1
1. 51-18N, 13-07E, Leipzig, DDR
2. 50-34N, 11-47E, Oschitz, Gera, DDR

OSNABRUECK, 1, 2
1. 52-16N, 08-03E, Niedersachsen, BRD

OSTERBURG, 1
1. 52-47N, 11-46E, Magdeburg, DDR

OSTERFELD, 1
1. 51-04N, 11-56E, Halle, DDR
2. 51-03N, 08-39E, Hessen, BRD
3. 51-30N, 06-53E, (section of city), Nordrhein-
Westfalen, BRD
4. 52-14N, 09-11E, (also called Osterfelde),
Niedersachsen, BRD
There are five farms of this name in Schleswig-
Holstein and Nordrhein-Westfalen, BRD.

OSTERITZ, Prussia, 3
1. 51-44N, 12-43E, Oesteritz, Halle, DDR

OSTERWITZ, 2
1. 51-58N, 10-43E, Osterwieck, Magdeburg, DDR

OSTNITZ, 3
Not found.

OSTROWO, Prussia, 2
1. 52-03N, 17-03E, Poland
2. 52-26N, 17-58E, Poland
3. 52-34N, 18-07E, Poland
4. 53-14N, 17-40E, Poland
5. 53-17N, 18-46E, Poland
6. 53-34N, 18-04E, Poland
7. 53-41N, 23-24E, Poland
8. 54-08N, 15-21E, (also called Wustrow; section
of city), Polish-occupied Germany

OTTENRIETH, 1
1. 49-41N, 12-19E, Bavaria, BRD
2. 48-55N, 09-49E, Ottenried, Baden-Wuerttemberg, BRD

OTTENSEN, 3
1. 52-22N, 09-18E, Niedersachsen, BRD
2. 53-27N, 09-40E, Niedersachsen, BRD
3. 53-33N, 09-55E, Hamburg, BRD

OTTERHAUSEN, 3
1. 50-25N, 12-06E, Otterhaus, Karl-Marx-Stadt, DDR

OTTERNDORF, 1
1. 53-56N, 20-39E, Ottendorf (Pol.=Radosty), Poland
2. 53-48N, 08-54E, Niedersachsen, BRD

PADERBORN, 3
1. 51-43N, 08-46E, Nordrhein-Westfalen, BRD

PAESNECK, 1, 2
1. 50-49N, 12-07E, Poesneck, Gera, DDR
2. 50-20N, 11-20E, Posseck, Bavaria, BRD
See also PESNECK

PAMPERIN, Mecklenburg, 2
1. 53-16N, 11-52E, Pampin, Schwerin, DDR
2. 53-31N, 10-56E, Pamprin, Schwerin, DDR

PANCKA, 2
There are four villages named Panki and one named Pankow in Poland.

PANTIN, 1
1. 53-40N, 10-37E, Panten, Schleswig-Holstein, BRD

PARBER, 1
1. 53-48N, 11-03E, Vitense-Parber, Rostock, DDR

PARCHAU, 1
1. 52-19N, 11-53E, Magdeburg, DDR
2. 51-29N, 15-57E, (Pol.=Parchow), Poland

PARCHIM, Mecklenburg, 1, 2, 3
1. 53-26N, 11-51E, Schwerin, DDR

PARIS, 1
1. 52-51N, 11-55E, (also called Parishof), Magdeburg, DDR

PARRWEISACH, PARWEISACH, 2
Not found.

PASSOW, 1
1. 53-09N, 14-06E, Frankfurt/Oder, DDR
2. 53-30N, 12-03E, Schwerin, DDR
3. 53-43N, 11-09E, Schwerin, DDR
4. 54-00N, 13-15E, Neubrandenburg, DDR

PAUSIN, 1
1. 52-38N, 13-02E, Potsdam, DDR

PEINE, Hannover, 2
1. 52-29N, 11-15E, Kolonie Peine (farm), Magdeburg, DDR
2. 52-19N, 10-14E, Niedersachsen, BRD

PELTZIG, Saxony, 2
Not found.

PENCKOW, 3
1. 53-27N, 12-29E, Penkow, Mecklenburg, DDR

PENNEWITZ, 1
1. 53-50N, 11-45E, Pennewitt, Schwerin, DDR
2. 50-40N, 11-03E, Suhl, DDR

PENZLIN, 2, 3
1. 53-17N, 12-15E, Potsdam, DDR
2. 53-30N, 13-05E, Neubrandenburg, DDR
3. 53-31N, 12-10E, Schwerin, DDR
4. 48-43N, 12-54E, Penzling, Bavaria, BRD

PERLEBERG, 1, 2
1. 53-04N, 11-52E, Schwerin, DDR

PERMUND, 2
Not found.

PESNECK, 1, 2
See also PAESNECK

PESTH [Hungary], 1, 2, 3

PETERSDORF, 1, 2, 3
1. 54-02N, 20-15E, (Pol.=Piotrowo), Poland
2. 54-10N, 17-34E, Polish-occupied Germany
There are 11 villages of this name in DDR; 7 in BRD.

PETERSHAGEN, Prussia, 2
1. 52-24N, 14-20E, Frankfurt/Oder, DDR
2. 52-31N, 13-47E, Frankfurt/Oder, DDR
3. 53-15N, 14-15E, Frankfurt/Oder, DDR
4. 52-47N, 12-23E, (farm), Potsdam, DDR
5. 54-13N, 20-30E, (Pol.=Pieszkowo), Poland
6. 54-15N, 19-09E, (Pol.=Zelichowo), Poland
7. 53-47N, 17-01E, (Pol.=Gdansk Pietraszek), Polish-occupied Germany
8. 52-23N, 08-58E, Nordrhein-Westfalen, BRD

PETROW, 1
Not found.

PETSCHKAU, 1
1. 54-02N, 12-18E, Petschow, Rostock, DDR
2. 53-51N, 22-42E, Petzkau (Pol.=Dudki), Poland

PFLANZVIRBACH, 1
1. 50-44N, 11-20E, Pflanzwirbach, Gera, DDR

PFUHL, 3
1. 48-25N, 10-02E, Bavaria, BRD
2. 50-40N, 07-59E, Rheinland-Pfalz, BRD

PHAZZONA, Hungary, 2

PHILADELPHIA, 1
1. 52-15N, 13-54E, Frankfurt/Oder, DDR

PILSEN, 1, 2
Probably Pilsen (Czech=Plzen) in Czechoslovakia.

PLAHSEN, 2
Not found.

PLANKENBERG, 3
1. 49-26N, 08-07E, (ridge), Rheinland-Pfalz, BRD

PLASSEW, 2
1. 52-23N, 12-53E, Plessow, Potsdam, DDR

PLASSIG? 3
Not found.

PLATE, 2
1. 53-33N, 11-30E, Schwerin, DDR
2. 53-48N, 15-16E, (also called Plathe), Polish-
   occupied Germany
3. 52-59N, 11-08E, Niedersachsen, BRD
4. 52-08N, 06-57E, (farm), Nordrhein-Westfalen,
   BRD

PLATHE, Prussia, 2
1. 52-46N, 11-26E, Magdeburg, DDR
2. 53-28N, 13-28E, Plath, Neubrandenburg, DDR
3. 53-48N, 15-16E, (also called Plate), Polish-
   occupied Germany

PLAU, Mecklenburg, 1
1. 53-27N, 12-16E, Schwerin, DDR
2. 50-47N, 10-54E, Plaue, Erfurt, DDR
3. 50-51N, 13-04E, Plaue, Karl-Marx-Stadt, DDR
4. 52-24N, 12-26E, Plaue, Potsdam, DDR

PLAUHAGEN, 2
1. 53-30N, 12-13E, Plauerhagen, Schwerin, DDR

PLAUSZIG, 2
1. 51-24N, 12-27E, Plaussig, Leipzig, DDR
2. 53-36N, 20-25E, Plautzig (Pol.=Pluski), Poland

PLESCHEN, 2
Not found.

PLOEN, 1
1. 50-34N, 12-24E, Plohn, Karl-Marx-Stadt, DDR
2. 54-10N, 10-26E, Schleswig-Holstein, BRD

POLJEWO, 2
Not found.

POLSEN, Prussia, 2
1. 53-10N, 13-59E, Polssen, Neubrandenburg, DDR

POLZIN, Prussia, 2
1. 51-43N, 13-18E, Polzen, Cottbus, DDR
2. 52-16N, 11-57E, Polzuhn, Magdeburg, DDR

POMEISKE, 1
1. 54-49N, 21-06E, Pomaski Wielkie, Poland

POMMERN, 3
1. 50-10N, 07-17E, Rheinland-Pfalz, BRD
2. 47-46N, 12-47E, Bavaria, BRD
Pommern (English=Pomerania) is the name of a Prussian province, now in Polish-occupied Germany.

POPPELAU, 1
Not found.

PORATZ, 1
1. 53-44N, 13-47E, Neubrandenburg, DDR
2. 49-29N, 22-14E, Poraz, Poland

POSEN, 1, 2, 3
1. 50-39N, 11-41E, Gera, DDR
2. 50-52N, 11-30E, Poesen, Gera, DDR
3. 52-25N, 16-58E, (Pol.=Poznan), Poland
Posen is also the name of a former Prussian province, now in Polish-occupied Germany.

POTSDAM, 2
1. 52-24N, 13-04E, Potsdam, DDR
2. 54-24N, 09-26E, (farm), Schleswig-Holstein, BRD

PRATAU? 3
1. 51-51N, 12-39E, Halle, DDR
2. 54-20N, 10-25E, Pratjau, Schleswig-Holstein,
   BRD

PREETZ, 2
1. 54-21N, 12-59E, Rostock, DDR
2. 54-21N, 13-38E, Rostock, DDR
3. 53-52N, 13-29E, Preetzen, Neubrandenburg, DDR
4. 54-14N, 10-17E, Schleswig-Holstein, BRD

PREILACK, PREILACKE, 3
1. 51-53N, 14-25E, Preilack, Cottbus, DDR

PRENZLAU, 3
1. 53-19N, 13-52E, Neubrandenburg, DDR

PRENZLIN, 2
1. 53-08N, 11-47E, Premslin, Schwerin, DDR

PREPWITZ, Bohemia [Czechoslovakia] 1

PRESBURG, 1
1. 50-03N, 07-53E, Presberg, Hessen, BRD
Pressburg, or Bratislava, is the capital of Slovakia
in Czechoslovakia.

PREUSSISCH EYLAU, 2
1. 53-36N, 19-34, now called Deutsch Eylau (Pol.=
   Iława), Poland

PREUSSISCH HOLLAND, 1
1. 54-04N, 19-40E, Preussen Holland (Pol.=Pasłek),
   Poland

PRIEGNITZ, 2
Not found.

PRITSCHEN, 1
1. 51-23N, 12-06E, Pritschoena, Halle, DDR
2. 51-39N, 14-05E, Pritzen, Cottbus, DDR
3. 48-57N, 09-43E, Pritschenhof, Baden-Wuerttemberg, BRD

PRITZWALD, 2
1. 54-06N, 13-40E, Rostock, DDR
2. 54-16N, 13-24E, Rostock, DDR

PRITZWALK, 1, 2
1. 53-09N, 12-11E, Potsdam, DDR

PROBFELD, 3
1. 48-40N, 11-22E, Bavaria, BRD

PROETTLIN, Prussia, 2
1. 53-12N, 11-34E, Schwerin, DDR

PROTSCHKENHAYN, 3
Not found.

PRUENEMUHLE, Mecklenburg, 3
Not found.

PUTTBUS, 3
1. 54-21N, 13-29E, Putbus, Rostock, DDR

PYRMONT, 1
1. 51-59N, 09-15E, (now called Bad Pyrmont),
   Niedersachsen, BRD

QUARITZ, 1
1. 53-50N, 11-49E, Qualitz, Schwerin, DDR

QUASSEL, Mecklenburg, 3
1. 53-20N, 11-05E, Schwerin, DDR

RABEN, 3
1. 52-03N, 12-35E, Potsdam, DDR
2. 48-03N, 08-11E, Baden-Wuerttemberg, BRD
3. 48-52N, 13-20E, Bavaria, BRD

RACHLITZ, Saxony, 2
1. 51-08N, 14-31E, Rachlau, Dresden, DDR
2. 51-21N, 14-17E, Rachlau, Cottbus, DDR
3. 51-02N, 13-43E, Raecknitz, Dresden, DDR
4. 51-26N, 12-23E, Rackwitz, Leipzig, DDR

RACKY, 2
1. 53-46N, 14-51E, Rackitt, Polish-occupied Germany

RADEGAST, Prussia, 3
1. 51-21N, 12-57E, Leipzig, DDR
2. 51-39N, 12-06E, Halle, DDR
3. 53-40N, 11-05E, Schwerin, DDR
4. 53-58N, 11-51E, Rostock, DDR
5. 53-20N, 10-43E, Niedersachsen, BRD

RADEGOSZ, 3
There are 15 villages and sections of cities named
Radgoszcz in Poland.

RAEBEL, 2
1. 52-50N, 12-02E, Magdeburg, DDR
2. 54-42N, 09-57E, Rabel, Schleswig-Holstein, BRD

RAGAZIN, 3
1. 51-59N, 12-17E, Ragoesen, Halle, DDR
2. 52-14N, 12-35E, Ragoesen, Potsdam, DDR

RAHDEN, 1
1. 52-04N, 14-27E, Raehden (lake), Frankfurt/Oder,
DDR
2. 52-26N, 08-37E, Nordrhein-Westfalen, BRD
3. 53-32N, 08-30E, Niedersachsen, BRD
4. 53-39N, 09-07E, Niedersachsen, BRD
5. 52-24N, 09-17E, Raehden, Niedersachsen, BRD
6. 52-26N, 08-36E, Raehden (farm), Nordrhein-Westfalen, BRD

RAIGERN, 2
Not found.

RALMA, 2
Not found.

RAMBOW, 2
1. 53-02N, 12-01E, Schwerin, DDR
2. 53-09N, 11-35E, Schwerin, DDR
3. 53-38N, 12-38E, Neubrandenburg, DDR
4. 53-50N, 11-26E, Rostock, DDR

RAMPE, 2
1. 53-41N, 11-29E, Schwerin, DDR

RANIS, 1, 3
1. 50-39N, 11-33E, Gera, DDR

RANSDORF, Prussia, 1
Not found.

RASTOW, Mecklenburg, 2
1. 53-27N, 11-26E, Schwerin, DDR

RATIBOR, 2
1. 53-44N, 13-47E, Rathebur, Neubrandenburg, DDR
2. 50-05N, 18-12E, (Pol.=Raciborz), Polish-occupied Germany

RATZEBURG, 1
1. 53-32N, 16-51E, Ratzebuhr, Polish-occupied Germany
2. 53-42N, 10-46E, Schleswig-Holstein, BRD

RAWITSCH, RAWITZ, 1
1. 51-37N, 16-52E, Rawitsch (Pol.=Rawicz), Poland
2. 51-29N, 19-25E, Rawicz, Poland

READING, Pennsylvania, U. S. A., 2

REBENTIN, 2
Not found.

RECHENBERG, Prussia, 1
1. 50-44N, 13-32E, Rechenberg-Bienemuehle, Karl-
Marx-Stadt, DDR
2. 53-50N, 21-23E, (Pol.=Kosewo), Poland
3. 49-03N, 10-09E, Baden-Wuerttemberg, BRD

RECHENZIEN, 3
1. 53-04N, 12-05E, Reckenthin, Potsdam, DDR
2. 54-14N, 11-42E, Reckenzin, Schwerin, DDR

RECHLIN, 2
1. 53-21N, 12-44E, Neubrandenburg, DDR

RECHMANNSDORF, 1
See REICHMANNSDORF

REDWITZ, 2
1. 50-10N, 11-12E, Redwitz an der Rodach, Bavaria
BRD
2. 50-00N, 12-05E, Marktredwitz, Bavaria, BRD

REGENSBURG, 2
1. 49-40N, 11-11E, Regensberg, Bavaria, BRD
2. 49-01N, 12-06E, Bavaria, BRD

REHAN, Bavaria, 2
1. 51-40N, 13-50E, Rehain, Cottbus, DDR
2. 51-49N, 12-55E, Rehain, Cottbus, DDR

REHNA, 2
1. 53-47N, 11-03E, Schwerin, DDR

REICHENAU, 2, 3
1. 50-48N, 13-35E, Dresden, DDR
2. 51-15N, 13-57E, Dresden, DDR
3. 53-35N, 20-05E, (Pol.=Rychnowo), Poland
4. 47-41N, 12-15E, Bavaria, BRD
5. 49-12N, 10-30E, Bavaria, BRD
6. 49-41N, 12-31E, Bavaria, BRD
7. 47-41N, 09-04E, (island), Baden-Wuerttemberg,
BRD

REICHENBACH, 1
1. 50-43N, 16-39E, Reichenbach in Schlesien, Polish-occupied Germany
2. 53-59N, 19-32E, (Pol.=Rychliki), Poland
There are 14 villages of this name in DDR; 35 in
BRD.

REICHENBACH, Saxony, 2
   See REICHENBACH

REICHMANSDORF, 1, 3
  1. 50-33N, 11-14E, Suhl, DDR
  2. 49-47N, 10-42E, Bavaria, BRD

REIFFENHAGEN, 1
  1. 51-24N, 09-59E, Reiffenhausen, Niedersachsen,
           BRD

REINSDORF, 1
  1. 51-15N, 13-37E, Reinersdorf, Dresden, DDR
  2. 53-19N, 09-54E, Niedersachsen, BRD

REINE, 1
  1. 52-03N, 09-10E, Niedersachsen, BRD

REINFELD, Holstein, 2
  1. 53-06N, 13-29E, (farm), Neubrandenburg, DDR
  2. 53-56N, 16-59E, Reinfeld Hammer, Polish-occu-
           pied Germany
  3. 53-50N, 10-29E, Schleswig-Holstein, BRD

REINSDORF, 3
  1. 53-19N, 09-54E, Reindorf, Niedersachsen, BRD
  There are 12 villages of this name in DDR.

REISDORF, 1
  1. 51-06N, 11-34E, Erfurt, DDR
  2. 48-31N, 11-37E, Bavaria, BRD
  3. 49-06N, 07-54E, Rheinland-Pfalz, BRD
  4. 51-04N, 06-32E, Nordrhein-Westfalen, BRD

REMBDEN, REMDEN, 1
  1. 50-46N, 11-13E, Remda, Gera, DDR

RENA, 1
  1. 51-04N, 10-04E, Renda, Hessen, BRD

RENDSBURG, Holstein, 1, 2
  1. 54-18N, 09-40E, Schleswig-Holstein, BRD

RESCHWITZ, Thuringia, 1, 2
  1. 50-37N, 11-23E, Gera, DDR

RETHEIM, 1
  1. 52-47N, 09-23E, Rethem, Niedersachsen, BRD

RETSCH, 1
  1. 54-21N, 20-56E, (Pol.=Redy), Poland

REUTLINGEN, 2
  1. 48-29N, 09-13E, Baden-Wuerttemberg, BRD

REWISENHOF, 3
  Not found.

RHEDA, Prussia, 1
  1. 54-40N, 18-28E, (stream), Poland
  2. 51-51N, 08-18E, Nordrhein-Westfalen, BRD
  3. 51-59N, 08-12E, (farm community), Nordrhein-
           Westfalen, BRD
  4. 51-50N, 06-42E, Rhede, Nordrhein-Westfalen, BRD
  5. 53-04N, 07-16E, Rhede, Niedersachsen, BRD

RHEINFELD, Holstein, 1
  1. 51-06N, 06-51E, Nordrhein-Westfalen, BRD

RHEINFELDEN, 3
  1. 47-34N, 07-48E, Baden-Wuerttemberg, BRD
  2. 49-54N, 08-28E, (also called Rheinfelderhof),
           Hessen, BRD

RHEINHAUSEN, 3
  1. 49-17N, 08-29E, Baden-Wuerttemberg, BRD
  2. 51-25N, 06-45E, Nordrhein-Westfalen, BRD

RIBNITZ, 1
  1. 53-51N, 13-47E, Neubrandenburg, DDR
  2. 54-15N, 12-28E, Ribnitz-Damgarten, Rostock, DDR

RIEGELSDORF, 2
  Not found.

RIEGERSDORF, 2
  Not found.

RIEPE, RIEPL, 1, 3
  1. 53-46N, 10-52E, Rieps, Schwerin, DDR
  2. 52-56N, 09-44E, Riepe, Niedersachsen, BRD
  3. 53-12N, 09-36E, Riepe, Niedersachsen, BRD
  4. 53-24N, 07-22E, Riepe, Niedersachsen, BRD

RIGA, 1
  1. 53-39N, 13-28E, Roga, Neubrandenburg, DDR
  2. 49-47N, 11-58E, Bavaria, BRD
  Riga is the capital of Latvia, now a republic of
  the U. S. S. R.

RINTELN, 2
  1. 52-11N, 09-05E, Niedersachsen, BRD

RIPEN, Denmark, 3
  1. 53-04N, 19-27E, Ripin (Pol.=Rypin), Poland

RITSCH, 1
  1. 53-42N, 09-25E, Niedersachsen, BRD

RITSCHUETZ, 3
  Not found

ROBEL, Mecklenburg, 1, 2
  See RAEBEL, ROEBEL

ROBERSBERG, 3
  1. 49-48N, 10-55E, Roebersdorf, Bavaria, BRD
  2. 54-23N, 10-15E, Roebsdorf, Schleswig-Holstein,
           BRD
  3. 48-22N, 11-15E, Roeckersberg, Bavaria, BRD

ROCHBERG, 3
  Not found.

ROCHOW, 1
  1. 53-43N, 14-03E, (also called Rochow Eins), Neu-
           brandenburg, DDR
  2. 54-15N, 21-59E, Rochau Ostpreussen (Pol.=Miculy)
           Poland

ROCK ISLAND, Illinois, U. S. A., 3

ROCKENDORF, 1
  1. 50-40N, 11-31E, Gera, DDR
  2. 51-26N, 11-56E, Halle, DDR

RODO, 1
  1. 53-28N, 20-18E, Rodau (Pol.=Rodowo), Poland
  There are 11 villages named Roda in DDR; 4 named
  Rodau in BRD.

RODWITZ, 2
  1. 51-06N, 14-27E, Rodewitz, Dresden, DDR
  2. 51-10N, 14-35E, Rodewitz, Dresden, DDR
  See also REDWITZ

ROEBEL, Mecklenburg, 1, 2
1. 53-23N, 12-36E, Neubrandenburg, DDR
2. 54-07N, 10-40E, Schleswig-Holstein, BRD

ROEBNITZ, 3
1. 50-39N, 11-26E, Roeblitz, Gera, DDR

ROEDELHEIM, 3
1. 50-09N, 08-39E, (section of city), Hessen, BRD

ROEHRENFAHRT, 2
1. 51-09N, 09-33E, Roehrenfurth, Hessen, BRD

ROEMHILD, Thuringia, 2, 3
1. 50-23N, 10-33E, Suhl, DDR
See also RONNHILD, HEINAMOF IN

ROEMPEN, 1
Not found.

ROETELMEIER, Bavaria, 2
1. 49-40N, 11-54E, Roetelweiher (or Roetelweiher-
schlag), Bavaria, BRD

ROGASEN, 2
1. 52-19N, 12-23E, Rogaesen, Potsdam, DDR
2. 52-13N, 12-06E, Rogaesen-Jerichow, Magdeburg,
DDR

ROHRBACH, 1
1. 50-15N, 10-30E, Karl-Marx-Stadt, DDR
2. 50-36N, 11-13E, Gera, DDR
3. 51-04N, 11-24E, Erfurt, DDR
4. 51-13N, 12-34E, Leipzig, DDR
5. 51-18N, 13-00E, Dresden, DDR
There are three villages named Rohrbeck in DDR; 34
in BRD.

ROMANSHOF, 1
1. 48-23N, 08-13E, Romaneshof, Baden-Wuerttemberg,
BRD

RONNER, 2
Not found.

RONNHILD, HEINAMOF IN, 3
1. 50-25N, 10-32E, Haina in Roemhild, Suhl, DDR
2. 50-59N, 10-32E, Haina, Erfurt, DDR
See also ROEMHILD

ROSENBERG, 1, 2
1. 53-40N, 11-13E, (farm), Schwerin, DDR
2. 50-53N, 18-26E, Polish-occupied Germany
3. 53-43N, 19-21E, (Pol.=Susz), Poland
4. 54-13N, 18-40E, (Pol.=Rozyny), Poland
There are 11 villages and farms of this name in BRD.

ROSENFELD, 3
1. 51-32N, 12-06E, Halle, DDR
2. 51-36N, 13-02E, Leipzig, DDR
3. 48-17N, 08-43E, Baden-Wuerttemberg, BRD
4. 54-17N, 10-16E, Schleswig-Holstein, BRD
5. 54-16N, 11-04E, (farm), Schleswig-Holstein, BRD

ROSENGARTH, 1
1. 52-21N, 14-28E, Rosengarten, Frankfurt/Oder, DDR
2. 54-18N, 13-23E, Rosengarten, Rostock, DDR
3. 53-55N, 20-19E, (Pol.=Rozynka), Poland
4. 54-15N, 20-11E, (Pol.=Rozaniec), Poland
There are six villages and farms named Rosengarten
in BRD.

ROSENKRANZ, 2
1. 53-56N, 18-54E, (Pol.=Roza), Poland
2. 54-54N, 08-45E, Schleswig-Holstein, BRD
3. 51-45N, 08-47E, (farm, also called Seskerbruch),
Nordrhein-Westfalen, BRD

ROSENLUBWITZ, 1
Not found.

ROSENTHAL, 1
There are 16 villages and farms of this name in
DDR; 11 in BRD.

ROSSIN, 2
1. 52-05N, 12-09E, Rosian, Magdeburg, DDR
2. 53-18N, 10-58E, Rosien, Schwerin, DDR
3. 51-20N, 12-01E, Roessen, Halle, DDR
4. 53-46N, 13-42E, Neubrandenburg, DDR

ROSSNOW, 1
1. 53-03N, 12-34E, Rossow, Potsdam, DDR
2. 53-05N, 12-35E, Rossow, Potsdam, DDR
3. 53-28N, 14-08E, Rossow, Neubrandenburg, DDR
4. 53-39N, 13-22E, Rossow, Neubrandenburg, DDR
5. 54-05N, 16-18E, Polish-occupied Germany

ROSTHAL, 3
1. 47-51N, 09-59E, Rostall, Baden-Wuerttemberg,
BRD

ROSTOCK, 1, 2, 3
1. 54-05N, 12-08E, Rostock, DDR

ROSTOCKE, 3
1. 49-48N, 20-43E, Rostoka (or Roztoka), Poland
2. 50-58N, 16-14E, Rostoka (or Rohnstock), Polish-
occupied Germany
3. 51-03N, 23-45E, Rostoka, Poland
4. 52-24N, 18-10E, Rostoka, Poland

ROTENBURG, 2
1. 54-05N, 17-59E, (Pol.=Rotembark), Poland
2. 52-00N, 15-25E, Rothenburg an der Oder, Polish-
occupied Germany
3. 50-59N, 09-43E, Rotenburg an der Fulda, Hessen,
BRD
4. 53-07N, 09-24E, Niedersachsen, BRD
See also ROTHENBURG

ROTENHAGEN BEI LUEBECK, 3
1. 52-06N, 08-25E, Nordrhein-Westfalen, BRD
See also LUEBECK

ROTH, 1
1. 50-22N, 11-02E, Suhl, DDR
2. 50-24N, 10-38E, Suhl, DDR
There are 24 villages and farms of this name in BRD.

ROTHEN, 2
1. 53-41N, 11-57E, Schwerin, DDR
2. 52-22N, 13-51E, Roethen, Frankfurt/Oder, DDR
3. 47-42N, 10-23E, Bavaria, BRD
4. 53-09N, 10-48E, Roethen (forester's lodge),
Niedersachsen, BRD

ROTHENBURG, Prussia, 2
1. 51-20N, 14-58E, (also called Rothenburg in Ober
Lausitz), Dresden, DDR
2. 51-39N, 11-45E, Halle, DDR
3. 53-32N, 14-04E, Neubrandenburg, DDR
4. 51-25N, 11-03E, (forester's lodge), Halle, DDR

ROTHENBURG, Prussia [continued]
5. 49-23N, 10-11E, Rothenburg ob der Tauber, Bavaria, BRD
6. 51-30N, 09-13E, Nordrhein-Westfalen, BRD
7. 49-51N, 12-13E, Bavaria, BRD
8. 50-19N, 11-46E, Bavaria, BRD
See also ROTENBURG

ROTHKIRCHEN, 1
1. 50-32N, 12-30E, Rothenkirchen, Karl-Marx-Stadt, DDR
2. 54-22N, 13-15E, Rostock, DDR
3. 51-46N, 09-50E, Rotenkirchen, Niedersachsen, BRD
4. 50-21N, 11-19E, Rothenkirchen, Bavaria, BRD
5. 50-43N, 09-42E, Rothenkirchen, Hessen, BRD

RUDOLSTADT, 1, 2
1. 50-43N, 11-20E, Gera, DDR

RUEST, 1, 2, 3
1. 48-16N, 07-44E, Rust, Baden-Wuerttemberg, BRD
2. 51-41N, 06-54E, Rueste, Nordrhein-Westfalen, BRD

RUHETHAT, Mecklenburg, 3
1. 51-20N, 14-33E, Ruhethal, Dresden, DDR
2. 53-25N, 11-03E, Ruhethal, Schwerin, DDR
There are five farms named Ruhethal (Ruhetal) in BRD.

RUHN, 2
1. 53-18N, 11-54E, Schwerin, DDR
2. 53-49N, 11-56E, Ruehn, Schwerin, DDR
3. 53-50N, 11-55E, Ruehn (farm), Schwerin, DDR
4. 51-31N, 07-57E, Ruhne, Nordrhein-Westfalen, BRD

RUKHAHN, 1
1. 50-51N, 13-49E, Rueckenhain, Dresden, DDR

RUMPENHAIN, 3
1. 53-31N, 12-58E, Rumpshagen, Neubrandenburg, DDR

RUNNSTADT, 2
1. 51-18N, 11-56E, Runstedt (or Runstaedt), Halle, DDR
2. 52-11N, 10-59E, Runstedt, Niedersachsen, BRD

RUPPERDORF, 2
Not found.

RUPPERSDORF, Saxony, 1, 2
1. 50-31N, 11-35E, Gera, DDR
2. 49-24N, 10-33E, Bavaria, BRD
3. 53-58N, 10-45E, Alt Ruppersdorf, Schleswig-Holstein, BRD

RUPPIN, 1
1. 52-57N, 21-22E, Rupin, Poland
2. 53-10N, 21-13E, Rupin, Poland
3. 53-28N, 21-56E, Rupin, Poland

SAAL, Bavaria, 1, 3
1. 54-19N, 12-30E, Rostock, DDR
2. 48-54N, 11-56E, (community), Bavaria, BRD
3. 49-28N, 07-15E, Schleswig-Holstein, BRD
4. 50-19N, 10-22E, Saal an der Saale, Bavaria, BRD
5. 51-14N, 07-57E, (farm), Nordrhein-Westfalen, BRD
6. 51-45N, 06-10E, (farming community) Nordrhein-Westfalen, BRD

SAALFELD, 1, 2, 3
1. 50-39N, 11-22E, Gera, DDR
2. 51-16N, 10-31E, Erfurt, DDR
3. 52-46N, 11-11E, Magdeburg, DDR
4. 53-50N, 19-36E, (Pol.=Zalewo), Poland

SACHSA, Prussia, 2
1. 49-18N, 10-24E, Sachsen, Bavaria, BRD
2. 49-18N, 10-39E, Sachsen, Bavaria, BRD
3. 47-51N, 10-58E, Sachsen (farm), Bavaria, BRD
4. 51-36N, 10-33E, now called Bad Sachsa, Niedersachsen, BRD

SACHSEN-WEIMAR, 1, 3
Probably the principality of Sachsen-Weimar is meant.

SAINT LOUIS [Missouri, U. S. A.] 2, 3

SAKOLKER, 1
Not found.

SALGAN, 3
1. 51-15N, 14-32E, Salga, Dresden, DDR
2. 48-08N, 10-29E, Salgen, Bavaria, BRD

SALZBURG, 3
1. 48-43N, 12-13E, Bavaria, BRD
2. 50-40N, 08-03E, Rheinland-Pfalz, BRD
3. 52-07N, 09-36E, Niedersachsen, BRD
4. 50-10N, 10-14E, (farm), Bavaria, BRD
Probably Salzburg, a major city in Austria, is meant.

SALZWEDEL, 1, 2, 3
1. 52-51N, 11-09E, Magdeburg, DDR
2. 54-11N, 22-30E, (Pol.=Drozdowka), Poland

SANDOMIERZ, Russia, 2
1. 50-41N, 21-45E, (also spelled Sandomir), Poland

SANDOMISS, Posen, 2
See SANDOMIERZ

SANGERHAUSEN, SANGERSHAUSEN, 1, 2
1. 51-28N, 11-18E, Sangerhausen, Halle, DDR

SANKT GALLEN, [Switzerland] 2

SANKT GEORG, 2
1. 53-33N, 13-15E, Neubrandenburg, DDR
2. 48-02N, 10-29E, Bavaria, BRD
3. 51-14N, 06-15E, Sankt Georg-Amern (section of city), Nordrhein-Westfalen, BRD
4. 53-33N, 10-01E, Hamburg, BRD
5. 48-24N, 13-19E, (farm), Bavaria, BRD

SANKT MARGARETHEN, Holstein, 1, 3
1. 53-54N, 09-15E, Schleswig-Holstein

SANKT MICHELN, Prussia, 2
1. 51-18N, 11-47E, (section of city), Halle, DDR

SANKT PETERSBURG, 1, 2
Probably Leningrad, U. S. S. R., is meant.

SANNEBORN, 1
See SONNEBORN

SARACZEWA, 2
Not found.

SARMENSDORF, Switzerland, 1

SASSBACH, 1
1- 48-43N, 13-35E, Bavaria, BRD

SATOW, 2, 3
1. 53-59N, 11-54E, (also called Satow-Niederhagen)
                  Rostock, DDR
2. 53-25N, 12-23E, Neubrandenburg, DDR

SAWADE, Prussia, 3
   There are 20 villages and sections of cities named
   Sawadden (Pol.=Zawada, Zawady) in Poland.

SCHAEDENRINKEL, 3
1. 53-51N, 18-53E, Schadewinkel (Pol.=Szadowka),
                  Poland

SCHAEFSTAEDT, 3
1. 51-23N, 11-46E, Schafstaedt, Halle, DDR
2. 54-05N, 09-18E, Schafstedt, Schleswig-Holstein,
                  BRD
3. 53-57N, 08-58E, Schafstedt, Schleswig-Holstein,
                  BRD

SCHAFFHAUSEN, 1, 3
1. 48-22N, 12-09E, (also Grossschaffhausen), Ba-
                  varia, BRD
2. 48-24N, 11-09E, Bavaria, BRD
3. 48-46N, 10-38E, Bavaria, BRD
4. 48-58N, 10-34E, Bavaria, BRD
5. 49-16N, 06-49E, Saar, BRD

SCHAMWECHT, 2
1. 52-41N, 08-56E, Schamwege, Niedersachsen, BRD

SCHARFFENOW, Prussia, 2
   Not found.

SCHARKY, 3
1. 51-00N, 18-41E, Szarki, Poland
2. 52-15N, 16-07E, Szarki, Poland
3. 54-22N, 20-17E, Szarki, Poland
4. 52-14N, 16-09E, Szarki Nowe (section of city)
                  Poland
5. 52-16N, 16-06E, Szarki Stare (section of city)
                  Poland

SCHARMBECK, Holstein, 3
1. 53-14N, 08-48E, (also called Osterholz-Scharm-
                  beck), Niedersachsen, BRD
2. 53-21N, 10-09E, Niedersachsen, BRD

SCHARPENORT, 2, 3
1. 54-18N, 18-39E, Scharfenort (Pol.=Ostrozek),
                  Poland

SCHELKINGEN, 1
1. 48-22N, 09-44E, Schelklingen, Baden-Wuerttem-
                  berg, BRD

SCHERKOW, 1
   Not found.

SCHERNEJAVA, 2
1. 54-10N, 18-30E, Scherniau (Pol.=Czerniewo),
                  Poland
2. 52-41N, 23-18E, Szernie, Poland

SCHIERITZ, 1
1. 51-12N, 13-24E, Dresden, DDR

SCHILDBERG, 2
1. 53-47N, 11-12E, Rostock, DDR

SCHILDE, 1
1. 53-03N, 11-46E, Schwerin, DDR
2. 52-17N, 11-42E, (farm), Magdeburg, DDR

SCHIRP, Dithmarschen, 3
   Not found.

SCHKEUDITZ, 2
1. 51-24N, 12-13E, Leipzig, DDR

SCHLAGERTHAL, Thuringia, 2
   Not found.

SCHLAGSDORF, Mecklenburg, 3
1. 51-55N, 14-41E, Cottbus, DDR
2. 53-44N, 10-50E, Schwerin, DDR
3. 54-30N, 11-04E, Schleswig-Holstein, BRD

SCHLESWIG, 1, 2, 3
1. 54-31N, 09-33E, Schleswig-Holstein, BRD

SCHLIEBEN, 1, 2
1. 51-43N, 13-23E, Cottbus, DDR

SCHLOETERSDORF, 2
   Not found.

SCHLOTTHEIM, 1
1. 51-15N, 10-40E, Schlotheim, Erfurt, DDR
2. 48-29N, 12-48E, Schlottham, Bavaria, BRD

SCHMALKALDEN, 3
1. 50-43N, 10-27E, Suhl, DDR

SCHMEGEL, 1, 3
   Not found.

SCHMIEDE, 2
1. 50-28N, 11-02E, (hill), Suhl, DDR
2. 50-48N, 11-23E, Schmieden, Gera, DDR
3. 54-19N, 18-34E, (Pol.=Kowale), Poland

SCHMIEDEBERG, 1
1. 53-09N, 13-57E, Frankfurt/Oder, DDR
2. 50-48N, 15-50E, Polish-occupied Germany
3. 53-50N, 09-45E, Schleswig-Holstein, BRD

SCHMIEDEFELD, 1
1. 51-05N, 14-04E, Dresden, DDR
2. 50-32N, 11-13E, Suhl, DDR
3. 50-37N, 10-50E, Schmiedefeld am Rennsteig, Suhl
                  BRD
4. 48-58N, 09-51E, Schmiedelfeld, Baden-Wuerttem-
                  berg, BRD

SCHMIEGEL, 1, 3
   Not found.

SCHMOELEN, Schmoelew?, 3
1. 51-21N, 12-44E, Schmoelen, Leipzig, DDR
2. 50-54N, 12-22E, Schmoelln, Leipzig, DDR
3. 51-08N, 14-14E, Schmoelln, Dresden, DDR
4. 53-18N, 14-06E, Schmoelln, Neubrandenburg, DDR
5. 50-53N, 12-23E, Schmoelln Nitzscka, Leipzig, DD

SCHNEIDEMUEHLE, 1
1. 53-09N, 16-45E, Schneidemuehl, Polish-occupied
                  Germany
2. 53-33N, 19-36E, Schneidemuehle Alteiche (Pol.=
                  Smolniki), Poland

SCHNITHRIGE, SCHNITTRIGE, 2
Not found.

SCHOENBERG, 1, 3
1. 51-04N, 15-04E, Polish-occupied Germany
2. 53-39N, 19-29E, (Pol.=Szymbark), Poland
3. 54-11N, 19-39E, (Pol.=Zastawno), Poland
There are 11 villages of this name in DDR; about
32 villages and farms of this name in BRD.

SCHOENBRUNN, 1, 2
There are nine villages and farms of this name in
DDR; 20 in BRD.

SCHOENEMARK, 1, 2
1. 52-54N, 12-19E, Schoenermark, Potsdam, DDR
2. 53-00N, 13-07E, Schoenermark, Potsdam, DDR
3. 53-07N, 14-02E, Schoenermark, Frankfurt/Oder,
   DDR
4. 53-20N, 13-43E, Schoenermark, Neubrandenburg,
   DDR
5. 51-55N, 08-56E, Nordrhein-Westfalen, BRD

SCHOENFELD, 2
There are four villages named Schoenefeld and 17
named Schoenfeld in DDR; five in Poland; nine in
BRD.

SCHOENINGEN, 1
1. 51-38N, 09-40E, Schoningen, Niedersachsen, BRD
2. 52-08N, 10-57E, Niedersachsen, BRD

SCHOENWALDE, 2
1. 51-59N, 13-46E, Cottbus, DDR
2. 52-28N, 11-48E, Magdeburg, DDR
3. 52-35N, 12-07E, Magdeburg, DDR
4. 52-37N, 13-08E, Potsdam, DDR
5. 52-41N, 13-26E, Frankfurt/Oder, DDR
6. 53-32N, 13-54E, Neubrandenburg, DDR
7. 51-39N, 15-04E, Polish-occupied Germany
8. 53-44N, 20-34E, (Pol.=Szczesne), Poland
9. 54-07N, 20-56E, (Pol.=Warmiany), Poland
10. 54-22N, 20-13E, (Pol.=Grabowiec), Poland
1. 54-11N, 10-45E, Schoenwalde am Bungsberg,
   Schleswig-Holstein, BRD

SCHOEPS, Prussia, 2
1. 50-50N, 11-36E, Gera, DDR
2. 51-09N, 14-45E, Dresden, DDR

SCHONDRA, 3
1. 50-16N, 09-52E, Bavaria

SCHONEMARK, 2
See SCHOENEMARK

SCHONLAMKE, Prussia, 2
1. 53-02N, 16-27E, Schoenlanke, Polish-occupied
   Germany

SCHOSSIN, Mecklenburg, 1
1. 53-33N, 11-13E, Schwerin, DDR

SCHREIBERSDORF, 3
1. 54-52N, 08-46E, Schreibersort (farm), Schleswig-
   Holstein, BRD

SCHWABACH, 1
1. 52-02N, 12-49E, Schwabeck, Potsdam, DDR
2. 49-20N, 11-02E, Bavaria
3. 48-26N, 08-21E, (farm), Baden-Wuerttemberg, BRD
4. 49-11N, 09-24E, Schwabbach, Baden-Wuerttemberg,
   BRD

SCHWABEROW, Mecklenburg, 2
1. 53-25N, 11-06E, Schwerin, DDR

SCHWABSTEDT, 1
1. 48-09N, 10-51E, Schwabstadl, Bavaria, BRD
2. 54-24N, 09-11E, Schleswig-Holstein, BRD

SCHWARTAU, 3
1. 53-24N, 10-45E, Schwartow, Schwerin, DDR
2. 53-54N, 10-43E, (stream), Schleswig-Holstein,
   BRD

SCHWARZBURG, 1
1. 50-38N, 11-12E, Gera, DDR
2. 53-56N, 12-13E, Schwarzberge (Pol.=Rydzewo),
   Poland
3. 49-35N, 12-13E, Schwarzberg, Bavaria, BRD
4. 48-31N, 11-53E, Schwarzberg (farm), Bavaria,
   BRD
5. 47-47N, 12-45E, Schwarzberg (farming community),
   Bavaria, BRD

SCHWARZENBERG-RUDOLSTADT, AMT GERINGEN, 1
1. 50-32N, 12-47E, Schwarzenberg (Landkreis), Karl-
   Marx-Stadt, DDR
2. 50-43N, 11-20E, Rudolstadt (Landkreis), Gera,
   DDR
[Amt Geringen not found.]
There are 15 villages and farms named Schwarzenberg in BRD. The above entry refers to the former
principality, no doubt.

SCHWEINFURT, 1
1. 51-27N, 13-24E, Schweinfurth, Dresden, DDR
2. 50-03N, 10-14E, Bavaria, BRD

SCHWEKOZNEN, 1
Not found.

SCHWERBORN, Prussia, 1
1. 51-02N, 11-04E, Erfurt, DDR

SCHWERCENZ, SCHWERSENZ, 1, 2
1. 47-39N, 08-22E, Schwerzen, Baden-Wuerttemberg,
   BRD

SCHWERIN, 1, 2, 3
1. 52-09N, 13-38E, Potsdam, DDR
2. 52-12N, 13-53E, Frankfurt/Oder, DDR
3. 53-38N, 11-23E, Schwerin, DDR
4. 52-36N, 15-30E, Polish-occupied Germany

SCHWERSITZ, 1
Not found.

SCHWESSOW, 2
See Schwessow, Kreis Greifenberg, in Clifford Neal
Smith, Nineteenth-Century Emigration of "Old Luther-
ans" from Eastern Germany (Mainly Pomerania and
Lower Silesia) to Australia, Canada, and the United
States (McNeal, AZ: Westland Publications, 1980).

SCHWIEBUS, 3
1. 52-15N, 15-32E, Polish-occupied Germany

SCONNING, Sweden, 3

SEEBERG, Hannover, 2
1. 52-33N, 13-41E, Frankfurt/Oder, DDR
2. 53-34N, 14-18E, (farm), Neubrandenburg, DDR
3. 48-29N, 11-51E, Bavaria, BRD
4. 47-55N, 12-48E, (farm), Bavaria, BRD
5. 54-18N, 10-02E, (farm), Schleswig-Holstein, BRD

SEEBERG [continued]
6. 54-31N, 09-59E, (farm), Schleswig-Holstein, BRD
7. 54-42N, 10-00E, (farm), Schleswig-Holstein, BRD
8. 51-34N, 10-09E, Seeburg, Niedersachsen, BRD
9. 48-06N, 12-12E, Seeburg, Bavaria, BRD
10. 48-27N, 09-27E, Seeburg, Baden-Wuerttemberg, BRD
11. 50-36N, 07-49E, Seeburg, Rheinland-Pfalz, BRD
12. 53-48N, 09-10E, Seeburg (farm), Niedersachsen, BRD

SEEBERGE, 3
1. 50-55N, 10-48E, Seebergen, Erfurt, DDR
2. 53-59N, 20-45E, Seeburg (Pol.=Jeziorany), Poland
3. 53-08N, 08-59E, Seebergen, Niedersachsen, BRD

SEEHAUSEN, Prussia, 1, 2, 3
1. 51-20N, 11-07E, Halle, DDR
2. 51-24N, 12-25E, Leipzig, DDR
3. 51-57N, 12-55E, Potsdam, DDR
4. 52-06N, 11-18E, Magdeburg, DDR
5. 52-53N, 11-45E, Magdeburg, DDR
6. 53-13N, 13-53E, Neubrandenburg, DDR
7. 54-07N, 21-58E, (Pol.=Jeziorowskie), Poland
8. 47-41N, 11-11E, Seehausen am Staffelsee, Bavaria, BRD
9. 53-07N, 08-43E, Bremen, BRD
10. 53-12N, 09-00E, Niedersachsen, BRD

SEESEN, Hannover, 2
1. 51-54N, 10-11E, Niedersachsen, BRD
2. 47-52N, 10-25E, (farm), Bavaria, BRD

SEGEBERG, Holstein, 1, 2, 3
1. 53-56N, 10-10E, now called Bad Segeberg, Schleswig-Holstein, BRD

SEIFERSDORF, 1
1. 50-46N, 12-48E, Karl-Marx-Stadt, DDR
2. 50-48N, 12-01E, Rostock, DDR
3. 50-56N, 13-39E, Dresden, DDR
4. 50-58N, 13-14E, Karl-Marx-Stadt, DDR
5. 51-01N, 12-42E, Leipzig, DDR
6. 51-05N, 13-12E, Leipzig, DDR
7. 51-08N, 12-54E, Leipzig, DDR
8. 51-10N, 13-53E, Dresden, DDR
9. 51-18N, 16-47E, Polish-occupied Germany

SEKKENDITZ, 2
Not found.

SELCHOW, Prussia, 2
1. 52-13N, 13-52E, Frankfurt/Oder, DDR
2. 52-22N, 13-28E, Potsdam, DDR

SELDIN, 2
Not found.

SENFTENBERG, 1
1. 51-31N, 14-01E, Cottbus, DDR

SESSLACH, 1
1. 50-11N, 10-51E, Bavaria, BRD

SETHERSMUEHLEN, Holstein, 1
Not found.

SETZDORF, 3
Not found.

SEVANGER, Norway, 2

SEVERIN, 1
1- 53-30N, 11-46E, Schwerin, DDR

SIBLINGEN, Switzerland, 1

SICHELKOW, 1
Not found.

SIEVERN, Hannover, 1
1. 53-30N, 08-36E, Niedersachsen, BRD

SILZ, 3
1. 53-31N, 12-26E, Neubrandenburg, DDR
2. 49-09N, 07-57E, Rheinland-Pfalz, BRD

SINZLEBEN, 2
1. 51-44N, 11-21E, Sinsleben, Halle, DDR

SITZERODE, Saxony, 1
1. 51-27N, 12-59E, Sitzenroda, Leipzig, DDR
2. 49-36N, 06-55E, Sitzerath, Saar, BRD

SKARABORGSLAEN, Sweden, 1

SLATE, Mecklenburg, 2
1. 53-24N, 11-52E, Schwerin, DDR

SOL, 2
1. 49-29N, 19-03E, Poland
2. 50-31N, 22-39E, Poland
3. 53-17N, 21-31E, Poland

SOLDIKOW, 2
Not found.

SOLDIN, Prussia, 2
1. 52-55N, 14-52E, Polish-occupied Germany

SOMMERFELD, 3
1. 51-21N, 12-30E, Leipzig, DDR
2. 52-48N, 13-02E, Potsdam, DDR
3. 54-22N, 13-00E, Rostock, DDR
4. 52-50N, 13-52E, Sommerfelde, Frankfurt/Oder, DDR
5. 51-48N, 14-58E, Polish-occupied Germany
6. 54-04N, 19-58E, (Pol.=Zabrowiec), Poland
7. 54-04N, 20-17E, (Pol.=Zagony), Poland

SONDERSHAUSEN, 1, 2
1. 51-22N, 10-52E, Erfurt, DDR

SONNEBERG, Prussia, 1, 2
1. 50-21N, 11-10E, Suhl, DDR
2. 51-02N, 14-31E, Dresden, DDR
3. 51-03N, 13-41E, Dresden, DDR
4. 53-48N, 19-14E, (Pol.=Gorowychy), Poland
There are 11 villages and farms named Sonnehberg in BRD.

SONNEBORN, 1
1. 51-00N, 10-35E, Erfurt, DDR
2. 53-51N, 19-53E, (Pol.=Słonecznik), Poland
3. 52-01N, 09-10E, Nordrhein-Westfalen, BRD
4. 51-10N, 07-54E, (farm), Nordrhein-Westfalen, BRD

SONNENBURG, 2
1. 52-45N, 14-02E, Frankfurt/Oder, DDR
2. 51-57N, 10-53E, (farm), Magdeburg, DDR
3. 52-33N, 14-48E, Polish-occupied Germany
4. 49-12N, 09-29E, (farm), Baden-Wuerttemberg, BRD
There are five villages named Sonnenberg in DDR; seven in BRD.

SORAU, 1
1. 51-05N, 13-30E, Sora, Dresden, DDR
2. 51-38N, 15-09E, Sorau in Nieder Lausitz, Polish occupied Germany

SPANDAU, 1, 2
1. 52-32N, 13-13E, (section of city), West Berlin, BRD
2. 52-07N, 09-57E, (farm), Niedersachsen, BRD

SPEYER, Bavaria, 1, 3
1. 49-19N, 08-26E, Rheinland-Pfalz, BRD

STACHAL, Saxony, 1
Not found.

STADE, 1, 2, 3
1. 51-03N, 07-50E, Nordrhein-Westfalen, BRD
2. 53-36N, 09-29E, Niedersachsen, BRD
3. 54-38N, 09-36E, (farm), Schleswig-Holstein, BRD

STADT ILM, Rudolstadt, 1, 3
See STADTILM

STADTILM, 1, 3
1. 50-46N, 11-05E, Erfurt, DDR

STAMELN, 2
1. 50-55N, 06-37E, Stammeln, Nordrhein-Westfalen, BRD

STANNSDORF, 1
Not found.

STARGAARD, STARGARD, 1, 2, 3
1. 53-30N, 13-19E, (also called Burg Stargard), Neubrandenburg, DDR
2. 53-58N, 18-33E, Starogard (also called Starogard Gdanski), Poland
3. 51-54N, 14-47E, Stargard Gubinski (also Stargardt), Polish-occupied Germany
4. 53-20N, 15-03E, (also called Stargard Szczecinski), Polish-occupied Germany
5. 52-02N, 21-39E, Starogrod, Poland
6. 53-19N, 18-23E, Starogrod, Poland

STAVENHAGEN, 2, 3
1. 53-42N, 12-54E, Neubrandenburg, DDR

STAZZONA, 2
Not found. See also PHAZZONA, Hungary

STEINBACH, 1
There are 12 villages of this name in DDR; about 65 villags and farms of this name in BRD.

STEINBECK, 2
1. 52-43N, 13-55E, Frankfurt/Oder, DDR
2. 53-23N, 11-42E, Schwerin, DDR
3. 53-35N, 12-03E, Schwerin, DDR
4. 53-43N, 12-14E, Schwerin, DDR
5. 54-00N, 11-09E, Rostock, DDR
6. 54-08N, 11-59E, Rostock, DDR
There are seven additional villages and farms of this name in BRD.

STEINFELD, 3
1. 50-22N, 10-44E, Suhl, BDR
2. 52-37N, 11-42E, Magdeburg, DDR
3. 53-02N, 13-25E, Neubrandenburg, DDR
4. 54-06N, 12-19E, Rostock, DDR
5. 54-12N, 12-49E, Rostock, DDR
6. 53-45N, 22-11E, Steinfelde (Pol.=Glabowskie), Poland
There are nine additional villages and farms of this name in BRD.

STEINFURTH, 2
1. 52-22N, 13-47E, Steinfurt, Frankfurt/Oder, DDR
2. 52-52N, 13-40E, Frankfurt/Oder, DDR
3. 53-58N, 13-39E, Rostock, DDR
4. 53-23N, 13-48E, (farm), Neubrandenburg, DDR
5. 51-09N, 06-32E, Steinforth, Nordrhein-Westfalen, BRD
6. 52-55N, 08-44E, Steinforth, Niedersachsen, BRD
7. 50-31N, 09-24E, Steinfurt, Hessen, BRD
8. 49-39N, 09-29E, Steinfurt, Baden-Wuerttemberg, BRD
9. 48-53N, 10-02E, Steinfurt (farm), Baden-Wuerttemberg, BRD
10. 48-49N, 12-50E, Bavaria, BRD
11. 50-47N, 06-13E, (section of city), Nordrhein-Westfalen, BRD
12. 53-32N, 10-09E, Hamburg, BRD
13. 54-18N, 10-01E, (farm), Schleswig-Holstein, BRD
14. 53-45N, 09-45E, (farm), Schleswig-Holstein, BRD

STERNBERG, 2, 3
1. 53-42N, 11-49E, Schwerin, DDR
2. 52-19N, 15-05E, Polish-occupied Germany
3. 54-03N, 20-30E, (Pol.=Stryjkowo), Poland
4. 49-11N, 11-33E, Bavaria, BRD
5. 50-02N, 09-07E, Bavaria, BRD
6. 50-16N, 10-34E, Sternberg in Grabfeld, Bavaria, BRD
7. 52-03N, 09-03E, Nordrhein-Westfalen, BRD
8. 53-37N, 09-25E, (farm), Niedersachsen, BRD

STERNKRUG, Mecklenburg, 2
1. 52-44N, 13-57E, Frankfurt/Oder, DDR
2. 53-52N, 11-18E, Rostock, DDR

STETTIN, 1, 2, 3
1. 53-25N, 14-35E, (Pol.=Szczecin), Polish-occupied Germany
There are numerous villages named Stetten in BRD.

STEUERMARK, Prussia, 2
Not found.

STEYER, Austria, 2

STOCKHOLM, [Sweden], 1, 2, 3

STOESSEN, 2
1. 51-06N, 11-56E, Halle, DDR

STOLLBERG, 1
1. 50-43N, 12-48E, Karl-Marx-Stadt, DDR
2. 48-33N, 13-42E, Bavaria, BRD
3. 54-39N, 08-55E, Schleswig-Holstein, BRD

STOLPE, 1
1. 52-40N, 13-16E, Potsdam, DDR
2. 52-58N, 12-26E, Potsdam, DDR
3. 52-59N, 14-07E, Frankfurt/Oder, DDR
4. 53-21N, 11-44E, Schwerin, DDR
5. 53-24N, 13-22E, Neubrandenburg, DDR
6. 53-52N, 13-34E, Neubrandenburg, DDR
7. 53-52N, 14-00E, Rostock, DDR
8. 54-27N, 17-02E, (also spelled Stolp), Polish-occupied Germany
9. 54-08N, 10-13E, Schleswig-Holstein, BRD
10. 54-09E, 10-47E, Schleswig-Holstein, BRD

STONE, Pose, 2
Not found.

STOVE, 3
1. 53-46N, 10-55E, Schwerin, DDR
2. 54-01N, 11-33E, Rostock, DDR
3. 53-25N, 14-25E, Stoeven, Polish-occupied Germany
4. 53-26N, 10-19E, Niedersachsen, BRD

STRADUN, 2
1. 51-36N, 14-18E, Stradow, Cottbus, DDR
2. 51-49N, 14-05E, Stradow, Cottbus, DDR
3. 53-36N, 19-30E, Stradem (Pol.=Stradomno), Poland
4. 50-22N, 20-29E, Stradow, Poland
5. 53-53N, 22-21E, Straduny, Poland

STRAHLENDORF, 1
1. 53-28N, 11-55E, Stralendorf, Schwerin, DDR
2. 53-35N, 11-18E, Stralendorf, Schwerin, DDR

STRALSUND, 1, 3
1. 54-18N, 13-06E, Rostock, DDR

STRASSBURG, 1, 2, 3
1. 53-31N, 13-45E, Strasburg, Neubrandenburg, DDR
2. 50-29N, 12-05E, Strassberg, Karl-Marx-Stadt,
DDR
3. 51-37N, 11-03E, Strassberg, Halle, DDR
4. 52-04N, 15-22E, (also Strassburg an der Oder),
Polish-occupied Germany
5. 49-33N, 08-51E, Hessen, BRD
6. 47-47N, 09-53E, (farm), Baden-Wuerttemberg, BRD
There are seven villages and farms named Strassberg
in BRD; also the city of Strassburg, now in France.

STRAUSSFURTH, Baden, 3
1. 51-10N, 10-59E, Straussfurt, Erfurt, DDR

STRELSEN, STRELSLEN, 2
Not found.

STRENZE, 1
1. 53-50N, 12-10E, Strenz, Schwerin, DDR

STRIEGAU, 3
1. 50-58N, 16-21E, Polish-occupied Germany

STRIEGE, 2
1. 52-30N, 06-43E, Striepe, Niedersachsen, BRD

STROPPEN, 2
1. 51-23N, 16-49E, Polish-occupied Germany

STUER, 2, 3
1. 52-52N, 09-03E, Niedersachsen, BRD

STUTTGART, 2, 3
1. 48-46N, 09-11E, Baden-Wuerttemberg, BRD
2. 47-40N, 08-53E, (farm), Baden-Wuerttemberg, BRD

SUCKAU, Prussia, 1
1. 53-19N, 10-57E, Sueckau, Schwerin, DDR
There are six villages named Suckow in DDR; 12
named Zukow in Poland.

SUCKWITZ, 2
1. 53-40N, 12-09E, Schwerin, DDR

SUELSDORF, 2
1. 52-01N, 11-34E, Suellsdorf, Magdeburg, DDR
2. 53-53N, 10-53E, Rostock, DDR
3. 54-21N, 10-57E, Sulsdorf, Schleswig-Holstein,
BRD
4. 54-28N, 11-03E, Sulsdorf, Schleswig-Holstein,
BRD

SUELZ, 2
1. 49-08N, 09-43E, Baden-Wuerttemberg, BRD
2. 50-55N, 06-55E, (section of city), Nordrhein-
Westfalen, BRD
There are also six villages and farms named Sulz
in BRD.

SUWALKY, Poland, 1
1. 54-06N, 22-56E, Suwałki (or Suwalkie), Poland

SUWANCK, 1
Not found.

SZARNAKOW, 2
Not found.

SZERD, 1
Not found.

SZIDONA, SZIDOWA, Prussia, 2
Not found.

TACKEN, 2
1. 53-11N, 12-00E, Schwerin, DDR
2. 53-09N, 09-12E, Taaken, Niedersachsen, BRD

TAMPOW, 1
Not found.

TANGENDORF, 2
1. 53-10N, 11-58E, Schwerin, DDR
2. 53-18N, 10-06E, Niedersachsen, BRD

TANGERMUNDE, 2
1. 52-33N, 11-57E, Tangermuende, Magdeburg, DDR

TANGSDORF, Saxony-Gotha, 1
1. 53-10N, 13-20E, Tangersdorf, Neubrandenburg,
DDR

TANNENRODE, 1
1. 50-52N, 11-15E, Tannroda, Erfurt, DDR
2. 50-07N, 11-48E, Tannenreuth, Bavaria, BRD

TANSBERG, 1
1. 51-14N, 12-27E, Tanzberg, Leipzig, DDR

TARAU, Saxony, 3
1. 51-45N, 19-59E, Taurow, Poland
2. 49-07N, 14-02E, Taurau (Czech=Tourov), Czechoslovakia

TARGAU, 1
See TORGAU

TARNOW, 3
1. 53-37N, 13-01E, Neubrandenburg, DDR
2. 53-47N, 12-01E, Schwerin, DDR
3. 50-35N, 18-05E, Tarnau, Polish-occupied Germany

TARNOWITZ, 2
1. 53-58N, 11-14E, Tarnewitz, Rostock, DDR
2. 50-26N, 18-50E, Tarnowice (also Tarnowice Stare)
Poland

TATUN, Prussia, 3
1. 51-56N, 11-28E, Tarthun, Magdeburg, DDR
2. 52-58N, 10-37E, Tatern, Niedersachsen, BRD

TAUCHWITZ, 1
1. 51-04N, 14-57E, Tauchritz, Dresden, DDR
2. 50-18N, 13-43E, Tauchowitz (Czech=Touchovice), Czechoslovakia

TAUER, 3
1. 51-19N, 14-38E, Dresden, DDR
2. 51-54N, 14-28E, Cottbus, DDR
3. 50-59N, 17-04E, Thauer, Polish-occupied Germany

TAURNOW, 3
1. 51-45N, 19-59E, Taurow, Poland
See also TARNOW

TAUTHEWALDE, Prussia, 2
1. 51-06N, 14-22E, Tautewalde, Dresden, DDR

TAWNOW? 3
1. 51-45N, 19-59E, Taurow, Poland
2. 41-40N, 06-31E, Tawern, Rheinland-Pfalz, BRD
3. 49-07N, 14-02E, Taurau (Czech=Tourov), Czechoslovakia
See also TARNOW

TEETZ, 2
1. 53-01N, 12-31E, Potsdam, DDR

TEHEROW, 1, 2
See TETEROW

TEMESWAR, Hungary, 1

TENER, 1
Not found.

TENNIS, Mecklenburg, 1
Not found.

TERGENTIN, 3
Not found.

TESDORFF, TESDORPF, TESSDORF, 2, 3
1. 53-33N, 10-52E, Testorf, Schwerin, DDR
2. 53-48N, 11-16E, Testorf, Rostock, DDR
3. 53-03N, 10-43E, Testorf, Niedersachsen, BRD
4. 54-15N, 10-47E, Testorf, Schleswig-Holstein, BRD

TESEROW, 1, 2
1. 53-49N, 13-12E, Tentzerow, Neubrandenburg, DDR
See also TETEROW

TESSIN, 1, 2
1. 53-24N, 10-51E, Schwerin, DDR
2. 53-34N, 11-02E, Schwerin, DDR
3. 53-43N, 11-35E, Schwerin, DDR
4. 54-02N, 12-28E, Rostock, DDR

TETENBUELL, Holstein, 1
1. 54-21N, 08-50E, Tetenbuel, Schleswig-Holstein, BRD

TETEROW, 1, 2
1. 53-47N, 12-34E, Neubrandenburg, DDR
See also TESEROW

TEUDITZ, 3
1. 51-17N, 12-06E, Halle, DDR

THARAND, 1
1. 50-59N, 13-35E, Tharandt, Dresden, DDR

THAROW? 3
1. 51-46N, 11-56E, Thurau, Halle, DDR
2. 53-49N, 13-33E, Thurow, Neubrandenburg, DDR
3. 53-58N, 13-32E, Thurow, Rostock, DDR
4. 53-23N, 13-11E, Thuerow, Neubrandenburg, DDR
5. 51-45N, 19-59E, Taurow, Poland

THIELBEEN, Prussia, 1
1. 52-51N, 11-29E, Thielbeer, Magdeburg, DDR

THIMETZ, 2
1. 50-18N, 11-35E, Thiemitz, Bavaria, BRD

THOMASBRUECK, 3
Not found.

THOMASBURG, Prussia, 1
1. 53-14N, 10-40E, (also called Thomasberg), Niedersachsen, BRD

THORE BEI ZERBST, Thuringia, 2
1. 50-53N, 10-57E, Thoerey, Erfurt, DDR

THORN, 1, 2
1. 50-46N, 12-33E, Thurm, Karl-Marx-Stadt, DDR
2. 53-02N, 18-36E, (Pol.=Torun), Poland
3. 52-20N, 08-56E, Thoren, Nordrhein-Westfalen, BRD
4. 52-41N, 09-45E, Thoeren, Niedersachsen, BRD

THUESDORF, 3
1. 51-06N, 11-30E, Halle, DDR

THUNIS, 1
Not found.

TIEFURT, 1
Not found.

TIEKOTSCHIN, Poland, 3
1. 52-01N, 19-11E, Tkaczew, Poland
2. 51-54N, 19-15E, Tkaczewska Gora, Poland

TIRSCHENREUTH, Bavaria, 2
1. 49-53N, 12-21E, Bavaria, BRD

TIRSCHTIEGEL, 3
1. 52-22N, 15-52E, Polish-occupied Germany

TISCHKAUER, Prussia, 1
Not found.

TONDERN, 1, 2
Not found.

TONKOEPINGSLAEN, Sweden, 1

TOPPER, 2
1. 52-16N, 15-15E, Polish-occupied Germany

TORGAU, Prussia, 1
1. 51-34N, 13-00E, Leipzig, DDR

TORSCHTIEGEL, 3
See TIRSCHTIEGEL

TRACHTELFINGEN, 3
See TROCHTELFINGEN

TREBA, Thuringia, 3
1. 50-31N, 12-17E, (stream), Karl-Marx-Stadt, DDR

TREFFURT, Holstein, 1
1. 51-08N, 10-14E, Erfurt, DDR

TRENDELBERG, Hannover, 2
1. 51-35N, 09-25E, Trendelburg, Hessen, BRD

TREPPELN, 2
There is a village of this name about 1 kilometer
southwest of the village of Kobbeln (52-06N, 14-39E)
Frankfurt/Oder, DDR.

TREPTOW, 2
1. 52-29N, 13-27E, (section of city), East Berlin,
DDR
2. 54-04N, 15-16E, Treptow an der Rega, Polish-
occupied Germany

TRIBBOW, 1
There was a village named Tribsow about 6 kilometers
northeast of Cammin (53-58N, 14-47E), Polish-occupied Germany.

TRIEGELHOF, 2
Not found.

TRIEST [TRIESTE, Austria, now free territory] 1

TROCHTELFINGEN, 3
1. 58-18N, 09-15E, Baden-Wuerttemberg, BRD
2. 48-51N, 10-24E, Baden-Wuerttemberg, BRD

TUETTLEBEN, 3
1. 50-57N, 10-48E, Erfurt, DDR

TUNGENHAUSEN, 3
1. 51-09N, 11-04E, Tunzenhausen, Erfurt, DDR
2. 54-06N, 20-05E, Tuengen (Pol.=Bogatzynskie),
Poland

TYROL [Austria] 1

UELITZ, 3
1. 51-53N, 11-40E, Uellnitz, Magdeburg, DDR
2. 51-36N, 22-07E, Ułez, Poland
3. 49-46N, 13-08E, Ullitz (Czech=Ulice), Czechoslovakia

UELSEN, UELZEN, 1
1. 51-32N, 07-43E, Uelzen, Nordrhein-Westfalen,
BRD
2. 52-58N, 10-34E, Uelzen, Niedersachsen, BRD

UETERSEN, 1, 2, 3
1. 53-41N, 09-40E, Schleswig-Holstein, BRD

UITWA, 1
1. 50-04N, 12-57E, Czechoslovakia

ULLENSDORF, ULLERSDORF, 1, 2
1. 51-06N, 13-29E, Ullendorf, Dresden, DDR
2. 50-43N, 13-24E, Ullersdorf, Karl-Marx-Stadt,
DDR
3. 51-05N, 13-54E, Ullersdorf, Dresden, DDR
4. 51-15N, 14-50E, Ullersdorf, Dresden, DDR
5. 52-02N, 14-23E, Ullersdorf, Frankfurt/Oder, DDR
6. 51-12N, 15-33E, Ullersdorf am Bober, Polish-
occupied Germany

UNIDENTIFIED, 2

UNTERBERNRIETH, Bavaria, 3
1. 49-40N, 12-23E, (farm), Bavaria, BRD

UNTERHAIN, 1
1. 50-38N, 11-08E, Gera, DDR

UNTERTUERKHEIM, 2
1. 48-47N, 09-16E, Baden-Wuerttemberg, BRD
2. 48-36N, 10-43E, Unterthuerkeim (or Unterthuer-
heim), Bavaria, BRD

UNTERWELLEBORN, UNTERWELLNBORN, 3
1. 50-39N, 11-26E, Unterwellenborn, Gera, DDR

UTERSHAUSEN, UTTERSHAUSEN, Hessen-Cassel, 1, 2
1. 51-05N, 09-20E, Uttershausen, Hessen, BRD

UTESTADT, Prussia, 3
Not found.

UTHSTADT, 1
1. 49-43N, 10-54E, Uttstadt, Bavaria, BRD

VAHINGEN, Wuerttemberg, 1
1. 48-44N, 09-06E, Vaihingen, Baden-Wuerttemberg,
BRD
2. 48-56N, 08-58E, Vaihingen an der Enz, Baden-
Wuerttemberg, BRD

VALKENBERG, 2
There are 13 villages and farms named Falkenberg
and Falkenburg in DDR; 3 in Polish-occupied Germany and Poland; 12 in BRD.

VAREL, 2
1. 53-11N, 09-30E, Niedersachsen, BRD
2. 53-24N, 08-08E, Niedersachsen, BRD
3. 52-37N, 08-44E, Varrel, Niedersachsen, BRD
4. 53-41N, 09-04E, Varrel, Niedersachsen, BRD

VECHTA, VECHTER, 2
1. 52-43N, 08-17E, Vechta, Niedersachsen, BRD

VECKENSTEDT, 1
1. 51-54N, 10-44E, Magdeburg, DDR

VENTSCHOW, 2
1. 53-47N, 11-34E, Schwerin, DDR

VERBOCA, Hungary, 1

VETSCHAU, 2
1. 51-47N, 14-04E, Cottbus, DDR
2. 50-49N, 06-02E, Nordrhein-Westfalen, BRD

VIETZ, Mecklenburg, 1
1. 53-28N, 11-14E, Viez, Schwerin, DDR
2. 52-40N, 14-54E, Polish-occupied Germany

VISSELBACH, 2
Not found.

VITKOVER, 2
Not found.

VOLKSTEDT, 1
1. 50-42N, 11-19E, (section of city), Gera, DDR
2. 51-34N, 11-34E, Halle, DDR

VOLLBUETTEL, 2
1. 52-25N, 10-29E, Niedersachsen, BRD

VOLLERSAADE, 1
1. 50-56N, 11-19E, Vollersroda, Erfurt, DDR
2. 51-04N, 10-02E, Volteroda, Erfurt, DDR
3. 53-20N, 08-55E, Vollersode, Niedersachsen, BRD

VOLSRADE, 1
1. 53-16N, 11-06E, Volzrade, Schwerin, DDR

VOLZENDORF, 2
1. 52-54N, 11-16E, Niedersachsen, BRD

VRETZ, Mecklenburg, 1
See VIETZ

WAEBZBACH, Bavaria, 2
Not found.

WAETEN, Mecklenburg, 2
Not found.

WAHLOW, 1, 3
Not found.

WAIMAR, 1
See WEIMAR

WAKENDORF, 2
1. 53-57N, 11-43E, Rostock, DDR
2. 54-15N, 10-17E, Schleswig-Holstein, BRD
3. 54-20N, 09-51E, Schleswig-Holstein, BRD
4. 53-52N, 10-22E, Wakendorf Eins, Schleswig-Holstein, BRD
5. 53-47N, 10-05E, Wakendorf Zwei, Schleswig-Holstein, BRD

WALD, 2
There are 23 villages and farms of this name in BRD, mainly in Baden-Wuerttemberg and Bavaria.

WALDAU, 1
1. 51-19N, 13-30E, Walda, Dresden, DDR
2. 50-30N, 10-50E, Suhl, DDR
3. 51-04N, 11-56E, Halle, DDR
4. 51-48N, 11-43E, Halle, DDR
5. 51-59N, 13-06E, (farm), Potsdam, DDR
6. 51-14N, 15-17E, Polish-occupied Germany
There are eight additional villages and farms of this name in BRD.

WALDBACH, Saxony, 3
1. 53-16N, 20-27E, Waldbeek (Pol.=Powierz), Poland
2. 49-10N, 09-24E, Baden-Wuerttemberg, BRD
3. 49-36N, 07-03E, Saar, BRD

WALDECK, 2
1. 50-55N, 11-47E, Gera, DDR
2. 52-26N, 13-49E, (section of city), Frankfurt/Oder, DDR
3. 54-02N, 12-13E, Rostock, DDR
4. 51-12N, 09-04E, Hessen, BRD
There are ten other villages and farms of this name in BRD.

WALDENBURG, 2
1. 50-53N, 12-36E, Karl-Marx-Stadt, DDR
2. 50-46N, 16-17E, Polish-occupied Germany
3. 49-11N, 09-38E, Baden-Wuerttemberg, BRD
4. 51-06N, 07-54E, (foresters' lodge) Nordrhein-Westfalen, BRD

WALDORF, WALLDORF, 1
1. 50-45N, 12-15E, Walddorf, Gera, DDR
2. 51-00N, 14-38E, Walddorf, Dresden, DDR
3. 51-25N, 14-52E, Walddorf, Cottbus, DDR
4. 50-37N, 10-23E, Walldorf, Suhl, DDR
5. 53-33N, 21-39E, Walddorf (Pol.=Przerosl) Poland
6. 53-40N, 21-28E, Walddorf (Pol.=Chostka) Poland
7. 54-13N, 19-13E, Walldorf (Pol.=Powalina) Poland
8. 50-23N, 06-37E, Waldorf, Nordrhein-Westfalen, BRD
9. 50-29N, 07-14E, Waldorf, Rheinland-Pfalz, BRD
10. 50-46N, 06-57E, Waldorf, Nordrhein-Westfalen, BRD
11. 49-20N, 08-39E, Walldorf, Baden-Wuerttemberg, BRD
12. 50-00N, 08-35E, Walldorf, Hessen, BRD

WALDTHUR, 1
See WALDTHURN

WALDTHURM, WALDTHURN, 1
1. 49-40N, 12-20E, Waldthurn, Bavaria, BRD

WALLBECK, WALLBEIK, 1
1. 50-38N, 10-24E, Wallbach, Suhl, DDR
2. 51-07N, 12-57E, Wallbach, Leipzig, DDR
3. 53-16N, 20-27E, Waldbeek (Pol.=Powierz) Poland
4. 53-33N, 09-06E, Wallbeck (or Wallbek)(stream), Niedersachsen, BRD
5. 47-34N, 07-55E, Wallbach, Hessen, BRD
6. 49-46N, 08-55E, Wallbach, Baden-Wuerttemberg, BRD

WALLENBURG, 2
1. 48-31N, 13-19E, Wallenberg (farm), Bavaria, BRD
2. 47-48N, 11-50E, Bavaria, BRD

WALLENDORF, 1
1. 50-32N, 11-12E, Suhl, DDR
2. 51-22N, 12-05E, Halle, DDR
3. 49-52N, 06-18E, Rheinland-Pfalz, BRD
4. 50-37N, 08-15E, Hessen, BRD

WALSCHLEBEN, WALSLEBEN, Saxony, 1, 2, 3
1. 51-04N, 10-56E, Walschleben, Erfurt, DDR
2. 52-46N, 11-51E, Walsleben, Magdeburg, DDR
3. 52-56N, 12-40E, Walsleben, Potsdam, DDR

WALTERSHAUSEN, Bavaria, 2
1. 50-54N, 10-34E, Erfurt, DDR
2. 53-22N, 20-18E, (Pol.=Rogozek), Poland
3. 50-21N, 10-24E, Bavaria, BRD

WAMKOW, 3
1. 53-37N, 11-50E, Wamckow, Schwerin, DDR

WANDSBEK, 1
1. 53-34N, 10-06E, (section of city), Hamburg, BRD

WANGEN, 2
1. 47-38N, 10-30E, Bavaria, BRD
2. 47-40N, 08-56E, Baden-Wuerttemberg, BRD
3. 47-41N, 09-50E, Baden-Wuerttemberg, BRD
4. 47-44N, 09-22E, Baden-Wuerttemberg, BRD
5. 47-58N, 09-21E, Baden-Wuerttemberg, BRD
6. 48-01N, 11-24E, Bavaria, BRD
7. 48-15N, 10-03E, Baden-Wuerttemberg, BRD
8. 48-36N, 11-21E, Bavaria, BRD
9. 48-43N, 09-36E, Baden-Wuerttemberg, BRD
10. 48-46N, 09-16E, (section of city), Baden-Wuerttemberg, BRD
11. 49-12N, 11-28E, Bavaria, BRD

WANGERIEHM, 1
Not found.

WANGERIN, 3
1. 53-59N, 11-25E, Wangern, Rostock, DDR
2. 53-32N, 15-33E, Polish-occupied Germany

WAREN, WARIN, 2, 3
1. 53-31N, 12-41E, Waren, Neubrandenburg, DDR
2. 53-48N, 11-42E, Warin, Schwerin, DDR

WARMBRUSEN? 3
1. 50-52N, 15-42E, Bad Warmbrunn, Polish-occupied Germany

WARNITZ, 2
1. 53-12N, 13-53E, Neubrandenburg, DDR
2. 53-40N, 11-21E, Schwerin, DDR

WARNOW, 1, 2, 3
1. 53-14N, 11-37E, Gross Warnow, Schwerin, DDR
2. 53-47N, 11-53E, Schwerin, DDR
3. 53-53N, 11-12E, Rostock, DDR

WARSCHAU, 1, 2
1. 52-15N, 21-00E, (Pol.=Warszawa), Poland

WASHINGTON [U. S. A.] 2

WEBERSTEDT, 2
1. 51-06N, 10-30E, Erfurt, DDR

WEDDINGSTEDT, 1
1. 54-14N, 09-06E, Schleswig-Holstein, BRD

WEDENDORFF, Mecklenburg, 1
1. 53-46N, 11-07E, Schwerin, DDR

WEDER, Prussia, 2
Not found.

WEGMAN, Gotha, 3
1. 47-44N, 12-28E, Wegmann (farm), Bavaria, BRD

WEIBZBACH, 2
Not found.

WEICHENRODT, Birkenfeld, 1
1. 48-36N, 11-26E, Weichenried, Bavaria, BRD

WEICKERSHEIM, 2
1. 50-35N, 09-01E, Weickartshain, Hessen, BRD

WEIDERSTAB, Prussia, 2
Not found.

WEIDNITZ, 2
1. 51-05N, 12-48E, Weiditz, Karl-Marx-Stadt, DDR
2. 51-14N, 14-18E, Weidlitz, Dresden, DDR
3. 50-09N, 11-14E, Bavaria, BRD

WEILEN, Denmark, 2
1. 51-13N, 18-33E, Weilun, Poland
2. 48-11N, 08-46E, Weilen unter den Rinnen, Baden-Wuerttemberg, BRD

WEILHEIM, 3
1. 48-01N, 12-44E, Weilham, Bavaria, BRD
2. 47-40N, 08-14E, Baden-Wuerttemberg, BRD
3. 47-50N, 11-09E, Bavaria, BRD
4. 48-01N, 08-47E, Baden-Wuerttemberg, BRD
5. 48-21N, 08-55E, Baden-Wuerttemberg, BRD
6. 48-29N, 09-02E, Baden-Wuerttemberg, BRD
7. 48-37N, 09-32E, Weilheim an der Teck, Baden-Wuerttemberg, BRD
8. 48-39N, 10-35E, Bavaria, BRD
9. 48-53N, 10-50E, Bavaria, BRD

WEIMAR, 1, 2, 3
1. 50-59N, 11-19E, Erfurt, DDR
2. 51-22N, 09-24E, Hessen, BRD

WEIMAR, Thuringia, 1
See WEIMAR

WEIMARSCHMINDE? 3
1. 50-33N, 10-12E, Weimarschmieden, Bavaria, BRD

WEIMERSDORF, Bavaria, 1
1. 50-20N, 11-03E, Bavaria, BRD

WEISCHWITZ, 1
1. 50-27N, 12-04E, Weischlitz, Karl-Marx-Stadt, DDR
2. 50-37N, 11-24E, Gera, DDR

WEISSENFELS, 2
1. 51-12N, 11-58E, Halle, DDR
2. 50-35N, 07-24E, Rheinland-Pfalz, BRD

WEISSENKUECHEN, 2
1. 48-52N, 11-12E, Weissenkirchen, Bavaria, BRD
2. 49-03N, 11-56E, Weissenkirchen, Bavaria, BRD

WEISSENSCHIRMBACH, 3
1. 51-19N, 11-33E, Halle, DDR

WEISSENSEE, 3
1. 51-11N, 11-04E, Erfurt, DDR
2. 52-33N, 13-28E, (section of city), East Berlin, DDR
3. 47-34N, 10-38E, (commune), Bavaria, BRD

WELLWARM, Bohemia, 1, 2
1. 50-17N, 14-14E, Welwarn (Czech=Velvary) Czecho-slovakia

WELMARN, 2
See WELLWARM

WENDORF, 2, 3
There are 13 villages of this name in DDR.

WENTDORF, 1
1. 51-54N, 13-33E, Cottbus, DDR
2. 53-02N, 11-40E, Schwerin, DDR
3. 49-23N, 10-48E, Wendsdorf, Bavaria, BRD
4. 54-25N, 10-18E, Wendtorf, Schleswig-Holstein, BRD
5. 52-07N, 08-55E, Wentorf, Nordrhein-Westfalen, BRD
6. 52-45N, 10-40E, Wentorf, Niedersachsen, BRD
7. 53-29N, 10-15E, Wentorf, Schleswig-Holstein, BRD
8. 53-41N, 10-28E, Wentorf, Schleswig-Holstein, BRD
9. 54-17N, 10-33E, Wentorf, Schleswig-Holstein, BRD
10. 54-23N, 09-46E, Wentorf (farming community), Schleswig-Holstein, BRD

WENZEN, 3
1. 52-34N, 11-07E, Wenze, Magdeburg, DDR
2. 54-16N, 21-51E, Wenzken, Poland
3. 51-52N, 09-49E, Niedersachsen, BRD

WERBEN, WERBER, Prussia, 2
1. 51-12N, 12-14E, Werben, Leipzig, DDR
2. 51-32N, 12-22E, Werben, Leipzig, DDR
3. 51-37N, 12-02E, Werben, Halle, DDR
4. 51-49N, 14-11E, Werben, Cottbus, DDR
5. 52-15N, 13-21E, Werben, Potsdam, DDR
6. 52-52N, 11-59E, Werben, Magdeburg, DDR
7. 53-14N, 14-54E, Werben, Polish-occupied Germany

WERDAU, 2
1. 50-26N, 12-19E, Werda, Karl-Marx-Stadt, DDR
2. 50-44N, 12-23E, Karl-Marx-Stadt, DDR
3. 51-33N, 13-02E, Leipzig, DDR

WERLE, 2
1. 53-16N, 11-40E, Schwerin, DDR
2. 53-54N, 12-05E, Schwerin, DDR

WERLHEIM, 3
Not found.

WESSENTIN, 2
1. 53-28N, 12-09E, Schwerin, DDR
2. 53-51N, 13-30E, Wussentin, Neubrandenburg, DDR

WEST RHODA, 1
1. 51-31N, 10-14E, Westerode, Niedersachsen, BRD
2. 51-54N, 10-34E, Westerode, Niedersachsen, BRD
3. 52-05N, 07-31E, Westerode (farming community),
   Nordrhein-Westfalen, BRD
4. 52-05N, 07-34E, Westerode (farming community),
   Nordrhein-Westfalen, BRD
5. 52-31N, 07-48E, Westeroden, Niedersachsen, BRD

WESTERVICK, Sweden, 1

WETTIN, 3
1. 51-35N, 11-48E, Halle, DDR

WEXSA, 1
Not found.

WICKENDORF, 1
1. 50-32N, 11-26E, Gera, DDR
2. 53-41N, 11-26E, Schwerin, DDR
3. 50-23N, 11-23E, Bavaria, BRD

WICKENRODT, 1
1. 51-28N, 11-08E, Wickerode, Halle, DDR
2. 51-15N, 09-44E, Wickenrode, Hessen, BRD
3. 49-49N, 07-21E, Rheinland-Pfalz, BRD

WIEDERSTRICH, 3
1. 51-40N, 11-32E, Wiederstadt, Halle, DDR

WIEN [Austria] 1, 2, 3

WIESAU, WIESAW, 1
1. 50-37N, 13-01E, Wiesa, Karl-Marx-Stadt, DDR
2. 51-15N, 14-07E, Wiesa, Dresden, DDR
3. 52-04N, 14-04E, Wiese, Cottbus, DDR
4. 52-14N, 14-36E, Wiesenau, Frankfurt/Oder, DDR
5. 51-18N, 15-34E, Polish-occupied Germany
6. 49-55N, 12-11E, Bavaria, BRD

WIESELBACH, WIESSELBACH, 2
1. 49-40N, 07-25E, Wieselbach, Rheinland-Pfalz, BRD

WILDENSPRING, 2
1. 50-36N, 11-04E, Suhl, DDR

WILERSHAUSEN, Hannover, 3
1. 54-06N, 13-12E, Willershusen, Rostock, DDR
2. 51-00N, 08-52E, Willershausen, Hessen, BRD
3. 51-02N, 10-11E, Willershausen, Hessen, BRD
4. 51-47N, 10-06E, Willershausen, Niedersachsen,
   BRD

WILLERNBACH, 1
1. 48-54N, 12-52E, Willersbach (farming community)
   Bavaria, BRD

WILLSTRUFF, 1
1. 51-03N, 13-32E, Wilsdruff, Dresden, DDR

WILMARS, 2
1. 50-30N, 10-15E, Willmars, Bavaria, BRD

WILMERSDORF, 1
1. 52-16N, 14-08E, Frankfurt/Oder, DDR
2. 52-24N, 14-16E, Frankfurt/Oder, DDR
3. 53-07N, 13-55E, Frankfurt/Oder, DDR
4. 53-10N, 12-18E, Potsdam, DDR

WILLSDORF, WILSDORF, 1
1. 51-03N, 14-00E, Wilschdorf, Dresden, DDR
2. 51-08N, 13-43E, Wilschdorf, Dresden, DDR
3. 51-01N, 11-39E, Wilsdorf, Gera, DDR
4. 51-11N, 11-45E, (foresters' lodge), Halle, DDR

WILSNACK, 3
1. 53-00N, 11-57E, Wilsnacker Forst (forest),
   Schwerin, DDR

WILSTER, 1
1. 52-26N, 07-28E, Wilsten, Niedersachsen, BRD
2. 53-55N, 09-23E, Schleswig-Holstein, BRD

WINSEN, Hannover, 3
1. 52-40N, 09-55E, Niedersachsen, BRD
2. 53-22N, 10-13E, Niedersachsen, BRD
3. 53-50N, 10-01E, Schleswig-Holstein, BRD

WINSEN, Prussia, 2
1. 53-23N, 20-36E, Winsken (Pol.=Wieckowo) Poland
2. 50-32N, 06-31E, Wintzen (farm), Nordrhein-Westfalen, BRD

WINZBACH, 3
Not found.

WISMAR, 1, 2, 3
1. 53-31N, 13-47E, Neubrandenburg, DDR
2. 53-34N, 11-28E, Rostock, DDR
3. 50-38N, 08-41E, Wissmar, Hessen, BRD

WISSENDORF, Mecklenburg, 2
1. 51-44N, 14-09E, Wiesendorf, Cottbus, DDR

WITGENDORF, 3
Not found.

WITTENBERG, 1, 2
1. 51-52N, 12-39E, Halle, DDR
2. 52-50N, 13-21E, (farm), Potsdam, DDR
3. 54-49N, 17-58E, Polish-occupied Germany
4. 47-39N, 09-41E, Baden-Wuerttemberg, BRD
5. 53-25N, 09-58E, Niedersachsen, BRD
6. 54-16N, 10-23E, Schleswig-Holstein, BRD
7. 52-04N, 08-27E, (farm), Nordrhein-Westfalen, BRD
8. 52-46N, 07-11E, (farm), Niedersachsen, BRD

WITTENBERGE, 2, 3
1. 53-00N, 11-45E, Schwerin, DDR
2. 53-08N, 07-52E, Niedersachsen, BRD
3. 53-34N, 09-45E, Wittenbergen, Hamburg, BRD
4. 53-56N, 09-40E, Wittenbergen, Schleswig-Hol-
        stein, BRD
5. 54-12N, 09-28E, Wittenbergen (farm), Schleswig-
        Holstein, BRD

WITTENBURG, WITTENBURGE, Mecklenburg, 1, 2, 3
1. 53-31N, 11-04E, Schwerin, DDR
2. 52-09N, 09-42E, Niedersachsen, BRD

WITTSTOCK, Prussia, 1, 2
1. 53-09N, 12-30E, Potsdam, DDR
2. 53-23N, 13-42E, Neubrandenburg, DDR

WITZENHAUSEN, 3
1. 51-20N, 09-52E, Hessen, BRD

WOETEN, Mecklenburg, 2, 3
1. 53-32N, 11-53E, Schwerin, DDR

WOLFFMANNSHAUSEN, WOLFMANSHAUSEN, 2
1. 50-26N, 10-28E, Wolfmannshausen, Suhl, DDR

WOLFSBERG, 1
1. 50-39N, 13-07E, Karl-Marx-Stadt, DDR
2. 50-47N, 10-22E, Suhl, DDR
3. 51-33N, 11-05E, Halle, DDR
4. 54-03N, 12-17E, Rostock, DDR
5. 50-57N, 13-01E, (farm), Karl-Marx-Stadt, DDR
There are 15 villages and farms of this name in BRD.

WOLFSHAGEN, 2
1. 53-09N, 12-01E, Schwerin, DDR
2. 53-27N, 13-39E, Neubrandenburg, DDR
3. 54-14N, 12-51E, Rostock, DDR
4. 52-34N, 13-45E, (farm), Frankfurt/Oder, DDR
5. 54-15N, 21-28E, (Pol.=Wilezyny), Poland
6. 51-55N, 10-19E, Niedersachsen, BRD

WOLGAST, 1
1. 54-03N, 13-46E, Rostock, DDR

WORMBRUSEN? 3
See WARMBRUSEN

WORMS, 2
1. 49-38N, 08-21E, Rheinland-Pfalz, BRD

WOSTEN, 2
See WOETEN

WOTZ, 1
1. 52-46N, 11-02E, Woetz, Magdeburg, DDR

WRESCHEN, Prussia/Posen, 1, 2
1. 53-23N, 13-32E, Wrechen, Neubrandenburg, DDR
2. 49-57N, 18-11E, Wreschin, Czechoslovakia

WRIEZEN, 2
1. 52-43N, 14-08E, Frankfurt/Oder, DDR

WUEBZBACH, Bavaria, 2
Not found.

WUENSCHENDORF, 3
1. 50-45N, 13-11E, Karl-Marx-Stadt, DDR
2. 50-48N, 12-06E, Gera, DDR
3. 50-53N, 12-30E, Karl-Marx-Stadt, DDR
4. 51-01N, 13-57E, Dresden, DDR
5. 51-21N, 11-51E, Halle, DDR
6. 49-50N, 11-24E, (farm), Bavaria, BRD

WUERZBURG, 3
1. 49-48N, 09-56E, Bavaria, BRD

WUESTEYERSDORFF, Saxony, 2
1. 52-32N, 14-03E, Wuestesieversdorf (farm), Frank-
        furt/Oder, DDR
2. 50-42N, 16-26E, Wuestewaltersdorf, Polish-occu-
        pied Germany

WULKEMIN, Mecklenburg, 2
1. 53-32N, 13-10E, Wulkenzin, Neubrandenburg, DDR

WULLBECK, 1
Not found.

WUNSIEDEL, 1, 2
1. 50-02N, 12-01E, Bavaria, BRD

WUNSTORF, 3
1. 52-10N, 13-28E, Wuensdorf, Potsdam, DDR
2. 52-26N, 09-25E, Niedersachsen, BRD

WUSEND? 3
1. 54-11N, 19-58E, Wusen (Pol.=Osetnik), Poland

WUSTERTHEROFEN, Mecklenburg, 3
Not found.

WUSTROW, 1, 2
1. 52-51N, 12-52E, Wustrau, Potsdam, DDR
2. 52-46N, 14-13E, (community), Frankfurt/Oder, DDR
3. 53-04N, 11-33E, Schwerin, DDR
4. 53-14N, 12-58E, Neubrandenburg, DDR
5. 53-29N, 13-09E, Neubrandenburg, DDR
6. 54-05N, 11-34E, (also called Ostseebad Wustrow)
        Rostock, DDR
7. 52-13N, 14-26E, (farm), Frankfurt/Oder, DDR
8. 54-08N, 15-21E, Polish-occupied Germany
9. 52-55N, 11-07E, Niedersachsen, BRD

XIAMS, 3
The X herein could stand for Christ, possibly the
village of Christanz (49-50N, 11-25E), Bavaria, BRD.

YERSBERG, Hessen-Cassel, 1
Not found.

YORKSROW, Prussia, 2
Not found.

YVERDON, 1
Not found.

ZACHOW, 1
1. 51-52N, 13-44E, Zaacko, Cottbus, DDR
2. 52-29N, 12-47E, Potsdam, DDR
3. 53-22N, 11-53E, Schwerin, DDR
4. 53-27N, 13-03E, Neubrandenburg, DDR
5. 53-26N, 13-12E, (foresters' lodge), Neubranden-
        burg, DDR

ZADELSDORF, 3
1. 50-40N, 11-57E, Gera, DDR

ZAGAJEWITZKY, ZAGRAJEWITZKY, Prussia, 3
1. 51-42N, 18-35E, Zagajew, Poland
2. 51-17N, 21-59E, Zagajdzie, Poland

ZARRENTIN, Mecklenburg, 1, 2
1. 53-55N, 13-45E, Neubrandenburg, DDR
2. 53-56N, 13-18E, Neubrandenburg, DDR
3. 54-00N, 13-12E, Neubrandenburg, DDR
4. 54-05N, 12-53E, Rostock, DDR
5. 54-27N, 13-00E, (also Zarrenzin), Rostock, DDR
6. 53-33N, 10-55E, Schwerin, DDR
7. 53-55N, 13-45E, Neubrandenburg, DDR
8. 54-00N, 13-12E, Neubrandenburg, DDR
9. 54-05N, 12-53E, Rostock, DDR
10. 54-27N, 13-00E, Rostock, DDR

ZDONY, 1
1. 51-35N, 18-55E, Zduny, Poland
2. 51-39N, 17-23E, Zduny, Poland
3. 51-44N, 18-10E, Zduny, Poland
4. 52-02N, 19-07E, Zduny, Poland
5. 52-09N, 19-49E, Zduny Koscielny, Poland
6. 53-08N, 19-33E, Zduny, Poland
7. 53-58N, 19-46E, Zduny, Poland
8. 54-00N, 18-38E, Zduny Osady (or Helenowo), Poland

ZDULY, 3
1. 50-10N, 14-27E, Zdiby, Czechoslovakia

ZECHAU, 2
1. 51-01N, 12-21E, Leipzig, DDR
2. 53-03N, 12-55E, Zechow, Potsdam, DDR
3. 53-24N, 13-10E, Zechow (foresters' lodge), Neubrandenburg, DDR
4. 52-44N, 15-19E, Zechow, Polish-occupied Germany

ZECHLIN, 3
1. 53-09N, 12-46E, Potsdam, DDR

ZEHNA, 1
1. 50-55N, 12-27E, Zehma, Leipzig, DDR
2. 53-43N, 12-09E, Schwerin, DDR

ZEITZ, 3
1. 51-03N, 12-09E, Halle, DDR
2. 51-58N, 11-48E, (farm), Magdeburg, DDR

ZELLA, ZELLA BEI GOTHA, 1, 3
1. 50-40N, 10-07E, Suhl, DDR
2. 50-40N, 10-41E, Suhl, DDR
3. 50-41N, 11-32E, Gera, DDR
4. 51-04N, 13-16E, Dresden, DDR
5. 51-17N, 10-22E, Erfurt, DDR

ZELLIN, 2, 3
1. 52-44N, 14-21E, Zelliner Loose (area), Frankfurt/Oder, DDR
2. 52-44N, 14-23E, Polish-occupied Germany

ZELLO, Thuringia, 1
1. 50-36N, 12-43E, Zelle, Karl-Marx-Stadt, DDR
2. 51-28N, 19-14E, Zelow, Poland
See also ZELLA

ZEMITZ, Sachsen-Dessau, 2
1. 51-40N, 12-07E, Zehmitz, Halle, DDR
2. 53-59N, 13-45E, Rostock, DDR

ZERRNIN, 2
1. 53-48N, 11-56E, Zernin, Schwerin, DDR

ZEULENRODE, 2
1. 50-39N, 11-59E, Zeulenroda, Gera, DDR

ZEWITZ, 2
1. 54-26N, 17-44E, Polish-occupied Germany

ZIEGELRADE, ZIEGELRODE, 2
1. 51-20N, 11-28E, Ziegelroda, Halle, DDR
2. 51-33N, 11-28E, Ziegelrode, Halle, DDR

ZIEGEMUECK, 2
See ZIEGENRUCK

ZIEGENRUECK, 3
1. 50-37N, 11-39E, Ziegenruck, Gera, DDR

ZIEGERSHEIM, 2
1. 50-55N, 11-37E, Ziegenhain, Gera, DDR
2. 51-08N, 13-18E, Ziegenhain, Dresden, DDR
3. 50-55N, 09-15E, Ziegenhain (also called Ziegenheim), Hessen, BRD
4. 50-41N, 07-32E, Ziegenhain (or Ziegenhahn), Rheinland-Pfalz, BRD

ZIEKE, Prussia, 2
1. 51-55N, 12-25E, Zieko, Halle, DDR

ZIERZOW, 2
1. 53-17N, 11-41E, Schwerin, DDR
2. 53-26N, 12-34E, Neubrandenburg, DDR

ZILCHAU, ZILLICHAU, 2
See ZUELCKOW; ZUELLICHAU

ZILZ, Silesia, 2
1. 50-23N, 17-39E, Zuelz, Polish-occupied Germany

ZIMERN, Saxony, 2
1. 51-00N, 11-38E, Zimmern, Gera, DDR
2. 51-05N, 10-34E, Zimmern, Erfurt, DDR
3. 47-56N, 08-43E, Zimmern, Baden-Wuerttemberg, BRD
4. 48-10N, 08-35E, Zimmern ob Rottweil, Baden-Wuerttemberg, BRD
5. 48-13N, 08-43E, Zimmern unter der Burg, Baden-Wuerttemberg, BRD
6. 48-19N, 08-57E, Baden-Wuerttemberg, BRD
7. 48-21N, 12-55E, Bavaria, BRD
8. 48-34N, 07-59E, Baden-Wuerttemberg, BRD
9. 48-49N, 09-53E, Baden-Wuerttemberg, BRD
10. 48-55N, 10-59E, Bavaria, BRD
11. 49-26N, 09-22E, Baden-Wuerttemberg, BRD
12. 49-36N, 09-47E, Baden-Wuerttemberg, BRD
13. 49-53N, 09-36E, Bavaria, BRD

ZIMMER, 2
Not found.

ZIMMERHAUSEN, 2
1. 49-04N, 09-40E, Zimmertshaus (farm), Baden-Wuerttemberg, BRD

ZIRCHAW, 3
1. 53-53N, 14-08E, Rostock, DDR
2. 54-22N, 13-19E, Zirkow, Rostock, DDR
3. 54-23N, 13-33E, Zirkow, Rostock, DDR

ZIRCKE, Prussia, 2
Not found.

ZITTITZ, 3
1. 54-25N, 13-28E, Zittvitz, Rostock, DDR

ZNIN, Prussia, 1
1. 52-51N, 17-44E, Poland

ZONNDORF, Prussia, 2
1. 53-00N, 13-41E, Zorndorf (foresters' lodge), Frankfurt/Oder, DDR

ZORBAU, 2
    1. 51-12N, 12-01E, Halle, DDR

ZSCHOPAN, 2
    1. 50-45N, 13-04E, Zschopau, Karl-Marx-Stadt, DDR
    2. 50-46N, 13-06E, Zschopenthal, Karl-Marx-Stadt, DDR

ZUELCKOW, 1
    1. 53-27N, 14-35E, Zuellchow, Polish-occupied Germany

ZUELLICHAU, 1, 2
    1. 52-05N, 15-37E, Polish-occupied Germany

ZUERICH, [Switzerland] 1

ZUROW, 3
    1. 53-52N, 11-37E, Rostock, DDR
    2. 50-47N, 19-24E, Zuraw (or Zoraw), Poland
    3. 51-31N, 18-24E, Zuraw, Poland
    4. 49-50N, 21-10E, Zurowa, Poland

ZWERGA, 1
    1. 49-52N, 11-58E, Zwergau, Bavaria, BRD

ZWICKAU, 1
    1. 50-44N, 12-30E, Karl-Marx-Stadt, DDR
    2. 50-46N, 11-49E, Zwackau, Gera, DDR

ZWIEFALTEN, 3
    1. 48-14N, 09-28E, Baden-Wuerttemberg, BRD